Frommer's®

Niagara Region

2nd Edition

by Melanie Chambers

D0107355

Here's what the critics say about Frommer's:

"Amazingly easy to use. Very portable, very complete."

—*Booklist*

"Detailed, accurate, and easy-to-read information for all price ranges."
—*Glamour Magazine*

"Hotel information is close to encyclopedic."

—*Des Moines Sunday Register*

"Frommer's Guides have a way of giving you a real feel for a place."
—*Knight Ridder Newspapers*

WILEY

John Wiley & Sons Canada, Ltd.

Published by:

John Wiley & Sons Canada, Ltd
6045 Freemont Blvd.
Mississauga, ON L5R 4J3

FROMMER'S is a registered trademark of Arthur Frommer. Used under license.

Library and Archives Canada Cataloguing in Publication Data

Chambers, Melanie
    Frommer's Niagara region / Melanie Chambers. — 2nd ed.

Includes index.

ISBN 978-0-470-15324-6

    1. Niagara Falls Region (N.Y. and Ont.) —Guidebooks. 2. Niagara Peninsula (Ont.) —Guidebooks. I. Title. II. Title: Niagara region.

FC3095.N5A3 2008   917.13'38045   C2008-907607-6

Executive Editor: Robert Hickey
Associate Editor: Gene Shannon
Project Manager: Elizabeth McCurdy
Project Coordinator: Lindsay Humphreys
Cartographer: Mapping Specialists
Vice President Publishing Services: Karen Bryan
Publishing Services Manager: Ian Koo
Production by Wiley Indianapolis Composition Services
Front cover photo: © Stockbyte/Getty Images
Back cover photo: © Matthew Plexman/Masterfile

Special Sales

For reseller information, including discounts and premium sales, please call our sales department: Tel. 416-646-7992. For press review copies, author interviews, or other publicity information, please contact our marketing department: Tel. 416-646-4584; Fax: 416-236-4448.

Manufactured in Canada

1 2 3 4 5 TRI 12 11 10 09 08

Contents

List of Maps

Acknowledgments

Thanks to my partner Tom who listened to my daily ramblings about Niagara and kept me fed while I typed the nights away. Thanks also to Louise Dearden, my former co-author and travel mentor—a little chocolate and wine makes everything better. Thank you very much to Robert Hickey, my editor, who helped me speak my mind. Lastly, thanks to my Niagara gal pal: here's to India and beyond.

An Invitation to the Reader

In researching this book, we discovered many wonderful places—hotels, restaurants, shops, and more. We're sure you'll find others. Please tell us about them, so we can share the information with your fellow travelers in upcoming editions. If you were disappointed with a recommendation, we'd love to know that, too. Please write to:

Frommer's Niagara Region, 2nd Edition
John Wiley & Sons Canada, Ltd. • 6045 Freemont Blvd. • Mississuaga, ON
L5R 4J3

An Additional Note

Please be advised that travel information is subject to change at any time—and this is especially true of prices. We therefore suggest that you write or call ahead for confirmation when making your travel plans. The authors, editors, and publisher cannot be held responsible for the experiences of readers while traveling. Your safety is important to us, however, so we encourage you to stay alert and be aware of your surroundings. Keep a close eye on cameras, purses, and wallets, all favorite targets of thieves and pickpockets.

About the Author

Since cycling solo from Amsterdam to Spain over a decade ago, **Melanie Chambers** has been struck with wanderlust. After graduation from Ryerson University's journalism program in 2001, she's been writing about her travels across the globe, often accompanied by her bike. Now the owner of a rambunctious Labrador Retriever, she's taken to hiking.

Frommer's Star Ratings, Icons & Abbreviations

Every hotel, restaurant, and attraction listing in this guide has been ranked for quality, value, service, amenities, and special features using a **star-rating system.** In country, state, and regional guides, we also rate towns and regions to help you narrow down your choices and budget your time accordingly. Hotels and restaurants are rated on a scale of zero (recommended) to three stars (exceptional). Attractions, shopping, nightlife, towns, and regions are rated according to the following scale: zero stars (recommended), one star (highly recommended), two stars (very highly recommended), and three stars (must-see).

In addition to the star-rating system, we also use **seven feature icons** that point you to the great deals, in-the-know advice, and unique experiences that separate travelers from tourists. Throughout the book, look for:

Finds	Special finds—those places only insiders know about
Fun Fact	Fun facts—details that make travelers more informed and their trips more fun
Kids	Best bets for kids and advice for the whole family
Moments	Special moments—those experiences that memories are made of
Overrated	Places or experiences not worth your time or money
Tips	Insider tips—great ways to save time and money
Value	Great values—where to get the best deals

The following **abbreviations** are used for credit cards:

AE	American Express	DISC	Discover	V	Visa
DC	Diners Club	MC	MasterCard		

Frommers.com

Now that you have the guidebook to a great trip, visit our website at **www.frommers.com** for travel information on more than 3,000 destinations. With features updated regularly, we give you instant access to the most current trip-planning information available. At Frommers.com, you'll also find the best prices on airfares, accommodations, and car rentals—and you can even book travel online through our travel booking partners. At Frommers.com, you'll also find the following:

- Online updates to our most popular guidebooks
- Vacation sweepstakes and contest giveaways
- Newsletter highlighting the hottest travel trends
- Online travel message boards with featured travel discussions

What's New in the Niagara Region

The falls in Niagara have always been the region's main attraction, but the wineries have become a major draw in their own right, with many visitors coming just for the vineyards. And to ensure every demographic and budget can partake in the wine experience—wine isn't just for the well to do—many new hotels and restaurants are offering affordable prices and varied experiences to draw in a younger crowd.

PLANNING YOUR TRIP Passport requirements have changed across Canada and the United States. The **Western Hemisphere Travel Initiative** requires that all U.S. citizens returning from Canada to the United States must show a valid passport. And if you make this trip frequently, the latest addition is a NEXUS card, which is a pre-approved Customs pass that allows users to forgo long Customs lineups and potentially lengthy checks. Before leaving home, U.S. citizens should check the latest regulations at **www.travel.state.gov**. These new regulations have meant a backlog of passport applications, so plan well in advance. All international visitors should check the **Citizenship and Immigration Canada** website, **www.cic.gc.ca**, for updated entry requirements.

Also, visitors to the Niagara region should be aware that the General Goods and Service (GST) tax has dropped from 7% to 5% but that visitors are no longer able to apply for tax rebates once they arrive home.

ACCOMMODATIONS To draw in a younger tourist, many new hotels are offering more affordable prices. The **Orchid Inn,** 390 Mary Street, Niagara-on-the-Lake (© **905/468-3871**), and the **Jordan House Tavern and Lodging,** 3751 Main Street, Jordan (© **800/701-8074**), may lack some frills—room service, spa services and fitness facilities for instance—but they offer good value.

Moving up the scale in price, **The Keefer Mansion,** 14 St. Davids St. W., Thorold (© **905/680-9581**), is good value and is a memorable historical bed-and-breakfast, offering fine dining. Kids will appreciate **The Great Wolf Lodge,** 3950 Victoria Ave., Niagara Falls (© **800/605-WOLF**), for its giant water park and cabinlike rooms.

DINING Affordability and good value are the reasoning behind many of the regions' new restaurants. The **Old Winery Restaurant,** 2228 Niagara Stone Rd., Niagara-on-the-Lake (© **905/468-8900**), is a perfect example, offering half-entrees in upbeat surroundings. **Echoes from Asia** (153 Hartzel Rd., St. Catharines (© **905/682-5807**), is another place to go for fresh and reasonably priced meals, despite the lackluster decor. And to keep up with the demand for organics, the **Green Bean Café and Oxygen Bar,** 224 St. Paul St., St. Catharines (© **905/688-0800**), is a new spot for the health conscious.

Two new spots in the city of Niagara Falls offer some variety to the dining scene. Niagara Falls' visitors looking for a bit of culture will sigh with relief at the **Krieghoff Gallery-Café,** 5470 Victoria Ave., Niagara Falls (© **905/358-9700**), which includes a small painting gallery of Cornelius Krieghoff's (1815–72) work, a menu of plate-sharing nibbles, and a good selection of local wines. The **Golden Lotus** in the Fallsview Casino, 6380 Fallsview Blvd, Niagara Falls (© **888/698-3888**), forgoes North American–style Chinese food for more authentic fare.

ATTRACTIONS   Something old gets a dusting off; something new will appeal to a thrill-seeking crowd. **Fort George** tours are now more hands-on and interesting; kids can now "enlist" in the army, and fascinating, lesser-known historical figures are featured in a more comprehensive historical tour. Amidst the overpriced attractions on Clifton Hill, the new **Niagara Skywheel** Ferris wheel at 53m (175 ft.) is worth the C$10 (US$9.50) just to see an aerial view of both the U.S. and Canadian falls. And for adventurous mountain bikers the **12-Mile Creek Trail** is a new, undulating, and sometimes steep path in St. Catharines.

WINERIES   Two of the regions' oldest wineries have gone through multimillion-dollar renovations: **Hillebrand,** 290 John St. E., Niagara-on-the-Lake (© **905/468-4578**), and **Inniskillin,** S.R. 66, R.R. 1, Niagara Pkwy., Niagara-on-the-Lake (© **888/466-4754**). Both wineries have not only increased the size of their facilities but they also have added specialized tours for the discerning wine drinkers.

Reif Estates Winery, 15608 Niagara Pkwy., Niagara-on-the-Lake (© **905/468-7738**), has also undergone an expansion that includes the regions' first wine sensory garden, featuring flowers and plants that mimic the smells found in popular wines.

SHOPPING   Americans looking to shop cheaply are already aware that the rising Canadian dollar means that the greenback won't travel as far in Canada as it used to. In fact, many Canadians are now crossing the border and taking advantage of lower U.S. prices. Canadian shops are fighting to retain customers, however, so sales are frequent.

Although some shops in the region have closed as a result of fewer American shoppers, two new stores opened in Niagara-on-the-Lake: **The Bark and Fitz,** 106 Queen St. (© **905/468-0305**), is a high-end store selling items for pampered pooches; and **Valleverde,** 55 Queen St., 5470 Victoria Ave., Niagara Falls (© **905/358-9700**), is a women's clothing store, featuring organics and natural materials.

AFTER DARK   Niagara Falls nightlife is gradually improving. The popular music and Asian-inspired decor at **Dragonfly,** 6380 Fallsview Blvd., Niagara Falls (© **905/356-4691**), in the Fallsview Casino, has well-dressed 20-somethings lining up every weekend to get in.

1

The Best of the Niagara Region

There's no doubt about it—the Falls are the main attraction in the Niagara region. And that's as it should be. The unfathomable amount of water catapulting over the river's edge is intense—not just at the larger Canadian falls, but on the American side as well. Charles Dickens poetically captured his first impression of the Falls, declaring, "Niagara was at once stamped upon my heart, an Image of Beauty. . . ." Thousands of visitors before him and millions after him have felt the same awe as they stood facing the majesty of the tumbling water.

If you're a first-time visitor, by all means plan to see the Falls first. But if you have the time to stay more than a day, or you're making a return visit, I strongly encourage you to venture beyond the thundering waters. You'll be pleasantly surprised by the diversity of the Niagara region.

Niagara has much to offer visitors in addition to the Falls. The picture-postcard, tree-lined streets of historic Niagara-on-the-Lake invite you to take a leisurely stroll. The town has gracious inns, great restaurants, a unique upscale shopping district, and world-class live theater. The wine region continues to add new wineries to its prestigious community of award-winning vintners every year, providing visitors with an eclectic variety of wine- and food-tasting experiences. The rich history of the region can be discovered through visits to the Welland Canal, the battlefields and other military sites of the War of 1812, the Freedom Trail of the escaping slaves from the southern United States, and the many museums and monuments. The natural environment is well stewarded, with numerous hiking and biking opportunities along the many pathways, parks, and conservation areas.

1 The Most Unforgettable Niagara Region Experiences

- **The Falls Up Close & Personal:** People have lost their lives trying to conquer the Falls; for the rest of us, it's enough to see the mighty water from behind (Journey Behind the Falls tour), from the front (*Maid of the Mist* tour), and even from above (helicopter ride). See chapter 7, "What to See & Do in the Niagara Region," p. 104.

- **The Falls by Night:** Experiencing the Falls in daylight is memorable, but the most remarkable sight is the nightly illuminations. An ever-changing palette of colors floods the American and Horseshoe Falls every evening at nightfall. See chapter 7, "What to See & Do in the Niagara Region," p. 104.

- **Dining Alfresco in the Vineyards:** The Niagara Peninsula serves up some lovely weather in the late spring, summer, and early fall that is perfect for outdoor dining. The only rule is to linger. See chapter 7, "What to See & Do in the Niagara Region," p. 104.

Niagara Region

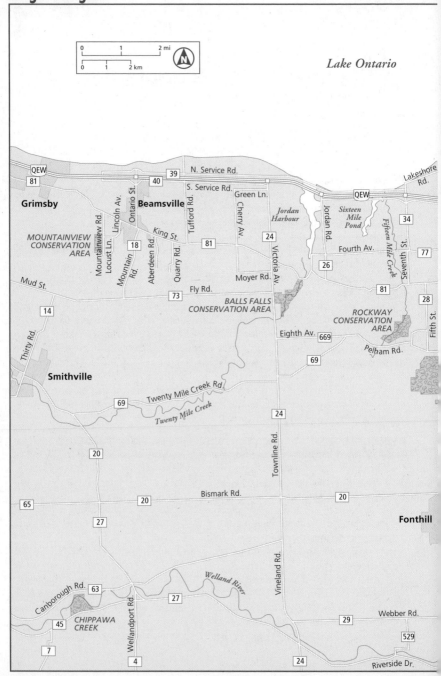

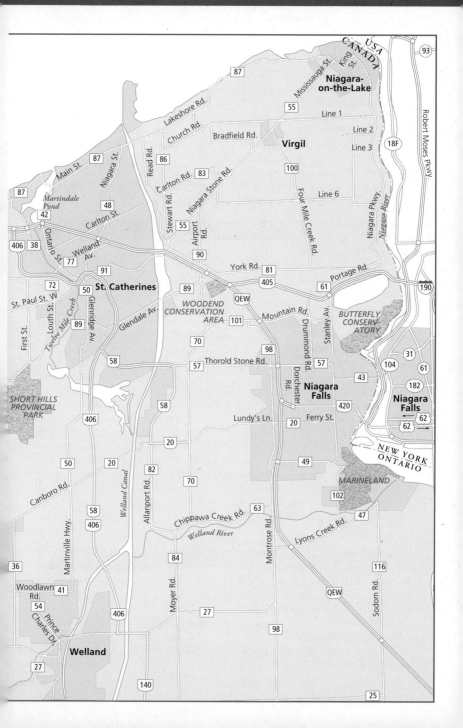

- **Spring Blooms & Blossoms:** The gentle climate of the Niagara region, influenced by its proximity to Lake Erie and Lake Ontario and the sheltering effect of the Niagara Escarpment, is particularly favorable for fruit-growing, in addition to its abundance of ornamental flowers, shrubs, and trees. Consequently, if you visit the region in spring and summer, you will be surrounded by blossoms in the acres of commercial orchards, and charmed by the beautiful formal displays in Niagara's many parks and gardens. See chapter 7, "What to See & Do in the Niagara Region," p. 104.

- **Immersing Yourself in History:** Niagara-on-the-Lake could easily have been a part of the U.S., if not for the decisive battle of 1812. A visit to one of the area's forts, including Fort Niagara and Fort George, will enrich your traveling experience. Bike- or wine-tour guides can also provide colorful historical background. See chapter 7, "What to See & Do in the Niagara Region," p. 112.

2 Best Splurge Hotels

- **Harbour House Hotel,** 85 Melville St., Niagara-on-the-Lake (© **905/ 468-4683**): A serene familiarity settles quite gently upon you at the Harbour House, making you feel like a welcome house guest rather than an overnight tourist. They provide home-away-from-home service such as goose down duvets, a complimentary DVD library, and wine and cheese tastings—you won't want to go home. See p. 70.

- **Sheraton Fallsview Hotel & Conference Center,** 6755 Fallsview Blvd., Niagara Falls, Ontario (© **905/374-1077**): For the ultimate sleepover that includes the Falls, check into a falls-view loft suite at the Sheraton Fallsview. Two-story-high windows capture the entire dramatic view. See p. 64.

- **Prince of Wales,** 6 Picton St., Niagara-on-the-Lake (© **905/468-3245**): You could sum up the Prince of Wales as luxury well done. The property's opulence makes guests feel like royalty: canopied beds, antiques, and thick, textured draperies are decadent and elegant. See p. 72.

- **Riverbend Inn,** 16104 Niagara Pkwy., Niagara-on-the-Lake (© **905/ 468-8829**): If you're looking for an intimate and gracious place to stay, the Riverbend Inn will please. The way this inn channels Southern charm, you could swear Scarlett O'Hara lived here. Sprawling staircases, chandeliers, balconies in some rooms, and fireplaces make this place unique. See p. 72.

3 Best Moderately Priced Hotels

- **Ramada Plaza Fallsview,** 6732 Fallsview Blvd., Niagara Falls, Ontario (© **905/356-1501**): Here you'll usually find the least expensive falls-view rooms in the city. The furniture is arranged so you can view the Falls from your bed. Just fling the curtains wide open and enjoy. The ceiling-to-floor-windows overlooking the Falls will make you feel like you can touch the water. There's also an observation deck, and a restaurant with a view. See p. 67.

- **Black Walnut Manor,** 4255 Victoria Ave., Vineland Station (© **905/562-8675**): There is nothing that compares with the Black Walnut in the entire Niagara region. An old farmstead property in the country, it is equipped with the upscale urban amenities of a downtown boutique hotel. See p. 76.

- **Keefer Mansion Inn,** 14 St. Davids St. W., Thorold, Ontario (*C* **905/ 680-9581**): Until local residents and the town brought this historical home back to life, it was almost demolished, due to years of neglect. Fully restored to its former grandeur, using original pieces such as door hinges and the fireplaces, today the inn lavishes guests with fine dining, a spa, and period-style rooms. See p. 81.
- **Old Bank House Historic Inn,** 10 Front St., Niagara-on-the-Lake (*C* **905/468-7136**): With such an

abundance of intriguing and charming historical properties in Niagara-on-the-Lake, choosing one to highlight seems grossly unfair. However, the Old Bank is a fine example of the type of accommodations you can expect to find in the town. It has a prime location close to the theater, shops, and restaurants, yet it's on a quiet street steps away from beautiful Simcoe Park and Lake Ontario. Rooms are nicely furnished in period decor, and a picturesque veranda runs along the front of the house. The property's historical secret is that it was the site of the first branch of the Bank of Canada—the original vault (now restored) is still in the house. See p. 73.

4 The Most Unforgettable Dining Experiences

- **LIV,** in the White Oak Conference Resort & Spa, Niagara-on-the-Lake (*C* **905/688-2550**): Surrender to the tranquillity and serenity of LIV. The spacious, airy dining room is draped with an abundance of soft, sheer white fabric. Simplicity rules. Food is presented as a work of art, each component thoughtfully placed in relation to the others. See p. 92.
- **Wellington Court,** 11 Wellington St., St. Catharines, Ontario (*C* **905/ 682-5518**): Tucked away in an old home on a sleepy street, Chef Erik Peacock has been serving the area's best local produce and wine for more than a decade. Inside the one-room restaurant, you'll find a memorable dining experience. See p. 100.
- **Stone Road Grille,** in the Garrison Plaza, corner of St. Mary Street and Mississauga Street, Niagara-on-the-Lake (*C* **905/468-3474**): Even the most jaded urban palate is rejuvenated at Stone Road Grille. You will find yourself alternately nodding

with satisfaction at the imaginative dishes and sighing with delight at the depth of the chef's understanding of how to marry flavors and textures. See p. 93.

- **Peninsula Ridge,** 5600 King St. W., Beamsville (*C* **905/563-0900**): The restaurant is located in a superbly restored red-brick Victorian manor, built in Queen Anne style. A distinctive turret and cedar-shingled roof add to the character of the property. Note the polished cherrywood staircase and red pine floors. Ask for a table facing the lake; you will see the gorgeous sunset as you dine, depending on the time of year. Try the prix-fixe lunch or five-course tasting menu paired with Niagara wines. See p. 99.
- **Terroir La Cachette,** 1339 Lakeshore Rd., Niagara-on-the-Lake (*C* **905/ 468-1222**): Although Terroir La Cachette's cuisine focuses on regional wines and ingredients, the French Provençal style of cooking that Quebecois chef Alain Levesque has

perfected remains at the heart of the restaurant's dishes. And French cuisine is rather thin on the ground in the Niagara region, so it's especially nice to find expertly prepared Provençal-inspired cuisine in a striking dining room, overlooking picturesque countryside, right in the middle of a winery. See p. 99.

- **Vineland Estates Winery Restaurant,** 3620 Moyer Rd., Vineland (© **888/846-3526**): One of the most consistently excellent restaurants in the Niagara region, Vineland Estates' dining room is also arguably the prettiest of the winery restaurants. The epicurean menu changes seasonally and makes good use of local ingredients. If you wish to indulge in a leisurely summer lunch, reserve a table on the shaded terrace; the view across the vineyards toward Lake Ontario is divine. See p. 99.

5 The Most Romantic Niagara Moments

- **Relaxing in bed in a luxury hotel with a view of the Falls illuminations:** The high-rise hotels on Fallsview Avenue in Niagara Falls, Ontario, have spectacular views of the Falls from many of their rooms. Try the Ramada Plaza Fallsview, which has an angled floor-to-ceiling wall of windows and king-size beds, or the Sheraton Fallsview Hotel & Conference Centre, which has stunning loft suites with a two-story wall of windows. See chapter 5, "Where to Stay," p. 67 and p. 64.
- **Taking a horse-drawn carriage ride:** The historical streets of Niagara-on-the-Lake are a picture-perfect setting for a romantic carriage ride in summer, when the gardens and hanging baskets are filled to overflowing with colorful blooms, or on a crisp, sunny winter day, bundled up under a blanket. See chapter 7, "What to See & Do in the Niagara Region," p. 128.
- **Hiking along the Bruce Trail on the Niagara Escarpment:** The Bruce Trail is an 850km (528-mile) meandering path. The Niagara Bruce Trail section runs between Beamsville and Queenston, overlooking the Niagara River. The trail passes through countless orchards and wineries, yet feels secluded and wild. Hikers can experience fantastic views, waterfalls, steep inclines, and lush fauna and flora. See chapter 7, "What to See & Do in the Niagara Region," p. 138.
- **Enjoying a leisurely meal on a winery patio, overlooking the vineyards:** There is no better way to dine than outdoors in the fresh air. A summer breeze, a glass of fine wine at your fingertips, and your amore—they all add up to a memorable experience. Try Peller Estates on a summer evening, when the terrace twinkles with candlelight, or Vineland Estates on a warm June afternoon, with the rolling vineyards spread out before you. See "Dine among the Vines" in chapter 8, p. 169.

6 The Best Things to Do for Free (or Almost)

- **Viewing the Falls from both sides of the border:** The best views of the Falls are enjoyed in Niagara Falls, Ontario, but you are free to stroll up and down the sidewalks along the Niagara Gorge on both sides of the Niagara River to view both sets of falls. See chapter 7, "What to See & Do in the Niagara Region," p. 104.

- **Enjoying the summer fireworks display over the Falls:** On Friday, Sunday, and holiday evenings at 10pm during the main tourist season (Victoria Day in May to Labour Day in Sept), there is a spectacular fireworks display over Niagara Falls. See chapter 7, "What to See & Do in the Niagara Region," p. 104.

- **Watching a ship go through the locks on the Welland Canal:** Lock 3 and Lock 7 are the best viewing locations. See chapter 7, "What to See & Do in the Niagara Region," p. 118.

- **Tasting wine at a winery tasting room:** Some wineries charge a nominal fee for each sample and a few ask for a donation to charity, but quite a number are free. However, there is a legal limit to the amount of wine a winery can serve a customer. See chapter 7, "What to See & Do in the Niagara Region," p. 104.

- **Strolling the Niagara Parks Commission Botanical Gardens:** These gardens are open all year. The displays of flowers, shrubs, and trees are deeply inspiring to gardeners and a delight to everyone who enters. See chapter 7, "What to See & Do in the Niagara Region," p. 130.

- **Hiking and biking your way around the Niagara Peninsula:** The Niagara region is rich in hiking and biking trails, conservation areas, and parklands. Take a leisurely stroll through groomed parks with formal flower displays, or visit a designated conservation zone such as Ball's Falls, Beamer Memorial Conservation Area, or Niagara Glen Nature Reserve. If you prefer a less structured environment, explore the 850km (528-mile) Bruce Trail, Canada's oldest and longest hiking trail. The southern terminus of the Bruce Trail is located in Queenston Heights Park. Follow the white blazes as the trail winds along the Niagara Escarpment, a prominent ridge that cuts through the Niagara region from east to west and has been designated a UNESCO World Biosphere Reserve. See chapter 7, "What to See & Do in the Niagara Region," p. 137.

7 Best Activities for Families

- *Maid of the Mist:* From the youngest to the oldest, everyone loves the *Maid of the Mist* tour. Schedule your visit early in the day (the first sailing is at 9am during peak season), before the lines begin to form. Put on the voluminous, recyclable blue rain poncho and prepare to be drenched by Niagara water. Head for the upper decks for the best views and the wettest, most authentic experience. The *Maid of the Mist* tours start on both sides of the border. See p. 106.

- **Cave of the Winds:** A wooden boardwalk takes visitors right to the base of the American Falls. Souvenir nonslip sandals and lightweight recyclable rain ponchos are provided. Tour hours have been extended so that tourists can see the illuminations and fireworks displays from unique vantage points on the boardwalk. See p. 111.

- **Butterfly Conservatory:** The conservatory, on the Niagara Parkway in Ontario, is a bright and airy rainforestlike environment, with a multilevel pathway (stroller and wheelchair accessible) that winds its way through the lush foliage. An amazing 2,000 tropical butterflies, representing 50 different species, live freely in the conservatory. The trick is to walk slowly and pause often, because the most rewarding sights are usually found through quiet observation. Even boisterous kids will enjoy the soothing atmosphere of this magical jungle. See p. 108.

- **Carousel at Lakeside Park:** One of the largest and best-preserved examples of a Looff menagerie carousel, the carousel at Lakeside Park on Lake Ontario in Old Port Dalhousie is a fantastic sight. Built in 1898, there are 69 carousel animals, arranged in four rings; and it costs only a nickel a ride! See p. 128

2

Planning Your Trip to the Niagara Region

Whether you're the kind of person that needs to plan every detail or you prefer to fly by the seat of your pants and let the trip plan itself as you go, taking the time to know the basics will ensure that you get the most out of the Niagara region in terms of visitor attractions, activities, and experiences. Considering today's increased travel security, which requires almost annual changes, it's in your best interest to understand the rules and requirements for transportation.

1 Visitor Information & Maps

FROM NORTH AMERICA

Within Canada, your starting point for information on the entire Niagara Region is the **Tourism Niagara** website at **www.tourismniagara.com**.

You can also access the expertise of the **Gateway Niagara Information Centre,** 424 South Service Rd., Queen Elizabeth Way, at Casablanca Boulevard in Grimsby (© **800/263-2988;** www.tourismniagara. com/gateway_niagara.html). Travel counselors can be reached between 8am and 8pm daily from July to August. The rest of the year, the phone lines are open between 9am and 6pm daily.

Niagara Falls Tourism, 5515 Stanley Ave., Niagara Falls, Ontario (© **800/56FALLS [563-2557]** or 905/356-6061; www.niagarafallstourism.com) has a wealth of information on accommodations, entertainment, events, golf, attractions, casinos, wedding planning, and travel in and around the city of Niagara Falls. Their travel counselors are available Monday to Friday from 8am to 6pm and weekends from 10am to 6pm year-round.

The **Niagara Parks Commission** is a self-financed agency of the Ontario government. They manage the immediate vicinity of the Falls and the Niagara River corridor, with the mandate of preserving and enhancing the natural beauty of the area. Their website offers valuable information on planning a visit to the area. Visit them at **www.niagaraparks.com,** or write for information to The Niagara Parks Commission, P.O. Box 150, Niagara Falls, Ontario, L2E 6T2.

Another excellent source of information on activities throughout the Niagara Region is the **Ontario Travel Centres.** Operated by the Ontario Ministry of Tourism, these centers offer provincial road maps, tourism guides, and attraction brochures. Give them a call at © **800/ONTARIO (668-2746)** or visit them online at **www.ontariotravel.net**. In the Niagara area, they can be found in **Fort Erie** at 315 Bertie St., just off the Queen Elizabeth Way at the Peace Bridge (© **905/871-3505**), in **Niagara Falls** at 5355 Stanley Ave. (west on Hwy. 420

from the Rainbow Bridge; (*C* **905/358-3221**), and in St. Catharines on the westbound Queen Elizabeth Way at the east end of Garden City Skyway (*C* **905/684-6354**).

For tourism information on Niagara Falls, New York, visit **Niagara Tourism and Convention Corporation,** 345 3rd St. suite 605, Niagara Falls, NY, 14303 (*C* **800/338-7890;** www.niagara-usa.com). They offer a free comprehensive travel guide that can be ordered online. For up-to-date maps of the Niagara area, visit **www.google.ca**.

FROM ABROAD

Visit the official travel site of the **Canadian Tourism Commission, www.keepexploring.ca,** and click on your country of residence to access customized visitor information, including advice on traveling to Canada and contact information for tour operators and travel agents in your country who specialize in Canada as a destination.

There are more than 300 Government of Canada diplomatic and consular missions overseas, which can provide information on traveling to Canada and direct you to the appropriate sources for tourist information. If your country of residence is not listed below, you can access the full directory online at **www.voyage.gc.ca**.

U.K.: The **Canadian High Commission,** 1 Grosvenor Sq., London W1K 4AB (*C* **0207/258-6600**).

Ireland: The **Canadian Embassy,** 65 St. Stephen's Green, Dublin 2 (*C* **01/417-4100**).

Australia: The **Canadian High Commission,** Commonwealth Avenue, Canberra, ACT 2600 (*C* **02/6270-4000**), or the Consulate General of Canada, Level 5, Quay West Building, 111 Harrington St., Sydney, NSW 2000 (*C* **02/9364-3000**). There are also Consulates in Perth and Melbourne.

New Zealand: The **Canadian High Commission,** 61 Molesworth St., Third Floor, Thorndon, Wellington (*C* **04/473-9577**).

South Africa: The **Canadian High Commission,** 1103 Arcadia St., Hatfield, Pretoria (*C* **012/422-3000**). There is also a Consulate General in Cape Town and a Consulate in Durban.

2 Entry Requirements

PASSPORTS

As of January 2008, all persons, including U.S. citizens, traveling by air, land, and sea may be required to show a passport, or a NEXUS card (a pre-approved passport document). The Western Hemisphere Travel Initiative mandate was created to strengthen border security, and as a result requirements have become more stringent.

The websites listed below provide downloadable passport applications as well as the current fees for processing passport applications. For an up-to-date, country-by-country listing of passport requirements around the world, go to the "Foreign Entry Requirement" Web page of the U.S. Department of State at **http://travel.state.gov**.

If you plan to drive into Canada, be sure to bring your car's registration papers and insurance documents. If you are traveling with children, make sure they have identification documents. Parents who share custody of their children should carry copies of the legal custody documents. If you are not the parent or legal guardian of children traveling with you, you should carry a written statement from the children's parent or guardian, granting permission for the children to travel to Canada under your supervision.

VISAS

For a complete list of countries and territories whose citizens require visas in order to enter Canada as visitors, visit **www.cic. gc.ca**.

MEDICAL REQUIREMENTS

For information on medical requirements and recommendations, see "Health," p. 26.

CUSTOMS

Generally, you are allowed to bring goods for personal use during your trip into Canada, although there are restrictions and controls on the importation of certain goods, such as firearms, ammunition, fireworks, meat and dairy products, animals, plants and plant products, firewood, fresh fruits and vegetables, and certain food and drug products. Outdoor sportsmen and women should note that fishing tackle can be brought into Canada, but the bearer must posses a nonresident license for the province where he or she plans to use it. However, there are severe restrictions on firearms and weapons, and visitors are strongly advised to contact the Canadian Firearms Centre, **www.cfc-cafc.gc.ca** (📞 **800/461-9999** within Canada, and 📞 **506/636-5064** from other countries), to verify the declaration process prior to travel.

If you meet the minimum age requirement of the province or territory in which you enter Canada (the age is 19 in Ontario), you can bring in, free of duty or taxes, no more than 1.14 liters (40 fl. oz.) of liquor, 1.5 liters (52 fl. oz.) of wine, or 24 containers of beer (355 ml/ 12. fl. oz. each). Visitors entering Ontario who are ages 19 or older can also bring up to 200 cigarettes, 50 cigars or cigarillos, 200 grams (7 oz.) of manufactured tobacco, and 200 tobacco sticks duty-free. Dogs and cats in good health can enter Canada from the U.S. with their owners, but you should bring a valid rabies vaccination certificate with you. Check with the **Canadian Food Inspection Agency's Import Service Centre** (📞 **800/835-4486**) if you wish to bring other kinds of animals from the U.S., or any animal from another country.

For more information on Customs matters, contact your nearest Canadian embassy or consulate, or call the **Automated Customs Information Service** (📞 **800/461-9999** from within Canada, or 204/983-3500 or 506/636-5064 from outside Canada). Information is available online from the **Canada Border Services Agency** at **www.cbsa-asfc.gc.ca**. Print publications can be ordered by calling 📞 **800/959-2221.**

3 When to Go

Hotel rooms fill up quickly during July and August, and also during major events such as Canada Day (July 1), Independence Day (July 4), and the Niagara Wine Festival (mid- to late September). If you plan to visit during these times, reserve accommodations several weeks or even months ahead. If you want to avoid the crowds but still maximize your chances of good weather, visit during the last week of August or first week of September. With the kids heading back to school and the Wine Festival not yet begun, this time of year is great for traveling to the Falls, if you want to avoid lineups and enjoy a little peace and quiet.

Note that several of the top Falls attractions, including the *Maid of the Mist* and the Cave of the Winds tours, operate only during the summer months. They open each year once the ice has melted in April or May, and end their season during the month of October.

THE CLIMATE

Spring in the Niagara region runs from late March to mid-May (although late

---

Tips **Nightly Illuminations**

The American Falls and the Horseshoe Falls are illuminated nightly throughout the year. All times posted are approximate and subject to change according to light conditions. April lights go on at 8:30pm and shut down at 11pm. During the peak tourist season, May 1 to August 24, the Falls are flooded with light between 9pm and midnight. From August 24 to September 30, lights are on at 8:30pm (off at midnights); and during October the Falls are lit at 7pm and the lights are switched off at midnight.

---

snowfalls may surprise visitors in April, and frosts are not uncommon in May). **Summer** temperatures are usually enjoyed from mid- to late May to mid-September. June, July, and August are the hottest months, with average highs of 79°F (26°C) and lows of 59°F (15°C). The **fall** season runs from mid-September to mid-November, although even October can be quite brisk. **Winter** spans November to March, with temperatures varying between 16°F (–8°C) and 39°F (4°C). Snowfall is abundant, and winter temperatures have been known to plunge well below 16°F (–8°C) some years.

Keep in mind that the Great Lakes can adversely affect local weather conditions, ranging from high humidity and sudden thunderstorms in the summer to lake-effect snow squalls and freezing rain in the winter. Lake Erie and, in particular, Lake Ontario are the main influence on the unique microclimate of the Niagara Peninsula, though, with a tendency to moderate summer heat and winter cold most years. The Niagara Escarpment also acts as a natural shelter against frost in the spring and fall. The weather can be somewhat unpredictable in this region, so I recommend packing some long-sleeved shirts for unexpectedly cool summer days and multiple layers to shed during a warm winter.

Visitors standing close to the Falls can get quite wet from the mist, especially if the wind is blowing in their direction. This can be welcome on a hot summer's day, but be prepared to don rain gear or even change into dry clothing. With the recent high-rise development around the Falls the mist has actually increased in the area, and you don't need to be that close to the water to get wet.

Niagara's Average Temperatures (°C/°F)

	Jan	Feb	Mar	Apr	May	June	July	Aug	Sept	Oct	Nov	Dec
High	–1/31	1/33	6/42	13/55	21/69	25/76	28/82	27/80	22/72	16/60	9/48	3/37
Low	–8/17	–8/17	–4/25	2/35	8/46	13/55	16/61	15/59	11/51	4/40	0/32	–5/23

HOLIDAYS

On most public holidays, banks, government offices, schools, and post offices are closed. Museums, retail stores, and restaurants vary widely in their policies for holiday openings and closings, so call before you go to avoid disappointment.

Note that some museums are closed on Mondays and Tuesdays outside of the peak summer months.

The Niagara Region celebrates the following holidays in Canada: New Year's Day (Jan 1), Good Friday and sometimes Easter Monday (Mar or Apr, dates vary each year), Victoria Day (Mon following the third weekend in May), Canada Day (July 1), Civic Holiday (first Mon in Aug), Labour Day (first Mon in Sept), Thanksgiving (second Mon in Oct),

Remembrance Day (Nov 11), Christmas Day (Dec 25), and Boxing Day (Dec 26).

The U.S. has a number of national holidays that differ from Canada. The most notable ones are Martin Luther King Jr. Day (third Mon in Jan), President's Day (third Mon in Feb), Memorial Day (last Mon in May), Independence Day (July 4), and Thanksgiving Day (last Thurs in Nov). On these dates, the Niagara region on the Canadian side of the border tends to swell with visitors just as it does during Canadian holidays.

NIAGARA REGION CALENDAR OF EVENTS

The following list of events will help you to plan your visit to the Niagara region. Even the largest, most successful events sometimes retire, a few events are biennial, and dates may change from those listed here. In addition to the following events, numerous smaller community and cultural events take place throughout the year. Contact the relevant tourist information center (see listings earlier in this chapter under "Visitor Information") to confirm details if a particular event is a major reason for your vacation.

For an exhaustive list of events beyond those listed here, check http://events.frommers.com, where you'll find a searchable, up-to-the-minute roster of what's happening in cities all over the world.

January

Niagara Icewine Festival. Mid-January, the Niagara region bustles with tours, tastings, and other activities related to harvesting of the grapes to make icewine. ✆ **905/688-0212. www.grapeandwine.com**.

April

Shaw Festival Season opens. The Shaw Festival exclusively produces the plays of George Bernard Shaw and his contemporaries, and plays set during Shaw's (very long) lifetime. The season runs from April to November, on three stages in Niagara-on-the-Lake. ✆ **800/511-7429. www.shawfest.com**.

Maple syrup season. When the daytime temperatures begin to climb above 32°F/0°C in late winter, the maple sap begins to run. Local farms offer tours of the "sugar bush," pancake breakfasts, and maple syrup products for sale. ✆ **905/682-0642. www.whitemeadowsfarms.com**.

May

Niagara Folk Arts Festival. This annual event is billed as Canada's oldest heritage festival, spanning more than 2 weeks in mid- to late May. Multicultural music, theater, dance, food, and traditions are celebrated. Held at various sites throughout the Niagara Region. ✆ **905/685-6589. www.folk-arts.ca**.

Opening Day at Fort Erie Racetrack. May 5 marks the beginning of the Fort Erie horseracing season that runs until November. ✆ **800/295-3770. www.forterieracing.com**.

June

Welland Rose Festival. Early June smells sweet as a variety of events lead up to the display and judging of the fairest roses in the land. ✆ **905/732-7673. www.wellandrosefestival.on.ca**.

Niagara New Vintage Festival. Dozens of Niagara wineries present the first taste of the season of their award-winning wines. Events are held in Jordan, St. Catharines, and other sites throughout the region. ✆ **905/688-0212. www.niagarawinefestival.ca**.

Beamsville Strawberry Festival. This festival, held the third week of June, features strawberry treats, live entertainment, crafters, car show, and more. Third weekend in June. ✆ **905/563-7274. www.strawberryfest.ca**.

July

Friendship Festival. This is a celebration of shared history and culture and friendship between Canada and the U.S. Events are held in Fort Erie, Ontario, and Buffalo, New York. © 888/333-1987. www.friendship festival.com.

Canada Day. Each July 1, Canadians gather in communities across the country to celebrate the nation's birthday. In the Niagara region, celebrations take place at the Falls and surrounding towns, including Port Dalhousie, Welland, St. Catharines, and Port Colborne.

Two Nations Celebration. This binational event, running from July 1 to July 4, celebrates the birth of two nations—Canada and the United States of America. Based in Queen Victoria Park, Niagara Falls, Ontario. © 877/NIA-PARK (642-7275). www.niagaraparks.com.

Battle of Chippawa Commemorative Ceremony. On July 5, the anniversary of the Battle of Chippawa is remembered at Chippawa Battlefield, Niagara Falls, with a memorial ceremony. © 877/NIA-PARK (642-7275).

Dragon Boat Festival. Held in late July on Martindale Pond, home of the Royal Canadian Henley Regatta in historical Port Dalhousie. Teams from Niagara and across the globe compete and raise funds for the St. Catharines Museum and the United Way. © 905/984-8880. www.stcatharinesdragon boat.org.

Niagara International Chamber Music Festival. Local churches, wineries, and museums host more than 30 concerts by internationally renowned artists. © 877/MUS-FEST (687-3378). www.niagaramusicfest.com.

Niagara Motorcycle Rally, Niagara Falls, New York. Bike enthusiasts can speak with custom bike builders, listen to live bands, compete in the chili cook-off, and buy swag from bike companies. www.buffalothrills.com/events/ev-festivalsevents/niagara motorcycle.htm.

August

Canal Days Marine Heritage Festival. On the Civic Holiday weekend (incorporating the first Mon in Aug), Port Colborne hosts this waterfront festival celebrating the community's marine heritage. © 888/PORT-FUN (767-8386). www.canaldays.ca.

Royal Canadian Henley Regatta. This annual rowing regatta draws more than 3,500 international competitors. Held on Martindale Pond, Port Dalhousie. © 905/937-1117. www.henleyregatta.ca.

Siege Reenactment at Old Fort Erie. This reenactment of the life and times of the battles during the War of 1812 includes camps, artillery and musket demonstrations, and drills. Held at the historic fort at Fort Erie. © 905/871-0540. www.oldforterie.com.

4 Getting There

BY PLANE

When visiting the Niagara region, you have a choice of arriving in Canada or the United States. The majority of the attractions are on the Canadian side, but the Buffalo Airport is closer to the Falls than either Pearson (Toronto) or Hamilton.

Most flights arrive at Pearson International Airport in northwest Toronto, approximately a 2-hour drive from Niagara Falls. The trip usually takes 30-plus minutes longer during the weekday peak commuter times: 7–9am and 4–7pm. If you can, fly into Hamilton—it's less busy.

If you're traveling with children, ask your air carrier in advance about child safety restraints, transport of strollers, times of meal service, availability of children's meals, and bulkhead seating (which has extra room to stretch out). Mention any food allergies or medical concerns.

Note that the term "direct flight" may include an en route stop but not an aircraft change.

ARRIVING IN CANADA

FROM THE U.S. Canada's only national airline, **Air Canada** (✆ 888/ 247-2262; www.aircanada.ca) operates direct flights to Toronto (Pearson Airport) from most major American cities and many smaller ones. It also flies from major cities around the world and operates connecting flights from other U.S. cities.

A major discount Canadian carrier servicing select routes is **WestJet** (✆ 888/ WEST-JET; www.westjet.com), with service between Toronto and San Francisco, Los Angeles, Phoenix, Palm Springs, Las Vegas, Hawaii, several Florida locations, and the Bahamas.

Among U.S. airlines, **American** (✆ 800/433-7300; www.aa.com) has daily direct flights from Chicago, Dallas, Miami, and New York. **United** (✆ 800/ 241-6522; www.united.com) has direct flights from Chicago, San Francisco, and Washington (Dulles); it's a code-share partner with Air Canada. **US Airways** (✆ 800/428-4322; www.usairways.com) operates directly into Toronto from a number of U.S. cities, notably Baltimore, Indianapolis, Philadelphia, and Pittsburgh. **Northwest** (✆ 800/225-2525; www.nwa.com) flies direct from Detroit and Minneapolis. **Delta** (✆ 800/221-1212; www.delta.com) flies direct from Atlanta and Cincinnati.

The Hamilton International Airport is smaller, which also means less busy, and it is closer to the Niagara region—it takes about 45 minutes to drive from the airport to Niagara Falls. WestJet flies into Hamilton from Orlando, Las Vegas, Los Angeles, Hawaii, Phoenix, and Palm Springs, Florida.

ARRIVING IN THE U.S.

WITHIN THE U.S. Niagara Falls International Airport is for charter and cargo planes only, so plan to fly into **Buffalo Niagara International Airport** (4200 Genesee St., Cheektowaga, NY; ✆ 716/630-6000; www.nfta.com/airport). The airport is served by a number of airlines, including **JetBlue** (✆ 800/ 538-2583; www.jetblue.com), which has lots of cheap one-way flights from other parts of New York; **AirTran Airways** (✆ 800/247-8726; www.airtran.com); **American** (✆ 800/433-7300; www.aa.com); **Continental** (✆ 800/525-0280; www.continental.com); **Comair/Delta Connection** (✆ 800/221-1212; www.comair.com); **Northwest** (✆ 800/225-2525; www.nwa.com); **Southwest** (✆ 800/435-9792; www.southwest.com); **United** (✆ 800/241-6522); www.ual.com); and **US Airways** (✆ 800/428-4322; www.usairways.com).

FROM CANADA Travelers whose departure city is within Canada are advised to fly to Toronto or Hamilton rather than Buffalo.

FROM ABROAD A number of major U.S. airlines fly into Buffalo Niagara International Airport (see "Within the U.S." above). Visitors arriving from abroad can make connections to Buffalo from several major U.S. cities, including Atlanta, Boston, Chicago, Detroit, and New York.

FLYING FOR LESS: TIPS FOR GETTING THE BEST AIRFARE

- Passengers who can book their ticket either **long in advance** or at the **last minute,** or who **fly midweek** or at **less-trafficked hours** may pay a fraction of the full fare. If your schedule is flexible, say so, and ask if you can secure a cheaper fare by changing your flight plans.

- Search the **Internet** for cheap fares. The most popular online travel agencies are **Travelocity.com** (http://travelocity.com), **Expedia.com** (www.expedia.com and www.expedia.ca), and **Orbitz.com** (www.orbitz.com). In the U.K., go to **Travelsupermarket** (© 0845/345-5708; www.travelsupermarket.com), a flight search engine that offers flight comparisons for the budget airlines whose seats often end up in bucket-shop sales. Other websites for booking airline tickets online include **Cheapflights. com, SmarterTravel.com, Priceline. com,** and **Opodo** (www.opodo.co. uk). Meta search sites (which find and then direct you to airline and hotel websites for booking) include **Sidestep.com** and **Kayak.com**—the latter includes fares for budget carriers such as JetBlue and Spirit as well as the major airlines. **Site59.com** is a great source for last-minute flights and getaways. In addition, most airlines offer online-only fares that even their phone agents know nothing about. British travelers should check **Flights International** (© 0800/0187050; www.flights-international.com) for deals on flights all over the world.

- Keep an eye on local newspapers for **promotional specials** or **fare wars,** when airlines lower prices on their most popular routes.

- Try to book a ticket **in its country of origin.** If you're planning a one-way flight from Johannesburg to New York, a South Africa–based travel agent will probably have the lowest fares. For foreign travelers on multi-leg trips, book in the country of the first leg; for example, book New York–Chicago–Montreal–New York in the U.S.

- Join **frequent-flier clubs.** Frequent-flier membership doesn't cost a cent, but it does entitle you to free tickets or upgrades when you amass the airline's required number of frequent-flier points. You don't even have to fly to earn points; **frequent-flier credit cards** can earn you thousands of miles for doing your everyday shopping. But keep in mind that award seats are limited, seats on popular routes are hard to snag, and more and more major airlines are cutting their expiration periods for mileage points—so check your airline's frequent-flier program so you don't lose your miles before you use them. *Inside tip:* Award seats are offered almost a year in advance, but seats also open up at the last minute, so if your travel plans are flexible, you may strike gold. To play the frequent-flier game to your best advantage, consult the community bulletin boards on **FlyerTalk** (www.flyertalk.com) or go to Randy Petersen's **Inside Flyer** (www.insideflyer.com). Petersen and friends review all the programs in detail and post regular updates on changes in policies and trends.

ARRIVING AT THE AIRPORT

Arriving at Pearson International Airport in Toronto, every passenger must pass through customs. Please see the Customs section (see p. 13 for more information). The general rule is anything sharp or liquid cannot be carried onboard. Customs officers will request to see your boarding pass and a valid passport. The lines may be longer for larger flights, but the Customs process generally takes about 10 minutes. If you possess a NEXUS card (a pre-approved Customs card), you can bypass lines but may still be subject to random searches. The NEXUS card is only available for U.S. and Canadian citizens. To apply, visit **www.cbsa-asfc.gc.ca**.

(Tips) Getting Through the Airport

- Arrive at the airport at least 1 hour before a domestic flight and 2 hours before an international flight. If you are traveling from the U.S., you can check the average wait times at your airport by going to the TSA **Security Checkpoint Wait Times** site (http://waittime.tsa.dhs.gov).
- Know what you can carry on and what you can't. For the latest updates on items you are prohibited to bring in carry-on luggage, go to **www.tsa.gov/travelers/airtravel**.
- Beat the ticket-counter lines by using the self-service electronic ticket kiosks at the airport or even printing out your boarding pass at home from the airline website. Using curbside check-in is also a smart way to avoid lines.
- Help speed up security before you're screened. Remove jackets, shoes, belt buckles, heavy jewelry, and watches and place them in your carry-on luggage or the security bins provided. Place keys, coins, cellphones, and pagers in a security bin. If you have metallic body parts, carry a note from your doctor. When possible, pack liquids in checked baggage.
- Use a TSA-approved lock for your checked luggage. Look for Travel Sentry certified locks at luggage or travel shops and Brookstone stores (or online at www.brookstone.com).

In terms of airport services, porters in red coats will assist inbound travelers with transportation (bus, limo, or taxis). Should you be approached in the terminal, do not accept transportation from individuals; these are unlicensed drivers who will charge a higher fee for taxi service. Inside the airport, information kiosks will assist with hotel, car rental, or currency needs. Most recently, travelers can order takeout at any restaurant participating in the "Made to Fly" program. Visit the website **www.gtaa.com/en/home** for details and a complete listing of services.

GETTING TO NIAGARA FROM THE AIRPORT

If you land at **Pearson International Airport** in Toronto, renting a car may be your best bet. However, there is an **airport express bus service** that will take you to the bus station and train station in downtown Toronto, where you can get transportation to the Niagara Region. The fare is C$16 (US$15) per adult one way. Car-rental companies with desks inside the terminals include **Avis, Budget, Dollar, Thrifty, Hertz, National,** and **Alamo.**

Car-rental companies at **Hamilton International Airport** include Avis, Hertz, and National.

Niagara Airbus (✆ **800/268-8111** in Canada, 716/835-8111 in Buffalo, or 716/625-6222 in Niagara Falls, New York; www.niagaraairbus.com) offers a flexible shuttle and taxi service from **Toronto (Pearson)** and **Buffalo Niagara International Airport** to any destination in the Niagara region in Canada and the Niagara Falls/Buffalo area in New York State. The one-way fare from Toronto Pearson Airport to Niagara Falls, Ontario, is C$60 (US$57). The company also serves **Hamilton airport** with individual taxi cabs rather than a shuttle service.

If you arrive at **Buffalo Niagara International Airport,** the closest airport to the Falls, the **ITA Shuttle** (✆ **800/551-9369;** www.buffaloairporttaxi.com) can take you from the airport to the

American side of the Falls for C$36 (US$34) per person each way or to the Canadian side for C$48 (US$46) per person each way. Children under 6 years old ride free. Reservations must be made at least 12 hours in advance and can be made online or by phone. If you prefer to rent a car, Avis, Budget, Hertz, and Enterprise all have rental counters at the airport.

BY CAR

When driving from the I-90 in **New York State,** take Route 290 to Route 190 to the Robert Moses Parkway. This will put you in downtown Niagara Falls, New York, and you'll see signs for the Rainbow Bridge to Canada. Other crossing points to Canada from the U.S. are between Lewiston, New York, and Queenston, Ontario, and between Buffalo, New York, and Fort Erie, Ontario.

Driving distances from major U.S. cities to Niagara Falls include Boston (774km/484 miles), Chicago (861km/538 miles), Detroit (384km/240 miles), New York (677km/423 miles), and Washington, D.C. (768km/480 miles).

From **Toronto,** take the Queen Elizabeth Way (signs read **QEW**) to Niagara via Hamilton and St. Catharines. Driving time is approximately 1½ to 2 hours, depending on traffic. Note that rush hour snarl-ups can considerably lengthen your trip when traveling from Toronto. If possible, avoid driving on major highways in the Toronto and Hamilton area between

7am and 10am and between 3:30pm and 6:30 pm.

From **Windsor** and **Detroit,** take Highway 401 East to Highway 403, then join the QEW to Niagara. Driving time from Windsor to Niagara Falls is approximately 4 to 4½ hours.

Exit from the QEW at Highway 55 if your destination is Niagara-on-the-Lake or if you would like to take the scenic route to Niagara Falls, which will lead you along the Niagara Parkway on the west side of the Niagara River. If you want to go straight to the Falls, continue on the QEW to Highway 420 and follow the signs. A third option is to continue on the QEW to Fort Erie, at the southern end of the Niagara River. You can visit the attractions in Fort Erie, and then make your way along the southern portion of the Niagara Parkway to the Falls, which is also a pretty drive.

Be sure to carry your driver's license and car registration and insurance documents if you plan to drive your own vehicle. If you are a member of the American Automobile Association (AAA) or the Canadian Automobile Association (CAA), you can get assistance by calling (© **905/984-8585;** www.caa.niagara.net).

If you decide to **rent a car,** try to make arrangements in advance to make sure the vehicle you want will be available. If you are traveling from outside Canada, you may obtain a reasonable discount by booking before you leave home. The rental fee depends on the type of car, but

---

Tips Don't Stow It—Ship It

Though pricey, it's sometimes worthwhile to travel luggage-free, particularly if you're toting sports equipment, meetings materials, or baby equipment. Specialists in door-to-door luggage delivery include **Virtual Bellhop** (www.virtual bellhop.com), **SkyCap International** (www.skycapinternational.com), **Luggage Express** (www.usxpluggageexpress.com), and **Sports Express** (www.sports express.com).

Flying with Film & Video

Never pack film—exposed or unexposed—in checked bags, because the new, more powerful scanners in airports can fog film. The film you carry with you can be damaged by scanners as well. In Canada, you can request hand inspections of film, which will be done "when circumstances permit" (www.catsa-acsta.gc.ca/english/travel_voyage/pbs_cpe.shtml). X-ray damage is cumulative; the faster the film and the more times you put it through a scanner, the more likely damage will occur. Film under 800 ASA is usually safe for up to five scans. If you're taking your film through additional scans, U.S. regulations permit you to demand hand inspections. In international airports, you're at the mercy of airport officials. On international flights, store your film in transparent baggies, so you can remove it easily before you go through scanners. Keep in mind that airports are not the only places where your camera may be scanned: Highly trafficked attractions are X-raying visitors' bags with increasing frequency.

Most photo supply stores sell protective pouches designed to block damaging X-rays. The pouches fit both film and loaded cameras. They should protect your film in checked baggage, but they also may raise alarms and result in a hand inspection.

You'll have little to worry about if you are traveling with **digital cameras.** Unlike film, which is sensitive to light, the digital camera and storage cards are not affected by airport X-rays, according to Nikon. Scanners used for carry-on luggage will not damage **videotape** in video cameras, but the magnetic fields emitted by the walk-through security gateways and handheld inspection wands will. Always place your loaded camcorder on the screening conveyor belt or have it hand-inspected. Be sure your batteries are charged as you may be required to turn the device on to ensure that it's what it appears to be.

a typical fee for a midsized car with automatic transmission is around C$50 (US$48) a day, plus taxes. This price will vary according to season, availability, and length of rental (a full week's rental will often give you a lower price than the daily rate multiplied by seven). The price quoted usually does not include insurance, but some credit card companies offer automatic insurance coverage if you charge the full amount of the car rental to the card (check with your credit card issuer before you travel). Be sure to read the fine print of the agreement and undertake a thorough visual check for damage before accepting the vehicle. Some companies add conditions that will boost your bill if you don't fulfill certain obligations, such as filling the gas tank before returning the car. Note that rental car companies customarily impose a minimum age of 25 for drivers, and some companies have a maximum age of 70 or 75.

BY TRAIN

Amtrak (✆ **800/USA-RAIL** [872-7245]; www.amtrak.com) and **VIA Rail Canada** (✆ **888/VIA-RAIL** [842-7245] or 416/366-8411; www.viarail.ca) operate trains between **Toronto** and **New York,** stopping in **Niagara Falls** and **St. Catharines** but not Niagara-on-the-Lake. Amtrak comes right into the Niagara Falls station in New York State at 27th Street and Lockport Road.

BY BUS

Greyhound Canada (© 800/661-8747) provides coast-to-coast service with connections to Niagara Falls. The local bus station is Niagara Transportation, 4555 Erie Ave., Niagara Falls, Ont. (© **905/357-2133**). Book online or obtain schedule and fare information at www. greyhound.ca. **Greyhound Lines, Inc.** (© **800/231-2222;** www.greyhound. com), provides bus service between the U.S. and Canada. The local bus station on the U.S. side is at Niagara Discount Souvenir, 303 Rainbow Blvd., Niagara Falls, NY (© **716/282-1765**).

Traveling by bus may be faster and cheaper than the train, and if you want to stop to visit towns along the way, bus routes may offer more flexibility. But there's also less space to stretch out, toilet facilities are meager, and meals are taken at roadside rest stops, so consider carefully, particularly if you're planning to bring children with you.

Investigate offers such as unlimited-travel passes and discount fares. It's tough to quote typical fares because bus companies, like airlines, are adopting yield-management strategies, resulting in frequent price changes depending on demand.

5 Money & Costs

It's always advisable to bring money in a variety of forms on a vacation: a mix of cash, credit cards, and traveler's checks. You should also exchange enough petty cash to cover airport incidentals, tipping, and transportation to your hotel before you leave home, or withdraw money upon arrival at an airport ATM.

In many international destinations, ATMs offer the best exchange rates. Avoid exchanging money at commercial exchange bureaus and hotels, which often have the highest transaction fees.

CURRENCY

The currency of Canada is the Canadian dollar, made up of 100¢. Paper currency comes in $5, $10, $20, $50, and $100 denominations. Coins come in 1¢, 5¢, 10¢, and 25¢ (penny, nickel, dime, and quarter) and $1 and $2 denominations.

The Canadian dollar is growing in strength; U.S. visitors will find that the heady days of highly favorable exchange rates have passed. At press time, the Canadian dollar was hovering around 95¢ in U.S. money, give or take a couple of points' variation. What this means is that your American money gets you about 5% more the moment you exchange it for local currency. By the time you read this book, however, the exchange rate will likely be one-to-one, or greater. The British pound has been sitting at around C$2.10 (US$2.10), translating into excellent value for visitors from the U.K. (You might want to visit a website such as **www.xe.com/ucc** for up-to-the-minute exchange-rate information.)

TAXES

Sales taxes are high in Ontario. You'll pay 13% tax on most retail items—a 5% federal goods and service tax (GST) and an 8% provincial sales tax (PST). Taxes for restaurant meals are even higher.

ATMS

The easiest and best way to get cash away from home is from an ATM (automated teller machine), sometimes referred to as a "cash machine," or a "cashpoint." The **Cirrus** (© 800/424-7787; www.master card.com) and **PLUS** (© 800/843-7587;

www.visa.com) networks span the globe. Go to your bank card's website to find ATM locations at your destination. Be sure you know your daily withdrawal limit before you depart.

Note: Many banks impose a fee every time you use a card at another bank's ATM, and that fee can be higher for international transactions (up to US$5 or more) than for domestic ones (where they're rarely more than US$2). In addition, the bank from which you withdraw cash may charge its own fee. For international withdrawal fees, ask your bank. Banks that are members of the **Global ATM Alliance** charge no transaction fees for cash withdrawals at other Alliance member ATMs; these include Bank of America, Scotiabank (Canada, Caribbean, and Mexico), Barclays (U.K. and parts of Africa), Deutsche Bank (Germany, Poland, Spain, and Italy), and BNP Paribus (France).

TRAVELER'S CHECKS

Traveler's checks are something of an anachronism from the days before the ATM made cash accessible at any time. Traveler's checks used to be the only sound alternative to traveling with dangerously large amounts of cash. They were as reliable as currency, but, unlike cash, could be replaced if lost or stolen.

These days, traveler's checks are less necessary because most cities have 24-hour ATMs that allow you to withdraw small amounts of cash as needed. However, keep in mind that you will likely be charged an ATM withdrawal fee if the bank is not your own, so if you're withdrawing money every day, you might be better off with traveler's checks—provided that you don't mind showing identification every time you want to cash one.

You can buy traveler's checks at most banks. They are offered in US and Canadian denominations of $5, $10, $20,

$50, and $100. Generally, you'll pay a service charge ranging from 1% to 4%.

The most popular traveler's checks are offered by **American Express** (☏ **800/807-6233,** or 800/221-7282 for card holders—this number accepts collect calls, offers service in several foreign languages, and exempts Amex gold and platinum cardholders from the 1% fee); **Visa** (☏ **800/732-1322**)—AAA members can obtain Visa checks for a $9.95 fee (for checks up to $1,500) at most AAA offices or by calling ☏ **866/339-3378;** and **MasterCard** (☏ **800/223-9920**).

Be sure to keep a record of the traveler's checks' serial numbers separate from your checks in the event that they are stolen or lost. You'll get a refund faster if you know the numbers.

American Express, Thomas Cook, Visa, and **MasterCard** offer **foreign currency traveler's checks,** useful if you're traveling to one country or to the Euro zone; they're accepted at locations where U.S.-dollar checks may not be.

Another option is the new prepaid traveler's check cards, reloadable cards that work much like debit cards but aren't linked to your checking account. The **American Express Travelers Cheque Card,** for example, requires a minimum deposit, sets a maximum balance, and has a one-time issuance fee of $14.95. You can withdraw money from an ATM (for a fee of $2.50 per transaction, not including bank fees), and the funds can be purchased in dollars, euros, or pounds. If you lose the card, your available funds will be refunded within 24 hours.

CREDIT CARDS

Credit cards are another safe way to carry money. They also provide a convenient record of all your expenses, and they generally offer relatively good exchange rates. You can withdraw cash advances from your credit cards at banks or ATMs, but high fees make credit card cash advances

Tips Dear Visa: I'm Off to Niagara!

Some credit card companies recommend that you notify them of any impending trip abroad so they don't become suspicious when the card is used numerous times in a foreign destination and block your charges. Even if you don't call your credit card company in advance, you can always call the card's toll-free emergency number (see "Credit Cards" above, or "Fast Facts" later in this chapter) if a charge is refused—a good reason to carry the phone number with you. But perhaps the most important lesson here is to carry more than one card with you on your trip; a card might not work for any number of reasons, so having a backup is the smart way to go.

a pricey way to get cash. Keep in mind that you'll pay interest from the moment of your withdrawal, even if you pay your monthly bills on time. Also, note that many banks now assess a 1% to 3% "transaction fee" on *all* charges you incur abroad (whether you're using the local currency or your native currency).

Almost every credit card company has an emergency toll-free number to call if you credit card is lost or stolen. This number is often printed on the card, so it is wise to print the number on a piece of paper and keep it safely stored separate from the card. The credit card company may be able to wire you a cash advance from

your credit card immediately, and in many places, they can deliver an emergency card in a day or two. In Canada, **MasterCard** holders should call ✆ **800/ MC-ASSIST (622-7747); Visa** customers should call ✆ **800/847-2911;** and **American Express** cardholders should call collect ✆ **336/393-1111.** Information is available online at **www.master card.com, www.visa.com,** and **www. americanexpress.com.** You can call a toll-free information directory at ✆ **800/555-1212** to get Canadian toll-free numbers. The best and quickest way to get assistance when you are in your home country is to call your card issuer.

6 Travel Insurance

The cost of travel insurance varies widely, depending on the destination, the cost and length of your trip, your age and health, and the type of trip you're taking, but expect to pay between 5% and 8% of the vacation itself. You can get estimates from various providers through **InsureMyTrip.com.** Enter your trip cost and dates, your age, and other information, for prices from more than a dozen companies.

TRIP-CANCELLATION INSURANCE

Trip-cancellation insurance helps you get your money back if you have to back out

of a trip, if you have to go home early, or if your travel supplier goes bankrupt. Allowed reasons for cancellation can range from sickness to natural disasters to government travel advisories that declare your destination unsafe for travel. Insurance policy details vary, so read the fine print; and make sure that your airline is on the list of carriers covered in case of bankruptcy. Protect yourself further by paying for the insurance with a credit card—you may, depending on the laws of your country, get your money back on goods and services not received if you report the loss within 60 days after the charge is listed on your credit card statement.

Note: Many tour operators, particularly those offering trips to remote or high-risk areas, include insurance in the cost of the trip or can arrange insurance policies through a partnering provider, a convenient and often cost-effective way for the traveler to obtain insurance. Make sure the tour company is a reputable one, however: Some experts suggest you avoid buying insurance from the tour or cruise company you're traveling with, saying it's better to buy from a third-party insurer than to put all your money in one place.

U.S. Citizens: For more information, contact one of the following recommended insurers: **Access America** (✆ 866/807-3982; www.accessamerica.com), **Travel Guard International** (✆ 800/826-4919; www.travelguard.com), **Travel Insured International** (✆ 800/243-3174; www.travelinsured.com), and **Travelex Insurance Services** (✆ 888/457-4602; www.travelex-insurance.com).

MEDICAL INSURANCE

Medical care in Ontario is provided to all residents through the Ontario Health Insurance Plan (OHIP), administered by the provincial government. Visitors from abroad are ineligible for OHIP coverage and should arrange for **health insurance** coverage before entering Canada. For more information, contact a private insurance company directly, or call the **Canadian Life and Health Insurance Association** (✆ 800/268-8099; www.clhia.ca). Canadian travelers are protected by their home province's health insurance plan for a limited time period. Check with your province's health insurance agency before traveling.

U.K. citizens who make more than one trip abroad per year may find an annual travel insurance policy works out cheaper. Check **www.moneysupermarket.com**, which compares prices across a wide range of providers for single- and multi-trip policies.

Most big travel agencies offer their own insurance and will probably try to sell you their package when you book a holiday. Think before you sign. **Britain's Consumers' Association** recommends that you insist on seeing the policy and reading the fine print before buying travel insurance. **The Association of British Insurers** (✆ 020/7600-3333; www.abi.org.uk) gives advice by phone and publishes *Holiday Insurance,* a free guide to policy provisions and prices. You might also shop around for better deals: Try **Columbus Direct** (✆ 0870/033-9988; www.columbusdirect.net).

LOST-LUGGAGE INSURANCE

On international flights (including U.S. portions of international trips), baggage coverage is limited to approximately C$21.14 per kg (US$9.07 per pound), up to approximately C$635 (US$603)

Travel in the Age of Bankruptcy

Airlines go bankrupt, so protect yourself by **buying your tickets with a credit card.** The Fair Credit Billing Act (a U.S. Act) guarantees that you can get your money back from the credit card company if a travel supplier goes under (and if you request the refund within 60 days of the bankruptcy). **Travel insurance** can also help, but make sure it covers against "carrier default" for your specific travel provider. And be aware that if a U.S. airline goes bust midtrip, a 2001 federal law requires other carriers to take you to your destination (albeit on a space-available basis) for a fee of no more than US$25, provided you rebook within 60 days of the cancellation.

per checked bag. If you plan to check items more valuable than what's covered by the standard liability, see if your homeowner's policy covers your valuables, get baggage insurance as part of your comprehensive travel-insurance package, or buy Travel Guard's "Bag-Trak" product.

If your luggage is lost, immediately file a lost-luggage claim at the airport, detailing the luggage contents. Most airlines require that you report delayed, damaged, or lost baggage within 4 hours of arrival. The airlines are required to deliver luggage, once found, directly to your house or destination free of charge.

7 Health

STAYING HEALTHY
GENERAL AVAILABILITY OF HEALTH CARE

Contact the **International Association for Medical Assistance to Travelers** (**IAMAT;** © **716/754-4883,** or 416/652-0137 in Canada; www.iamat.org) for tips on travel and health concerns in the countries you're visiting, and for lists of local, English-speaking doctors. The **United States Centers for Disease Control and Prevention** (© **800/311-3435;** www.cdc.gov) provides up-to-date information on health hazards by region or country and offers tips on food safety. **Travel Health Online** (www.tripprep.com), sponsored by a consortium of travel medicine practitioners, may also offer helpful advice on traveling abroad. In Canada, visitors can find medical travel advisory information at the **Public Health Agency**'s website at **www.phac-aspc.gc.ca.**

WHAT TO DO IF YOU GET SICK AWAY FROM HOME

For non-life-threatening emergencies that require a physician consultation, go to a **walk-in clinic.** These clinics operate just as the name implies—you walk in and wait your turn to see a doctor. Look in the Yellow Pages or ask your hotel to recommend one. Some doctors will make house calls to your hotel. Payment procedures and opening hours vary among clinics, so call ahead and ask about their billing policy for nonresidents of Ontario or Canada.

Most clinics will accept health cards from other provinces, although Quebec residents may be required to pay cash and obtain reimbursement from their provincial government. Out-of-country patients may be required to pay cash—checks or credit cards may not be accepted.

If you are suffering from a serious medical problem and are unable to wait to be seen at a walk-in clinic, visit the

---

Healthy Travels to You

The following government websites offer up-to-date health-related travel advice.
- **Australia:** www.dfat.gov.au/travel
- **Canada:** The Health Canada home page, www.phac-aspc.gc.ca, offers no direct links to travel information. For more comprehensive information, try www.phac-aspc.gc.ca (the Public Health Agency) instead, whose site has a "Travel Health" section.
- **U.K.:** www.dh.gov.uk/en/Policyandguidance/Healthadvicefortravellers/index.htm
- **U.S.:** wwwn.cdc.gov/travel

Avoiding "Economy-Class Syndrome"

Deep vein thrombosis, or as it's known in the world of flying, "economy-class syndrome," is a blood clot that develops in a deep vein. It's a potentially deadly condition that can be caused by sitting in cramped conditions—such as an airplane cabin—for too long. During a flight (especially a long-haul flight), get up, walk around, and stretch your legs every 60 to 90 minutes to keep your blood flowing. Other preventive measures include frequent flexing of the legs while sitting, drinking lots of water, and avoiding alcohol and sleeping pills. If you have a history of deep vein thrombosis, heart disease, or other conditions that put you at high risk, some experts recommend wearing compression stockings or taking anticoagulants when you fly; always ask your physician about the best course for you. Symptoms of deep vein thrombosis include leg pain or swelling, or even shortness of breath.

nearest hospital emergency room. Emergency rooms operate on a triage system, where patients are assessed upon arrival and those who need care the most urgently are seen first. Hospitals and emergency numbers are listed under "Fast Facts: Niagara Region" in chapter 4.

Ontario emergency rooms are extremely busy and wait times for nonurgent cases are typically several hours. If at all possible, use the walk-in clinics. For minor health problems, consult a **pharmacist.** These professionals are trained in health consultation and will recommend whether you should see a doctor about your particular condition. Many pharmacies are open evenings and weekends and advertise their hours in the Yellow Pages.

If you suffer from a chronic illness, consult your doctor before your departure. For such conditions as epilepsy, diabetes, or heart problems, wear a **MedicAlert identification tag** (✆ **800/668-1507,** or www.medicalert.ca in Canada; ✆ **888/633-4298,** or www.medicalert.org in the U.S.), which will immediately alert doctors to your condition and give them access to your records through MedicAlert's 24-hour hotline.

Pack prescription medications in your carry-on luggage, and carry prescription medications in their original containers with pharmacy labels—otherwise they may not make it through airport security. Also bring along copies of your prescriptions in case you lose your pills or run out. Don't forget an extra pair of contact lenses or prescription glasses. Carry the generic name of prescription medicines, in case a local pharmacist is unfamiliar with the brand name.

For domestic trips, most reliable health-care plans provide coverage if you get sick away from home. For travel abroad, you may have to pay all medical costs up front and be reimbursed later. See "Medical Insurance," above.

Medicare and Medicaid do not provide coverage for medical costs outside the U.S. Before leaving home, find out what medical services your health insurance covers. To protect yourself, consider buying medical travel insurance (see "Medical Insurance," under "Travel Insurance," above).

Very few health insurance plans pay for medical evacuation back to the U.S. (which can cost US$10,000 and up). A number of companies offer medical evacuation services anywhere in the world. If you're ever hospitalized more than 150 miles from home, **MedjetAssist** (✆ **800/527-7478;** www.medjetassistance.com) will pick you up and fly you to the hospital of your choice virtually anywhere in the world in a medically equipped and staffed aircraft 24 hours day, 7 days a week. Annual memberships are US$225 individual, US$350 family; you can also purchase short-term memberships.

We list **hospitals** and **emergency numbers** under "Fast Facts," p. 55.

8 Safety

The Niagara region is generally safe for visitors, but be alert and use common sense, particularly late at night. That said, it's never a good idea to take your safety for granted. Take the same precautions you would in any crowded district—women should carry a shoulder bag diagonally across one shoulder and men should carry their wallets in a secure place, not stuffed in their back pocket. Use the neck or wrist strap of cameras and other electronic equipment. Don't flaunt quantities of expensive jewelry or wads of bills. Keep a few small bills handy and put the remainder in a concealed place.

At the hotel, keep the door locked and use the bolt when you're inside. Before you answer the door, make sure you know who it is. If it's an unexpected visit from room service or maintenance, don't be embarrassed to call the front desk to make sure it's legitimate. Remember that the staff have passkeys, and your room is frequently opened when you're not there. Use the in-room safe for cash, traveler's checks, and other valuables. If there's no safe in your room, inquire about using the hotel safe.

In light of global concern surrounding terrorist attacks, unattended bags or suspicious-looking packages in public places should be reported.

9 Specialized Travel Resources

TRAVELERS WITH DISABILITIES

Most disabilities shouldn't stop anyone from traveling. There are more options and resources out there than ever before.

To find out which attractions, accommodations, and restaurants in the Niagara region are accessible to people with disabilities, refer to **Accessible Niagara,** an annual guide available from local Visitor Information Centers, or visit their website at **www.accessibleniagara.com**. The guide covers accommodations, tourist attractions, parks, religious facilities, restaurants, shopping malls, retail stores, wineries, and transportation. On the U.S. side, find **www.cqc.state.ny.us**, the **New York State Commission on Quality of Care and Advocacy for Persons with Disabilities.**

Blind and visually impaired travelers can obtain information on how to make the most of their trip to Niagara by calling the **Canadian National Institute for the Blind (CNIB) Information Centre** (© 905/688-0022; www.cnib.ca) or the **American Foundation for the Blind** (© 800/232-5463; www.afb.org).

Organizations that offer a vast range of resources and assistance to disabled travelers include **MossRehab** (© 800/CALL-MOSS; www.mossresourcenet.org), the **American Foundation for the Blind** (**AFB;** © 800/232-5463; www.afb.org), and **SATH (Society for Accessible Travel & Hospitality;** © 212/447-7284; www.sath.org). **AirAmbulanceCard.com** is now partnered with SATH and allows you to preselect top-notch hospitals in case of an emergency.

For more information specifically targeted to travelers with disabilities, the community website **www.accesstotravel.gc.ca** has destination guides and several regular columns on accessible travel. Also check out the quarterly magazine *Emerging Horizons* (www.emerginghorizons.com)

and *Open World* magazine, published by SATH (see above).

GAY & LESBIAN TRAVELERS

The International Gay and Lesbian Travel Association (IGLTA; © **800/448-8550** or 954/776-2626; www.iglta.org) is the trade association for the gay and lesbian travel industry, and offers an online directory of gay- and lesbian-friendly travel businesses and tour operators.

Canada is one of the world's most progressive countries, and the December 2004 Supreme Court of Canada's Equal Marriage decision demonstrated the country's commitment to human rights and strengthened the country's position as a gay-friendly travel destination. For gay-friendly accommodations, bars, and restaurants in the Niagara area, visit **www.gaycanada.com** or **www.gayniagara.com**. Details of the region's annual Pride Weekend, held in St. Catharines in June, are posted on the Gay Niagara website. The Canadian website **GayTraveler** (http://gaytraveler.ca) offers ideas and advice for gay travel all over the world. On the U.S. side, see **www.gayjourney.com/hotels/us_ny.htm**.

SENIOR TRAVEL

Some attractions and accommodations offer special rates or discounts for seniors, so always mention that fact when you make your travel arrangements. Carry a form of photo ID that includes your birth date. Becoming a member of a senior's organization may earn you a discount on travel arrangements. Consider joining the **Canadian Association of Retired Persons (CARP),** 27 Queen St. E., Ste. 1304, Toronto, Ont. M5C 2M6 (© **800/363-9736;** www.carp.ca). The website has a comprehensive travel section for members, which features hotels, packages, transportation, and travel insurance. The U.S. equivalent is **AARP** (formerly known as the American Association of Retired Persons), 601 E. St. NW, Washington, DC 20049 (© **888/687-2277;** www.aarp.org). Members get discounts on hotels, airfares, and car rentals. AARP offers members a wide range of benefits, including *AARP: The Magazine* and a monthly newsletter. Anyone over age 50 can join.

Recommended publications offering travel resources and discounts for seniors include the quarterly magazine *Travel 50 & Beyond* (www.travel50andbeyond.com) and the bestselling paperback *Unbelievably Good Deals and Great Adventures that You Absolutely Can't Get Unless You're Over 50 2005–2006, 16th Edition* (McGraw-Hill), by Joann Rattner Heilman.

FAMILY TRAVEL

Luckily for visitors with kids in tow, the Niagara region has a good selection of hotels with suite accommodation, which are equipped with kitchenettes or full kitchens and one or two bedrooms; some have two bathrooms. You get the advantage of food-preparation facilities and accommodation for the entire family in one unit, which are important considerations when you have young children with you. When booking your accommodation, always ask if family packages are available.

When you're deciding which time of year to visit, try to schedule your trip during school vacation periods, which in Ontario run for 2 weeks during Christmas/New Year, 1 week in mid-March, and the months of July and August. Special events and festivals particularly aimed at families are held at various museums and other locations during school holidays.

To locate accommodations, restaurants, and attractions that are particularly kid-friendly, refer to the "Kids" icon throughout this guide.

Recommended family-travel Internet sites include **Family Travel Forum** (www.familytravelforum.com), a comprehensive site that offers customized trip planning; **Family Travel Network** (www.familytravelnetwork.com), an award-winning site that offers travel features, deals, and tips; **Traveling Internationally with Your Kids** (www.travelwithyourkids.com), a comprehensive site offering sound advice for long-distance and international travel with children; and **Family Travel Files** (www.thefamilytravelfiles.com), which offers an online magazine and a directory of off-the-beaten-path tours and tour operators for families.

WOMEN TRAVELERS

Check out the award-winning website **Journeywoman** (www.journeywoman.com), a "real life" women's travel-information network where you can sign up for a free e-mail newsletter and get advice on everything from etiquette and dress to safety. The travel guide *Safety and Security for Women Who Travel* by Sheila Swan and Peter Laufer (Travelers' Tales Guides), offering common-sense tips on safe travel, was updated in 2004.

STUDENT TRAVEL

The **International Student Travel Confederation** (ISTC; www.istc.org) was formed in 1949 to make travel around the world more affordable for students. Check out its website for comprehensive travel services information and details on how to get an **International Student Identity Card (ISIC),** which qualifies students for substantial savings on rail passes, plane tickets, entrance fees, and more. It also provides students with basic health and life insurance and a 24-hour helpline. The card is valid for a maximum of 18 months. You can apply for the card online or in person at **STA Travel** (© 800/781-4040 in North America; www.statravel.com), the biggest student travel agency in the world; check out the website to locate STA Travel offices worldwide. If you're no longer a student but are still under age 26, you can get an **International Youth Travel Card (IYTC)** from the same people, which entitles you to some discounts. **Travel CUTS** (© 800/592-2887; www.travelcuts.com) offers similar services for both Canadians and U.S. residents. Irish students may prefer to turn to **USIT** (© 01/602-1904; www.usit.ie), an Ireland-based specialist in student, youth, and independent travel.

Students who would like to attend lectures, seminars, concerts, and other events can contact **Brock University,** 500 Glenridge Ave., St. Catharines (© 905/688-5550; www.brocku.ca) or **Niagara College** (© 905/641-2252; www.niagarac.on.ca) for information on all campuses (Welland, St. Catharines, Niagara Falls, and Grimsby).

10 Sustainable Tourism/Ecotourism

Each time you take a flight or drive a car, CO_2 is released into the atmosphere. You can help neutralize this danger to our planet through "carbon offsetting"—paying someone to reduce your CO_2 emissions by the same amount you've added. Carbon offsets can be purchased in the U.S. from companies such as **Carbonfund.org** (www.carbonfund.org) and **TerraPass** (www.terrapass.org), and from **Climate Care** (www.climatecare.org) in the U.K.

To get a comprehensive appreciation of the land in Niagara, **Niagara Nature Tours** (www.niagaranaturetours.ca) offers tours that delve into the geology and even the soil—known for producing high-quality vinifera grapes—of the Niagara region. Open since 1996, environmentalist and agriculture/horticulture expert

Frommers.com: The Complete Travel Resource

It should go without saying, but we highly recommend **Frommers.com**, voted Best Travel Site by *PC Magazine*. We think you'll find our expert advice and tips; independent reviews of hotels, restaurants, attractions, and preferred shopping and nightlife venues; vacation giveaways; and online booking tool indispensable before, during, and after your travels. We publish the complete contents of over 128 travel guides in our **Destinations** section, covering nearly 3,800 places worldwide to help you plan your trip. Each weekday, we publish original articles reporting on **Deals and News** via our free Frommers.com **newsletter** to help you save time and money and travel smarter. We're betting you'll find our new **Events** listings (http://events.frommers.com) an invaluable resource; it's an up-to-the-minute roster of what's happening in cities everywhere, including concerts, festivals, lectures, and more. We've also added weekly **podcasts, interactive maps,** and hundreds of new images across the site. Check out our **Travel Talk** area featuring **message boards** where you can join in conversations with thousands of fellow Frommer's travelers and post your trip report once you return.

Carla Carlson leads visitors through an informative and healthy tour of the area. Starting and ending in Toronto, **Something's Afoot** (www.somethingsafoot.com) offers adventure eco tours through the Niagara Region that include accommodation for 2- to 5-night stays on specific dates only.

Although one could argue that any vacation that includes an airplane flight can't be truly "green," you can go on holiday and still contribute positively to the environment. You can offset carbon emissions from your flight in other ways. Choose forward-looking companies that embrace responsible development practices, helping preserve destinations for the future by working alongside local people. An increasing number of sustainable tourism initiatives can help you plan a family trip and leave as small a "footprint" as possible on the places you visit.

Responsible Travel (www.responsibletravel.com) is a great source of sustainable travel ideas run by a spokesperson for responsible tourism in the travel industry. **Sustainable Travel International** (www.sustainabletravelinternational.org) promotes responsible tourism practices and issues an annual "Green Gear & Gift Guide."

You can find eco-friendly travel tips, statistics, and touring companies and associations—listed by destination under "Travel Choice"—at the **International Ecotourism Society** website, www.ecotourism.org. Also check out **Conservation International** (www.conservation.org), which, with *National Geographic Traveler,* annually presents **World Legacy Awards** (www.nationalgeographic.com/traveler/worldlegacy_winners.html) to those travel tour operators, businesses, organizations, and places that have made a significant contribution to sustainable tourism. **Ecotravel.com** is part online magazine and part eco-directory that lets you search for touring companies in several categories (water-based, land-based, spiritually oriented, and so on).

11 Staying Connected

TELEPHONES

If you're making a local call from anywhere in Niagara—for example, from Jordan to Niagara Falls—you must prefix the seven-digit phone number with 905.

To call Niagara:

1. Dial the international access code: 011 from the U.S.; 00 from the U.K., Ireland, or New Zealand; or 0011 from Australia.
2. Dial the country code 011.
3. Dial the city code 905 and then the number.

To make international calls from Niagara:

1. Dial 011 and then the country code (U.S. or Canada 1, U.K. 44, Ireland 353, Australia 61, New Zealand 64).
2. Next you dial 1 plus the area code and number. For example, if you wanted to call the British Embassy in Washington, D.C., you would dial 1-202/588-7800.

For directory assistance: Dial ✆ **411** if you're looking for a number inside Ontario, and dial ✆ **0** (a $5 charge applies) for numbers to all other countries.

For operator assistance: If you need operator assistance in making a call, dial ✆ **0** for local call assistance or overseas help.

Toll-free numbers: Numbers beginning with 866 and 877 are toll-free in Canada, but calling a 1-800 number in the States from Niagara is not toll-free. In fact, it costs the same as an overseas call.

CELLPHONES

The three letters that define much of the world's wireless capabilities are **GSM** (Global System for Mobile Communications), a big, seamless network that makes for easy cross-border cellphone use throughout Europe and dozens of other countries worldwide. In the U.S., T-Mobile, AT&T Wireless, and Cingular use this quasi-universal system; in Canada, Microcell and some Rogers customers are GSM, and all Europeans and most Australians use GSM. GSM phones function with a removable plastic SIM card, encoded with your phone number and account information. If your cellphone is on a GSM system, and you have a world-capable multiband phone such as many Sony Ericsson, Motorola, or Samsung models, you can make and receive calls across civilized areas around much of the

---

Tips **Hey, Google, Did You Get My Text Message?**

It's bound to happen: The day you leave this guidebook back at the hotel for an unencumbered stroll through Niagara-on-the-Lake, you'll forget the address of the lunch spot you had earmarked. If you're traveling with a mobile device, send a text message to ✆ **466/453-GOOGLE** for a lightning-fast response. For instance, type "Fort George" and within 10 seconds you'll receive a text message with the address and phone number. This nifty trick works in a range of search categories: Look up weather ("weather St. Catharines"), language translations ("translate goodbye in French"), currency conversions ("10 USD in Canadian dollars"), movie times ("Harry Potter 60605"), and more. If your search results are off, be more specific ("Copacabana Brazilian Steak House Niagara Falls Ontario"). For more tips and search options, see www.google.com/intl/en_us/mobile. Regular text-messaging charges apply.

Online Traveler's Toolbox

Veteran travelers usually carry some essential items to make their trips easier. Following is a selection of handy online tools to bookmark and use.

- **Airplane Seating and Food:** Find out which seats to reserve and which to avoid (and more) on all major domestic airlines at **www.seatguru.com**. And check out the type of meal (with photos) you'll likely be served on airlines around the world at **www.airlinemeals.net**.
- **ATM Locator:** www.mastercard.com
- **Foreign Languages for Travelers** (www.travlang.com): Learn basic terms in more than 70 languages and click on any underlined phrase to hear what it sounds like.
- **Maps: Mapquest** (www.mapquest.com), the best of the mapping sites, lets you choose a specific address or destination, and in seconds will return a map and detailed directions.
- **Weather: Intellicast** (www.intellicast.com) and **Weather.com** (www.weather.com) give weather forecasts for all 50 states and for cities around the world.

globe. Just call your wireless operator and ask for "international roaming" to be activated on your account. Unfortunately, per-minute charges can be high—usually US$1 to $1.50 in Western Europe and up to US$5 in places such as Russia and Indonesia.

For many, **renting** a phone is a good idea. While you can rent a phone from any number of overseas sites, including kiosks at airports and at car-rental agencies, we suggest renting the phone before you leave home. North Americans can rent one before leaving home from **InTouch USA** (© **800/872-7626;** www.intouchglobal.com) or **RoadPost** (© **888/290-1606** or 905/272-5665; www.roadpost.com). InTouch will also, for free, advise you on whether your existing phone will work overseas; simply call © **703/222-7161** between 9am and 4pm EST, or go to **http://intouchglobal.com/travel.htm**.

VOICE-OVER INTERNET PROTOCOL (VOIP)

If you have Web access while traveling, you might consider a broadband-based telephone service (in technical terms, **Voice over Internet protocol,** or **VoIP**) such as Skype (www.skype.com) or Vonage (www.vonage.com), which allows you to make free international calls if you use their services from your laptop or in a cybercafe. The people you're calling must also use the service for it to work; check the sites for details.

INTERNET/E-MAIL WITHOUT YOUR OWN COMPUTER

To find cybercafes in your destination, check **www.cybercaptive.com** and **www.cybercafe.com**.

Most major airports have **Internet kiosks** that provide basic Web access for a per-minute fee that's usually higher than cybercafe prices. Check out copy shops, such as **Kinko's** (FedEx Kinko's), which offer computer stations with fully loaded software (as well as Wi-Fi).

WITH YOUR OWN COMPUTER

More and more hotels, resorts, airports, cafes, and retailers are going **Wi-Fi**

Tips **Ask Before You Go**

Before you invest in a package deal or an escorted tour:

- Always ask about the **cancellation policy.** Can you get your money back? Is there a deposit required?
- Ask about the **accommodations choices and prices** for each. Then look up the hotels' reviews in a Frommer's guide and check their rates online for your specific dates of travel. Also find out what types of rooms are offered.
- Request a complete **schedule** (escorted tours only).
- Ask about the **size** and demographics of the group (escorted tours only).
- Discuss what is included in the **price** (transportation, meals, tips, airport transfers, etc.; escorted tours only).
- Finally, look for **hidden expenses.** Ask whether airport departure fees and taxes, for example, are included in the total cost—they rarely are.

(wireless fidelity), becoming "hotspots" that offer free Wi-Fi access or charge a small fee for usage. Most laptops sold today have built-in wireless capability. To find public Wi-Fi hotspots at your destination, go to **www.jiwire.com**; its Hotspot Finder holds the world's largest directory of public wireless hotspots.

T-Mobile Hotspot (www.t-mobile.com/hotspot) serves up wireless connections at more than 1,000 Starbucks coffee shops across the U.S. and Canada. **Boingo** (www.boingo.com) and **Wayport** (www.wayport.com) have set up networks in airports and high-end hotel lobbies. Wireless Internet is available for C$8.95 (US$8.50) per day at the Hamilton International Airport. Once you're out of the airport, UPS stores have in store Internet access at computer terminals. For all Canadian locations, check the website at **www.ups.ca**.

For dial-up access, most business-class hotels throughout the world offer dataports for laptop modems, and a few thousand hotels in Europe now offer free high-speed Internet access.

Wherever you go, bring a **connection kit** of the right power and phone adapters, a spare phone cord, and a spare Ethernet network cable—or find out whether your hotel supplies them to guests.

The electrical current in Canada is the same as the U.S.: 110V to 120V AC; the adapter is type B.

12 Tips on Accommodations

SURFING FOR HOTELS

In addition to the online travel booking sites **Travelocity, Expedia, Orbitz, Priceline,** and **Hotwire,** you can book hotels through **Hotels.com, Quikbook** (www.quikbook.com), and **Travelaxe** (www.travelaxe.net).

HotelChatter.com is a daily webzine offering smart coverage and critiques of hotels worldwide. Go to **TripAdvisor.com** or **HotelShark.com** for helpful independent consumer reviews of hotels and resort properties.

It's a good idea to **get a confirmation number** and **make a printout** of any online booking transaction.

In the Niagara region, accommodation packages and hotel reservations can be made online by visiting **www.tourismniagara.com**. Detailed contact information for accommodations throughout the region can be found on this site. For the

Niagara Falls area, you can also visit **www.niagarafallstourism.com**. If you want to stay in the pretty town of Niagara-on-the-Lake (only a 20-minute drive from the Falls), visit **www.niagaraonthe lake.com**.

SAVING ON YOUR HOTEL ROOM

With a plethora of accommodations in the area, there are many resources to find the perfect spot. And, with a little know-how, you can help lower the room price. To start your search, you can view photos and descriptions of B&Bs, hotels, inns, and private vacation homes. The local **Chamber of Commerce Accommodation Booking Service** (© **905/468-4263**) will make a reservation for you at one of more than 200 properties, or you can book online at **www.niagaraonthe lake.com** under accommodations. Another useful site for B&B accommodations is **www.bbcanada.com**.

The **rack rate** is the maximum rate that a hotel charges for a room. Hardly anybody pays this price, however, except in high season or on holidays. To lower the cost of your room:

- **Ask about special rates or other discounts.** You may qualify for corporate, student, military, senior, frequent flier, trade union, or other discounts.
- **Dial direct.** When booking a room in a chain hotel, you'll often get a better deal by calling the individual hotel's reservation desk rather than the chain's main number.
- **Book online.** Many hotels offer Internet-only discounts, or supply rooms to Priceline, Hotwire, or Expedia at rates much lower than the ones you can get through the hotel itself.
- **Remember the law of supply and demand.** You can save big on hotel rooms by traveling in a destination's off-season or shoulder seasons, when rates typically drop, even at luxury properties.
- **Look into group or long-stay discounts.** If you come as part of a large group, you should be able to negotiate a bargain rate. Likewise, if you're planning a long stay (at least 5 days), you might qualify for a discount. As a general rule, expect 1 night free after a 7-night stay.
- **Sidestep excess surcharges and hidden costs.** Many hotels have adopted the unpleasant practice of nickel-and-diming its guests with opaque surcharges. When you book a room, ask what is included in the room rate, and what is extra. Avoid dialing direct from hotel phones, which can have exorbitant rates. And don't be tempted by the room's minibar offerings: Most hotels charge through the nose for water, soda, and snacks. Finally, ask about local taxes and service charges, which can increase the cost of a room by 15% or more.
- **Consider enrolling in hotel chains' "frequent-stay" programs,** which are upping the ante lately to win the loyalty of repeat customers. Frequent guests can now accumulate points or credits to earn free hotel nights, airline miles, in-room amenities, merchandise, tickets to concerts and events, discounts on sporting facilities—and even credit toward stock in the participating hotel, in the case of the Jameson Inn hotel group. Perks are awarded not only by many chain hotels and motels (Hilton HHonors, Marriott Rewards, Wyndham ByRequest, to name a few), but individual inns and B&Bs. Many chain hotels partner with other hotel chains, car-rental firms, airlines, and credit-card companies to give consumers additional incentive to do repeat business.

Tips for Digital Travel Photography

- **Take along a spare camera—or two.** Even if you've been anointed the "official" photographer of your travel group, encourage others in your party to carry their own cameras and provide fresh perspectives—and backup. Your photographic "second unit" may include you in a few shots so you're not the invisible person of the trip.

- **Stock up on digital film cards.** At home, it's easy to copy pictures from your memory cards to your computer as they fill up. During your travels, cards seem to fill up more quickly. Take along enough digital film for your entire trip or, at a minimum, enough for at least a few days' of shooting. At intervals, you can copy images to CDs. Many camera stores and souvenir shops offer this service, and a growing number of mass merchandisers have walk-up kiosks you can use to make prints or create CDs during your travels.

- **Share and share alike.** No need to wait until you get home to share your photos. You can upload a gallery's worth to an online photo sharing service. Just find an Internet cafe where the computers have card readers, or connect your camera to the computer with a cable. You can find online photo sharing services that cost little or nothing at **www.clickherefree. com.** You can also use America Online's Your Pictures service, or commercial enterprises that give you free or low-cost photo sharing: Kodak's EasyShare gallery (www.kodak.com), Flickr (www.flickr.com), Snapfish (www.snapfish.com), or Shutterfly (www.shutterfly.com).

- **Add voice annotations to your photos.** Many digital cameras allow you to add voice annotations to your shots after they're taken. These serve as excellent reminders and documentation. One castle or cathedral may look like another after a long tour; your voice notes will help you distinguish them.

- **Experiment!** Travel is a great time to try out new techniques. Take photos at night, resting your camera on a handy wall or other support as your self-timer trips the shutter for a long exposure. Try close-ups of flowers, crafts, wildlife, or maybe the exotic cuisine you're about to consume. Discover action photography—shoot the countryside from trains, buses, or cars. With a digital camera, you can experiment and then erase your mistakes.

—From Travel Photography Digital Field Guide,
1st edition *(John Wiley & Sons, 2006)*

LANDING THE BEST ROOM

Somebody has to get the best room in the house. It might as well be you. You can start by joining the hotel's frequent-guest program, which may make you eligible for upgrades. A hotel-branded credit card usually gives its owner "silver" or "gold" status in frequent-guest programs for free. Always ask about a corner room. They're often larger and quieter, with more windows and light, and they often cost the same as standard rooms. When you make your reservation, ask if the hotel is renovating; if it is, request a room away from the construction. Ask about nonsmoking rooms and rooms with views. Be sure to request your choice of twin, queen- or king-size bed. If you're a light sleeper, ask for a quiet room away from vending or ice machines, elevators, restaurants, bars, and dance clubs. Ask for a room that has been recently renovated or refurbished.

If you aren't happy with your room when you arrive, ask for another one. Most lodgings will be willing to accommodate you.

3

Suggested Itineraries for the Niagara Region

Everyone thinks first of the Falls, which are, without a doubt, the primary reason most tourists visit the Niagara region. And if you've never seen them, then certainly they should be your first priority. Second on your list should be Niagara-on-the-Lake, an elegant, small Ontario town with exquisite accommodations, excellent shopping and dining, and the renowned Shaw Festival Theatre. The Niagara region is also the proud home of a well-respected wine industry, and those with a penchant for good food and wine could spend anything from an afternoon to a week exploring the wine country. Sidling up to the accessible locks of the Welland Canal is another worthwhile experience. In between, there are villages, bicycle trails, and nature preserves that will add variety to your schedule and allow you to discover delights of the Niagara region you might otherwise never realize were on the doorstep of the world's best-known waterfalls.

Note: These itineraries have been set up for visitors who come to Niagara during the prime tourist season between April and October. Many, but not all, of the attractions are open in the winter months, and Niagara under snow can be a magical winter wonder. However, please call ahead (or check chapter 7, "What to See & Do in the Niagara Region") if you are planning to visit outside the main tourist season and there are specific attractions or itineraries you wish to include.

1 The Best of Niagara Falls in 1 day

Seeing the sights of Niagara in 1 day requires an early start, discipline, and stamina, but it's quite doable. Start on the Canadian side, since it is on this side of the river that you get the gorgeous panorama of both the American and Horseshoe falls. First, park your car in an all-day parking lot, and then buy one of the tourist passes. The large lot on the Niagara Parkway, south of the Horseshoe Falls in Canada, is recommended because you can purchase your **Great Gorge Adventure Pass** at the kiosk there and take the People Mover (unlimited transport for the day is included with the pass) right from the parking lot to the Falls and other attractions. *Start: Maid of the Mist on the Canadian side.*

❶ The *Maid of the Mist*
Although your first instinct will be to rush to the side of the river and stare at the Falls, head straight for the *Maid of the Mist* for two reasons. First, during the

boat trip you will immediately feel the immense power of the water and get a deep appreciation of the size and grandeur of both the American and Canadian falls. Second, you will avoid the

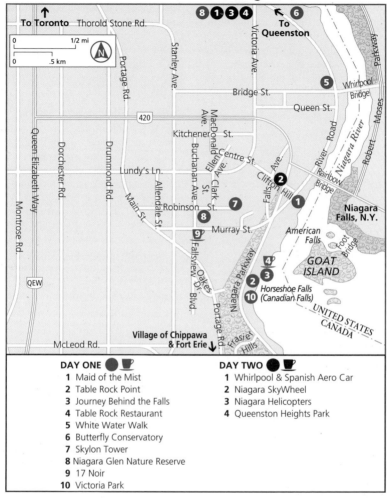

To Toronto Thorold Stone Rd.

To Queenston

DAY ONE ● ☕
1 Maid of the Mist
2 Table Rock Point
3 Journey Behind the Falls
4 Table Rock Restaurant
5 White Water Walk
6 Butterfly Conservatory
7 Skylon Tower
8 Niagara Glen Nature Reserve
9 17 Noir
10 Victoria Park

DAY TWO ● ☕
1 Whirlpool & Spanish Aero Car
2 Niagara SkyWheel
3 Niagara Helicopters
4 Queenston Heights Park

lines, which get longer as the day goes on. Grab a spot on the starboard side of the boat (that's the right-hand side, for you landlubbers)—you'll get closer to the Horseshoe Falls and will still have great views of the American Falls on your return to the dock. See p. 106.

❷ The Falls by Day

After you alight from the *Maid of the Mist*'s dock, walk south along the edge of the Niagara River to Table Rock Point.

Now is the time to drink in the views and marvel at the thundering waters of Niagara from the safety of the shore. Get out your camera—and don't be shy to ask a fellow tourist to take a picture of you with the Falls in the background. You'll probably be asked to do the same thing!

❸ Journey Behind the Falls

Now it's time to plunge down into the gorge on foot. Use your Great Gorge Adventure Pass in Canada and enter Table

Rock House to take the Journey Behind the Falls tour. Walk through tunnels bored into the rock behind the Horseshoe Falls and emerge onto the lower balcony at the northern edge. This is where you will feel the power of the Horseshoe Falls at its mightiest.

4 TAKE A BREAK
Take a food/beverage break at the **Table Rock Restaurant,** 6650 Niagara Pkwy., Niagara Falls (© 905/354-3631—another spot that has a spectacular view of the Falls.

5 White Water Walk

Jump on the People Mover and ride north to the White Water Walk attraction. An elevator takes you on a deep plunge to the bottom of the Niagara Gorge. A boardwalk along the edge of the base of the gorge brings you face to face with one of the world's wildest stretches of white water. See p. 110.

6 Butterfly Conservatory

Take the People Mover to the Butterfly Conservatory, a delightful place to visit for an hour or so. The Conservatory doubles as the display greenhouse for the Niagara Parks Botanical Gardens and is blessed with an abundance of natural light. The butterflies spend a considerable amount of time resting, so it's a great place to bring your camera.

7 Skylon Tower or Konica Minolta Tower

The aerial view of the Falls offers a unique and panoramic perspective. You're literally on top of the Falls. Take the People Mover to the Incline Railway, situated opposite

Table Rock House terminus. If you have a Great Gorge Adventure Pass, the trip is free; otherwise you will have to pay a small fee to ride up the cliff. Once at the top, walk farther up the hill to Fallsview Boulevard, and turn right (north) for the Skylon Tower (p. 106 and 107).

8 Niagara Glen Nature Reserve

On the east side of the Niagara Parkway, a short drive north of the whirlpool, you'll find the Niagara Glen Nature Reserve, which features a series of seven linked trails, ranging in length from .4km (¼ mile) to 3.3km (2 miles). Note that each of the paths, or access to them, is steep in places—River Path is the flattest, but you need to descend the cliff to reach it. Alternatively—or in addition, if you just love to be outdoors—you can stroll the Niagara Parks Botanical Gardens, just a little farther north on the west side of the Parkway. See p. 141.

9 TAKE A BREAK
In the Fallsview Boulevard area, you can choose from a variety of dining options. For casual fine-dining in a casino-themed restaurant (it resembles a roulette table), I recommend **17 Noir,** 6380 Fallsview Blvd., Niagara Falls, Ont. (© 888/WINFALL). See p. 84. There are several family-style and roadhouse restaurants in the immediate area, if your tastes run more to that type of food.

10 The Falls by Night

When darkness falls, both Falls will be magically illuminated in a flood of rainbow colors. Take another tower trip, or walk down into Victoria Park and view the light show from the Canadian shore of the Niagara Gorge.

2 The Best of the Niagara Region in 2 Days

Head north on the Niagara Parkway by car or the Niagara-on-the-Lake Shuttle (see chapter 4, "Getting to Know the Niagara Region"). Marvel at the whirlpool in the Niagara Gorge, and then enjoy the beauty of the public areas of the Niagara Parks

Commission by exploring the Botanical Gardens or taking a leisurely ramble through the Niagara Glen Nature Reserve before heading to historic Queenston Heights Park, scene of one of the most famous battles of the War of 1812. Explore Niagara-on-the-Lake, including the quaint shops and restaurants along Queen Street. Fill your afternoon with a visit to Fort George, live theater at the Shaw Festival, or a thrill ride along the Niagara Gorge Rapids on a jet boat. ***Start:*** *Niagara Parkway, alongside Victoria Park.*

❶ Whirlpool & Spanish Aero Car

A vintage metal carriage, suspended on cables above the whirlpool phenomenon in the Niagara Gorge, takes passengers on a 1km (half-mile) round-trip overlooking the whirlpool. See p. 109.

❷ Niagara SkyWheel

For a mere C$10 (US$9.50), ride the giant Ferris wheel on Clifton Hill. Heated in the winter and cooled in the summer, the gondola ride overlooks the Falls and into New York. The 7-minute ride does three loops in all.

❸ Helicopter Ride

After seeing the Falls from below, underneath, and behind, the next step is to see the giant from above. Starting near the gorge, the ride swoops over the gorge, over the Falls, down the Welland Canal, and back. See p. 125.

❹ Queenston Heights Park

Queenston Heights Park has a variety of facilities and attractions for visitors. View Brock's Monument (under repair with no set reopening date at press time) and the Laura Secord Monument. Take a 45-minute self-guided walking tour of the battleground of the War of 1812's Battle of Queenston Heights, or enjoy the mature shade trees and grassy open spaces of the park, perfect for ballgames and family fun. See p. 131.

❺ TAKE A BREAK

If you're looking for an early lunch, **Queenston Heights Restaurant,** located right in the park, enjoys beautiful open vistas looking north along the Niagara River toward Lake Ontario. Lunch, afternoon tea, and dinner are served, and a children's menu is available (14184 Niagara Pkwy, Queenston, Ontario; ✆ 905/ 262-4274). See p. 84. If you have a picnic basket with you, enjoy lunch on one of the many picnic tables throughout the park.

❻ Shaw Festival Afternoon Performance

I recommend booking tickets in advance if you wish to see a performance at the world-renowned Shaw Festival. The Shaw has three theaters in Niagara-on-the-Lake, and presents plays written by George Bernard Shaw and his contemporaries, along with plays set during the period of Shaw's lifetime. See p. 187.

❼ Niagara World Wine Tours

Biking through little-known trails in the woods and behind the vineyards, with breaks for tastings, is a relaxing way to visit the wineries. At some wineries, you can drink wine straight from the barrel and then compare it with the mature wine in the bottle. If you opt for a tour with lunch, you can sit under a shaded tree and eat a homemade lunch with your new wine buddies. See p. 142.

❽ Queen Street Shopping

The best boutique shopping in Niagara is to be found along Queen Street in Niagara-on-the-Lake; the shops spill onto the side streets along the route. The street gets crowded in the summer months, but the shops are quaint, unique, and entertaining. See chapter 9, "Shopping."

TAKE A BREAK
There are plenty of places to buy a tasty bakery treat, ice cream, or cold drink along Queen Street. Or take the time to enjoy afternoon tea; try the **Prince of Wales Hotel**, 6 Picton St., Niagara-on-the-Lake (✆ 888/669-5566).

❿ Fort George

Fort George is a reconstructed British fort that served as military headquarters in the past and played a key role in the War of 1812. Highlights of the fort include the reconstructed guardhouse, officers' quarters, flag bastion, blockhouses, and Brock's bastion, the fort's most strategic artillery battery (p. 114).

⓫ The Leafy Side Streets—by Foot or Horse & Carriage

The graceful and pleasant streets of Niagara-on-the-Lake's Heritage District—the "Old Town"—are laid out in a grid fashion, making it simple to find your way around. Just head down any side street off the main shopping district on Queen Street and you will find quaint streets lined with impressively restored historic homes. You can pick up a map of the town at the Niagara-on-the-Lake Visitor & Convention Bureau, at 26 Queen St. Sentinel Carriages will take you around town in a horse-drawn carriage, passing by places of historic interest on the way.

TAKE A BREAK
If you have tickets for an evening Shaw performance, then make a reservation for an early dinner for around 5:30pm, which will allow you time to walk to the theater afterward without having to rush. If you *aren't* going to the theater, then wait until around 7pm, when the pretheater crowds have thinned out; you will enjoy a more peaceful and relaxed meal. Try **Zee's Patio & Grill**, right across the street from the main theater, 92 Picton St., Niagara-on-the-Lake (✆ 906/468-5715). If you are looking for a quiet place for a drink in the evening, try one of the hotel bars.

3 The Best of the Niagara Region in 3 Days

On the third day, you can really begin to get to know Niagara, and make your itinerary more personal. Start your day with a tour of the local wineries. The Welland Canal is well worth a visit, but only if you have your own vehicle to drive to one of the two main viewing locations *and* a ship will be entering or leaving the lock you choose to view at a convenient time. See chapter 7, "What to See & Do in the Niagara Region," for how to find the shipping traffic schedule for the day of your visit. Finally, drop in to the pretty villages of Old Port Dalhousie or Jordan, and enjoy life at a slower pace for the afternoon. ***Start:*** *Park at Strewn Winery on Lakeshore Rd. in Niagara-on-the-Lake, then make your way west to the escarpment and outlying wineries.*

❶ The Niagara Peninsula Wine Route

Visit the wineries in the morning (10am is the almost universal opening time), before the crowds arrive. Remember, you're tasting 1-ounce samples, and it's perfectly acceptable to spit the wine out after tasting, so don't get in a twist about

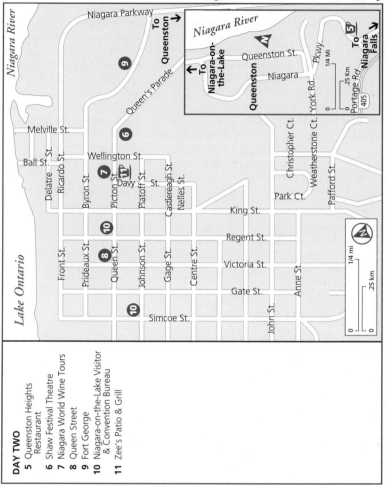

drinking before noon. You are likely to have the tasting bar staff all to yourself, which means you can linger, ask questions, and generally have a more relaxing time. Check out chapter 8, "The Wine-Country Experience," for more details.

TAKE A BREAK
If you're looking for a winery lunch, **Terroir La Cachette Restaurant & Wine Bar,** at Strewn Winery, 1339 Lakeshore Rd., Niagara-on-the-Lake (☏ **905/468-1222**), offers excellent Provençal cuisine at reasonable prices and tends to be a little more casual than most of the region's winery restaurants.

❸ Welland Canal Lock 3 or Lock 7

Viewing complexes have been created for the public to watch the "salties" (ocean-going ships) and "lakers" (those ships that sail the Great Lakes) at Thorold Lock 7 Viewing Complex, where you can watch the ships climb up and down the escarpment at a series of three twinned locks, and get a close-up view of Lock 7 in operation. There is a tourist information center and small cafe at this location (p. 118). The Welland Canal Centre is located at Lock 3, which is also home to the St. Catharines Museum (p. 118).

❹ Old Port Dalhousie

Browse the village shops and take a stroll along the waterfront. If you have kids in tow, they will enjoy the antique carousel in the park along Lake Ontario's shoreline.

⑤ TAKE A BREAK
By now you'll probably be ready for lunch. Try **Spice of Life,** 12 Lock St., Port Dalhousie (✆ 905/ 937-9027) for a unique taste not found in the wineries.

❻ Twenty Valley

Shop in the boutiques of Jordan Village, enjoy the rolling hills, woodlands, and meandering streams of the countryside, or experience the hospitality of the many wineries in this area. The Bruce Trail blazes through the Twenty Valley's southern end, circumnavigating Ball's Falls and passing within sipping distance of several wineries.

⑦ TAKE A BREAK
If you want to experience an authentic wine-country dinner, call for reservations at **On the Twenty Restaurant,** 3836 Main St., Jordan Village, Ont. (✆ **905/562-7313**). See p. 98. Be adventurous and ask whether a tasting menu is on offer.

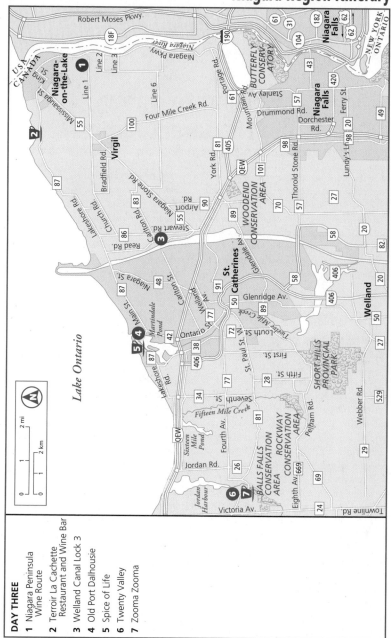

4

Getting to Know the Niagara Region

The name *Niagara* is synonymous with the Falls, and indeed the extraordinary power of the seventh forgotten wonder of the natural world is often the biggest draw for visitors to the Niagara region. But the Niagara region has much more to offer. You can step into the commercial maze of Niagara Falls, Ontario, and its sister city Niagara Falls, New York, or escape along the Niagara River Parkway into an oasis of groomed greenery.

For those exhausted by the force of the Falls and the city's exuberant tackiness, a journey of discovery to the rest of the Niagara region will provide welcome relief. The historical town of Niagara-on-the-Lake, the rolling vineyards and fragrant orchards of Niagara's agricultural heart, and the friendly communities strung along the mighty Welland Canal are reasons enough to venture beyond the Falls.

1 Orientation

VISITOR INFORMATION

In the city of Niagara Falls, Ontario, visit **Niagara Falls Tourism** at 5515 Stanley Ave. (© **800/563-2557;** www.niagarafallstourism.com). Other major tourism offices include **Niagara-on-the-Lake Visitor and Convention Bureau,** 26 Queen St., Courthouse Building, Lower Level, Niagara-on-the-Lake (© **905/468-1950;** www.niagaraonthelake.com); St Catharines Tourism Services, 1932 Welland Canals Pkwy., St. Catharines (© **800/305-5134;** www.stcatharineslock3museum.ca); and **Thorold Lock 7 Information & Viewing Centre,** 50 Chapel St. S., Thorold (© **905/680-9477;** www.thorold.com).

If you are traveling by car, drop in to one of the **Ontario Travel Centres: Niagara Falls** at 5355 Stanley Ave. (west on Hwy. 420 from the Rainbow Bridge; © **905/358-3221**), **Fort Erie** at 350 Bertie St., Unit 1, just off the Queen Elizabeth Way (QEW; © **905/871-3505**), or in **St. Catharines** at 251 York Rd., RR#4 (westbound QEW at east end of Garden City Skyway; © **905/684-6354**). If you are arriving in the Niagara region along the Queen Elizabeth Way, you can also visit **Gateway Niagara Information Centre** at 424 S. Service Rd., QEW at Casablanca Boulevard, at the Grimsby exit (© **905/945-5444**).

On the American side, the **Niagara Tourism and Convention Corporation** is at 345 Third St., Suite 605, Niagara Falls, NY (© **800/338-7890** or 716/282-8992; www.niagara-usa.com). Office hours are Monday to Friday from 8:30am to 5pm.

PUBLICATIONS & WEBSITES

The daily newspapers are *Niagara Falls Review, St. Catharines Standard, Fort Erie Review, Port Colborne Tribune,* and *Welland Tribune.* Several smaller communities publish weekly newspapers. *Niagara This Week* is a free local paper that carries local news and a listing of community events in its "It's Happening" section. Also published is the smaller *Free Daily Press.* Both are available at tourist information centers. On the U.S. side, you'll find two dailies: *The Niagara Gazette* and *The Tonawanda News. The Current* is a free weekly. Online sources of information on the Niagara region include **www.tourismniagara.com**, **www.niagarafallstourism.com**, **www.info niagara.com**, **www.niagaraparks.com**, and **www.niagarapeninsula.com**. For information more closely tied to specific areas and towns, visit the websites of the tourist information centers listed in "Visitor Information," above.

LAYOUT OF THE REGION

The **Niagara region** is a peninsula bordered by **Lake Ontario** to the north, the **Niagara River** to the east, and **Lake Erie** to the south. A ridge of land known as the **Niagara Escarpment,** characterized by a steep face on one side and a gentle slope on the other, rises from Queenston on the Niagara River and runs east to west through the region. The other major physical structure in the landscape is the **Welland Canal,** which connects Lake Ontario with Lake Erie via a series of eight locks, and roughly divides the region in half. At the head of the Canal sits the port city of **St. Catharines.** Moving south along the Canal, **Thorold,** with its Lock 7 Viewing Complex, is the next major place of interest. Farther south is the city of **Welland.** Finally, at the connection with Lake Erie lies the marine city of **Port Colborne.**

The **Falls** are situated midway along the Niagara River, which connects Lake Ontario and Lake Erie. They consist of two main waterfalls. The **American Falls** (which are, appropriately, located on U.S. soil) dramatically cascade onto tons of fallen rock that lie at the base of the waterfall. The **Horseshoe Falls,** located across the border in Canada, send clouds of mist into the air from their concave center. Afternoon sunlight creates a rainbow in the swirling droplets of water.

The cities of **Niagara Falls, Ontario,** and **Niagara Falls, New York,** cluster around the Falls on either side of the border, connected by the **Rainbow Bridge,** just downstream from the American Falls. Farther downstream, the **Lewiston–Queenston Bridge** provides another span across the **Niagara River.** Where the Niagara River flows into Lake Ontario proudly sits the town of **Niagara-on-the-Lake,** once the capital of Upper Canada.

At the opposite end of the Niagara River, the city of **Buffalo** lies on the southwestern edge of Lake Erie and the Niagara River, with the town of **Fort Erie** across the river in Canada. The **Buffalo–Fort Erie Peace Bridge** transports vehicular and foot traffic at this border crossing.

The major highway in the region is the Queen Elizabeth Way (QEW), which runs along the western shore of Lake Ontario from Toronto, turning south as it makes its way through St. Catharines and eventually linking with I-190 across the border in Buffalo. Feeder highways siphon traffic off the QEW into St. Catharines (Hwy. 406), the Lewiston–Queenston Bridge to the U.S. (Hwy. 405), and Niagara Falls, Ontario (Hwy. 420).

The Niagara Escarpment

The **Niagara Escarpment** forms the backbone of the Niagara Peninsula. The unique natural features of the escarpment and its ecological importance have been recognized by the United Nations Education, Scientific, and Cultural Organization (UNESCO), and the escarpment has been duly designated as a **Man and the Biosphere Reserve**. The designation has elevated the escarpment's significance, joining the growing ranks of Biosphere Reserves that include the Galapagos Islands, the Serengeti National Park, and the Florida Everglades.

The Niagara Escarpment is a 1,050km (650-mile), crescent-shaped *cuesta*—a ridge formed by inclined rock strata, with a gentle slope on one side and a steep slope on the other. Its origin lies in New York State, south of Rochester. The ridge extends into Canada, running through Queenston on the Niagara River, bisecting the Niagara region from east to west, and then traveling north before plunging into Lake Huron. It eventually ends at the Door Peninsula in Wisconsin, in the Midwestern United States.

The southern part of the escarpment, which contains the section that is found in Niagara, is located in Canada's warmest region, the **Carolinian Canada Zone**. It is a fragile ecosystem containing roughly one-quarter of the country's population and half of the endangered species—in an area that represents less than one-quarter of 1% of Canada's total landmass. This region is one of the most threatened of all Ontario's natural areas, and numerous organizations are involved in the preservation and conservation of the Niagara Escarpment's natural and cultural heritage.

The **Bruce Trail** follows the Niagara Escarpment through Ontario from Queenston Heights in the south to Tobermory at the northern tip of the Bruce Peninsula. The trail, which is marked by white blazes painted on trees, fence posts, and rocks, links parks and conservation areas along the route. The path is steep and rocky in places, but its rugged beauty, accented by waterfalls tumbling over the dolostone cliffs, is worth the effort. The trail offers a welcome escape from the urban landscape and agricultural development that cover much of the Niagara region.

The **winegrowing area** in the Niagara region is the sheltered section of land between Lake Ontario's south shore and the Niagara Escarpment, running from just west of Grimsby all the way to the Niagara River. An official **Wine Route Map** is available and the route is clearly marked with signposts along the roadways.

THE REGION IN BRIEF
Niagara Falls, Ontario, Canada

The Niagara Falls area is the hub of the region. This is where you will find the mighty "thundering waters" of the powerful American Falls and the spectacular Canadian Horseshoe Falls. The Niagara Falls district welcomes a mind-boggling 14 million visitors each year, and it's got the amenities to prove it: Skyscraper hotels look over dozens of eateries on top of the hill in the Fallsview District.

Anchoring the hotel district, Clifton Hill exudes a boisterous carnival atmosphere. A protected strip of land lies between the Falls and the commercial mayhem of the city of Niagara Falls. The Niagara Parks Commission is the steward of this oasis, which provides a mix of immaculately groomed lawns and flowerbeds along the edge of the Falls and the Niagara Gorge. The world-famous *Maid of the Mist* tour boat can be boarded here. Traveling north along the western bank of the Niagara River, the scenic Niagara Parkway links Niagara Falls and Niagara-on-the-Lake by road, passing by the Niagara Parks Botanical Gardens, Butterfly Conservatory, Niagara Glen Nature Area, Floral Clock, McFarland House, Queenston Heights, Sir Adam Beck 2 Generating Station, and other places of interest.

Niagara Falls, New York, U.S.

You can take in the view of the Falls from the American side and also see the pre-falls rapids. The district includes the Niagara Falls State Park, the oldest state park in the United States. There are a number of other tourist attractions on the American side, including the *Maid of the Mist* (which launched here in 1846), Cave of the Winds, a boardwalk constructed next to the American Falls, and an observation tower. The infrastructure for tourists is not as well developed in Niagara Falls, New York, as it is in Niagara Falls, Ontario, however, so if you start your Niagara visit on the U.S. side of the border, it's well worth crossing to Canada.

Niagara-on-the-Lake

Only a 1½-hour drive from Toronto, Canada's largest city, lies one of North America's prettiest and best-preserved 19th-century villages. The streets of Niagara-on-the-Lake are lined with mature trees. Dozens of immaculately restored and maintained historical brick and clapboard homes grace the town. The town center is home to the Shaw Festival, boutique shopping, B&Bs, inns, and a choice of fine restaurants. On the edges of the town you'll find a number of wineries, as well as Fort George National Historic Site. If you like elegance and don't mind the bustle of tourists stepping out of packed tour buses during the busy summer months, base yourself in Niagara-on-the-Lake and tour the region from here.

Wine Route

The Niagara Peninsula is home to more than 60 wineries and is the largest designated viticultural area in Canada. The region is divided into three areas, each of which offers a variety of accommodations, primarily in B&Bs and inns, and restaurants ranging from exquisite winery cuisine to cozy tea shops and delicious ethnic fare.

Grimsby and Beamsville are the farthest west. This plateau of fertile land, which lies between the escarpment ridge and Lake Ontario, runs from Grimsby to just west of St. Catharines.

Jordan and Vineland is the next region you will meet as you travel east. This area offers art galleries, unique

---

(*Fun Fact*   **The Falls are Falling**

Scientists speculate that at the present rate of erosion the Falls will no longer exist in 50,000 years, although a river will still flow between Lake Erie and Lake Ontario.

shopping in quaint villages, and follows the Bruce Trail, which at 850km (528 miles) is Ontario's longest footpath. The Bruce Trail can be accessed from several wineries that back onto the Niagara Escarpment. (Grimsby, Beamsville, Jordan and Vineland are all part of an area known as "The Bench.")

Niagara-on-the-Lake is the third viticultural area in Niagara (see above).

Welland Canal Corridor & Fort Erie

St. Catharines is the largest city in the Niagara region. The city has two main heritage districts—downtown St. Catharines (encompassing Queen Street Heritage District and Yates Street District, which feature fine examples of historical residential architecture) and the lakeside village of Port Dalhousie. St. Catharines is known as the "Garden City," due to its surrounding vineyards, gardens, nurseries, and farmland. The Welland Canals Centre is located at Lock 3 along the Welland Canal.

Thorold, south of St. Catharines, offers another visitor-friendly viewing point, the Lock 7 Viewing Complex. The Twinned Flight Locks, which raise and lower ships up and down the Niagara Escarpment (42m/140 ft.), are also located in Thorold. With downtown revitalization plans underway, which will result in new stores and the restoration of the Keefer Mansion Inn, overlooking the town, this town is an ugly duckling on its way to becoming a swan.

Welland is the next city along the canal. Canada's Rose city, Welland hosts a Rose Festival each summer. Recreational trails run alongside the canal here. Merritt Island, a haven for outdoor enthusiasts, is a highlight of the area.

Port Colborne is the community situated at the mouth of the Welland Canal and Lake Erie. The city's signature event is the Canal Days Marine Heritage Festival.

Fort Erie lies on the banks of the Niagara River, overlooking Buffalo and just a few minutes from the Peace Bridge. Attractions include Historic Fort Erie, Fort Erie Historical Museum, Ridgeway Battlefield Site, Fort Erie Railroad Museum, Mahoney Dolls' House Gallery, The Slave Quarters, and Fort Erie Racetrack.

2 Getting Around

BY CAR

A car is necessary if you wish to tour the entire region during your visit, but you do not need a car to get around in Niagara Falls. Public transit is not available between Niagara Falls and Niagara-on-the-Lake, but a shuttle bus runs between the bus terminal and certain hotels in Niagara Falls to Fort George in Niagara-on-the-Lake (© 800/667-0256 or 905/358-3232). The bus leaves in the morning and returns in the late afternoon. Niagara-on-the-Lake is small enough that you don't need a car. Wine country tours can be arranged through tour companies. See chapter 8 for details.

Fun Fact

The brilliant green color of the Niagara River comes from dissolved minerals and finely ground rock, mostly from the limestone riverbed but also from the shale and sandstone under the limestone cap at the Falls.

DRIVING RULES In Ontario, a right turn on a red light is permitted after coming to a complete stop, unless posted otherwise, provided you yield to oncoming traffic and pedestrians. Wearing your seat belt is compulsory. Fines for riding without a seat belt are substantial. Speed limits are posted and must be obeyed at all times. Always stop when pedestrians are using the crosswalks, and watch for pedestrians crossing against the lights. Radar detectors are illegal. American drivers should note the difference in speed limits—Canadian signs are calculated in kilometers per hour, while U.S. signs are in miles per hour. Use the kilometer display on your speedometer or, if your car doesn't have one, divide the kilometers by 1.6 to obtain the mileage.

PARKING Parking meters generally accept quarters, loonies, and toonies. Always read the signs posted near parking meters to find out if there are any parking restrictions. If you must leave your vehicle on a city street overnight, ask hotel staff or your B&B host whether there are parking restrictions. Parking meters are available in the city of Niagara Falls, New York, but I recommend that you park your vehicle in the Niagara Falls State Park. Meters are plentiful on both the U.S. and Canadian sides. Meter payment is required 7 days a week.

For parking at the Falls, you can leave your vehicle at the **Rapids View Parking Lot** for C$6.50 (US$6.20) (south of the Horseshoe Falls on the Niagara Parkway). The price includes a free shuttle to and from the Falls. Other options include purchasing a **People Mover Pass** at the parking lot (C$7.50/US$7.10 adults, C$5/US$4.75 children 6–12; see below), which allows you unlimited on/off privileges on the People Mover transit system that runs between Table Rock, at the Horseshoe Falls, and The Floral Clock, north of the Niagara Gorge along the Niagara Parkway. The People Mover stops at most of the major tourist attractions along the route, including the *Maid of the Mist,* American Falls, Whitewater Walk, Whirlpool Aero Car, Botanical Gardens & Butterfly Conservatory, and the Floral Clock. You can also elect to purchase a **Niagara Falls and Great Gorge Adventure Pass** at the parking lot (C$40/US$38 adults, C$25/US$24 children 6–12). This pass includes entry to major attractions and access to the People Mover for a single, discounted price. Additional parking is available opposite the Horseshoe Falls (all day for a single fee ranging between C$12/US$11 and C$18US$17), and at the Niagara Parks Floral Showhouse, south of the Horseshoe Falls (Apr–Nov C$3/US$2.85 per hour to a maximum of C$12/US$11; free in the winter). You will find a number of all-day parking lots with the reasonable fee of around C$5 (US$4.75) in the Fallsview district at the top of the escarpment. From here, you can take footpaths down to the Falls (ask your parking

Getting Married

If you want to join the ranks of millions of romantic couples who have made the big leap, to get married near the Falls that is, there are dozens of organizations eager to help you and your beloved tie the knot in Niagara. If you've done the deed elsewhere and you're considering a post-wedding getaway, the Honeymoon Capital of the World awaits, complete with heart-shaped tubs in a plethora of motel rooms (see chapter 5, "Where to Stay," for a look at the region's coziest love nests). And for same-sex couples, the Niagara region is quickly becoming a popular destination.

Wedding Services   Niagara Falls Tourism has compiled a list of local photographers, wedding planners, florists, limos, and other wedding services. You can access this list at **www.infoniagara.com/services/weddings/index.html**.

Same-sex couples   After you have obtained a license from City Hall, head to the Sheraton Fallsview Hotel & Conference Centre (6755 Fallsview Blvd.; © **800/618-9059**) for a ceremony, reception, or honeymoon. For more information, visit **www.gayniagara.com**.

Venues   The **Niagara Parks Commission** (5881 Dunn St., Niagara Falls, Ont.; © **877/642-7275**; www.niagaraparks.com) offers six beautiful outdoor locations for wedding ceremonies. **Oakes Garden Theatre** features graceful architecture and beautiful gardens, with the Bridal Veil Falls in full view across the Niagara Gorge. The Victorian-style lattice **wedding arbor** in the **Botanical Gardens** is a popular spot, as is the secluded **willow pond,** with its quaint wooden bridge. The elegant **Floral Showhouse Gardens & Tropical Foyer,** surrounded by tall grasses and ponds, is the newest venue. Farther from the Falls, you will find the **Laura Secord Monument** at Queenston Heights and the **Mather Arch** in the town of Fort Erie. Weddings are also held at the **Queenston Chapel,** an 1862 white clapboard chapel that features oak pews and stained-glass windows.

Other popular wedding venues include **Niagara Fallsview Weddings,** located at the top of the Konica Minolta Tower overlooking the Falls. With the Pinnacle Restaurant and the Ramada Plaza Hotel located in the same

attendant for directions, since these paths are not well signposted), or travel on the Incline Railway (see below for details).

BY PUBLIC TRANSPORTATION

BUS   Niagara Transit operates throughout the city of Niagara Falls and surrounding communities, including service to Brock University and Niagara College. The bus station is located at 4320 Bridge St., Niagara Falls, Ont. (© **905/356-1179**; www.niagara transit.com). The buses operate on an exact-fare basis: C$2.25 (US$2.15) adults, C$2 (US$1.90) students and seniors, and C$1 (US95¢) children; ages 5 and under ride free. Buses run regularly until midnight. Welland Transit has regular routes, and the last run tower, you can arrange the ceremony, reception, and honeymoon all in one location. You'll find the Tower at 6733 Fallsview Blvd., Niagara Falls, Ont. (© **866/325-5785** or 905/356-1501). **Niagara Fallsview Weddings** (Niagara Falls, Ontario; © **866/325-5785**) offers a wedding on the 25th floor of the Konica Minolta Tower (at the Ramada Hotel) with almost floor-to-ceiling windows overlooking the mouth of the Canadian Falls. The **Little Wedding Chapel** (7701 Lundy's Lane, Niagara Falls, Ont.; © **800/463-0884** or 905/357-0266) features candlelit services performed by licensed ministers and elegant white pews with seating for 40 people. **Niagara Weddings Canada** (5669 Main St., Niagara Falls, Ont.; © **866/645-1714**) performs wedding ceremonies in various locations in the Niagara area, including the gazebo in **Niagara-on-the-Lake,** overlooking Lake Ontario. They also operate the **Wayside Chapel,** a tiny chapel beside the Niagara Parkway that holds a maximum of 10 people. **Two Hearts Wedding Chapel** (5127 Victoria Ave., Niagara Falls, Ont.; © **866/251-1115** or 905/371-3204) is close to the Falls and City Hall. Religious and civil candlelight services are available. **The Wedding Company of Niagara** (6053 Franklin Ave., Niagara Falls, Ont.; © **877/641-3111** or 905/371-3695) offers services in their chapel and off-site. If you would like to hold your wedding ceremony or reception in wine country, many of the wineries now host weddings. Make your inquiries directly with the wineries. See chapter 8 for contact information.

Marriage licenses   Licenses must be obtained prior to the ceremony and are valid for 3 months from the date of issue. You can apply in person for a marriage license at City Hall, Clerks Department, 4310 Queen St., Niagara Falls, Ont. (© **905/356-7521**). The fee is C$100 (US$95), although the price is subject to change, and must be paid in cash or by debit card. Both parties must be 18 years of age or over to obtain a license. Applicants who are 16 or 17 years of age must have parental consent. Two pieces of identification—a birth certificate or valid passport only and photo ID (original documents only)—must be produced. Note that while same-sex marriages are recognized in Canada, they may not be accepted as legal in other countries.

is 10:30pm (160 E. Main St.; © **905/732-6844,** ext. 6; www.welland.ca/Transit/index.asp). The City of St. Catharines Transit Commission has regular bus routes and also services Thorold, with limited services in Niagara-on-the-Lake (© **905/687-5555;** www.yourbus.com). The last St. Catharines bus leaves at 11:45pm. Niagara Falls, New York, runs buses via the Niagara Frontier Transportation Authority (© **716/855-7300;** www.nfta.com). Rates depend on zones crossed, starting at C$1.60 (US$1.50) within one zone to a maximum of C$2.40 (US$2.25) for four zones.

THE FALLS SHUTTLE   Owned and operated by the Niagara Transit Commission, the Falls Shuttle passes by tourist accommodations properties in the Lundy's

---

Fun Fact

The name "Niagara" has evolved from the North American Native word *Onguiaahra,* most often translated as "the strait," although the more poetic phrase "thunder of waters" is frequently attributed.

Lane and River Road district. The **Red Line** serves Lundy's Lane, the Via Rail Station, the Bus Terminal, the Falls, and points of interest along the Niagara Gorge. The **Blue Line** serves the Fallsview area, including the Konica Minolta Tower, Skylon Tower, and Clifton Hill, traveling as far as Marineland. When the fireworks display over the Falls is in operation, every Friday and Sunday (10pm) and holidays from May 24 until September, a special **fireworks shuttle** takes tourists to the brink of the Falls. Fare is C$6 (US$5.70) per adult, and tickets are available from shuttle bus drivers, the Niagara Bus Terminal, and most lodgings.

PEOPLE MOVER ⚡   This public transportation system, operated by the Niagara Parks Commission between April and October, is highly recommended for visitors to Niagara Falls. The spotless and air-conditioned buses shuttle between the main terminal beside Table Rock Plaza to the Horseshoe Falls and Queenston Heights Park along the Niagara River. Buses operate daily between April and October, although first and last trip times vary by season. All-day passes are available, which allow visitors to hop on and off at will. For more information call ✆ **905/357-9340.** The people mover departs every 20 minutes and costs C$7.50 (US$7.10) adults, C$4.50 (US$4.30) children 6 to 12, and children 5 and under are free. A pass includes unlimited rides on the Incline Railway.

INCLINE RAILWAY   This open-air car transports pedestrians up and down the cliff between the Fallsview tourist area and the Horseshoe Falls. The cost is C$2 (US$1.90) per trip, or unlimited access with the purchase of a People Mover Day Pass.

BY BICYCLE

If you are fit and healthy, getting around rural Niagara (the wine country, Niagara Parkway, and Niagara-on-the-Lake) can be very enjoyable during the summer and early fall months. As a tourist, riding a bicycle is not practical in the larger towns because the roadways heavily favor vehicular traffic. For bicycle rental information and tips on touring, see chapter 7, "What to See & Do in the Niagara Region."

BY TAXI

You can hail a taxi on the street, but you'll also readily find one at taxi stands in front of major hotels. You can also summon a taxi by phone: ✆ **905/357-4000** for **Niagara Falls Taxi,** or ✆ **905/685-5463** for **5-0 Transportation.** Other cab companies are listed in the Yellow Pages. On the American side, call **LaSalle Cab Dispatch Service** (✆ **716/284-8833**).

5-0 SHUTTLE   For service between Niagara Falls and Niagara-on-the-Lake, you can use the 5-0 Transportation shuttle bus. Pickup is at major hotels in Niagara Falls and the Niagara Falls Bus Terminal. One-way fare is C$10 (US$9.50) adult and C$5 (US$4.75) child. For more information call ✆ **800/667-0256** or 905/358-3232 (**www.5-0taxi.com**).

FAST FACTS: Niagara Region

Airport For general inquiries, and for information on flights, baggage, and air freight, call the appropriate airline company (see "Getting There" in chapter 2). You can also obtain general information from the airport switchboards and on the relevant websites: **Toronto (Pearson) Airport** (✆ **866/207-1690** for all terminals, or locally 416/247-7678 for Terminal 1 and 416/776-5100 for Terminal 3; www.gtaa.com); **Hamilton International Airport** (✆ **905/679-1999**; www.flyhi. ca); **Buffalo Niagara International Airport** (✆ **716/630-6000**; www.buffaloairport. com); or **Niagara Falls International Airport,** which is located at Niagara Falls Boulevard at Porter Road, Niagara Falls, New York (✆ **716/297-4494**; www.nfta.com/nfairport). For information on transportation from the airports to Niagara, see "Getting There" in chapter 2.

Air Travel Complaints The Canadian Transportation Agency handles unresolved passenger complaints against air carriers. Information and complaint forms are available at **www.cta-otc.gc.ca**. For more information call the **Canadian Transportation Agency** (✆ **888/222-2592**). You can also contact the **Travel Industry Council of Ontario,** a provincial government authority that deals with consumer matters, including travel, at ✆ **888/451-8426** or 905/624-6241 (www. tico.on.ca). In the United States, contact the **Aviation Consumer Protection Division** to file a complaint (✆ **202/366-2220** to complain about U.S. airline service; http://airconsumer.ost.dot.gov).

American Express For card member services, including traveler's checks and lost or stolen cards, call ✆ **800/528/4800** (call ✆ **363/393-1111** collect only if your card is lost or stolen). There is an **American Express Affiliated Travel Agency,** which provides travel and financial services, at World Wide Travel One, 3714 Portage Rd., Niagara Falls, Ont. (✆ **905/353-8400**).

Area Codes The telephone area code for the Niagara region is 905. The area code in Niagara Falls, New York, is 716.

ATMs Walk-up cash machines that link to the Cirrus or PLUS networks can be found every few blocks at various bank branches. You can also get cash advances against your MasterCard or Visa at an ATM, but you'll need a separate personal identification number (PIN) to access this service, and will likely be charged interest from the time of withdrawal. ATMs generally charge a fee for each withdrawal unless the machine is operated by your own banking institution. Various convenience stores (U.S. and Canadian) also have ATMs.

Babysitting Hotel concierge or front desk staff can usually supply names and phone numbers of reliable sitters.

Business Hours Most **stores** are open Monday to Saturday from 9:30 or 10am to 6pm, and many have extended hours one or more evenings. Sunday opening hours are generally from noon to 5pm, although some stores open at 11am and others are closed all day. **Banks** generally open at 10am and close by 4pm, with extended hours one or more evenings; some are open Saturdays. **Restaurants** generally open at 11 or 11:30am for lunch and around 5pm for dinner, although many stay open all day. Hours for **attractions and museums** vary considerably depending on the season; refer to chapter 7, "What to See & Do in the Niagara Region," for individual opening hours. **U.S. banking** hours are generally 9am to 5pm Monday through Thursday, 9am to 6pm Friday, and Saturday 9am to 1pm.

Car Rentals See "Getting Around," earlier in this chapter.

Climate See "When to Go" in chapter 2.

Currency Exchange Generally, the best place to exchange your currency is at a bank or by obtaining local currency through an ATM. The Table Rock House Plaza, located on the Niagara Parkway, near the lip of the Horseshoe Falls, has a currency exchange center open 7 days a week (✆ **905/358-3268**). There is a currency exchange facility at **Niagara Clifton Currency Exchange** (4943 Clifton Hill, Niagara Falls, Ont.; ✆ **800/668-8840**).

Dentists For emergency dental care, ask the front desk staff or concierge at your hotel for the name of the nearest dentist, or call the **Ontario Dental Association** Monday through Friday 8:30am to 4:30pm (✆ **416/922-3900**). In the United States, contact the **American Dental Association** for information (✆ **312/440-2500**).

Directory Assistance For numbers within the same area code, call ✆ **411, in the U.S. and Canada.** For other numbers, call ✆ **555-1212**, prefixed by the area code of the number you're searching for. There is a charge for these services. In the U.S. call "0" for the operator to get a long-distance number.

Disability Services Many of Niagara's museums and public buildings, as well as many theaters and restaurants, are accessible to travelers with disabilities. For details, refer to **Accessible Niagara** (www.accessibleniagara.com). For more information, see "Travelers with Disabilities" in chapter 2.

Doctors Ask hotel staff or the concierge to help you locate a doctor. Some physicians will visit hotels. Walk-in clinics are available to out-of-province and international visitors, but be prepared to pay for services on the spot with cash. You will find walk-in medical clinics listed in the local Yellow Pages directory. For more information, see "Health & Safety" in chapter 2.

Documents See "Entry Requirements" in chapter 2.

Driving Rules See "Getting Around," earlier in this chapter.

Drugstores **Shopper's Drug Mart** has two late-night locations. Both are open until midnight 7 days a week: 6240 Lundy's Lane, Niagara Falls, Ont. (✆ **905/354-3845**), and 111 Fourth Ave. (Ridley Square) in St. Catharines (✆ **905/641-2244**). If you are a U.S. resident wanting a prescription filled, you must obtain a prescription from an Ontario-licensed doctor. In Niagara Falls, New York, **Walgreens Drug Store** (1202 Pine Ave.; ✆ **716/285-0281**) is open 8am to 10pm Monday through Friday, Saturday 9am to 6pm, and Sunday 10am to 6pm. Visit Tonawanda—a 15-minute drive from Niagara Falls—for a 24-hour **Walgreens** (2601 Sheridan Dr.; ✆ **716/835-3346**).

Electricity It's the same as in the United States—110V to 115V, AC.

Embassies & Consulates All embassies in Canada (more than 100 in total) are located in Ottawa; consulates are primarily located in Toronto, Montreal, and

Vancouver. Embassies include the **Australian High Commission,** 50 O'Connor St., Suite 710, Ottawa, Ont., K1P 6L2 (© **613/236-0841**); the **British High Commission,** 80 Elgin St., Ottawa, Ont., K1P 5K7 (© **613/237-1530**); the **Embassy of Ireland,** 130 Albert St., Ottawa, Ont., K1P 5G4 (© **613/233-6281**); the **New Zealand High Commission,** 727–99 Bank St., Ottawa, Ont., K1P 6G3 (© **613/238-5991**); the **South African High Commission,** 15 Sussex Dr., Ottawa, Ont., K1M 1M8 (© **613/744-0330**); and the **Embassy of the United States of America,** 490 Sussex Dr., Ottawa, Ont., K1N 1G8 (© **613/238-5335;** http://ottawa.usembassy.gov for general inquiries).

Emergencies Call © **911** emergency services for fire, police, or ambulance. For the **Ontario Regional Poison Information Centre,** call © **800/268-9017.** For the **Western New York Regional Poison Control Center,** call © **800/222-1222.** When in Ontario, call **Telehealth Ontario** © **866/797-0000** to speak with a registered nurse and have health questions answered, including whether your health situation should be deemed an emergency, urgent care, or regular consultation.

Eyeglasses For same-day service (perhaps as quick as 1 hour) on most prescriptions, try **Precision Optical,** Niagara Square, 7555 Montrose Rd. N., Niagara Falls, Ont. (© **905/356-5955**) or **Lenscrafters** in the Pen Centre shopping center at 221 Glendale Ave., St. Catharines (© **905/682-8000**). In New York, visit **Sterling Optical** at 8962 Porter Rd. (© **715/297-4994**).

Hospitals Emergency services are available at **Greater Niagara General Hospital,** 5546 Portage Rd., Niagara Falls, Ont. (© **905/358-0171**), and **St. Catharines General Hospital,** 142 Queenston St., St. Catharines (© **905/684-7271**). Ontario hospital emergency rooms are extremely busy and wait times for nonurgent cases are typically several hours. If at all possible, use a walk-in clinic; for more information see "Health & Safety" in chapter 2. On the U.S. side, **Niagara Falls Memorial Medical Center** offers emergency services (621 10th St.; © **716/278-4000,** or 716/278-4394 emergency room).

Internet Access New wireless hotspots are popping up all over the place, so if you're equipped with the technology, you should find it fairly easy to go online. Otherwise, try the public library. See "Libraries," below. **UPS Stores** offering paid Internet access include locations in St. Catharines at the Pendale Plaza, 210 Glendale Ave. (© **905/682-5310**); in Niagara Falls at the Doubletree Resort Lodge & Spa (see chapter 5), and at 4025 Dorchester Rd. (© **905/357-4348**); in Fort Erie, 1243 Garrison Rd. (© **905/994-8339**); and at the Welland Plaza, 200 Fitch St. (© **905/788-9993**).

Kids Help Phone Kids or teens in distress can call © **800/668-6868** for help.

Laundry & Dry Cleaning Most hotels provide same-day laundry and dry-cleaning services or have coin-operated laundry facilities.

Libraries In Ontario, the main branch of the Niagara Falls public library is located at 4848 Victoria Ave. (© **905/356-8080;** www.nfpl.library.on.ca). The main branch of the St. Catharines public library is at 54 Church St. (© **905/688-6103**). In Niagara-on-the-Lake, you'll find the library at 10 Anderson Lane (© **905/468-2023**). Online databases, local history materials, and local photo galleries are just some of the resources available. In the U.S., visit the Niagara Falls Public Library (1425 Main St.; ℭ **716/286-4899**).

Liquor You must be **19 years of age or older** to consume or purchase alcohol in Ontario. Bars and retail stores are strict about enforcing the law and will ask for proof of age, at their discretion. The **Liquor Control Board of Ontario (LCBO)** sells wine, spirits, and beer. Beer is also available through the Beer Store, with numerous locations in the Niagara region. Niagara wines may also be purchased at individual wineries by the bottle or case. You must be **21 years of age or older** to consume or purchase alcohol in the United States. Beer, and sometimes wine, can be purchased at local convenience stores. Liquor is sold through private proprietors.

Mail Mailing letters and postcards within Canada costs C52¢ (US49¢). Postage for letters and postcards sent from Canada to the United States costs C93¢ (US88¢), and overseas C$1.55 (US$1.50).

Newspapers & Magazines The daily newspapers are the ***Niagara Falls Review, St. Catharines Standard, Fort Erie Times, Port Colborne Tribune,*** and the ***Welland Tribune.*** Several smaller communities publish weekly newspapers. For entertainment listings in the St. Catharines area, pick up a copy of ***The Downtowner*** or ***Pulse St. Catharines. The Brock Press*** is Brock University's student newspaper. ***Niagara Life*** is a glossy magazine featuring the personalities of the region. There are two local dailies in Niagara Falls, New York: the ***Niagara Gazette*** and the ***Tonawanda News. The Current*** is a free weekly.

Police In a life-threatening emergency or to report a crime in progress or a traffic accident that involves injuries or a vehicle that cannot be driven, call ℭ **911.** Non-emergency inquiries should be directed to ℭ **905/688-4111.** The **Niagara Falls Police Department** in New York can be reached at ℭ **716/286-4711** for non-emergency inquiries.

Post Offices Many convenience stores and drugstores offer postal services, and some have a separate counter for shipping packages during regular business hours. Look for the sign in the store window advertising such services. You will also find **Canada Post** outlets at 4500 Queen St. in Niagara Falls (ℭ **905/374-6667**), 4 Queen St. in St. Catharines (ℭ **905/688-4064**), and 117 Queen St. in Niagara-on-the-Lake (ℭ **905/468-3208**). For general information and delivery inquiries, call ℭ **800/267-1177.** For postal code information, call ℭ **900/565-2633** (there is a charge for this service). Visitors can look up Canadian postal codes for free at **www.canadapost.ca.** On the U.S. side, there are more than a half-dozen United States Postal Service locations in Niagara Falls—look for the blue-and-red storefront signage. For general information, as well as zip codes, visit **www.usps.com.** Central locations include 2020 Pine Ave. (front A) and 615 Main St. Call ℭ **800/ASK-USPS** for hours and other locations.

Public Transit Information For information on public transit, see "Getting Around," earlier in this chapter.

Radio The **Canadian Broadcasting Corporation (CBC)** broadcasts on **99.1 FM.**
CFLZ 91.9 FM is operated by the Niagara Parks Commission and provides information about events, attractions, and bridges. Soft-rock tunes are played on
CHRE FM-Light 105.7. For news and talk radio, tune in to **AM610 CKTB.** Adult
contemporary music is featured on **CHSC AM1220** and **CKEY FM 101.1.** For
country music fans, there's **Spirit 91.7 FM/CHOW.** Fans of sports and '70s music
should check out **CJRN AM 710.** Album-oriented rock takes the stage on **97.7
HTZ-FM.** Tune in to **AM930 WBEN** from Buffalo for news, traffic, weather, and
sports. **WBFO FM88.7** plays jazz, the blues, and news. The local rock station is
KISS FM 98.5.

Safety The Niagara region is generally safe for visitors. That said, it's never a
good idea to take your safety for granted. In a region that welcomes 14 million
visitors each year, it's wise to be alert and use common sense, particularly late
at night. Keep a look out for pickpockets and thieves.

Taxes Canada's national Goods and Services Tax (GST) is 5%. In Ontario there
is a provincial retail sales tax (PST) of 8% on most goods; certain purchases, such
as groceries and children's clothing, are exempt from provincial sales tax. The
accommodations tax is 5%.

In Niagara Falls, New York, sales tax is 8% on all goods and accommodations.
There are no duty-free stores in the U.S. To receive a tax refund on goods, visitors can receive tax-free purchases only if they ship their purchases home at
the time of purchase. For more information, visit **www.tax.state.ny.us**, or call
© **800/972-1233.**

Taxis See "Getting Around," earlier in this chapter.

Telephone A local call from a telephone booth costs C25¢; Canadian and U.S.
coins are accepted at face value. Watch out for hotel surcharges on local and
long-distance phone calls; often a local call will cost at least C$1 (US95¢) from a
hotel room. Canada and the United States are on the same long-distance system—to make a long-distance call between the two countries, use the area codes
as you would at home. The international prefix for Canada and the US is 1. Phone
cards can be purchased at convenience stores and drugstores.

Time Niagara is on **eastern standard time. Daylight saving time** is in effect
from the second Sunday in March (clocks are moved ahead 1 hr.) to the first
Sunday in November (clocks are moved back 1 hr.).

Tipping Basically, it's the same as in major U.S. cities—15% in restaurants (up
to 20% in higher-end restaurants or for exceptional service and food), 10% to
15% for taxis, C$1 (US95¢) per bag for porters, C$2 (US$1.90) per day for hotel
housekeepers.

Weather For the weather forecast, check the daily newspaper, catch a radio
broadcast, or tune in to the Weather Channel on TV. Some hotels post this
information at the front desk.

Moments **A Little Peace, Please**

It can be quite a challenge to escape the crush of people jostling for prime viewing positions alongside the Falls, but there are a couple of places where you can avoid the crowds and still be wowed by the force of the water.

On the Canadian side, head to **Navy Island,** located opposite Ussher's Creek in Chippawa, at the northern tip of Grand Island closest to the Canadian shore. Home to French, British, and Canadian rebels and farmers, Navy Island was considered for both the 1960 World's Fair and the home of the United Nations, although neither plan came to fruition. The island now serves as a refuge for many species of wildlife, including deer. It's a popular spot for fishers, nature lovers, bird-watchers, and campers. The vegetation is lush, and in the summer you may be rewarded by the discovery of wild raspberries and grapes. The wide variety of trees includes pawpaw, oak, hickory, and blue beech. Be careful when venturing on a hike, though—the island also plays host to poison ivy. (Navy Island is only accessible in your own personal watercraft—there are no boat rentals or public transportation to the island.)

On the American side, head to **Three Sisters Islands,** tiny islands that jut out from Goat Island. You'll be close enough to the swirling rapids to dip your toes in, but take care near the water's edge, and keep children with you at all times. Looking out over the rapids in this spot, it's easy to forget the crowds of people behind you.

5

Where to Stay

To oblige millions of visitors a year, the Niagara Region offers a wide range of accommodation options. Although places can get quite pricey during the high season, more and more moderate accommodations have popped up recently. But be wary of the roadside motels—although their prices may be desirable, some haven't seen a cleaning rag in a long time.

For those traveling with children I strongly recommend staying in a one- or two-bedroom suite with kitchenette facilities if your budget will allow, or hunt down a self-contained cottage in Niagara-on-the-Lake or along the shores of Lake Ontario. In return for your investment, you'll get a comfortable base with space for everyone to spread out, a place to make meals on your own schedule (you'll also save money by not having to eat out all the time), and usually more than one TV. You may even get some private time once the kids are asleep, when you can enjoy a glass of wine with your spouse as you watch the spectacular nightly illumination of the Falls. Couples looking for a more romantic getaway will do well to base themselves at an inn or B&B in Niagara-on-the-Lake or in the wine country and tour the region by car or bicycle.

Many of the properties listed in this chapter are clustered around the Falls themselves, or in the beautiful, serene setting of Niagara-on-the-Lake. Wine-country choices abound, with everything from luxurious inns to cozy cottages for two and friendly B&Bs. If you are looking for somewhere off the beaten tourist path, head for Port Dalhousie or watch the majestic lakers and ocean-going freighters glide past your balcony alongside the Welland Canal.

PARKING   If you have a vehicle with you, remember to factor in parking charges when estimating the cost of your accommodations if you plan to stay at one of the larger properties close to the Falls. Hotel parking rates at these locations vary from C$5 (US$4.75) to C$20 (US$19) per night.

AN IMPORTANT NOTE ON PRICES The prices quoted in this chapter are generally a range from the cheapest low-season rate up to corporate or rack rates (rack rates are the highest posted rates, although rooms are rarely sold at the full rack rate). In each listing, the prices include accommodations for two adults sharing. Discounts can result in a dramatic drop in the rate, typically anywhere from 10% to 50%.

Almost every hotelier I spoke with mentioned that weekend specials or family packages are available at various times throughout the year. Note also that 5% accommodations tax and 6% GST (Goods and Services Tax) are required by law to be added to your bill.

A NOTE TO NONSMOKERS   Happily, many of the properties in the Niagara Region are entirely or almost entirely nonsmoking, partly due to a reduced demand for smoking rooms and partly due to the increasing trend toward smoking bylaws that prohibit smoking in public places. Typically 10% of the rooms in any given hotel are reserved for smokers.

However, people who want a smoke-free environment should make that clear when reserving a room. Rooms for smokers are often clustered together at one end of the hallway, and the rooms and even the hallways adjacent to those areas tend to smell strongly of tobacco smoke, even in the cleanest hotels. Never assume that you'll get a smoke-free room if you don't specifically request one.

A NOTE ABOUT POOLS   Please be aware that hotel pools are almost always **not** supervised by hotel staff. If you have children with you, make sure they are under your direct supervision in pool areas at all times.

BED-AND-BREAKFASTS   The Niagara region, in particular Niagara-on-the-Lake and the River Road district in the city of Niagara Falls, has an abundance of gracious, older homes, many of which have been transformed into charming B&Bs. For the most part, B&Bs are located in quiet residential neighborhoods with tree-lined streets. If you're traveling solo or as a couple, then a B&B presents an economical and delightful alternative to a hotel room, but families will usually need to rent two rooms to secure enough sleeping area, and that must be taken into account when estimating costs. Also, be aware that B&Bs and inns are usually geared to adult visitors. Many homes have expensive antiques on display and guests are expecting a quiet, restful stay. If you have children with you and they're young, boisterous, or both, then you're better off in a family-oriented property.

During the busy summer season, some bed-and-breakfasts require a 2-night minimum stay. If one is full, hosts are more than happy to suggest another in the area; most of them know each other and are pleased to recommend one nearby.

REDUCING YOUR ROOM RATE
Always ask for a deal. Corporate discounts, club memberships (CAA, AAA, and others), and discounts linked to credit cards are just a few of the ways you can get a lower price. Rates between June and August are decidedly higher than the rest of the year and fluctuate wildly depending on the particular week; if any events are scheduled that increase the rates, try the following week. Weekend rates and getaway packages for couples and families are often available. Packages may include golf, spa treatments, attraction tickets or discounts, restaurant coupons, or other money-saving deals.

1 Niagara Falls, Ontario and New York

With 14 million visitors to the Falls every year, you would expect the vicinity to be awash in hotels and motels—and you'd be right, at least on the Canadian side. There are fewer choices on U.S. soil.

Accommodations range from huge chains to quaint B&Bs to seedy motels. In general, hotels are much nicer on the Canadian side, although the Canadians have their share of dodgy digs (thankfully, these are easy to spot by their general outward appearance). In Niagara Falls, New York, your best bet is to pamper yourself at the elegant Red Coach Inn adjacent to the Niagara Falls State Park and within view of the Niagara River rapids. If that is too much of a squeeze on the finances, head up Niagara Falls Boulevard (Hwy. 62), where a number of chain hotels have staked their claim. The **Super 8,** 7680 Niagara Falls Blvd. (© 716/283-3151) and **Econolodge,** 2000 Niagara Falls Blvd. (© 716/694-6696) on this stretch of road are good choices—both properties are relatively recently built and are clean and bright.

The Niagara Falls area caters well to families, and the major hotels in town on the Canadian side woo honeymooners with packages galore. Staying in Niagara Falls

Niagara Falls Accommodations

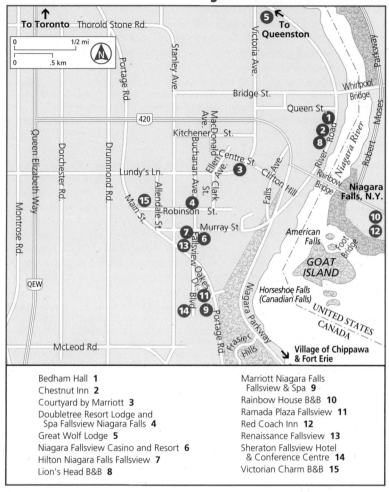

Bedham Hall **1**
Chestnut Inn **2**
Courtyard by Marriott **3**
Doubletree Resort Lodge and
  Spa Fallsview Niagara Falls **4**
Great Wolf Lodge **5**
Niagara Fallsview Casino and Resort **6**
Hilton Niagara Falls Fallsview **7**
Lion's Head B&B **8**

Marriott Niagara Falls
  Fallsview & Spa **9**
Rainbow House B&B **10**
Ramada Plaza Fallsview **11**
Red Coach Inn **12**
Renaissance Fallsview **13**
Sheraton Fallsview Hotel
  & Conference Centre **14**
Victorian Charm B&B **15**

means a lot of chain restaurants and nightlife, which centers on the carnival atmosphere of Clifton Hill and the glitz of the casinos—if that excites you, then the Falls is the place to be. Otherwise, you will find the much quieter atmosphere of Niagara-on-the-Lake or the tranquillity of the wine country more attractive.

VERY EXPENSIVE

Hilton Niagara Falls Fallsview ✹✹ *Kids*   Family focused, this monstrous 512-room hotel has an Adventure Pool, which includes a 930-sq.-m (10,000-sq.-ft.) pool complete with a waterslide and cascading waterfall. Above the pool, parents can work out in a fitness area. Kids can also play in the neighboring arcade. Rooms are generously proportioned—the idea is that each room can hold a good-size family if needed. Choose from rooms offering city views, or a view of the Canadian or U.S. falls—these are the real attraction, not the plain decor in the rooms. A unique feature in all suites is a two-person Jacuzzi tub with French doors opening up into the main bedroom. For families who travel en masse, a family suite offers two adjoining rooms (one king-size bed in one room and two queen-size beds in the other) with a connecting door. Room prices are cheaper when booked online or by phone in advance.

6361 Fallsview Blvd., Niagara Falls, Ont. ℂ **888/370-0325** or 905/354-7887. Fax 905/374-6707. www.niagarafalls hilton.com. 512 units. C$99–C$400 (US$94–US$380) double; suites from C$129 (US$123). Weekend packages are available. AE, DC, MC, V. Valet and self-parking C$20 (US$19). **Amenities:** Restaurant; bar; coffee shop; pool; golf nearby; exercise room; spa; Jacuzzi, sauna; video arcade; concierge; separate tour/activity desk; business center; shopping arcade; limited room service; massage; babysitting. *In room:* A/C, TV w/pay movies, dataport, coffeemaker, hair dryer, iron.

Marriott Niagara Falls Fallsview & Spa 🅇🅇 *(Kids)* Families traveling with children will love the entertainment possibilities—a pool, a PlayStation in the rooms, a game room, a clear view of the Falls from the rooms (including the fireworks display held on summer weekends). Holiday packages for families may include popcorn and movie night, complimentary tickets to one or more local attractions, and a magician's workshop. There are family shows in the on-site live theater and a kids' club to keep the little darlings busy. The hotel is only 90m (300 ft.) from the Falls and built in a curving design that allows virtually every room an unobstructed view. Even the standard rooms are generously sized with large bathrooms; upgraded rooms let you take a whirlpool bath with the Falls just a glance away.

6740 Fallsview Blvd., Niagara Falls, Ont. ℂ **888/501-8916** or 905/357-7300. Fax 905/357-0490. www.niagarafalls marriott.com. 427 units. C$120–C$460 (US$114–US$437) double; suites from C$189 (US$180). Packages available. AE, DC, DISC, MC, V. Valet parking C$20 (US$19). **Amenities:** Restaurant; lounge; large indoor pool; exercise room; spa; 2 Jacuzzis; sauna; children's programs; game room; concierge; tour desk; courtesy car; business center; limited room service; massage; babysitting; laundry service; same-day dry cleaning; executive-level rooms. *In room:* A/C, TV w/pay movies, dataport, minibar, coffeemaker, hair dryer, iron, safe.

Sheraton Fallsview Hotel & Conference Centre 🅇 At the far end of Fallsview Boulevard, away from the hustle of the casino area, lies the Sheraton Fallsview. Rooms on the upper floors have the best views of the Falls, with floor-to-ceiling windows. Rooms are basic and clean—with a new hotel feel. Falls-view rooms cost a premium; without the view, the rooms are quite ordinary. All rooms feature the signature Sheraton "Sweet Sleeper" beds, which are among the most comfortable, luxurious beds anywhere. There's also a Sheraton club floor where guests can relax, browse the Internet, eat breakfast, and nibble on hors d'oeuvres. Families are also welcomed here, with several packages; during Christmas and March breaks, a kids' club operates daily from noon to 9pm.

6755 Fallsview Blvd., Niagara Falls, Ont. ℂ **905/374-1077.** www.sheraton.com/fallsview. 402 units. C$99–C$349 (US$94–US$332) standard double; C$209–C$609 (US$199–US$579) suite. Children 18 and under stay free in parent's room. AE, DC, DISC, MC, V. Self-parking C$10–C$20 (US$9.50–US$19); valet parking C$25 (US$24). Dogs up to 36kg (80 lb.) accepted, C$25 (US$24) per stay. **Amenities:** 3 restaurants; bar; indoor pool; golf course nearby; exercise room; hot tub; sauna; limited children's programming; concierge; shuttle for local area; business center; limited room service; massage; babysitting; laundry service; dry cleaning; executive floor. *In room:* A/C, TV w/pay movies, dataport, coffeemaker, hair dryer, iron.

EXPENSIVE

Courtyard by Marriott 🅇 A great place to sleep but not necessarily linger. The standard rooms are similar to many chain hotels: they're clean and large but are slightly generic without any frills. But there's loads of space in these rooms and a variety of options to upgrade—presidential suites offer a Jacuzzi and fireplace, and king-size suites include a whirlpool bath for two in the room. The entire family can stay in a two-room family suite that sleeps up to six. This newer hotel is great for families; there are many amenities, such as an indoor pool with whirlpool and outdoor pool with slide, and the large Keg Restaurant. It's a great location: next to all the attractions of the Falls, without being too immersed in the mayhem of Clifton Hill.

5950 Victoria Ave., Niagara Falls, Ont. ℭ **800/321-2211** or 905/358-3083. Fax 905/358-8720. www.nfcourtyard. com. 258 units. June–Aug C$99–C$299 (US$94–US$284) double, C$159–C$369(US$151–US$351) suite. Sept–May C$70–C$350 (US$66–US$332) double, C$100–C$400 (US$95–US$380) suite. Packages available. AE, DC, MC, V. Self-parking June–Aug C$8 (US$7.60), other times free. **Amenities:** Indoor/outdoor pool; small exercise room; Jacuzzi; sauna; children's programs; game room; tour desk; limited room service; laundry service; coin-op laundry; same-day dry cleaning. *In room:* A/C, TV w/pay movies, Wi-Fi, dataport, coffeemaker, hair dryer, iron, safe.

Doubletree Resort Lodge & Spa Fallsview Niagara Falls ★★

The foyer of this hotel has a ski-lodge-resort feel—expansive ceilings decorated with wooden beams and an abundance of fieldstone. The opulent feeling continues at the Five Lakes Spa AVEDA. Beyond these elegant touches the rooms are standard hotel fare—but spacious and warmly decorated in cherry and burgundy wood furniture. And despite its big-hotel feel, each room is decorated with local art and black-and-white photos of Ontario from days gone by. There's an outside hot tub in the summer surrounded by trees from Ontario's Algonquin Park. A new art gallery, called the Ochre Gallery, features beautiful Canadian landscape art and totem poles from British Columbia.

6039 Fallsview Blvd., Niagara Falls, Ont. ℭ **800/730-8609** or 905/358-3817. Fax 905/358-3680. www.niagarafalls doubletree.com. 224 units. C$99–C$299 (US$94–US$284) double; suites from C$119 (US$113). Children 18 and under stay free in parent's room. Weekend packages are available. AE, DC, MC, V. Self-parking C$10 (US$9.50). **Amenities:** Restaurant; pub; coffee shop; indoor pool; golf nearby; exercise room; spa; seasonal hot tub; sauna; video arcade; concierge; seasonal activity desk; business center; limited room service; massage; babysitting; same-day laundry/dry cleaning service (Mon–Fri only). *In room:* A/C, TV w/pay movies, dataport, coffeemaker, hair dryer, iron.

Great Wolf Lodge ★★ *(Kids)*

"Can we stay longer?" is a refrain I often overheard kids asking their parents at this kid-inspired lodge. From the entrance with its animatronic talking moose, tree, and bear, to the rooms large enough to run laps in, kids rule here; parents are just along for the ride. The main attraction is over 9,300 sq. m (100,000 sq. ft.) of waterslides and pools. Get some extreme air on rollercoaster-style water slides, or try the wicked Vortex that whirls you around in a giant tub. Rides and wading pools are available for the wee ones also. The morning is the least busy—after noon, lines form and congestion starts in the locker rooms.

The kid-focused fun continues into the rooms, many of which feature a segregated sleeping area with bunk beds. To save on money, many families double or triple up and stay in the larger family rooms, including the giant Family Suite with two queen beds and a sofa sleeper. For more luxury, there's the Loft Fireplace Suite, with three queen beds, one in the upstairs loft. Rooms are kid-proofed with no loose figurines and no sharp table edges. Although the rooms are big, the bathrooms might be a squeeze for two or more who want to brush their teeth at the same time.

If your head starts to spin from running after your kids, there's a spa and a tranquil room with a waterfall. For babysitting, 3 hours costs C$20 (US$19) at the Cub Club, where kids can make crafts, play video games, or watch movies. There are seven eateries—including ice cream, pizza, and homemade fudge—but beware: it's not healthy food and it is expensive. Wristbands, which act as room keys, can also be loaded up with money for kids to spend at will. Rates include water-park passes and parking.

3950 Victoria Ave., Niagara Falls, Ont. **800/605-WOLF** or 905/354-4888. www.greatwolflodge.com. 406 units. C$199–C$799 (US$190–US$759). C$20 ($US19) extra person. Packages available. AE, DC, MC, V. Self-parking free. **Amenities:** 2 restaurants, 3 snack bars (one seasonal), pizza takeout, 2 coffee shops, bar; pools (indoor/outdoor); 18-hole minigolf; health club; spa; adult-only Jacuzzi; hot tub; video arcade; children's center; concierge; tour desk; business center; gift shop; salon; massage; babysitting. *In room:* A/C, TV w/pay movies, Wi-Fi, dataport, fridge, microwave, coffeemaker, hairdryer, iron, safe.

Niagara Fallsview Casino Resort ★★   If you want to be pampered, try this upscale Canadian version of Las Vegas. This casino is a self-contained biosphere of hedonism. The rooms, however, although nicely decorated in burgundy and green earth tones, are pretty standard hotel fare. The standard Diplomat rooms are quite small, and I recommend upgrading to the Deluxe, which has more room. Jacuzzis are found in all suites. The falls-view rooms boast great views.

The real fun is outside the rooms, however: the bright, white-tiled pool area, with large tropical plants and glass windows, feels like an exotic spa. To get the full spa treatment, walk down the hall from the pool, for pedicures and therapeutic massages. Next door is an impressive workout room—all-new machines face four large flatscreen TVs. Staff come by frequently with fresh towels for guests. Jacuzzis are located in all suites, as well as in the spa and pool areas. Everything feels new and flashy throughout the resort.

6380 Fallsview Blvd., Niagara Falls, Ont. ⓒ **888/FALLSVU** or 905/358-3255. www.fallsviewcasinoresort.com. 374 units. C$149–C$449 (US$142–US$427). AE, DC, MC, V. Self-parking C$20 (US$19), or free with Fallsview Players Advantage Club membership (membership free). Small pets accepted. **Amenities:** 10 restaurants; 4 bars; casino; pool; golf nearby; exercise room; Jacuzzi; sauna; bike rental; concierge; business center; shopping arcade; salon; 24-hour room service; massage; babysitting; laundry service; same-day dry cleaning; executive floor. *In room:* A/C, TV w/ pay movies, dataport, coffeemaker, hairdryer, iron, safe.

Red Coach Inn ★★   This 1920s-era Tudor-style hotel with its distinctive gabled roof is the most luxurious property on the American side of the Falls by a nautical mile, and its individuality is worth crossing the border for. The prices are set at a reasonable level for the high standard of service and room amenities, and the restaurant is worth eating in. Located just across the street from the Niagara River rapids, you're at the gateway of Niagara Falls State Park's attractions. The standard rooms are rather small and basic; I'd recommend staying in one of the suites, which are more like apartments, with full kitchens, dining tables, and comfortable furniture. Suites also enjoy a view of the rapids, separate bedroom, and spacious bathrooms. The feel of the place is like an English country house.

2 Buffalo Ave., Niagara Falls, NY. ⓒ **800/282-1459** or 716/282-1459. www.redcoach.com. 19 units. C$119–C$215 (US$94–US$204) double; C$155–C$431 (US$147–US$409) suite. Packages available. AE, DISC, MC, V. **Amenities:** Restaurant; lounge. In room: A/C, TV/VCR, dataport, fridge, coffeemaker, hair dryer.

Renaissance Fallsview ★   Bright reds and yellows liven up this large hotel, which is a good bet for families. Adjoining rooms mean parents can have some peace and quiet, while kids can talk all night. Rooms are very spacious, particularly the Executive Fallsview, with two doubles (or a king-size) in one room adjoined to a room with another two queen-size—not to mention a great view of the Horseshoe Falls. Or for the adults, choose from a spacious deluxe room with Jacuzzi (heart-shape tubs are optional) and king-size bed. Kids 12 and under receive half-price meals and 5 and under eat free. Cribs and rollaway beds are complimentary. Squash and racquetball are available beside the small gym, which is in need of better ventilation. Located in the heart of Niagara Falls, there is a convenient catwalk attached to the casino, which is loaded with more restaurants, shops, and spa services.

6455 Fallsview Blvd., Niagara Falls, Ont. ℃ **800/363-3255** or 905/357-5200. Fax 905/357-7487. www.renaissance fallsview.com. 262 units. C$89–C$299 (US$85–US$284) double; suites from C$129 (US$123). Children 18 and under stay free in parent's room. Weekend packages are available. AE, DC, MC, V. Valet parking C$20 (US$19). **Amenities:** 2 restaurants; lounge; pool; golf nearby; exercise room; Jacuzzi; sauna; children's programs; game room; seasonal concierge; business center; shopping arcade attached via catwalk to casino; limited room service; massage; babysitting; same-day dry cleaning; executive floor. *In room:* A/C, TV w/pay movies, fridge available C$10 (US$9.50), coffeemaker, hair dryer, iron.

MODERATE

Bedham Hall 🍴   Old-country decor meets relaxing amenities of the 21st century. Mature guests will appreciate fireplaces and Jacuzzis (except in the Buckingham Room) added to spacious rooms, with sizable bathrooms that feature Crabtree & Evelyn products. Flowery wallpaper and dainty touches abound. The Windsor Room, on the third floor, is decked out with a four-poster bed and a separate living area overlooking the gorge. The Buckingham Room is the smallest but most charming, with a sitting room located in the turret of the house, opposite stairs leading from the sitting room directly to the bedroom. In the yellow and blue (feels like royalty) breakfast area downstairs, guests can eat at the communal table or at a table for two near the window near the gorge. The host is an informative concierge and will whip up eggs, any style, for breakfast.

4835 River Rd., Niagara Falls, Ont. ℃ **877/374-8515** or 905/374-8515. Fax 905/374-9189. www.bedhamhall.com. 4 units. C$95–C$160 (US$90–US$152). Packages available. Rates include breakfast. MC, V. Free parking. **Amenities:** Spa services arranged; same-day laundry service (fee). *In room:* A/C, TV/DVD, Wi-Fi, dataport, fridge, coffeemaker, hairdryer, iron, no phone.

Chestnut Inn 🍴   No frills and plain decor but good value with some good add-ons. Parents will appreciate the Grey Room—no one above or underneath to hear the pitter-patter of little feet. Every room except the loft has a single bed built into the curved windows—perfect for wee ones. Likewise, a large front lawn with gazebo and a pool in the back allows kids to be kids, or adults to linger. There are private patios for every room; all rooms are also equipped with electric fireplaces. A communal room has tea and coffee, as well as a hairdryer and iron. There's plenty of common space in the living and sun room, full of wicker chairs, with decks of cards and books. Breakfast is continental—shreddies and corn flakes—but also features apple cinnamon French toast—the house specialty.

4983 River Rd., Niagara Falls, Ont. ℃ **905/374-4616**. www.chestnutinnbb.com. 4 units. C$100–C$120 (US$95–US$114). C$35 (US$33) for extra person. Rates include breakfast. MC, V. Free parking. **Amenities:** Outdoor pool. *In room:* A/C, TV, no phone.

Ramada Plaza Fallsview 🍴 *Value*   A landmark of Ontario's Niagara Falls skyline for decades, the Ramada Plaza Fallsview Hotel features a mere 42 guest rooms, all in a pod at the top of the Konica Minolta Tower Centre. This gives the property a distinctive boutique hotel feel. It's a great place for a quiet weekend getaway—just try not to think about the fact that all the rooms are suspended hundreds of feet above the lobby, with only a concrete elevator shaft linking them to the ground.

The lobby has been recently refurbished in a minimalist style. The rooms, which are quite comfortably appointed, have switched to taupe walls with burgundy chairs and accents that feel like any other brand hotel but are quite large. The falls-view rooms have fabulous views, but the quirky room shapes, with their outward-leaning windows, can give you quite a dizzy turn. The location on Fallsview Boulevard is convenient for walking to the Falls, riding the Incline Railway to the base of the hill, or heading out for dinner or to one of the casinos. Guests have access to the exercise room and pool at the Radisson Hotel. Weddings are a specialty. Staff are courteous and efficient.

6732 Fallsview Blvd., Niagara Falls, Ont. ℂ **866/325-5784** or 905/356-1501. Fax 905/356-8245. www.niagaratower.com. 42 units. Queen or king C$69–C$309 (US$66–US$294). AE, DC, MC, V. Valet parking C$15 (US$14). **Amenities:** Restaurant; bar; golf course nearby; limited room service; same-day laundry and dry cleaning. *In room:* A/C, TV, dataport, fridge, coffeemaker, hair dryer, iron, safe.

Victorian Charm B&B *(Value (Kids*   Starched embroidered linens, a piano in the foyer, and a turret combine to make the name appropriate. The Garden Room—my favorite—has a terrace overlooking the garden, a remote-controlled fireplace, and an air-jet therapeutic tub. Decorated with white wicker furniture and yellow walls, it's an airy and fresh room. The Grande Room has a mini–living space with sofa and bathtub in the room, while the bathroom is located immediately outside the door. Owner Anne Marie, the mother of five children, is happy to cater to the little ones—there is a brand-new crib, and a carriage and stroller are ready to go for a jaunt through the quiet residential area, only a short walk from the casino and Falls. For breakfast, the Belgian waffles with fruit from Anne Marie's organic garden (or preserves in the winter) are tasty, as are the crepes with whipped cream and maple syrup. *Note:* This establishment is entirely nonsmoking.

6039 Culp St., Niagara Falls, Ont. ℂ **877/794-6758** or 905/357-4221. Fax 905/357-9115. www.victoriancharmbb.com. 5 units. C$120–C$185 (US$114–US$176) double. Rates include breakfast. Weekly rates 1 day free. AE, MC, V. Free parking. **Amenities:** Golf nearby; spa services available in room; Jacuzzi; free train station pickup/drop off; massage; babysitting; coin-op washers/dryers. *In room:* A/C, TV/VCR, dataport, fridge, coffeemaker, hair dryer, no phone.

INEXPENSIVE

Lion's Head B&B *(★★*   This historical bed-and-breakfast hasn't changed structurally since 1910. Overlooking the gorge, it's a cozy retreat from the bright lights and tall buildings of downtown Niagara Falls, which is only a 10-minute walk away. Each room is decorated in keeping with its artist namesake—the coral pink walls and dark wood furniture in the Georgia O'Keeffe Room are decidedly bohemian, while the luminescent yellows of the van Gogh are as bright as a sunflower. The third-floor French Quarters room offers privacy for a couple with its own entrance, while friends can be accommodated in an adjacent room.

The eclectic, funky decor throughout the home reflects owner Helena Harrington's effervescent personality and world travels, as does her breakfast menu, which is constantly changing; recent dishes include stuffed tomatoes with asiago cheese and her signature poached pears with orange spice glaze and yogurt topping. And don't expect plain old table sugar—hers is imported from France, and the maple syrup hails from Quebec. More added touches in the rooms include goose-down bedding and Italian ceramic tiles—all handpicked by Helena, who goes to painstaking lengths to get the color and feel of every room exactly to her liking. The B&B is entirely nonsmoking.

5239 River Rd., Niagara Falls, Ont. ℂ **905/374-1681**. www.lionsheadbb.com. 5 units. C$100–C$195 (US$95–US$119) double. Rates include breakfast. AE, MC, V. Free parking. **Amenities:** Golf nearby; massage. *In room:* A/C, hair dryer, iron.

Rainbow House B&B   This historical Victorian home has wrought-iron beds, embroidered doilies, stained-glass windows, and heaps of charming clutter. Think whitewashed wicker furniture and lots of collectables. Owner Laura Lee takes pride in her cozy home and has made it extremely cheery and welcoming. Standard rooms offer better value than the suite. If you get the urge to get hitched in the honeymoon

---

Kids Family-Friendly Sleepovers

Where can you take the kids and have fun at the same time? You'll find a warm welcome at **Victorian Charm B&B,** 6039 Culp St., Niagara Falls, Ont. (✆ **877/794-6758**). Crib, carriage, and stroller are waiting for your little one. Crepes and Belgian waffles will put a smile on sleepy faces. If your kids like nonstop entertainment, head for the **Marriott Niagara Falls Fallsview & Spa,** 6740 Fallsview Blvd., Niagara Falls, Ont. (✆ **888/501-8916**). With a pool, game room, kids' club, live family theater, PlayStation, and movie and popcorn nights, your children will play hard and sleep well. For a country vacation, experience the charm of the farm at **Feast of Fields Organic Vineyard B&B Cottage,** 3403 11th St., Jordan, Ont. (✆ **905/562-0151**). This self-contained two-bedroom cottage with full kitchen is part of a restored farmhouse (ca. 1835). The surrounding paddocks are inhabited not only by horses and cows, but also llamas and a peacock or two.

---

capital of the world, there is a wedding chapel conveniently located on the premises. This property is best suited to adults and older children; no smoking is allowed.

423 Rainbow Blvd. S., Niagara Falls, NY 14303. ✆ **800/724-3536** or 716/282-1135. Fax 716/292-1135. www.rainbow housebb.com. 4 units. C$66–C$150 (US$63–US$143) double. Packages available. Rates include breakfast. MC, V. Free parking. *In room:* A/C, hair dryer, iron.

2 Niagara-on-the-Lake

Niagara-on-the-Lake, with its historical streets, fine choice of restaurants, and boutique shopping, is an attractive place to spend a night or two. Adult vacationers without children in tow will find the town to be a welcome contrast to the razzmatazz of Niagara Falls.

There are hundreds of B&Bs in Niagara-on-the-Lake, and many of them are meticulously restored historical properties. In addition, there are a number of luxurious inns from which to choose. Don't let the plethora of accommodations lull you into thinking you can breeze into town and find somewhere to stay on a whim, though. Niagara-on-the-Lake is highly popular for overnight stays, particularly in the summer months, and there is often no room at the inn (or the B&B, or the guest cottage). Although you are strongly advised to book ahead, the consistency of the quality of properties in this area is quite remarkable, and you are extremely unlikely to be disappointed wherever you end up staying. You'll find that proprietors and staff are experienced in hosting guests and eager to share knowledge of the area that will enhance your vacation, whatever your special interests and needs may be.

VERY EXPENSIVE

Charles Inn ✦✦   Built shortly after the War of 1812 and full of history, this grand Georgian-style inn, with sweeping verandas and stately gardens, takes you back to a simpler time, nicely overlaid with modern amenities. If Scarlett and Rhett were around, you'd find them here on a romantic getaway. My favorite room was originally the kitchen: The Verandah Room still has the original fireplace and cast-iron bake oven—you can still smell the bread cinders if you take a good whiff inside; the room also backs out onto the sweeping veranda. Most rooms have a fireplace (gas or wood-burning) to add to the ambience, although the smaller rooms (Magnolia, Renoir, Apple, and Sunflower) do not. The Verandah Room and the Richardson Room feel like a step back in time, with four-poster beds and antique furniture, whereas other rooms such as the Magnolia, Safari, and Poppy feature modern, elegant decor. Bed linens are 300-thread-count Egyptian cotton, while the duvets and pillows are down-filled. Creaking floors and wooden antique furniture throughout the property add to the experience—you could swear former owner Charles Richardson is smiling down at you. After supper in the fine-dining restaurant, sip cognac on a bar stool at the newly constructed oak bar in the lounge. If you want to be active, the backyard spills onto the Niagara-on-the-Lake golf course, one of the oldest in North America. Breakfast includes seasonal freshly squeezed orange juice from gigantic Osage trees surrounding the property. Wedding ceremony services are available on-site. The inn is entirely nonsmoking.

209 Queen St., Niagara-on-the-Lake, Ont., L0S 1J0 © 866/556-8883 or 905/468-4588. www.charlesinn.ca. 12 units. C$99–C$325 (US$94–US$309) double. Weekend packages are available. AE, MC, V. Free parking. **Amenities:** Restaurant; lounge; enclosed veranda dining year-round; golf course next door; limited room service; massage; babysitting. In room: A/C, dataport, coffeemaker, hair dryer, iron, no phone.

Harbour House Hotel 🐾🐾

Harbour House is tucked away on a quiet street close to the marina, bike paths, and Lake Ontario, yet an easy walk to the center of the historical district of Niagara-on-the-Lake and the Shaw Festival Theatre. A refined tranquillity settles upon you from the moment you enter the main door.

The rooms are well-appointed, with quality amenities: Frette robes, soft throws to cuddle up in next to the fire, and Judith Jackson bathing products. And the best treat of all is that you will experience one of the most comfortable beds you have ever slept in, thanks to the Mount Orford feather bed (filled with hypoallergenic duck feathers) laid on top of the mattress. Lightweight white goose-down duvets and pillows and 300-thread-count Egyptian cotton linens complete the slumber kit. Note that those with feather allergies can request that a room be converted to non–feather bedding.

There is a cozy sitting room with fireplace, an intriguing selection of books, and a complimentary DVD lending library. At the cocktail hour, wines from local wineries are on hand, accompanied by Harbour House potted cheese. A hearty and healthy buffet breakfast is served in a pretty room overlooking the secluded patio. What sets Harbour House apart is its friendly yet impeccable service, its serene atmosphere, and those heavenly beds. No smoking is allowed on the premises.

85 Melville St., Niagara-on-the-Lake, Ont., L0S 1J0 © 866/277-6677 or 905/468-4683. Fax 905/468-0366. www.harbourhousehotel.ca. 31 units. C$199–C$335 (US$190–US$318) double; C$310 (US$295) and up suite packages available. Rates include breakfast. AE, MC, V. Free parking. Pets allowed in two specific guest rooms, C$25 (US$24) per day. **Amenities:** Bike rentals; concierge; courtesy shuttle; business services; limited room service; massage; babysitting; same-day laundry; dry cleaning. In room: A/C, TV, dataport, coffeemaker, hair dryer, iron.

Pillar and Post 🐾

The phrase "rustic charm" comes to mind as you stroll the corridors of the Pillar and Post, with its expanses of exposed brick, post-and-beam structures, and original windows, which have been preserved where possible. The inn's rooms are laid out in a U-shape around a central courtyard with lovely gardens.

Guest room decor has been updated to feel more contemporary: black and white photographs, plasma TVs, and fresh white bedspreads contrast with the dark furniture.

Birdsong Chalet **1**
Charles Inn **2**
Clover Field House
   Bed and Breakfast **3**
Harbour House Hotel **4**
Orchid Inn **5**
Old Bank House **6**
Pillar and Post **7**
Prince of Wales **8**
Everheart Country Manor **9**

Deluxe rooms have fireplaces, while premium rooms have a fireplace and jetted tub. Rooms facing the courtyard have better views than the ones facing the outdoor parking lot. Rooms can feel a little cramped. Likewise, rooms in some wings have larger bathrooms than others; request a more spacious one if that's important to you. The real highlight of this inn is the spa—The 100 Fountain Spa completed a $2-million renovation that includes an indoor and outdoor area. An indoor open concept allows guests to linger in the lounge area while waiting between treatments.

The dining room is heavy on wood; the food and service are more than satisfactory (see chapter 6, "Where to Dine," for more details). The inn is popular with families and also hosts a lot of weddings.

48 John St., Niagara-on-the-Lake, Ont., L0S 1J0. © 888/669-5566 or 905/468-2123. Fax 905/468-3551. www.vintage-hotels.com. 122 units. From C$225 (US$214) double; from C$425 (US$404) suite. AE, DC, DISC, MC, V. Free parking. **Amenities:** Restaurant; bar; indoor and outdoor pools; spa; Jacuzzi; sauna; bike rental; concierge; shuttle available; business center; babysitting; same-day dry cleaning. *In room:* A/C, TV w/pay movies, minibar, hair dryer, iron, safe.

Prince of Wales 🛇🛇   As the flagship property in the old town of Niagara-on-the-Lake, standing in prime position at the southeast corner of Picton Street and King Street, this place is quintessential Victorian; it feels like a dollhouse. Rooms are individually decorated, drawing their inspiration from days gone by, with an abundance of floral fabrics, antiques, and complemented by reproductions and 21st-century amenities. Traditional and deluxe guest rooms are quite cramped; the premium and suites have a separate living area. Bathrooms are also small but are bright and clean. English afternoon tea is offered in the Drawing Room.

6 Picton St., Niagara-on-the-Lake, Ont., L0S 1J0. © 888/669-5566 or 905/468-3246. Fax 905/468-5521. www.vintageinns.com. 110 units. From C$225 (US$214) double. Packages available. AE, DC, DISC, MC, V. Valet parking C$5 (US$4.75); self-parking free. Pets accepted. **Amenities:** Restaurant; cafe; bar; lounge; indoor pool; health club; spa; Jacuzzi; bike rental; concierge; shuttle available; business center; room service; babysitting; same-day dry cleaning. *In room:* A/C, TV w/pay movies, Wi-Fi, dataport, minibar, hair dryer, iron, safe.

Riverbend Inn & Vineyard 🛇🛇🛇   With only 21 guest rooms, this inn is an intimate and gracious property. Rooms are larger than average and all have fireplaces. Corner rooms have several windows, offering different views over the vineyards and surrounding greenery; a few rooms have private balconies. Due to its semirural location on the Niagara Parkway at the southern edge of Niagara-on-the-Lake, views are lovely from all rooms. Bathrooms are spacious. A magnificent chandelier hangs in the front foyer. Riverbend has 17 acres of vineyards, and its neighbor Reif Estates Winery manages the maintenance of the vineyards and production of the wine—the first vintage was released in 2006. The dining room has won praise for its cuisine, and rightly so. Open for breakfast, lunch, and dinner for nonresidents as well as inn guests, the restaurant offers an eclectic cuisine in the expert hands of resident chef Chris Smythe, blending local products with Southern style. Service in the restaurant and at the front desk is friendly and polished—many of the staff have been working for the proprietors since long before the Riverbend was born, and their loyalty and enthusiasm shine through. If you're looking for a romantic getaway, this place will please.

16104 Niagara River Pkwy., Niagara-on-the-Lake, Ont., L0S 1J0. © 905/468-8866. Fax 905/468-8829. www.riverbendinn.ca. 21 units. C$260–C$325 (US$247–US$309) double; C$375 (US$356) suite. Kids 10 and under stay free in parent's room. C$25 (US$24) per extra person 11 years and over in room. AE, MC, V. Free parking. **Amenities:** Restaurant; bar; bike rental; business services; limited room service; massage; babysitting. *In room:* A/C, TV, dataport, hair dryer.

White Oaks Conference Resort & Spa 🛇   Striving to be the ultimate in a combined resort/spa/conference center, White Oaks has a list of facilities, amenities, and

Just for Two

Looking for a romantic retreat? You'll find life is a bed of roses at the **Black Walnut Manor** (4255 Victoria Ave., Vineland, Ont.; 🕐 **800/859-4786**), the **Gracewood Inn** (16052 Niagara Parkway, Niagara-on-the-Lake, Ont.; 🕐 **905/468-9658**), the **Riverbend Inn** (16104 Niagara Parkway, Niagara-on-the-Lake, Ont.; 🕐 **905/468-8866**), and the **Sheraton Fallsview Hotel & Conference Centre** (6755 Fallsview Blvd., Niagara Falls, Ont.; 🕐 **905/374-1077**).

activities as long as your arm. Their spa offers skin-care treatments, massage, hydrotherapy, and a variety of retreat packages. Self-indulgence is the order of the day. Fitness nuts will lap up private sessions with personal trainers and Pilates instructors. Rooms are spacious, swathed in muted earth tones, and all have either a sunrise or sunset view. Ask for a room facing the nicely landscaped gardens rather than the parking lot. Also, lower-priced superior rooms are quite a bit smaller than the tower rooms (35 sq. m/377 sq. ft. versus 51 sq. m/549 sq. ft.). The entire property has an exclusive, yet austere, "club" feel. There is no smoking allowed here.

253 Taylor Rd., Niagara-on-the-Lake, Ont., L0S 1J0 🕐 800/263-5766 or 905/688-2550. www.whiteoaksresort.com. 220 units. C$165–C$289 (US$157–US$275) double; C$195–C$439 (US$185–US$417) suite. Children 12 and under stay free in parent's room. AE, MC, V. Free parking. **Amenities:** 2 restaurants; indoor pool; golf course; indoor tennis courts; health club; spa; hot tub; sauna; bike rental; concierge; business center; room service; massage; babysitting; same-day laundry and dry cleaning; executive rooms. *In room:* A/C, TV w/pay movies, Wi-Fi, dataport, bar, coffeemaker, hairdryer, iron, safe.

EXPENSIVE

Grand Victorian B&B 🕢   This enormous mansion on the Niagara Parkway was built in the Victorian era in the Queen Anne Revival style as a rebellion against the boxy, crowded Victorian architectural fashion of the day. Evidence of Quaker influences can be seen throughout the property. Each room is individually decorated and appointed; all are charming. A pretty sunroom/conservatory was added in 1899 and now serves as a breakfast nook for guests. The interior has a very open, airy feel, with high ceilings and an open floor plan allowing flow through the main-floor rooms. The property is popular for weddings; it's also a great place to stay for lovers of historical homes and antiques. The owner has acquired a considerable collection of antique furniture from Europe and North America over the years, in addition to a number of items from her grandmother's seaside homes in England, including draperies and china. The property is TV- and smoke-free.

15618 Niagara Pkwy., Niagara-on-the-Lake, Ont., L0S 1J0. 🕐 905/468-0997. Fax 905/468-1551. www.grandvictorian. ca. 6 units. C$170–C$220 (US$162–US$209) room; C$225 (US$214) suite. MC, V. Free parking. **Amenities:** Outdoor tennis court; bike rental; business services; massage. *In room:* A/C, no phone.

The Old Bank House 🕢   If you traveled the world and returned with a piece of each country—be it Asian textiles, Chinese vases, or even brightly colored contemporary Parisian paintings, you'd find yourself in this eclectic house with its own history. The two-story Georgian home, built around 1817, has a direct view of old Fort Niagara across the river and was originally the first branch of the Bank of Canada. In 1902, the Prince and Princess of Wales stayed here. The comfortable sitting room features a cozy fireplace and three separate dining areas. Upstairs, the Arbour Room features French-style flowered wallpaper and a big oval mirror with red velvet chairs. The Pine Room has French doors leading out to a shared patio, while the high-ceilinged Cedar Room—open to bright sunlight—has a private patio. Walking through the uneven, creaky hardwood floors to the front entrance, you'll find a guestbook under the nose of the house mascot—a stuffed eland (moose-like animal) from South Africa named Master Ted. He is the guardian of this quiet, contemplative place and a friend of the owners, Judy and Michael, who are gracious and warm.

10 Front St., Niagara-on-the-Lake, Ont., L0S 1J0. **C** **877/468-7136** or 905/468-7136. www.oldbankhouse.com. 9 units. C$145–C$225 (US$138–US$214) double. Rates include breakfast. AE, MC, V. Free parking. **Amenities:** Jacuzzi. *In room:* A/C, no phone.

MODERATE

Everheart Country Manor Frazzled parents or business types will appreciate the seclusion here in the sleepy town of Queenston at the foot of the Brock monument, off the Niagara Parkway. Guests are able to chat with others on the wrap-around patio, or they can find a secluded table out in the sunken gardens throughout the large property. There's an indoor pool, Jacuzzis, and a fireplace in every room, and plenty of living space. Each room has character: The French doors of the Riverview Suite open to reveal the Niagara River, letting in lots of natural light; while the Garden View Suite, decorated in burgundy, feels like a gentlemen's club. The Turret Room is great for couples, with two chairs and a dining table in the turret. There's a small communal kitchen area—a separate room—that has a fridge for the day's food shopping that also includes complimentary pop, water, and coffee. Here, you can also find a selection of movies to watch in your room. Choose your own breakfast the night before—it includes great coffee and fresh fruit to start; you can eat in the dining room or in one of the many areas outside. Former Torontonians Doug and Joyce are wonderful conversationalists, but they also respect guests' desire for privacy should you want it.

137 Queenston St., Queenston. **C** **866/284-0544** or 905/262-5444, L0S 1L0. www.everheart.ca. 3 units. C$125–C$180 (US$119–US$172). C$30 (US$29) extra person. MC, V. Free parking. **Amenities:** indoor pool; golf nearby; massage arranged. *In room:* A/C, TV/VCR (2 w/DVD), Wi-Fi, hairdryer, iron, no phone.

Shaw Club The decor is sleek and minimalist: chic black furniture, bamboo plants, and steel accents. But it also has a home-away-from-home feel: DVDs and Italian coffees (espressos and cappuccinos) are complimentary in the lobby. Goldfish in the rooms also add a colorful touch. Rooms are quite cramped but they're full of cool gadgets: an iPod docking station, plasma TV, another TV in the bathroom, and a DVD/CD player. Other touches include 300-count Egyptian cotton linens, down pillows and duvet, and a gigantic showerhead. The king suite with fireplace has its own balcony, wet bar, double soaker tub, and living room. Downstairs features Zee's Patio and Grill, which includes an outdoor wraparound patio to see theatergoers heading to the Shaw Theatre across the street.

92 Picton Street, Niagara-on-the-Lake. **C** **800/511-7070** or 905/468-5711. Fax 905/468-4988. www.shawclub.com. 30 units. C$99–C$455 ($US94–US$432). Packages available. Breakfast included. AE, DC, MC, V. Free parking. Pet accepted for C$25 (US$24) per night. **Amenities:** Restaurant; lounge; golf nearby; exercise room; spa; concierge; courtesy shuttle; limited room service; babysitting arranged. *In room:* A/C, TV/DVD w/pay movies (free DVD library), Wi-Fi, dataport, fridge, coffeemaker, hair dryer, iron, safe.

INEXPENSIVE

Birdsong Chalet 🌟 *(Finds* Crickets chirp at night and the rooster crows in the morning at this Swiss chalet hidden in wine country. Centrally located 10 minutes from downtown Niagara-on-the-Lake, and minutes from several wineries, this place feels like an island. Inside, the rooms remind me of my grandmother's cottage—small, tacky, and flowery but cozy. Bathrooms are a squeeze: the Morning Glory Room has only a shower while the Wisteria Room has a tub/shower. The upstairs breakfast area is full of knickknacks, figurines, and plants. Guests can also picnic on the banks of the man-made pond and garden. Breakfast includes fresh seasonal produce from their garden (frozen for winter visitors). A common area includes a kitchenette with fridge, coffeemaker, hairdryer, and iron.

982 Line 6, Niagara-on-the-Lake, Ont., L0S 1J0 ✆ **905/262-5080.** www.birdsongchaletniagara.com. 2 units. C$89–C$119 (US$85–US$113). Rates include breakfast. **Amenities:** Golf course nearby; massage arranged. *In room:* A/C, TV/DVD (Morning Glory only), no phones.

Clover Field House Bed and Breakfast 🌟 Down the road from the epicenter of Niagara-on-the-Lake is this home, decorated with pictures of ski trips and family on the wall that add personality. Out back is a dense garden full of sitting areas and vines. Inside, rooms are also quite cramped with queen beds and table and chairs in every room. Vine-covered patios for every room offer private retreats. The deluxe suite has the most room with a separate living room, private entrance, and private courtyard outside. Whirlpool tubs are also in every room. Breakfasts are a high point and include fresh fruit, yogurt, and a hot dish. Guests are invited to bring furry dog friends to play with the owners' two sheep dogs. This establishment is entirely nonsmoking.

1879 Lakeshore Rd., Niagara-on-the-Lake, Ont., L0S 1J0 ✆ **905/468-7377.** Fax 905/468-0293. www.cloverfieldhouse.com. 3 units. C$135–C$225 (US$128–US$214); C$199 (US$190) for 1 night year-round. Discounts for multiple nights. **Amenities:** Free bike use. *In room:* A/C, fridge, coffeemaker, hairdryer, iron, stereo.

Orchid Inn 🌟 *(Value* One of this inn's main selling points is its location, set back from the throngs of tourists on the main street in Niagara-on-the-Lake. Industrial carpet and officelike hallways contribute to a generic feeling; the rooms are also basic but bright and clean, decorated in lemony yellows with bamboo accents and dark furniture. Bathrooms are exceptionally spacious with whirlpool tubs. Afternoon tea is offered from May to October.

390 Mary St., Niagara-on-the Lake, Ont., L0S 1J0 ✆ **905/468-3871.** www.orchidinn.ca. 9 units. C$100–C$210 (US$95–US$200). Packages available. Rates include breakfast for 2. AE, MC, V. Free parking. **Amenities:** Restaurant; golf nearby; limited spa; massage arranged. *In room:* A/C, TV, Wi-Fi, dataport, coffeemaker, hairdryer, iron, no phone.

3 Wine Country

The choice of accommodations in wine country is as diverse as the wineries themselves. Each has a distinctive personality and ambience. The list below is a representative sample of the best of the region, although there are many more lovely properties nestled among the vines.

VERY EXPENSIVE

Inn on the Twenty 🌟🌟 This upscale inn in Jordan features a variety of guest room and suite styles in a converted sugar warehouse and nearby buildings, including two small adjoining cottages and a historical home with three rustic suites. All the main-inn suites have gas fireplaces, comfortable seating areas, and Jacuzzi tubs. Some suites have private gardens. The room decor is an artistic blend of antiques and contemporary accessories. Bathrooms are spacious and luxuriously appointed. The Inn is located in the center of the compact, fashionable commercial area in Jordan Village, with gift shops, art galleries, designer clothing stores, and antiques retailers only a step away. Breakfast is served in the renowned On the Twenty Restaurant on the other side of the street from the guest accommodations. Please note that the reception desk is on the second floor of the main inn building. If you require assistance with your luggage, you'll need to climb the stairs to the lobby to alert the staff. The property is nonsmoking.

3845 Main St., Jordan, Ont., L0S 1J0. © **800/701-8074** or 905/562-5336. Fax 905/562-0009. www.innonthetwenty. com. 29 units. C$169–C$289 (US$161–US$275) and up regular suite; C$239–C$359 (US$227–US$341) and up deluxe and cottage suites. Rates include breakfast. Children under 12 may share parent's room; C$40 (US$38) per rollaway bed per night. AE, DC, MC, V. Free parking. **Amenities:** Restaurant; bar; spa; bike rental; business services; shopping arcade; limited room service; massage; babysitting; same-day laundry service. *In room:* A/C, TV/VCR, hair dryer, iron.

EXPENSIVE

Black Walnut Manor 🏛🏛   Billing itself as an urban oasis in the heart of wine country, Black Walnut Manor undeniably has a sophisticated atmosphere. The twist is that the three spacious en-suite guest rooms are decorated in cool, modern, ultrachic style, yet the property is a historical homestead set in the rolling hills near the village of Vineland. The rooms are named to evoke a feeling of tranquillity and restfulness— "Retreat," "Return," and "Relax." Two of the rooms have private rooftop terraces. The most luxurious and romantic room (and also the most expensive, natch) is "Retreat," with its king-size bed draped in graceful sheers, an air-jet tub, and a shower large enough for two. The proprietor's distinctive personality touches everything in the house, from her dog (trained to stay at paw's length from the guests) to the black-and-white photographs shot on a trip to Paris, to the eclectic dining-room decor, with its mix of 1940s dining chairs, antique silver tea service, and brushed-aluminum light fixture suspended above the table. Thoughtful touches that add to guests' comfort include amenities bags filled with essential toiletries to replace those forgotten-at-home items, fluffy bathrobes, and wineglasses and corkscrews in the rooms. There is a wine fridge in the common room that guests can use to chill their winery purchases. The inn is nonsmoking.

4255 Victoria Ave., Vineland, Ont., L0R 2E0 © **800/859-4786** or 905/562-8675. www.blackwalnutmanor.com. 3 units. C$150–C$205 (US$143–US$195) double. Children ages 3 and up in parent's room C$25 (US$24) per night. AE, MC, V. Free parking. **Amenities:** Bikes available for use free of charge. *In room:* A/C, TV/VCR, hair dryer, no phone.

Feast of Fields Organic Vineyard B&B Cottage 🏛 *Finds Kids Value*   A unique experience awaits at Feast of Fields. As you drive up the laneway to this working farm, you are likely to pass horses and cows in the adjacent fields. Curious peacocks may form a welcoming committee—they roam free on the grounds. Around the back of the restored farmhouse (ca. 1835), llamas hang their necks over a gated pen and seem to smile at you. The farmhouse has been restored to a self-contained bed-and-breakfast cottage with full kitchen, sitting room, and two bedrooms upstairs. A queen-size sofa bed in the sitting room can be used for sleeping, thereby providing accommodation for up to six guests in total. This is a tranquil countryside location, yet close to a number of Niagara wineries—Rockway Glen and Trillium are two of the nearest. You can join the Bruce Trail in a 10- to 15-minute leisurely walk from the cottage. Hikers'

Niagara Region Accommodations

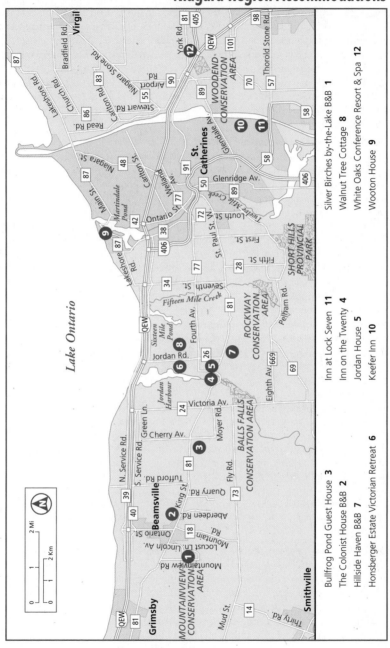

Silver Birches by-the-Lake B&B **1**
Walnut Tree Cottage **8**
White Oaks Conference Resort & Spa **12**
Wooton House **9**

Inn at Lock Seven **11**
Inn on the Twenty **4**
Jordan House **5**
Keefer Inn **10**

Bullfrog Pond Guest House **3**
The Colonist House B&B **2**
Hillside Haven B&B **7**
Honsberger Estate Victorian Retreat **6**

packages are offered, and the proprietor will drop off and pick up hikers who are interested in exploring different parts of the Bruce Trail on different days. Wine made from the farmer's organic grapes is available in limited quantities. The kitchen is stocked with organic products for guests to prepare their own breakfast. There is no smoking at this accommodation.

3403 11th St., Jordan, Ont., L2R 6P7. (📞 905/562-0151. www.feast-of-fields.ca/bandb. 2-bed cottage with queen-size sofa bed in sitting room. C$149–C$175 (US$142–US$166) 2 guests; C$35–C$50 (US$33–US$48) each additional guest to maximum of 6 guests in the cottage. MC, V. Free parking. **Amenities:** Bicycles available free by prior arrangement; washer/dryers. *In cottage:* A/C (bedrooms only), TV, dataport, kitchen, coffeemaker, hair dryer, iron, no phone.

Honsberger Estate Victorian Retreat 🍷   This 560-sq.-m (6,000-sq.-ft.) Victorian country house is one of the finest examples of its type in the Niagara region. The Honsberger Estate is located on a 40-acre working farm, with orchards gracing the fields leading up the sweeping drive to the home. The bedrooms are arranged in two separate wings on the second floor, with four bedrooms in one wing and two bedrooms in the other. This arrangement is ideal for a multifamily or multigeneration holiday, or for a wedding party. Booking the entire property is quite commonplace, but bookings are also accepted for a minimum of eight guests (a full house is 12 guests). Breakfast is included with the rates, but for an extra cost the proprietor will arrange for a chef to prepare dinner, which is served in the formal dining room. The grounds of the estate are peaceful and relaxing, with plenty of mature shade trees and even an old-fashioned wooden-seated swing, suspended by ropes strung on a sturdy tree branch. If you've ever wanted to play the part of a country squire and gentrified family, this is the place for you. This property is best suited to adults; older children accepted with prior arrangement. There is no smoking allowed.

4060 Jordan Rd., Jordan Station, Ont., L0S 1J0. (📞 **905/562-6789**. Fax 905/227-4663. www.honsbergerestate.com. C$200 (US$190) double. **Amenities:** Massage. *In room:* A/C, dataport, iron, no phone.

MODERATE

Jordan House Tavern and Lodging 🍷 *Value*   This refurbished industrial building is an inexpensive alternative to some of the high-priced inns in the area. All rooms have queen beds and a flatscreen television. Studio rooms are tight for space; for more room there are three executive rooms with an electric fireplace, pull-out sofa, full tub, and a small desk. Rooms facing west have a nice sunset view. While the rest of the town shuts down after 6pm, there's free live music every Friday night at the bar downstairs.

3751 Main Street, Jordan, Ont., L0R 1S0 (📞 **800/701-8074** or 905/562-9591. www.jordanhouse.ca. 14 units. C$99–C$170, (US$94–US$162). Packages available. AE, DC, MC, V. Self-parking free. **Amenities:** Restaurant; golf nearby; massage arranged; concierge; limited room service; same-day laundry service. In room: A/C, TV, dataport, coffeemaker, hairdryer, iron.

Silver Birches by-the-Lake B&B   Silver Birches is much more than a B&B. Its level of comfort and amenities puts it more in the league of a country house or inn. With its large outdoor swimming pool, luxury indoor hot tub, tennis court, and 1.2 hectare (3 acres) of park-like gardens, you will feel relaxed and pampered. You can extend the pleasure by prebooking a four-course gourmet dinner prepared by owners and hosts Paul and Leah Padfield (a minimum of four guests are required to book a dinner). Or take advantage of one of their many packages, put together in partnership with local wineries, restaurants, and theaters. Families can book the two-bedroom suite, which sleeps up to seven and has a private bathroom. Three other bedrooms, each with en-suite and individual decor, are located on the second floor. Gorgeous sunrises flood the sky above Lake Ontario and can be seen from the front porch—if you're awake early enough to enjoy them. This bed-and-breakfast is nonsmoking.

4902 Mountain View Rd., Beamsville, Ont., L0R 1B3. ℂ 905/563-9479. www.silverbirchesbythelake.com. 5 units. C$125–C$135 (US$119–US$128) double; suite from C$235 (US$223) based on 4 sharing. AE, MC, V. Free parking. Inquire about children. **Amenities:** Outdoor pool; outdoor tennis; indoor hot tub; bikes available free of charge; laundry service C$10 (US$9.50). *In room:* Dataport, hair dryer.

Walnut Tree Cottage   Tucked away in the center of Jordan Village among the mature shade trees, Walnut Tree Cottage actually offers a choice of two accommodations: a tiny romantic guesthouse for two, or a suite in the main house next door where the proprietor lives. The cottage is a delightfully private retreat. Skylights in the cathedral ceiling flood the room with light—this is a former artist's studio. A pretty garden at the rear is available for guests' use. The cottage features a king-size bed, a fireplace, and a kitchenette with toaster, microwave, fridge, and small table with two chairs. At Walnut Tree, you may be on your own without interacting with anyone— a blessing first thing in the morning. Breakfast can be enjoyed in privacy in the cottage: order the night before and the proprietor will leave a picnic basket on your front doorstep in the morning. If you're staying in the house, you have the option of eating on the deck or in the dining room, or you also may have a basket. Neither accommodation allows smoking.

3797 Main St., Jordan Village, Ont., L0R 1S0. ℂ **905/562-8144**. www.bbcanada.com/walnuttreecottage.ca. 2 units (1 room, 1 cottage). C$120–C$140 (US$114–$US133). MC, V. Free parking. **Amenities:** Fridge in house; coffeemaker in cottage. *In room:* A/C, TV, no phone.

INEXPENSIVE

Bullfrog Pond Guest House   If you like walking, whether it's a stroll to one of the nearby wineries or hiking the Bruce Trail, this is a good place to base yourself. The proprietors will cheerfully pack a picnic basket if you're heading out on an adventure by foot, on bicycles (there are several on-site for guests' use), or in your car. The guest accommodations are accessed at the rear of the house and are on ground level, so no steps to climb up and down. There is a common room with limited kitchen facilities and a cozy sitting area, and a hallway leading to the comfortable en-suite bedrooms, both with fireplaces. Rooms feature Mennonite furniture, homemade quilts, and simple decor—it feels like Grandma's house. Guests are welcome to enjoy the .4-hectare (1-acre) sweep of lawns and flower gardens and the outdoor patio. You might luck out and arrive on a day when the proprietor has just baked a batch of her delicious chocolate chip cookies. You may not smoke here.

3801 Cherry Ave., Vineland, Ont., L0R 2C0. ℂ **905/562-1232**. www.bullfrogpond.com. 3 units. C$115–C$130 (US$109–US$124) double. C$25 (US$24) for extra person. MC, V. Free parking. **Amenities:** Bikes available at no charge. *In room:* A/C, TV/VCR, hair dryer, iron, no phone.

The Colonist House B&B   Those with a passion for history or who are simply curious about the past will revel in The Colonist House. Not only is the 165-year-old property an exceptional example of an original two-story timber-framed, plank-walled home built in the Colonial Georgian style, but also the owners, Lloyd and Jennifer Haines, are descendants of the original 1798 Mennonite settlers of the area. Jennifer's ancestors' family home is now on exhibit on the grounds of the Jordan Historical Museum of the Twenty. The Haineses are gentle, welcoming hosts who are pleased to discuss local history, whether it's Colonist House, their own family, or local events. The guest rooms are accessed through the rear garden and have their own private hallway with windows overlooking the garden. A coffee bar for guests' use has thoughtfully been placed in the hall. No stairs to climb—unlike most B&Bs. An eclectic mix of antiques and contemporary furniture and accessories fill the modestly sized bedrooms, each with compact en-suite bathroom. A pretty deck at the rear has seating for warm summer days and evenings. The property is entirely nonsmoking.

4924 King St., Beamsville, Ont., L0R 1B0. ☎ 905/563-7838. www.colonisthouse.com. 2 units. C$110 (US$105) double. MC, V. Free parking. *In room:* A/C, TV, Wi-Fi, hair dryer, no phone.

Hillside Haven B&B *Value*   Nestled among the rolling hillsides of Niagara's wine-country back roads, this secluded country property features a unique loft in an outbuilding separate from the owners' home. It's a perfect setting for a romantic weekend getaway. The comfortably furnished accommodations include a fully equipped kitchen for those who like to cook for themselves—with the wealth of fresh local produce available during the growing season, why wouldn't you? Rates include a thoughtfully stocked fridge and pantry so you can fix your own breakfast on a schedule that suits you and enjoy it in privacy. The large one-room apartment has a queen-size bed in an alcove and a comfortable couch for relaxing. Guests are invited to use the spacious deck and pool adjacent to the main house at any time. The Bruce Trail is on your doorstep, and there is plenty of opportunity to enjoy leisurely bike rides along the quiet country roads (bikes available for use). The flower gardens are a rainbow of color in the summer, and fall is spectacular—the property lies in an area heavily populated with deciduous trees that blaze orange, yellow, and red. Winery dinner packages are available, which include a shuttle service to and from the restaurant. No smoking is allowed.

3496 17th St., R.R. 1, St. Catharines, Ont., L2R 6P7. ☎ 905/562-7021. www.hillsidehaven.com. 1 unit (self-contained). C$110 (US$105) 1-night stay; C$195 (US$189) 2-night stay. Rates include breakfast. MC, V. Free parking. **Amenities:** Outdoor pool. *In room:* A/C, TV/VCR, dataport, coffeemaker, hair dryer, iron, no phone.

4 Welland Canal Corridor

The village of Port Dalhousie has a handful of bed-and-breakfast properties if you'd like to stay over and enjoy an evening at the community theater, or if you just want to stroll along the lakeshore and relax. For shipping enthusiasts, the Inn at Lock 7 is an ideal base—the ships pass right by the balconies of the building.

INEXPENSIVE

Inn at Lock Seven   Watch international ocean freighters and tankers from your outdoor balcony. The Welland Canal water route—a link between the St. Lawrence and the Great Lakes—has seen more than two billion tons of cargo pass through since opening in 1959. Guests receive "The ABC's of the Seaway" and quickly become boat nerds, say owners Ed Kuiper and Patty Szoldra. Formerly the Lock Motel, this bed-and-breakfast is a mix of both styles: room walls are concrete and have simple matching bedspreads and curtains like a motel, while Patty and Ed have added their personal B&B touch—Patty sells her pottery wares in the gift shop, while Ed will take guests on motorcycle rides or a scuba dive. Only 15 minutes from the popular tourist destinations, this is a great jumping-off point to local wineries that won't break the bank. Set in a residential locale—enjoy some peace and quiet.

24 Chapel St. S., Thorold, Ont., L2V 2C6. ℂ **877/INN-LOCK7** (877/465-6257). www.innatlock7.com. 24 units. C$69–C$119 (US$66–US$113) double. Rates include breakfast. AE, DC, MC, V. Free parking. *In room:* A/C, TV, no phone.

Keefer Mansion Inn ★★ *Value*   Every nook and cranny has a personality in this place—complete with a shelf that opens up to a staircase on the third floor. Overlooking the town of Thorold, the Keefer Mansion is one of the finest inns in the Niagara region for its amenities and wonderful history. Slated for demolition only a few short years ago, today the impeccable restored inn is a symbol of what can happen when residents believe in their heritage. Built in 1886, it has been touched by many aspects of Canada history and in most recent times it served as a hospital. Today there's a glass cabinet full of house treasures including vials of morphine (when it was a hospital) to a funeral bill (only $200 to die in 1908). The grand curving staircase is the showcase with the dining rooms on both the left and right; there are wooden fireplaces on both sides and a bar with stools on the right. Upstairs, all rooms are named after homeowners' of the Keefer Mansion and town icons. Rooms facing the Welland Canal have the best views, such as the very spacious George Keefer room: a four-poster bed draped with fabric and a large wardrobe are elegant and grand pieces. And on the third floor, originally a ballroom, rooms have fantastic birds-eye views of the town or canal. The most cozy and unique room is the Hugh Keefer, which has half stone walls and angled ceilings; the panoramic view of the canal is the best in the house. There are also two rooms dedicated to a spa for massages and a fine dining restaurant below. Months after my stay, I still can't stop thinking about this place.

14 St. Davids St. West, Thorold, Ont., L2V 2K9. ℂ **905/680-9581.** www.keefermansion.com. 9 units. Double C$150–C$219 (US$143–US$209). Packages available. Breakfast included. AE, MC, V. Free parking. **Amenities:** Restaurant; golf nearby; spa; concierge; limited room service; babysitting can be arranged; washers/dryers, same-day laundry service. *In room:* A/C, TV/DVD, dataport, hairdryer, iron.

Wooton House B&B   The pubs, lake marina, shops, and live theater of historical Port Dalhousie are all within walking distance of this charming home built in 1885. Watch world-class rowing on Martindale Pond from the lawn as you eat your Wooton House waffles with fresh-fruit topping. The "View with a Room" room has a balcony overlooking Lake Ontario. Ideal for a long stay, this unit has its own kitchen and dining area, complete with microwave and en-suite bathroom with Jacuzzi. Discounts are available for longer stays. If you're the bookish type, you'll appreciate the library room, with its skylight and built-in shelves full of classics. All rooms offer cable TV and are accessed through a private entrance. All beds are queen-size four-posters. Niagara-on-the-Lake and Niagara Falls are only a 15-minute drive away. The cozy corner room has an adjacent private bathroom.

2 Elgin St., St. Catharines, Ont., L2N 5G3. ℂ **905/937-4696.** www.wootonhouse.com. 3 units. C$90–C$150 (US$86–US$143) double. Rates include breakfast. Free parking. *In room:* TV, no phone.

6

Where to Dine

Dining in Niagara tends to fall into two categories—pricey but extremely good, or mundane and reliable. The former includes the excellent restaurants in Niagara's wine country, and more recently, St. Catharines, which is a favorite destination with locals. Niagara Falls is peppered with a plethora of chains that have firmly established themselves in an area that sees 14 million tourists annually, many of whom just want fuel to keep their feet going as they are herded from attraction to attraction.

The range of dining experiences in the region is wide. You can enjoy a leisurely lunch on a shady terrace with the lush vineyards spread out around you, dine by candlelight as you marvel at the rainbow colors of the illuminated Horseshoe and American Falls, or lounge around in a diner, eating pancakes and bacon washed down with a bottomless mug of coffee.

DINING NOTES Dining out in Niagara does not have to be an expensive venture, but be aware that taxes are high. Meals are subject to 8% provincial sales tax and 6% GST, so when you factor in an average tip, a whopping 27% is added to the bill. Tipping is usually left to the diner's discretion, although some establishments add 15% to the bill for parties of six or more.

Pay attention to the wine prices in restaurants—they can be quite high, even for the local Niagara wines. Don't be surprised to find your favorite vintage at double the price you'd pay at the liquor store or sometimes even at the winery. Savvy diners can take note of wine prices in the winery boutiques and compare them with those on the wine list in their chosen restaurant in order to better gauge how much markup has been applied. Note that a 10% liquor tax is added to alcoholic beverage purchases.

If you find a bottle of wine from a winery that you want to bring to supper, some Ontario restaurants participate in the BYOB (bring your own bottle) program. At the time of publication, 13 Niagara region restaurants offer this service—for a complete list visit **www. bringmywine.ca**. Diners can bring their bottle of wine, provided it's not offered on the restaurants' wine list. Diners pay a corkage fee—this pays for servers to open and serve your bottle; corkage fees range between C$12 (US$11) and C$25 (US$24) and during the winter season, some restaurants offer no-corkage fees—call ahead to find out. No partially consumed bottles allowed. Visit the site for a full list of rules, which includes informing the restaurant you intend to bring your own bottle, before you arrive.

Hours vary quite markedly between summer and winter. The "high season," when opening hours are long, runs approximately from May to October for restaurants. Some restaurants close 1 day or more during the week in the winter months. You should always call ahead if you have chosen a particular restaurant, in order to avoid disappointment.

1 Restaurants by Cuisine

AMERICAN

Hard Rock Cafe (Niagara Falls, Ontario, $$, p. 88)

Rainforest Café (Niagara Falls, Ontario, $$, p. 88)

Red Coach Inn ✪ (Niagara Falls, New York, $$, p. 90)

Terrapin Grille ✪ (Niagara Falls, Ontario, $$$$, p. 86)

ASIAN

Echoes from Asia (Welland Canal Corridor, $$, p. 101)

Ginger Restaurant ✪ (Niagara-on-the-Lake, $$, p. 94)

The Golden Lotus ✪✪ (Niagara Falls, Ontario, $$$, p. 86)

BAKERY

Willow Cakes and Pastries (Niagara-on-the-Lake, $, p. 96)

BISTRO/CAFE

The Epicurean Restaurant (Niagara-on-the-Lake, $$$, p. 92)

The Krieghoff Gallery-Café (Niagara Falls, Ontario, $$, p. 88)

The Pie Plate ✪ (Niagara-on-the-Lake, $, p. 96)

Zooma Zooma Café ✪ (Wine Country, $$, p. 100)

CANADIAN

Shaw Café and Wine Bar (Niagara-on-the-Lake, $$$, p. 93)

Queenston Heights Restaurant ✪ (Niagara Falls, Ontario, $$$$, p. 84)

Tiara Restaurant ✪✪ (Niagara-on-the-Lake, $$$$, p. 92)

Zest ✪ (Fonthill, $$$$, p. 103)

CONTEMPORARY

Charles Inn Restaurant ✪✪✪ (Niagara-on-the-Lake, Ontario, $$$$, p. 90)

17 Noir ✪✪ (Niagara Falls, Ontario, $$$$, p. 84)

Wolfgang Puck Grand Café Niagara ✪ (Niagara Falls, Ontario, $$$, p. 87)

CONTINENTAL

The Restaurant at Vineland Estates Winery ✪✪ (Wine Country, $$$$, p. 99)

DINER

Bob Evans Farms Restaurant (Niagara Falls, New York, $$, p. 87)

Falls Manor Motel and Restaurant ✪ (Niagara Falls, Ontario, $$, p. 88)

Little Red Rooster (Niagara-on-the-Lake, $$, p. 94)

ECLECTIC

Pow Wow ✪ (Welland Canal Corridor, $$, p. 101)

Stone Road Grille ✪✪ (Niagara-on-the-Lake, $$$, p. 93)

Zee's Patio & Grill ✪✪ (Niagara-on-the-Lake, $$$, p. 93)

FRENCH

Peller Estates Winery Restaurant ✪✪ (Wine Country, $$$$, p. 98)

The Restaurant at Peninsula Ridge ✪✪ (Wine Country, $$$$, p. 99)

Terroir La Cachette ✪✪ (Wine Country, $$$, p. 99)

INTERNATIONAL

LIV Restaurant ✪✪ (Niagara-on-the-Lake, $$$$, p. 92)

The Epicurean Restaurant (Niagara-on-the-Lake, $$$, p. 92)

Wellington Court ✪✪ (Welland Canal Corridor, $$$, p. 100)

ITALIAN

The Capri (Niagara Falls, Ontario, $$$, p. 86)

Carpaccio Restaurant and Wine Bar ✪ (Niagara Falls, Ontario, $$$, p. 86)

The Old Winery ✪ (Niagara-on-the-Lake, $$, p. 94)

PIZZA

Zappi's (Kids) (Niagara Falls, Ontario, $$, p. 90)

PUB

Olde Angel Inn Pub and Restaurant (Niagara-on-the-Lake, $$$, p. 94)

REGIONAL CUISINE

Hillebrand Vineyard Café 🏵🏵 (Wine Country, $$$$, p. 98)

Niagara Culinary Institute Dining Room 🏵 (Wine Country, $$, p. 100)

On the Twenty Restaurant 🏵🏵 (Wine Country, $$$$, p. 98)

Peller Estates Winery Restaurant 🏵🏵 (Wine Country, $$$$, p. 98)

Queenston Heights Restaurant 🏵 (Niagara Falls, Ontario, $$$$, p. 84)

The Restaurant at Peninsula Ridge 🏵🏵 (Wine Country, $$$$, p. 99)

Stone Road Grille 🏵🏵 (Niagara-on-the-Lake, $$$, p. 93)

Terroir La Cachette 🏵🏵 (Wine Country, $$$, p. 99)

Wellington Court 🏵🏵 (Welland Canal Corridor, $$$, p. 100)

STEAKHOUSE

The Keg 🏵 (Niagara Falls, Ontario, $$$, p. 87)

VEGETARIAN

Green Bean Café and Oxygen Bar 🏵 (Welland Canal Corridor, $$, p. 103)

Spice of Life (Welland Canal Corridor, $$, p. 101)

2 Niagara Falls, Ontario and New York

There's a restaurant wherever you look in Niagara Falls. Sadly, I wouldn't want to eat at most of them. Even locals hop in their cars to drive to St. Catharines for a good meal. Fast-food signs and roadhouse grille signs dominate the skyline, but hooray for the great Italian restaurants that save the day. And don't be fooled by some of the restaurants that offer the best views of the Falls—in many cases, the view is only meant to distract you from your unsatisfying meal.

Most of the tourist amenities, including restaurants, are concentrated on the Canadian side of the Falls.

VERY EXPENSIVE

Queenston Heights Restaurant 🏵 REGIONAL/CANADIAN   Perched above the Niagara River, the dining room of this restaurant is in the heart of Queenston Heights Park. The a la carte menu, which features a variety of cuisines, is well intentioned but uninspired. However, I highly recommend the tasting menu, which begins with three starters—a few bites per portion. You'll get a taste of fresh herbs on top of such items as seared tuna, ravioli, or smoked salmon; the sauces on many dishes are locally inspired, using such ingredients as Baco noir, icewine, and local cherries. The tasting menu includes lamb and chicken entrees, also prepared with local sauces and herbs. The white tablecloths, giant painting of the Falls hanging over the stone fireplace, and the panoramic windows make this place feel like a dining room at a well-heeled country club. Service is efficient, if a little distant. Your best bet is to enjoy the patio view with a glass of wine and selections from the tasting menu.

14184 Niagara Pkwy., Queenston, Ont. © **905/262-4274.** Reservations recommended. Main courses C$15–C$34 (US$14–US$32). AE, DC, MC, V. Mar–Dec daily 11am–9pm.

17 Noir 🏵🏵 CONTEMPORARY   It only makes sense that the Fallsview Casino has a restaurant that pays homage to gambling and the good life. Decorated in reds and blacks to mimic a roulette table, the room has fuzzy felt chairs and round tables. You'll feel like a high roller here—I chatted with Canadian acting icon Gordon Pinsent, who

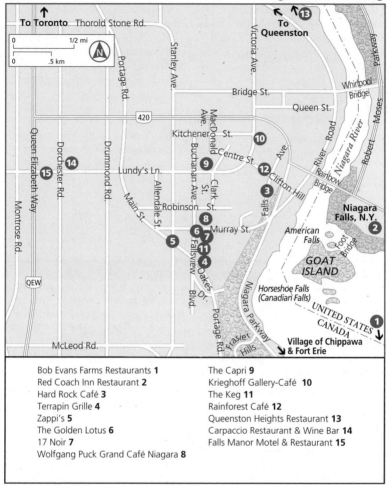

Niagara Falls Dining

Bob Evans Farms Restaurants **1**	The Capri **9**
Red Coach Inn Restaurant **2**	Krieghoff Gallery-Café **10**
Hard Rock Café **3**	The Keg **11**
Terrapin Grille **4**	Rainforest Café **12**
Zappi's **5**	Queenston Heights Restaurant **13**
The Golden Lotus **6**	Carpaccio Restaurant & Wine Bar **14**
17 Noir **7**	Falls Manor Motel & Restaurant **15**
Wolfgang Puck Grand Café Niagara **8**	

was a few tables over. The menu hasn't changed much since its opening but that has allowed the chef time to perfect each dish, allowing flavors to come through even on the simplest of menu items. A staid foie gras gets a pick-me-up with tequila-lime jelly, and a simple squash soup is a great blend of puréed squash with creamy butter, which brings out the sweetness of the vegetable. And for fish lovers, I recommend an organic Irish salmon filet cooked to your liking, just like a steak. The salmon is perched on top of fingerling potatoes, double smoked bacon, and shallot veal reduction. The frozen banana soufflé with walnuts is a rare find for desserts. Downstairs from the dining room, have a seat at the sushi and noodle bar, which is open late. Watch the Japanese master sushi chefs (two on staff) prepare delicacies right in front of your eyes.

6380 Fallsview Blvd. Niagara Falls, Ont. ✆ **888/WINFALL**. Reservations recommended. Dining room C$35–C$47 (US$33–US$45). AE, MC, V. Dining room daily 5–11pm; sushi and noodle bar daily 11am–4am.

Terrapin Grille ⑆ AMERICAN   While it does not boast the boldest of menus, thanks to a talented French chef on board, some ordinary fare gets a nice touch-up: the filet mignon meets béarnaise sauce, and Asian herbs with cilantro and chile are rubbed on sea bass with a raspberry reduction. Main entrees are well prepared, but the side dishes are a bit dull. The extensive wine list features Niagara wines. The view from your chair is one of the best in the city: with a wall of windows facing the panorama, every diner gets a piece of the action. Booths facing the Falls are cozy for couples, while calming music plays in the background. With its high-class atmosphere, this restaurant is your best bet for Fallsview dining, if you can't leave the area.

6740 Fallsview Blvd., Niagara Falls, Ont. ⓒ 905/357-7300. Reservations recommended. Main courses C$28–C$85 (US$27–US$81). AE, DC, MC, V. Mon–Thurs 6:30–11am and 11:30am–11pm; Fri 6:30–11am and 12:30–11pm; Sat–Sun 6:30am–11pm.

EXPENSIVE

The Capri ITALIAN   This Niagara Falls landmark has been dishing up hearty portions of Italian fare for more than 40 years—the illuminated vertical restaurant sign, outlined in theater-style light bulbs, gives away its age, but no one seems to mind the time-warp feel—the place is usually quite busy, with locals and tourists alike. Their specialty is pasta that is North Americanized—try to imagine a brick-size plate of lasagna with slightly soggy noodles—so be aware that this place is more quantity than quality. You can also find a variety of veal and chicken dishes on the menu. It's a far cry from fine dining, but if you're hungry, it will fit the bill. Conventional lovebirds may like to try the "Honeymoon Special," featuring two New York strip loin steaks served with sautéed mushrooms, tossed salad, choice of dessert, and tea or coffee for C$59 (US$56).

5439 Ferry St., Niagara Falls, Ont. ⓒ **905/354-7519.** Main courses C$12–C$37 (US$11–US$35). AE, DC, MC, V. Mon–Fri 11am–10pm; Sat–Sun 4–10pm.

Carpaccio Restaurant and Wine Bar ⑆ ITALIAN   This place is consistently good. The rich, earthy tones of the decor make the dining space welcoming and comfortable. There's not much to find fault with here. I highly recommend the thin-crust brick-oven pizzas, especially the *Quattro stagioni,* which features tomatoes, mozzarella, artichokes, black olives, mushrooms, and prosciutto. The pizzas are not as good as Wolfgang Puck's, but this place offers a more extensive selection of Italian fare. There are several main-course chicken and veal dishes to choose from, and the tiramisu is the city's finest. If you are a wine aficionado, hang out in the wine bar and let someone else drive—Carpaccio has more than 300 wines on its list, with 3-ounce tasting glasses available for a handful of selections.

6840 Lundy's Lane, Niagara Falls, Ont. ⓒ **905/371-2063.** Reservations recommended Sat. Main courses C$16–$30 (US$15–US$29). AE, DC, MC, V. Summer Mon–Fri 11:30am–11pm, Sat–Sun 4pm–midnight; winter Mon–Fri 11:30am–10pm, Sat–Sun 4–11pm.

The Golden Lotus ⑆⑆ ASIAN   This is the closest I've been to China without crossing continents—there's not a deep-fried chicken ball or chow mien noodle in sight. There is, however, food for the adventurous eater: homemade noodles swimming in spicy beef soup, seafood dumpling with shark's fin soup (who would have guessed that shark tastes like mushrooms?), and my new Chinese favorite, chicken and roasted duck in congee, which looks like oatmeal but is rice boiled in a savory broth. Over 200 menu items include North American–style food for the delicate eater. There's a buffet during lunch hour. With bright violet tablecloths and Easter-colored

Try a Tasting Menu

A tasting menu is an adventure for the senses as well as the imagination. Carefully created by the *chef de cuisine,* a tasting menu will incorporate local seasonal produce in a presentation of a series of small portion courses, often matched with wines. In some restaurants, the menu is set; in others you can choose among dishes. Advance notice is required at some establishments. If you are eager to experience a tasting menu, ask about availability when you call to make your reservation.

circular lamps, it feels very contemporary; located inside a glass dome in part of the Fallsview Casino, one side of the restaurant follows the circular shape overlooking a fountain and the Falls in the background. Word to the wise: drinking Chinese tea will undercut the spicy foods.

6380 Fallsview Blvd., Niagara Falls, Ont. (C) 888/698-3888. AE, MC, V. Reservations recommended for supper. Main dishes C$15–C$150 (US$14–US$143). Mon–Fri 11am–2am; Sat–Sun 10am–2am.

The Keg ⋆ STEAKHOUSE   Dark ambience complemented by a stone fireplace— this chain restaurant will pleasantly surprise you. Steak comes cooked just the way you like it—it's their specialty. Choose from steak combinations with ribs and seafood or try the impeccable steak cuts such as sirloin, New York, and prime rib. But don't hold back. Try other items such as the baked garlic shrimp or the crab, Parmesan, and spinach dip. Baked goat cheese is warm and smooth, while steak and lobster—even though it's Atlantic frozen—is quite good. Yes, it's a steakhouse, but you'll leave impressed because whether you ask for well done or rare, it's done exactly how you want it.

5950 Victoria Ave., Niagara Falls, Ont. (C) 905/353-4022. Main courses C$17–$C43 (US$16–US$41). AE, DC, MC, V. Summer noon–1am daily; winter Sun–Thurs noon–midnight, Fri–Sat noon–1am.

Wolfgang Puck Grand Café Niagara ⋆ CONTEMPORARY   The Niagara outpost of Puck's culinary empire is still one of the most consistently good restaurants in the area. The thin crust pizzas are by far the best in the region; a simple tomato and mozzarella outshines even the real Italian pizzas in the Falls. At the time of publication, the menu changed; thank goodness the pizzas made the cut because fresh and simple ingredients do it every time. Another survivor of the revised menu, the salmon—topped with almonds and served with a celery root puree—is served slightly moist with few added flavors to obstruct the taste. For appetizers, I suggest fried calamari with roasted tomato and lemon. The decor and staff are in tune with the food, smartly turned out, sleek, clean, and chic. Upstairs is the new Sky Lounge featuring local bands. The lounge is open from 10pm until 2am Thursday until Saturday.

6300 Fallsview Blvd., Unit A, Niagara Falls, Ont. (C) 905/354-5000. Reservations recommended on weekends. Main courses C$14–C$38 (US$13–US$36). AE, MC, V. Summer Sun–Thurs noon–11pm, Fri–Sat noon–midnight; winter Sun–Mon noon–9pm, Tues–Thurs noon–10pm, Fri–Sat noon–11pm. Call ahead as winter hours may vary.

MODERATE

Bob Evans Farms Restaurant DINER   Yes, it is a chain, but it's a darn good, reliable one. Their all-day breakfast dishes range from C$4 (US$3.80) to C$10 (US$9.50). Main courses are generous in portion size and are likely to evoke happy but long-forgotten memories of hot gravy, mashed potatoes, and meatloaf in older folk. Service is fast and friendly. If you phone ahead, you can order entire home-style meals to go and whole pies.

6543 Niagara Falls Blvd. (southeast corner of Hwy. 62 and Interstate 90), Niagara Falls, NY. ✆ 716/283-2965. Main courses C$8–C$12 (US$7.60–US$11). Daily 6am–9pm.

Falls Manor Motel and Restaurant ★ DINER
Drive down Lundy's Lane until you see the big chicken. The Falls Manor Motel and Restaurant has been family owned and operated since 1953—that's a lot of roasted chicken. Falls Manor serves comfort food with a capital C, and they really know how to deliver. Kettle-cooked barbecue ribs, pepper steak with mashed potatoes and gravy, toasted club sandwiches, hot corned beef, grilled cheese—this is food from the '50s, and it is fab. A bottomless mug of coffee is just C$1.60 (US$1.50). The Hungry Jack breakfast is amazing value at C$7.50 (US$7.10)—two each of eggs, bacon, and sausage, plus a slice of Canadian peameal bacon, potatoes, and toast. The Belgian waffles are crisp, sweet, and filling. Seniors' portions are available for those over age 60—you get a little less on your plate and a little less on your check. The front section of the restaurant is cozy, but if the tables are full, there are plenty more in the back room and on an outdoor terrace at the rear.

7104 Lundy's Lane, Niagara Falls, Ont. ✆ 888/693-9357 or 905/358-3211. Main courses C$8–C$17 (US$7.60–US$16). AE, DC, MC, V. Summer Sun–Thurs 6am–9pm, Fri–Sat 6am–10pm; winter Sun–Thurs 6am–8pm, Fri–Sat 6am–9pm.

Hard Rock Cafe ⓚⁱᵈˢ AMERICAN
Situated at the main entrance to Casino Niagara, this upbeat, rockin' restaurant is full of music memorabilia and filling, good food. The menu is enormous and features barbecue favorites, such as a hickory barbecue bacon burger, and entrees such as New York strip steak or blackened chicken pasta. Top it all off with a good old-fashioned hot fudge sundae. If you're a night owl, stop in for a hearty fix of eats until 2am. The food is average but it takes a back seat to the wild scenery and high energy.

6705 Fallsview Ave., Niagara Falls, Ont. ✆ 905/356-7625. Main courses C$14–C$30 (US$13–US$29). AE, DC, MC, V. Daily 11am–2am. U.S. location: 33 Prospect St., Niagara Falls, NY. ✆ 716/282-0007. Sun–Thurs 11am–11pm; Fri–Sat 11am–midnight.

The Krieghoff Gallery-Café BISTRO/CAFE
I recommend this place more for its atmosphere than its food (it serves platters, light fare, and dessert brought in from a local pastry shop). Dubbed a cultural cafe, it's a drastic change from the fast-food mentality on nearby Clifton Hill. Inside, crisp white tablecloths and bench-back seating is refined. With an extensive local wine list, you can escape the mayhem of the Falls here. On the menu are bite-sized pastries (cream puffs filled with amaretto custard; chocolate shortbread) and platters for sharing, including smoked salmon with crackers, bread and crème fraîche, or the Niagara charcuterie plate with a selection of salami, prosciutto, and dry cured meat with sweet onions and a baguette. The menu also has a few sandwiches. There's also an artisanal cheese plate to have with your local wine. Named after artist Cornelius Krieghoff (1815–72), the in-house gallery features paintings of early Canadian settlers and North American Natives. Free educational tours through the gallery are offered in six languages.

5470 Victoria Ave., Niagara Falls, Ont. ✆ 905/358-9700. www.krieghoff.ca Platters C$13–C$17 (US$12–US$16). AE, MC, V. Daily 10am–midnight.

Rainforest Café ⓚⁱᵈˢ AMERICAN
This place is the epicenter of chaos on Clifton Hill—leave the overpriced rides and kitsch for an equally overpriced restaurant. But the kids will appreciate the tropical setting: thunderstorms and animatronic gorillas,

Finds Fallsview Dining

Although there is no question that one of the essential ingredients of a satisfying dining experience is a memorable setting, there is an important distinction to be made between the ambience of the surroundings and a view from a window or terrace. People seem to get caught up in a fantasy of eating a meal while romantically gazing at a beautiful panorama. In the case of the Falls, the tons of cascading water grab all the attention, leaving very little for your dinner, so it's best to treat the two as separate activities unless you have already had your fill of the spectacle and can restrain yourself to the occasional glance. One exception to this point of view is the romance angle as tackled by the **Sheraton Fallsview (see Where to Stay).** Book a room or loft suite with a glassed-in alcove overlooking the Falls, and ask the hotel to set you up a table for two in the alcove for one of their special in-room dinners.

There are several restaurants in town, of course, which have chosen to capitalize on one of the world's most famous scenic vistas. For those who like to view and chew, here's a taste of where to do it.

Edgewater's Tap & Grill (*©* **905/356-2217**) is one of the Niagara Parks Commission's restaurants. The second-floor dining room features indoor and outdoor dining. Try the **Terrapin Grille,** the Niagara Falls Marriott Fallsview's restaurant (p. 86). Finally, the two observation towers each have a fallsview dining room. The Konica Minolta Tower Centre (6732 Fallsview Blvd.; *©* **905/356-1501**), which hosts the Ramada Plaza Fallsview Hotel, has the **Pinnacle Restaurant,** which has a great view, but I wouldn't recommend eating here. You'll find this retro structure tucked in between recently constructed high-rise blocks, but don't be fooled—the views from the hotel rooms, observation deck, and restaurant are unobstructed. The distinctive **Skylon Tower** (5200 Robinson St.; *©* **905/356-2651**) has a revolving restaurant that completes each revolution in 1 hour, giving you a view of the Falls for approximately half that time.

Of these offerings, the better food is probably found at Terrapin Grille, but expect to pay dearly for it. Reservations are recommended at all of these locations to avoid disappointment. Check the time of the illuminations before booking if you want them to be an integral part of your dinner.

snakes, and elephants entertain with their antics at regular intervals. Perhaps the theatrics are trying to mask the food? Bruschetta comes out cold, fries are not fresh, and burgers are more bun than beef. The best option is the tropical smoothies, which are nutritious and come in a variety of flavors such as coconut with strawberry. The Niagara Falls Rainforest Café features a live shark exhibit (free) and promises daily encounters with live animals.

Get your wallet ready for more than the check; the Rainforest Café shop has mountains of brightly colored Rainforest-themed merchandise, including an extensive line of private-label Rainforest Café clothing and more toys than Santa's sack.

5785 Falls Ave. Niagara Falls, Ont. ℂ **905/374-2233**. Main courses C$10–C$26 (US$9.50–US$25). AE, DC, MC, V. Sun–Thurs 11am–10pm; Fri–Sat 11am–midnight.

Red Coach Inn Restaurant ✦ AMERICAN   The decor is all deep, dark wood and subdued tapestry, and the view toward the Niagara River rapids is a treat. Dine on the veranda in warm weather. The restaurant is exceedingly traditional and exudes a formal atmosphere; the food is likewise standard (heavy on the meats and potato fare) but is quite good. Menu highlights include Black Angus steak (several cuts), scallops, Australian lobster tail, and swordfish. Choose from dozens of toppers and sides, including fruit salsa, mushroom and Marsala wine sauce, smoked tomato coulis, chive cream cheese, or roasted red pepper. The service is genuine and personable—they'll remember your name at the end of the meal. If you're a wine lover, this isn't your place. There are only two selections, and they're both international.

2 Buffalo Ave., Niagara Falls, NY. ℂ **800/282-1459** or 716/282-1459. www.redcoach.com. Reservations recommended. Main courses C$16–C$30 (US$15–US$29). AE, MC, V. Summer Mon–Thurs 11:30am–10pm, Fri 4–11pm, Sat 11:30am–11pm, Sun noon–10pm; winter Mon–Thurs 11:30am–2:30pm and 5–9pm, Fri–Sat 11:30am–10pm, Sun noon–9pm.

Zappi's ⟨Kids⟩ PIZZA   Families will appreciate this pizzeria, around since 1971, with red-and-white-checked tablecloths, that gets a little rowdy at suppertime—just like at home. There's also more than just pizza: salads run the gamut from Caesar to Greek, and traditional Italian dishes include lasagna, calzone, and pasta primavera. Pizzas come in a huge variety, including the Diavolo for meat lovers topped with bacon, ham, and pepperoni. The White Greek includes feta and olives, while the Four Cheeses will skyrocket your cholesterol with provolone, mozzarella, Romano, and Parmesan cheeses.

6663 Stanley Ave., Niagara Falls, Ont. ℂ **905/357-7100**. www.zappis.com. Main dishes C$9–C$19 (US$8.55–US$18). AE, MC, V. Mon–Sat 11am–midnight; Sun 3–10pm.

3 Niagara-on-the-Lake

The town of Niagara-on-the-Lake, with its pastiche market of theater patrons, boutique shopping brigade, and lovers of historic homes, has an eclectic assortment of restaurants. Whether you are looking for an Old-English-style pub, an elegant Victorian dining room, a bright and breezy outdoor patio, or a small-town diner, you'll find it here. If you're torn between choices of where to eat, ask for opinions from your B&B host or hotel staff—they are knowledgeable about local restaurants and will be eager to share their recommendations with you. Some of the hotels and inns in town will provide a shuttle service to and from restaurants in the evening upon request, saving you hunting for an unfamiliar address and allowing you the indulgence of a glass or two of local wine.

VERY EXPENSIVE

Charles Inn Restaurant ✦✦✦ CONTEMPORARY   Set in a 1832 Georgian-style house, this restaurant is a throwback to gracious service and an elegant romantic dining experience; expect to linger for a few hours. On the seasonal menu that uses only Canadian ingredients, each taste and flavor comes through without impeding the others. A simple starter soup, cream of chanterelle, is balanced with a drop of rosemary oil in the center. The marinated and roasted loin of Cervena venison is served with chestnut puree, ragout of spiced pear, yellow beans, black trumpet mushroom, and

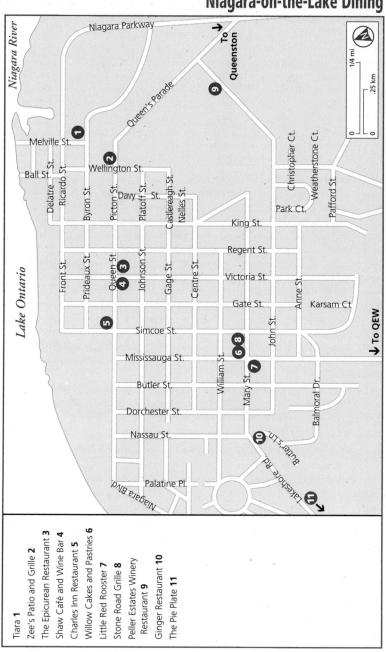

Tiara **1**
Zee's Patio and Grille **2**
The Epicurean Restaurant **3**
Shaw Café and Wine Bar **4**
Charles Inn Restaurant **5**
Willow Cakes and Pastries **6**
Little Red Rooster **7**
Stone Road Grille **8**
Peller Estates Winery
Restaurant **9**
Ginger Restaurant **10**
The Pie Plate **11**

potato rosti. The cheese plate offers farmhouse cheeses such as *Fourme d'Ambert*, a French cheese made from raw cow's milk, or 5-year-aged English white cheddar. It's a menu that is worth the premium price, with a tasteful parallel in the decor: calm persimmon-colored walls, two large fireplaces, white crown molding, and replica chandeliers from the old apothecary. In the summer, enjoy a candlelit dinner on the veranda, overlooking the gardens and golf course, or have an afternoon tea with scones and preserves. In the winter, a glass of port goes down smooth in front of the lounge's fireplace decorated in dark, warm wood.

209 Queen St., Box 642, Niagara-on-the-Lake, Ont. © 866/556-8883 or 905/468-4588. www.charlesinn.ca. Reservations recommended, especially for summer. Main courses C$25–C$35 (US$24–US$33). AE, DC, MC, V. Summer daily 7:30–10am, 11am–4pm, and 5–9pm; winter Wed–Sun 5–9pm.

LIV Restaurant ★★ INTERNATIONAL   Sink back in the exceedingly tall black chairs, accompanied by New Age music. Waiters bring hot towels and an amuse-bouche to get you in the pampered mood. Southeast Asian flavors are sprinkled throughout the menu in ingredients such as mahimahi, jasmine rice, and cilantro. Natural ingredients are emphasized; the breakfast menu is the healthiest and tastiest in the area, featuring organic quinoa with dates, dried cherries, and soy milk; egg-white omelet with feta, tomato, and onion; toasted gluten-free bread and local preserves; and homemade oatmeal buttermilk pancakes with a fruit smoothie or eggs Benedict, but with Virginia ham. Dinners are equally appealing. Each dish is artfully constructed: my entree of grilled scallops balanced on crisp bread was topped with yellow pepper–and-coconut coulis, with sweet crawfish on the side. Rice is tucked into a banana leaf and mixed with cilantro and coconut. And don't think LIV is beyond pizza—but pizza LIV-style, topped with cured duck, caramelized onion, roasted garlic, walnut, and warmed Camembert. The wine list is impressive, featuring 22 choices, mostly local.

253 Taylor Rd. (inside White Oaks Conference Resort & Spa), Niagara-on-the-Lake, Ont. © 800/263-5766 or 905/688-2550. Reservations required in summer, recommended in winter. Main courses C$26–C$45 (US$25–US$43). AE, DC, MC, V. Summer daily 7am–2pm and 5–10pm; winter Sun–Thurs 7am–2pm, Fri–Sat 7am–2pm and 5–10pm.

Tiara Restaurant ★★ CANADIAN   Candelabras on the wall and tapestry draperies make this formal dining room feel like an exquisite dollhouse with a traditionally elegant menu to match. Located in the stately Queen's Landing Inn, Tiara is filled with light that streams in through a bank of windows overlooking the historic Niagara-on-the-Lake harbor. The menu is heavy on the Canadian classics, featuring items such as Maritime lobster, Quebec foie gras, and Alberta steaks. Tiara isn't taking too many culinary risks, but the dishes are prepared well. The butter-poached P.E.I. lobster topped with sweet corn risotto is sumptuously decadent. The butterscotch crème brûlée may seem old fashioned, but the preparation is creamy and smooth. Waitstaff are warm and an in-house wine expert will impart an encyclopedia of wine facts to ensure the perfect meal accompaniment. You'll be well cared for.

155 Byron St., Niagara-on-the-lake, Ont. © 888/669-5566. Reservations recommended. Main courses C$32–C$45 (US$30–US$43). AE, MC, V. Daily 7–10:30am, 11am–2pm, and 5–9pm.

EXPENSIVE

The Epicurean Restaurant INTERNATIONAL/BISTRO/CAFE   This bistro eatery has two faces—a laid-back, come-on-up counter at the front entrance, with sandwiches and daily specials chalked on a blackboard for daytime diners, and a casual fine-dining section at the rear that opens onto a gorgeous shaded patio for evening patrons. Perfect for a hot summer day, the cold tomato soup (gazpacho) tastes like it was made from fruit picked straight off the vines, and the extra-large portion of quiche makes this a good spot to get a healthy meal. The Epicurean offers simple dishes in a less formal atmosphere than some of its neighbors. The dinner menu includes suggestions for wine matched to each course. Dessert is decadent, such as warm chocolate cake with crème anglaise and butterscotch sauce.

84 Queen St., Niagara-on-the-Lake, Ont. © 905/468-0288. Reservations recommended. Main courses C$19–C$25 (US$18–US$24). MC, V. Summer daily 9am–9pm; winter Wed–Sun 9am–9pm.

The Shaw Café & Wine Bar CANADIAN   Although this cafe can be on the expensive side, it offers some good light-lunch options; if you want to people-watch, the patio looks on to the town's busiest street. Lunch choices include inventive salads and wraps, and a large assortment of cakes and pastries is also available. For those tired of wine tasting, a flight of locally brewed beers is offered. Dinner is also served here, with entrees including braised lamb and blackened catfish, but it's not the cafe's strong suit.

92 Queen St., Niagara-on-the-Lake, Ont. © **888/669-5566** or 905/468-4772. Main courses C$15–C$22 (US$14–US$21). Summer daily 10am–11:30pm; winter Mon–Fri 10am–6pm, Sat–Sun 10am–9pm.

Stone Road Grille ✦✦ *(Finds* REGIONAL/ECLECTIC   Located in a generic strip mall with a sign that reads REST (ask a server for the story), this place is anything but generic. Inside, waitresses sporting stylish black dresses and funky shoes attend to guests like it's a large dinner party—there's lots of talking and jazzy music in the background. Regulars come for the imaginative dishes and funky atmosphere, which is hip and young. Two standouts are roasted king mushroom and spinach on a chickpea blini—which has the consistency of polenta—with artichoke chips; and salmon with sea asparagus, chardonnay ribbons, and braised bok choy. Fresh ingredients are mainstays, as are fun combinations—an entree called Three Little Pigs features small portions of various pieces of pork jazzed up with innovative spices and tastes. And for the sweet tooth, chocolate mousse, slightly baked to give it a chewy exterior, is topped with a crispy meringue and drizzled with a hint of caramel passion fruit sauce. Too bad you can't lick the plate. And now you can order to go at the next-door takeout counter that offers pizzas and build-your-own gourmet sandwiches.

In the Garrison Plaza, corner of Mary St. and Mississauga St., Niagara-on-the-Lake, Ont. © **905/468-3474.** Main courses C$18–C$25 (US$17–US$24). MC, V. Summer Tues–Fri 11:30am–2pm and 5–10pm, Sat–Sun 5–10pm; winter Tues–Fri 11:30am–2pm and 5–9pm, Fri–Sat 5–10pm; Sun 5–9pm.

Zee's Patio & Grill ✦✦ ECLECTIC   One of the best dining experiences in the region, Zee's manages to be just casual enough in its atmosphere to entice diners to relax and just sophisticated enough to please patrons with its service and food; it's enough to make Torontonian foodies make the 90-minute trek in traffic. The menu begins with appetizers such as a popcorn shrimp, crusted in coconut and touched up with a sweet soy, lime, and chile dipping sauce. The sauces or spices are not overdone, to let the quality of the food come through; beef comes with a simple red wine and shallot beef jus, and Quebec foie gras is complemented by a pinot noir reduction. The beef burger, on the lunch menu, is a good example of the ordinary made extraordinary, with a slice of aged cheddar on top of ground organic sirloin. Service is crisp and enthusiastic without becoming overly chummy. Servers have a solid knowledge of local wines and are willing to guide you through tasting some, if you so desire. The selection of Canadian artisanal cheeses is superb. Enjoy a series of red wines to accompany your cheese plate and settle in for an indulgent evening.

92 Picton St., Niagara-on-the-Lake, Ont. ☎ 905/468-5715. www.zees.ca. Reservations recommended. AE, MC, V. Main courses C$19–$C29 (US$18–US$28). Summer Tues–Sat 7:30am–midnight, Sun–Mon 7:30am–9pm; winter Mon–Tues 5–9pm, Thurs–Sun noon–9pm.

MODERATE

Ginger Restaurant ☆ *Value* ASIAN   Asian (Thai, Chinese, Malaysian) cuisine is presented in a North American style here. Favorites include a filet of salmon on top of soba noodles dressed with soy sesame glaze, chicken stir fry (bok choy, sweet peppers), teriyaki beef served with vegetables and steamed rice, or house-made Canton-style barbecued pork with Singapore noodles. It's a small one-room restaurant on the main floor of the Orchid Inn. Simple black-and-white photographs of Hong Kong and other cities line the walls. The service is gracious in this family-run restaurant.

390 Mary St., Niagara-on-the-Lake, Ont. ☎ 905/468-3871. AE, MC, V. Main dishes C$16–C$23 (US$15–US$22). Daily noon–2pm and 5–9pm.

Little Red Rooster *Value* DINER   This spacious down-home diner is filled with comfy upholstered banquettes and booths. Popular with locals, it's a perfect spot to drop in and relax. If you're looking for cheap eats, you've found the place. Homey menu items include pork chops with apple sauce, liver and onions, toasted western sandwiches, and french fries with gravy. Home-baked pies, old-fashioned milkshakes, and ice-cream sundaes round out the sweet stuff. All-day breakfast with two eggs and bacon, ham, or sausage is only C$4 (US$3.80), and the kids' menu for 10 and under is just C$5 (US$4.75) for a main course, small drink, and ice cream sundae.

271 Mary St., Niagara-on-the-Lake, Ont. ☎ 905/468-3072. Main courses C$4–C$13 (US$3.80–US$12). MC, V. Daily 7am–8pm.

Olde Angel Inn Pub and Restaurant PUB   One of the oldest operating inns—and one of the only places up past bedtime in the area—they serve traditional hearty pub grub and a good variety of microbrews from beyond and locally. Over 16 draft beers are available, including their own lager and red, Creemore Springs lager, and Toronto's own Steam Whistle Pilsner. Imported beers include Guinness Stout, Kilkenny Cream, and Stella Artois. Every Friday and Saturday, tap your feet to local musicians. Choose from English menu staples such as shepherd's pie, fish and chips, and bangers and mash—this last offering is delicious rather than alarming. Bangers and mash is a dish featuring pork sausage and garlic mashed potatoes with Guinness gravy. The pub also has North American roadhouse munchies such as bruschetta and spring rolls. A great place to relax and unwind.

224 Regent St. (in the Market Square), Niagara-on-the-Lake, Ont. ☎ 905/468-3411. Main courses C$9–C$25 (US$8.55–US$24). AE, MC, V. Daily 11:30am–1am.

Old Winery Restaurant ☆ *Value* ITALIAN   Finally! Niagara-on-the-Lake has a restaurant with a sophisticated menu in a cool atmosphere that won't break the bank.

Cooking Up a Storm in Niagara

Would-be iron chefs and weekend kitchen wizards will be pleased to discover the culinary playgrounds of the Niagara region. Spurred by the growth of the wine industry, cooking classes for weekend kitchen warriors have sprung up across the area.

The Wine Country Cooking School (1339 Lakeshore Rd., Niagara-on-the-Lake, Ont.; ✆ **905/468-8304**) is Canada's first winery cooking school. Based at Strewn Winery, the cooking school highlights the close relationship between food and wine in its teaching philosophy. Its bright, airy classroom, featuring an entire bank of windows along one wall, is a pleasure to work in. Cooking stations designed for pairs of cooks to work together are equipped with utensils and appliances that will make home cooks sigh with delight. A separate dining room is available for students to enjoy their creations, matched with wines from Strewn's cellars. Strewn's winemaker and guest speakers often attend the dinners. Packages are available that include dinner at Terroir la Cachette, Strewn's winery restaurant, and overnight accommodations in nearby Niagara-on-the-Lake.

The Good Earth Cooking School (4556 Lincoln Ave., Beamsville, Ont.; ✆ **905/563-7856**) is run by Nicolette Novak, a walking encyclopedia of the land and its fruits. "When people come down the rickety lane through the orchards, I want them to forget their stress and tune out for 3 hours." And that's just what you'll do—no more than 12 guests sit around the kitchen island and watch local chefs demonstrate how to make easy-to-replicate dishes. Don't be intimidated—Nicolette is a jeans and T-shirt kind of lady, and her open-cupboard kitchen is a gateway to good food no matter what your experience level. But do book ahead: spring classes are posted online in February, and often fill up within a month. In the summer, sit outside and enjoy the demonstration beside the stone hearth. Classes also include hands-on courses, 2-day team-building events, and kitchen parties.

Niagara Culinary Institute (Glendale Campus, 135 Taylor Rd., Niagara-on-the-Lake, Ont.; ✆ **905/735-2211**) is part of the Hospitality and Tourism Division at Niagara College. They offer a variety of courses, ranging from half-day courses in desserts and other delights to full-day classes in soup-making and a three-session bread-making course. More extensive part-time classes leading to certification in various aspects of the hospitality and tourism industry are also available, including sommelier training.

L'Escoffier (17 Lloyd St., St. Catharines, Ont.; ✆ **905/685-7881**) is a retail kitchenware destination with a teaching kitchen on the premises. Local chefs teach evening classes in food preparation, presentation, and how to pair food and wine.

Located in a restored brick warehouse, this place is the area's best bet for a refined meal on a budget. Reminiscent of an Italian trattoria, the atmosphere is lively and the food is simple Italian with some North American favorites thrown in. There's pizza from the wood-burning oven, several homemade pasta dishes, and organic steaks. As a plus, the restaurant offers half-size entrees. Appetizers are also simple but flavorful: prosciutto and peaches come with a dab of olive oil, and spicy mayonnaise adds zap to potato crab cakes. The bar is a great place to linger for a glass of wine and people-watching. The wine list is vast, covering all the major international wine hot spots—Australia, France, California, and Italy—as well as a vast number of local wineries. I also like that they carry many varieties by the glass—eight choices for reds and eight for whites.

2228 Niagara Stone Rd., Niagara-on-the-Lake, Ont. (*C*) **905/468-8900**. www.theoldwineryrestaurant.com. Main courses C$8–C$24 (US$7.60–US$23). Sun–Thurs 11:30am–10pm; Fri–Sat 11:30am–10pm.

INEXPENSIVE

The Pie Plate *←* BISTRO/CAFE   The sign outside has the daily pie posted. That's because they only serve what's in season (except for the winter, of course). As the best pie destination in the region, you can expect fresh strawberry, blueberry, cherry, and my personal favorite, peach, baked in a delicate flaky crust that makes Grandma's seem store bought. Light lunches are also available. The Guinness and sirloin beef pot pie main dish is a nice precursor to a dessert pie, as is the turkey burger, thin-crust pizzas, or fish tacos: two homemade soft corn tortillas stuffed with tilapia, fresh salsa, and cabbage. There are also cinnamon buns and other baked goods. Located in an old Victorian home with creaky hardwood floors, it feels like going to Grandma's. Dine in one of two small rooms with jellybean-colored chairs, if you want to take in the wafts of freshly baked pie emanating from the kitchen. Outside, wrought iron chairs line the gabled patio. Newly licensed: wine and pie couldn't make a better combo.

1516 Niagara Stone Rd., Niagara-on-the-Lake, Ont. (*C*) **905/468-9-PIE**. Most courses under C$12 (US$11). Tue–Sat 8am–9pm; Sun 10am–4pm.

Willow Cakes and Pastries BAKERY   This is a delightful little place to duck in for a quick coffee and a simple homemade croissant or a skillfully prepared dessert. Beware: the thick buttery filling from the butter tart will spill onto your fingers and your napkin—just make sure it ends up in your mouth. The pastries are light yet loaded with sinful calories. Quiche, *pain au chocolat,* banana bread, *petits fours,* and more are on display in the brightly lit glass-fronted cabinets. The array of artisanal breads is extensive. The shop has the feel of a chic French patisserie, but the distinctive charm of small-town Ontario shines through. A few small bistro tables are available, or you can grab takeout to enjoy outdoors.

242 Mary St., Niagara-on-the-Lake, Ont. (*C*) **905/468-2745**. Most items under C$10 (US$9.50). AE, MC, V. Summer daily 8am–7:30pm; winter daily 8am–6pm.

4 Wine Country

The renaissance of the Niagara region's wine industry in the late 1980s and early 1990s attracted considerable interest from a handful of talented chefs. These chefs, with their innovative approach to cuisine and intimate understanding of the connection between the land and the cooking pot, nurtured the fledgling wine-country restaurant industry. Today, it is quite reasonable to expect good food on your travels through Niagara's vineyards. The bar is constantly being raised by the restaurateurs themselves, whose enthusiasm for food and wine continues to drive the industry to new heights. Relax, savor, and enjoy.

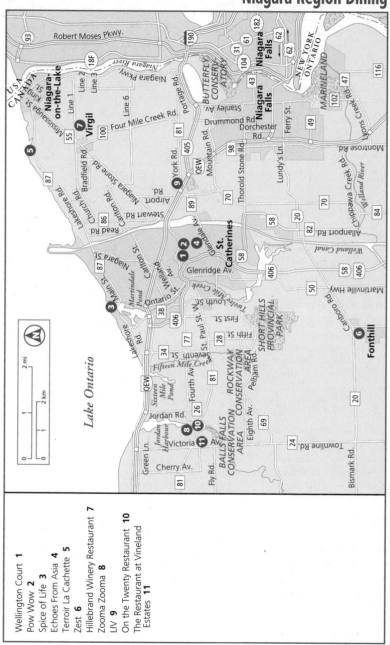

Wellington Court **1**
Pow Wow **2**
Spice of Life **3**
Echoes From Asia **4**
Terroir La Cachette **5**
Zest **6**
Hillebrand Winery Restaurant **7**
Zooma Zooma **8**
LIV **9**
On the Twenty Restaurant **10**
The Restaurant at Vineland Estates **11**

VERY EXPENSIVE

Hillebrand Vineyard Café ★★ REGIONAL   A large chunk of the $3-million winery renovation in 2007 went into overhauling the restaurant and the menu; what was good was made great. The menu changes seasonally, and the accompaniments almost daily. "You'll never see a strawberry on our menu in January," the waiter informs me. I began with seven varieties of local hothouse heirloom tomatoes—purple, green, and red—wedged between slices of goat cheese, washed down with a crisp Sauvignon Blanc Artist Series limited edition. Entrees offered during my visit included homemade ravioli with asparagus and goat cheese and the St. Canut smoked and sugar-glazed pork. I highly recommend the Tour of Niagara, which allows you to sample three entrees. On less busy nights, guests are invited to sample bottles inside the climate-controlled wine room.

1249 Niagara Stone Rd., R.R. 2, Niagara-on-the-Lake, Ont. ② **905/468-7123**. www.hillebrand.com. Reservations recommended. Main courses C$24–C$42 (US$23–US$40). AE, DC, MC, V. Summer daily 11:30am–3pm and 5–9pm; winter daily noon–2:30pm and 5:30–9pm.

On the Twenty Restaurant ★★ REGIONAL   As the pioneer of Niagara's estate winery restaurants, On the Twenty has a lot to live up to, and the restaurant has achieved consistency in the quality of its food over the years. Its approach to cuisine is similar to many of the wineries'; fresh local ingredients permeate the menu. What sets this place apart is its romantic ambience. Situated in quaint Jordan Village, it's a relaxing retreat from the busy wineries; after supper, feel free to make it a weekend destination and stay at the Inn on the Twenty across the street, which is associated with the restaurant. Each dish is carefully crafted and each ingredient thoughtfully chosen. The salads were some of the most imaginative I've had in the region, featuring several tastes and textures: baby greens wrapped in prosciutto were surrounded by slices of Bartlett pear with blue cheese and drizzled with pomegranate vinaigrette; a Gewürztraminer was paired with blue cheese and buttermilk dressing. I cooed over the seared organic salmon with fingerling potatoes, warm goat cheese, roasted almonds, and Meyer lemon butter. The wine list covers all the bases—Cave Spring Cellars' (also associated with the restaurant) own vintages, a good range of other Canadian wines, mostly Niagara, and choices from other wine regions of the world. Warm colors, soft lighting, and a pastoral view from the rear windows over Twenty Mile Creek combine to provide an intimate atmosphere. Service is professional and courteous.

3836 Main St., Jordan Village, Ont. ② **905/562-7313**. Reservations recommended. Main courses C$23–C$40. (US$22–US$38). AE, MC, V. Daily 11:30am–3pm and 5–9pm.

Peller Estates Winery Restaurant ★★ FRENCH/REGIONAL   Diners looking for an adventurous meal should experience Peller's tasting menu in an unpretentious and inviting room. The restaurant looks out over the vineyards, and its oak and cherrywood finishes and warm cream walls are soothing. An ever-changing menu, to keep up with the seasons, is fresh and creative. Their tasting menu is one of the finest in the region—Chef Jason Parsons has a bit of fun with each dish. Standouts served during my visit included the foie gras cheesecake topped with apple; a lobster truffle; and an audacious dish consisting of, from top to bottom, scallop, aged cheddar, braised beef short rib, zucchini confit, and toasted brioche, all sitting on a small bed of leeks braised in cabernet. The dessert continued the playful tone, with a new take on a camping favorite: icewine cherry s'mores. Enjoy the cheese garden on warmer days between 1 and 6pm.

Each server is trained in wine tasting, with mandatory continuing education. Ask for wine to accompany to any dish and feel free to inquire about basic wine knowledge.

290 John St. E., Niagara-on-the-Lake, Ont. © **888/673-5537**. www.peller.com. Reservations recommended. Main courses C$24–C$42 (US$23–US$40). AE, MC, V. Summer daily noon–3pm and 5–9pm; winter daily noon–3pm and 5:30–8:30pm.

The Restaurant at Peninsula Ridge ✴✴ FRENCH/REGIONAL In this restored red brick Victorian home, diners are cloistered into cozy compartments and served an eclectic mix of local food that's an adventure to eat. Spinach Frangelico cream soup with herbed ricotta crostini and a hint of cocoa olive oil sounds good and tastes even better. I'm still talking about the Muscovy duck breast marinated in sauvignon blanc—the wine gives the rich meat a light kick. I strongly recommend the five-course tasting menu, matched with wines (the total amount of wine served is two glasses—not excessive by any means). Ask for a table facing the lake, which, depending on the time of year, will allow you to watch the sun set as you dine. The restaurant also offers the best Sunday brunch in the winery region, leagues above your typical ham and eggs: scrambled eggs with lobster and sautéed mushrooms are flavored with tarragon vermouth and truffle oil. Lunch on the patio is also exemplary.

5600 King St. W., Beamsville, Ont. © **905/563-0900**. Main courses C$25–C$40 (US$24–US$38). AE, DC, MC, V. Wed–Sun 11:30am–3pm and 5–9pm; Sun brunch 11am–3pm.

The Restaurant at Vineland Estates Winery ✴✴ CONTINENTAL The bucolic surroundings—a vineyard amidst rolling hills set in an old Mennonite village—make a visit here an event. The menu, which changes seasonally and makes good use of local ingredients, is traditional fine dining fare but it's accented with subtle changes and fresh additions. Instead of a mushy risotto, Vineland's version is slightly less moist and has many fresh herbs and flavors coming through; likewise, the tomato risotto uses smoked, sun-dried, and fresh garden tomatoes for a new twist. With many appetizers and choices, it's fun to order two or three different plates. Vineland's version of a tasting menu is a five-course creative dinner, which costs C$70 (US$67); add another C$30 (US$29) if you opt for paired wines. A prix-fixe three-course lunch is excellent value at C$35 (US$33)—match with wines for another C$20 (US$19). Unfortunately, the wine selection, besides the winery's own, is sparse: they only carry wine from nearby Tawse Winery and a few international selections.

3620 Moyer Rd., Vineland, Ont. © **888/846-3526**. Reservations required on summer weekends; recommended in winter. Main courses C$24–C$36 (US$23–US$34). AE, DC, MC, V. Summer daily 11:30am–2:30pm and 5–8:30pm; winter Wed–Sun noon–2pm and 5:30–8:30pm.

EXPENSIVE

Terroir La Cachette ✴✴ FRENCH/REGIONAL The region's best French cuisine joins forces with fresh Niagara produce in Quebecois chef Alan Levesque's dishes. Sautéed shrimp pairs with a French fennel noisette butter; duck confit meets a local marinated honey glaze mushroom salad. Typical of a French menu, there is a focus on meat and sauces, albeit less heavy; highlights include an organic salmon with dill and Berkshire ham in a preserved lemon broth, and grilled veal with a smacking strong Gorgonzola. The meals' side dishes, which consist of ordinary greens with a few vegetables, take a back seat to the main fare. Large, panoramic picture windows overlook the Four Mile Creek. The restaurant is located inside Strewn Winery, and although the ownership is independent, there is a strong relationship between the restaurant and the winery; a great selection of Strewn wines is available. Other Niagara wines are on the list: whites include Featherstone, Daniel Lenko, and Stoney Ridge; and reds are available from Creekside, Palatine Hills, and Malivoire.

1339 Lakeshore Rd., Niagara-on-the-Lake, Ont. (located inside Strewn Winery). © **905/468-1222.** Reservations recommended. Main courses C$21–C$32 (US$20–US$30). AE, DC, MC, V. Summer Mon–Fri 11:30am–3:30pm and 5–9pm, Sat 11:30am–10pm, Sun 11:30am–9pm; winter Wed–Sat 11:30am–3:30pm and 5–9pm, Sun 11:30am–3:30pm and 5–8pm.

MODERATE

The Niagara Culinary Institute Dining Room 🖈 *Value* REGIONAL   Meet the
next Jamie Oliver at the dining room of the Glendale Campus of Niagara College. Students enrolled in the Hospitality and Tourism Division assist in menu design, work in the kitchen, and perform front-of-house duties as part of their course requirements. With dishes such as chilled cucumber and dill soup with crème fraîche and pâté de champagne with chardonnay jelly and toast, the restaurant aims high and meets expectations, but for a lot less money. A three-course prix-fixe lunch is just C$24 (US$23), and a four-course prix-fixe dinner at C$39 (US$37) is a great value. Fresh herbs are supplied by the college's horticultural students, and the wine list features wines made by students at the Niagara College Teaching Winery, along with bottles from almost a dozen Niagara wineries. Most bottles are priced under the C$30 (US$29) mark. The restaurant features panoramic windows and a casual atmosphere; student servers are charming and eager to please.

135 Taylor Rd., Niagara-on-the-Lake, Ont. © **905/641-2252.** Reservations recommended. Main courses C$17–C$19 (US$16–US$18). AE, MC, V Lunch Tues–Sun 11:30am–2pm; dinner Wed–Fri 5–9pm, Sat 5–9:30pm.

Zooma Zooma Café 🖈 BISTRO/CAFE   This is a great place for a light, casual
lunch or midafternoon pick-me-up if you are touring wine country or hitting Jordan for its boutique shops, galleries, and antiques retailers. Striking acidic tones of chartreuse, orange, and fuchsia wake up your senses before the first sip of espresso or cappuccino passes your lips. Their grilled vegetable pizza—with sweet peppers, zucchini, and eggplant—is a highlight as is the warm brie with apricot Riesling jelly on flatbread. A regular concert series of music on the patio makes for a great summer night.

3839 Main St., Jordan, Ont. © **905/562-6280.** Main courses C$8–C$14 (US$7.60–US$13). AE, MC, V. Sun–Thurs 10am–6pm; Fri 10am–10pm; Sat 10am–5pm. Live music. Winter daily 10am–5pm.

5 Welland Canal Corridor

The Welland Canal corridor takes in the communities of Old Port Dalhousie on the shores of Lake Ontario, the city of St. Catharines, and the town of Welland, among others. If you're exploring the area, or traversing it on the way to or from Niagara Falls, here are a few places you might like to stop for a bite to eat or a longer, more elaborate meal.

EXPENSIVE

Wellington Court 🖈🖈 REGIONAL   Local artists' paintings tastefully decorate the
intimate rooms and photographs line the hallway of this restaurant, located in an Edwardian town house where the chef's mother was raised. If you're a seasoned restaurant aficionado, you won't be bored here by the predictable. In this modest 40-seat restaurant, the menu has some original pairings that are pleasantly surprising. For instance, grilled tuna is paired with a chile-hot guacamole, while lamb is combined

with lentils and a coconut curry. For appetizers, they make their own pâté on dried cranberry crostini with pear compote. Menu items change with the seasons. Complement your dinner with a fine selection of regional wines. The waitstaff is subtle, floating in and out without interrupting a word of conversation.

11 Wellington St., St. Catharines, Ont. ℂ 905/682-5518. www.wellington-court.com. Reservations recommended. Main courses C$20–C$30 (US$19–US$29). AE, DC, MC, V. Tues–Sat 11:30am–2:30pm and 5–9:30pm.

MODERATE

Echoes from Asia *Value* ASIAN Locals of all kinds—businessmen, teenagers, and girlfriends—gather in this former fast-food restaurant for a taste of Thailand and Vietnam. The decor hasn't changed much since the fast food checked out, but the food is stellar. A huge menu offers curries such as an intensely spicy warrior beef or red chicken curry. A chile logo indicates spiciness: choose from a mild single chile all the way up to a "make your ears steam" four chiles. The selection of soups is also broad: the pho rice noodle soup with brisket and flank steak, accented with basil, bean sprouts, chile peppers, and lime is phenomenal for only C$8 (US$7.60). The power lunch for C$7 (US$6.65) includes generous portions of red curry, vegetables, house egg noodles, and spicy basil chicken. I like to wash it down with a mango shake, followed by deep-fried bananas drizzled with honey. Most dishes can be prepared vegetarian.

153 Hartzel Rd., St. Catharines, Ont. ℂ 905/682-5807. Main dishes C$7–C$18 (US$6.65–US$17). AE, MC, V. Mon 11am–9pm; Tues–Fri 11am–10pm; Sat noon–10pm; Sun 4–9pm.

Pow Wow *Finds* ECLECTIC When local chefs and winery employees want to exhale, they come here. The food isn't fine dining, but it's what chefs like: simple combinations that let the taste come through. The menu is extensive—a good mix of fish, meat, and pastas. The Komodo Dragon is a mix of Japanese udon noodles and sweet and spicy teriyaki sauce, loaded up with crunchy vegetables and tender beef tenderloin strips. The spicy Moroccan grouper is served on an herbed rice cake with passion fruit and pomegranate reduction. Starters include the popular firecracker shrimp, fried with sweet chiles, cashews, saffron, lemon, and lime. Tin painted ceilings, slanted hardwood floors, and partial brick walls make you think you're in a funky neighborhood in New York.

165 St. Paul St., St. Catharines, Ont. ℂ 905/688-3106. www.powwowrestaurant.com. Main courses C$15–C$27 (US$14–US$26). AE, MC, V. Summer Tues–Fri 11:30am–9pm, Fri–Sat 11:30am–10pm; Winter Also open Mondays.

Spice of Life Restaurant and Catering Services VEGETARIAN Wine country aside, much of the Niagara region's cuisine is stuck in the mire of standard North American fare. Spice of Life dares to specialize in vegetarian, vegan, and gluten-free dishes—but note that steak is on the menu for any carnivores who might be lurking in your dining party. The eclectic appetizers include Chef Sue's samosas, a tasty concoction of spiced potatoes and green peas with fresh herbs wrapped in homemade pastry, served with a dollop of Niagara peach and pepper chutney. Hand-wrapped spring rolls come stuffed with Niagara potatoes and carrots, accented by South Asian spices and drizzled with raspberry coulis. Salads, pizza (available in vegetarian, vegan, and gluten-free forms), and pasta round out the menu. Sue also makes a killer mango cheesecake. Niagara wines are available by the glass or bottle.

12 Lock St., Port Dalhousie, St. Catharines, Ont. ℂ 905/937-9027. Reservations recommended. Main courses C$15–C$30 (US$14–US$29). AE, DC, MC, V. Summer daily 11:30am–3:30pm and 5–11pm; winter Thurs–Sat 11:30am–2:30pm and 5–8:30pm.

Tips   Where to Stock Up for a Picnic—And Where to Enjoy It

With its lush green spaces, the Niagara region is ideal for a picnic. Here are a few places that will help you stock the perfect picnic hamper with delicious nosh.

Head down to **DeLuca's Cheesemarket and Deli** on Niagara Stone Road, south of the Old Town (2017 Niagara Stone Rd., in the Forum Galleries Building, Niagara-on-the-Lake, Ont.; ℂ 905/468-2555). Under the direction of one of Niagara's most renowned chefs, Tony DeLuca (former executive chef of Hillebrand Estates Winery), this friendly gourmet emporium has an exceptional selection of cheeses. Picnic baskets, box lunches, and sandwiches are made to order to take out. Artisanal bread, charcuterie, and antipasti are all delicious. The latest cheese store, the **Upper Canadian Cheese**, in Jordan (4159 Jordan Rd., Jordan Station, Ont.; ℂ 905/562-9730), offers two of their own cheeses—Comfort Cream is a semisoft rind cheese with an intense buttery taste, while the Niagara Gold has a washed rind with a mellower butter taste and nutty undertones. There's also a number of condiments such as cabernet jelly and gourmet crackers.

Order a picnic from the **Shaw Festival Greenroom** chefs (Shaw Festival Box Office, 10 Queen's Parade, Niagara-on-the-Lake, Ont.; ℂ 800/511-7429). Book when you order your theater tickets or up to 24 hours in advance of pickup time. If you're in the vicinity of Port Dalhousie, drop in to **Olson Foods and Bakery** (17 Lock St., Unit 112, Port Dalhousie, St. Catharines; ℂ 905/938-8490). Well-known local pastry chef Anna Olson and her staff prepare yummy artisanal breads and divine desserts. Olson also stocks a first-rate variety of European and Canadian cheeses. Gourmet pantry items and upscale kitchen gifts are also available. Most recently she began making sandwiches that can be packed to go.

Just a few minutes south of Niagara-on-the-Lake, on the Niagara Parkway, you'll find **Kurtz Orchards Gourmet Marketplace** (16006 Niagara Pkwy.; ℂ 905/466-2937). This large food market and gourmet gift store has plenty of sampling stations, so you can try before you buy.

As you drive along the Niagara region's rural roads, you will find many **roadside fruit stands** during the harvest season. Some are more substantial than others and stock additional food and beverage items.

If you are touring the wineries, keep your eyes open when you browse the **winery boutiques.** Many of them keep on hand a few loaves of local artisanal bread, packets of gourmet crackers, and a limited selection of cheeses for purchase.

As for where to enjoy your picnic—turn to "Parks & Gardens" or "Hiking & Biking" in chapter 7, "What to See & Do in the Niagara Region," and choose an idyllic swath of green on which to spread your picnic blanket, recline gracefully, and while the afternoon away.

INEXPENSIVE

Green Bean Café and Oxygen Bar ⚹ VEGETARIAN   The Green Bean offers eco-friendly food that tastes good and doesn't harm the earth. This laid-back, incense-burning restaurant is all about feeling good; organic tomatoes used for the bruschetta are hand cut and not processed to ensure full flavor. Does it make a difference? Yes. There's veggie, vegan, and meat dishes, including a meaty-tasting vegan chili and a satisfying pasta sacchettini (cambozola cheese–filled pasta) with tomato and mushroom sauce. Choose from a huge list of coffees—including green bean cool steam—or a plethora of herbal teas. At the bar, I inhaled oxygen for half an hour via a nose tube. It was hard to tell if I got energetic from the coffee or the extra O2, but it cleared out the sinuses!

224 St. Paul St., St. Catharines, Ont. © **905/688-0800.** Main courses C$7–C$14 (US$6.65–US$13). AE, MC, V. Mon–Thurs 11am–8pm; Fri–Sat 11am–9pm.

6 Fonthill

The village of Fonthill is home to of the odd restaurant whose reputation extends to the far reaches of the Niagara region.

VERY EXPENSIVE

Zest ⚹ CANADIAN   Many Torontonians make the 2-hour trek to this restaurant, and I can see why. With the curtains drawn to hide the derelict buildings across the street, inside is a veritable cooking show set in a sophisticated restaurant full of ambience: distinctive teal blue walls, blonde wood floors, and comfy leatherette-upholstered chairs that you'll have to turn to face the open kitchen where chefs skillfully concoct your meal. Using his Southeast Asian experiences, co-owner Chef Michael Pasto prepares modern Canadian cuisine and has a particular flair for fish entrees. Mains include baked striped bass with a simple grilled corn salsa and potato. Meat dishes are well done (grilled beef strip loin with foie gras butter, and a potato on the side stuffed with bacon and triple cheese), but the fish is the reason to come. The wine list is informative and a pleasure to read, with columns for the wine, vintage, origin, tasting notes, and price by the bottle and the glass. A glance from left to right sums up each wine in a flash. A good representation of Niagara grape varietals forms the backbone of the list—with *vitis vinifera* leading the way—although a French hybrid or two have bravely worked their way into the list.

1469 Pelham St., Fonthill, Ont. © **905/892-6474.** www.zestfonthill.com. Reservations recommended. Main courses C$24–C$32 (US$23–US$30). MC, V. Tues–Fri 11:30am–3pm and 5:30–9pm; Sat 5:30–9pm.

7

What to See & Do in the Niagara Region

The Niagara region has much to offer visitors. Naturally, first timers flock to the Falls, and quite rightly. Once you have had your fill of the Falls, the area is full of historical venues, child-friendly rides, lush parks, and some of Canada's best vineyards. Many attractions are concentrated in the twin cities of Niagara Falls, Ontario, and Niagara Falls, New York, on either side of the border. The pretty town of Niagara-on-the-Lake, with its stately tree-lined streets and superbly restored and preserved historical homes, excellent live theater, and unique shopping, should be high on your list of priorities—it is one of my favorite places to visit in Canada. And no trip to Niagara is complete without a visit to the wine country to taste the award-winning VQA Ontario wines and sample the exceptional winery restaurant cuisine featuring local produce (an entire chapter is devoted to the wine region; see chapter 8, "The Wine-Country Experience").

As you delve into this chapter, you will get a good grasp of the top attractions in Niagara—a mosaic of museums, historical landmarks, galleries in which to while away an hour or two, and a smattering of the gaudy and the garish. I've also highlighted some activities that are ideal for families traveling with children. There are also many beautiful parks and gardens, which flourish in the unique microclimate of the Niagara Peninsula. Outdoor enthusiasts will find plenty of opportunities to enjoy hiking, cycling, and pastimes such as golf. Finally, I have listed some organized tours, and even provided a few self-guided ones.

Note that some advance planning may be required, since a few attractions eat up a fair bit of time, while others involve some driving. Call ahead to confirm admission hours, too—admission hours are very seasonal in the area, and can change up to 10 times during the course of the year.

1 The Top Attractions

ON THE CANADIAN SIDE

HORSESHOE FALLS ★★★

Two key factors draw visitors in the millions to the Horseshoe Falls, or the Canadian Falls as they are also known. One is the sheer magnitude of the volume of water that flows along the Upper Niagara River and cascades over the U-shaped rock shelf into the Niagara Gorge below; the other is the fact that you can get so thrillingly close to this remarkable natural display. There are numerous vantage points, each of which will give you a different experience, different emotions, and different souvenir snapshots to take home. To fully absorb the enormousness of this natural wonder, take in as

Niagara Falls Attractions

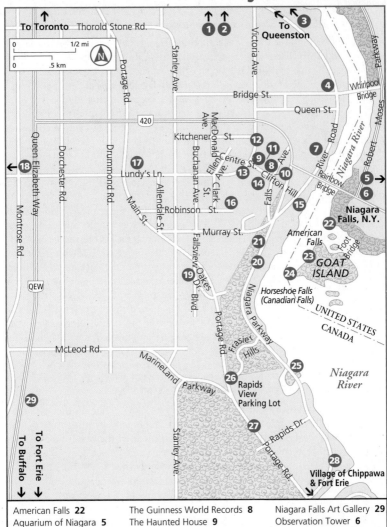

many of these as you can. Top it off with the spectacle of the illuminations. If you are only in the area for a day trip, don't go home until you've seen the Falls by night.

Maid of the Mist ✶✶✶ *Kids*   A trip on the *Maid of the Mist* is a must for first-time visitors to the Falls. These small tour boats have been thrilling visitors to the Falls since 1846, when the first coal-fired steamboat equipped with two tall smoke stacks chugged daringly close to the thundering wall of water. Today, the original family still runs it.

Before climbing aboard, you will be handed a large blue rain poncho (it's voluminous enough to cover even a backpack should you be sporting one). You can drop the poncho into the recycling bin on the way out after your trip, but you might be better off keeping it as a souvenir. You might even want to keep it on, as a protector against the mist that often drifts (or blows!) in from the Horseshoe Falls at Table Rock House, a few hundred yards upstream from the *Maid of the Mist* boat launch. Another piece of advice: resist the urge to bring out the electronics to record the event—you're better off with a waterproof disposable camera.

I must pass on a tip: Get a spot on the upper deck of the starboard side of the boat (landlubbers, that's the right-hand side). Most people crowd to the other side, eager to catch a close-up glimpse of the American Falls as soon as the boat leaves the dock. However, the Canadian *Maid* cautiously approaches the Horseshoe Falls with her starboard side closest to the waterfall, and then veers left to return to the dock, thereby rewarding starboard passengers with a close-up of the Horseshoe Falls, followed by a panoramic sweep past the American Falls as it returns to the dock. Stay below decks and you will miss the action. The trip is short, about half an hour, so get your cameras snapping right away. If you are visiting during July or August, schedule your boat ride for early- to mid-morning (the first sailing is at 9am during peak season), before the lines begin to form.

5920 River Rd., Niagara Falls, Ont. (near the foot of Clifton Hill). ✆ **905/358-0311.** www.maidofthemist.com. Admission C$14 (US$13) adults, C$8.60 (US$8.20) children 6–12, free for children 5 and under. Daily Apr–late Oct (opening date depends on ice conditions in the river). Sailing times vary by season: first trip of the day is at 9am in peak season, 9:45am in spring and fall; last boat sails between 4:45 and 7:45pm.

Konica Minolta Tower Centre *Finds*

Everyone wants a ride on the "yellow bug" that creeps up the outside of the Skylon Tower. But quietly standing to attention on Fallsview Boulevard, sandwiched in and overshadowed by the recent high-rise development on this stretch of the hotel district, the Konica Minolta Tower is an excellent place to view the Falls. Enter the minimalist, modestly sized lobby and purchase tickets to ride the elevator (alas, this one is enclosed by a mundane shaft) 160m (525 ft.) to the 25th floor, where you can view the Falls through a wall of outwardly angled glass, specially coated with a nonglare finish for better-quality photos. The room is carpeted, so there are no howling winds to contend with as you are likely to experience on the outdoor deck of the Skylon Tower, and if you go early in the morning you may have the entire viewing deck to yourself, since many of the hotel guests are still in the breakfast room and few other tourists are likely to be in the area at that time of day. Really early risers can watch the sunrise. Views of the illuminated Falls are also spectacular from this viewpoint. Hotel guests have free access to the tower.

6732 Fallsview Blvd., Niagara Falls, Ont. ✆ **866/325-5784** or 905/356-1501. www.niagaratower.com. Admission C$4.50 (US$4.30) adults, C$2.50 (US$2.40) children 6–12, free for children 6 and under. Tickets can be purchased in advance or at front reception desk of hotel. Daily 7am–11pm.

Journey Behind the Falls

This self-guided tour takes you through tunnels bored into the rock behind the Canadian Falls, so if you suffer from claustrophobia, give this

Fun Fact **Niagara Trivia—Facts and Figures**

- The difference in elevation between Lake Erie and Lake Ontario is about 99m (325 ft.), with half of that difference occurring at the Falls themselves.
- The Niagara River, which connects Lake Erie and Lake Ontario, is about 58km (36 miles) long.
- At Grand Island, the Niagara River divides into two channels—the Chippawa (Canadian) channel on the west, which carries approximately 60% of the total river flow, and the Tonawanda (American) channel on the east.
- The deepest section of the Niagara River is immediately below the Falls. The depth of the river here is equal to the height of the Falls—52m (170 ft.).
- There are some 500 other waterfalls in the world that have a greater elevation than Niagara Falls. However, many of them have relatively little water flow. The grandeur of Niagara Falls is attributed to a combination of its height, water volume, and picturesque setting.

a miss—some people seem to find the idea of walking in a tunnel underneath the Falls quite unnerving. There are a couple of short offshoots from the main tunnel where you can peer through openings cut into the rock literally behind the Horseshoe Falls. There is not much to see except a wall of water, but it is nonetheless exhilarating to be on the "other side" of the mighty cascade.

The absolutely best part of the tour, though, is to venture outside onto the lower balcony at the northern edge of the base of the Falls. You will get wetter than wet (much more so than on the *Maid of the Mist*), but it is more than worth the inconvenience. Recyclable rain ponchos are provided (yellow, instead of the blue ones for the boat ride), but you're still likely to get drenched in spray or a rogue cascade of water depending on the wind direction and strength. Of all the ways and means you can access the Horseshoe Falls, this is the place where you will feel the power of the Falls at its mightiest. The roar of the water is thrilling beyond compare.

The Journey Behind the Falls is one of the attractions included in the Great Gorge Adventure Pass. During peak season, the attraction operates on a timed entry system with a maximum number of visitors allowed through at any one time. You can visit the ticket booth early in the day and prebook your entry time, saving you the inconvenience and frustration of standing in line.

6650 Niagara River Pkwy., Niagara Falls, Ont. (inside the Table Rock Complex). (C) **877/642-7275.** www.niagara parks.com/nfgg/behindthefalls.php. Admission C$12 (US$11) adults, C$7.20 (US$6.85) children 6–12, free for children 5 and under. Sun–Fri 9am–7:30pm; Sat 9am–8:30pm. Last ticket sold 30 min. before closing.

Skylon Tower *Overrated*   One of the most distinctive structures on the skyline on the Canadian side of Niagara Falls is the 236m-high (775-ft.) Skylon Tower. Built in 1965, it dominated the landscape on the hill above the Falls for more than 30 years. In recent years, increasingly taller hotels have been sprouting up in the district, but the Skylon still attracts attention—it's almost a landmark. The brightly painted elevators

Tips Best-Value Canadian Niagara Falls Experiences

Take advantage of the special package put together by the Niagara Parks Commission, experience the top attractions, save a bundle, and avoid lines all at the same time. The **Niagara Falls Great Gorge Adventure Pass**, available between May and October, grants you entry to the *Maid of the Mist,* **Journey Behind the Falls, White Water Walk,** and the **Butterfly Conservatory.** Included with the pass is all-day transportation on the **People Mover** bus and **Incline Railway** that connect the Fallsview area on top of the hill with the complex in front of the Horseshoe Falls at the bottom. The price of just C$41 (US$39) adults and C$26 (US$25) children 6 to 12 (free for kids 5 and under) is a fantastic bargain.

Between November and April, you can buy a **Winter Magic Pass,** which grants you entry to **Journey Behind the Falls, Niagara Parks Butterfly Conservatory, IMAX Theatre** *Legends and Daredevils* movie, and the **Bird Kingdom** at the Niagara Falls Aviary. The Winter Magic Pass costs C$27 (US$26) adults and C$16 (US$15) children 6 to 12 (free for kids 5 and under). Coupons are included with the Winter Magic Pass that give you discounts on admission to the Skylon Tower and Niagara Helicopter Tours rides. In 2005, audio tours at the Journey Behind the Falls and the Butterfly Conservatory were added to the package at no extra cost. Another advantage is the ability to prebook your entry time to the attractions at peak tourist periods. Rather than wasting time standing in line on busy days, use the People Mover to drop in to the attractions and book your visit for later in the day.

that crawl up the outside of the tower are affectionately known as "yellow bugs." The view is panoramic, covering both the US and the Canadian falls, but the journey to get there—stuffed in an elevator with tourists—isn't fun; you can get similar views from a restaurant nearby. In addition to the indoor viewing area, there is an outdoor deck protected by a wire mesh screen. Be prepared for windy conditions outside, even if there is only a slight breeze at ground level. At the base of the tower there is a maze of shops selling trinkets and a cavernous arcade zone, which can be overflowing with tourists. Ticket prices are rather high—if you are planning to ascend the tower, I recommend dropping in to **Niagara Falls Tourism** (5515 Stanley Ave.; ✆ **905/356-5567**) to find out whether discount coupons are available (often there are booklets that have coupons for many of the attractions not included in the Great Gorge Adventure Pass), or ask at your hotel.

5200 Robinson St., Niagara Falls, Ont. ✆ 905/356-2651. www.skylon.com. Admission C$11 (US$10) adults, C$6 (US$5.70) children 12 and under. Summer daily 8am–midnight; winter daily 11am–9pm.

BEYOND THE FALLS

Butterfly Conservatory A visit to the Butterfly Conservatory can be combined with a leisurely stroll around the Niagara Parks Botanical Gardens, as the building is located right on the grounds. The Conservatory is a bright and airy rainforestlike environment that is carefully climate-controlled. A multilevel pathway (stroller and wheelchair accessible) winds its way through the lush foliage. Two thousand tropical butterflies, representing 50 different species, live freely in the Conservatory.

This is an absolutely delightful place to spend an hour or so. The trick is to walk slowly and pause often, since the most rewarding discoveries are usually found through quiet observation. Often the butterflies will land on visitors, but it is important not to touch them because they are extremely delicate and easily injured. It can be quite comical to see butterflies hitching a ride on the hat or shoulder of the person in front of you, who may be wandering around completely unaware of their natural adornment. There is a butterfly "nursery" with an observation window looking onto several stages of metamorphosis, and the window is opened several times daily to allow newly emerged butterflies to enter their new home in the Conservatory.

There is an abundance of natural light, and since the butterflies spend a considerable amount of time resting (you might almost believe they are posing for photos), it is a great place to bring your camera. The Conservatory doubles as the display greenhouse for the Niagara Parks Botanical Gardens. With more than 100 exotic plants in its tropical plant collection, the Conservatory also provides a rare opportunity to come into close contact with plants rarely seen in the Northern Hemisphere, and another reason for photographers to indulge in their passion.

The Conservatory is serviced by the People Mover bus and is one of the attractions included in the Great Gorge Adventure Pass. Due to space restrictions, the number of visitors allowed into the Conservatory at any one time is limited, and during peak season you may have to wait before entering.

2405 Niagara River Pkwy., Niagara Falls, Ont. (C) **877/642-7275**. www.niagaraparks.com/nature/butterfly.php. Admission C$11 (US$10) adults, C$6.50 (US$6.20) children 6–12, free for children 5 and under. Daily 9am–5pm. Closed Dec. 25. Last ticket sold 30 min. before closing.

Whirlpool Aero Car   Often called the Spanish Aero Car, because it was designed by Spanish engineer Leonardo Torres Quevedo and built in Bilboa, Spain, the Whirlpool Aero Car takes visitors on a hair-raising trip 75m (246 ft.) above the Niagara Gorge. Suspended between two points on the Canadian shore of the Niagara River, six sturdy cables support the uniquely crafted carriage, which holds 40 standing passengers. The car crawls along the cables on a 1km (half-mile) round-trip between Colt's Point and Thompson's Point, allowing tourists a bird's eye view of the natural phenomenon of the Niagara Whirlpool. Although the car remains in its original form from when it began operating in 1916, the wheels, electric circuits, and track cable suspension system were modernized in the 1980s. The trip is only 10 minutes long, and you can see the whirlpool from the land, so if it's a busy day and the line is long, consider giving this attraction a miss. The winding stairwell that leads to the entrance to the aero car can be stifling on a hot day, despite the roof covering that

---

(*Tips* **Catch the Rainbow**

If you want to gaze upon the rainbow in the mist of the Horseshoe Falls, you need to view the Falls from the Canadian shore during the afternoon. Sunlight slants through the water droplets dancing in the air in mid- to late afternoon, depending on the time of year, creating the mystical band of color that is such a profound symbol of the wonder of nature.

> **Fun Fact** **The Old Scow**
>
> If you look upriver from the Horseshoe Falls and scan the surface of the turbulent water, you will see an old scow that became stuck on the shoals way back in 1918. The scow, a flat-bottomed boat used for transporting cargo to and from ships, broke loose from its tugboat. Two men were stranded onboard as the scow made its way with increasing speed toward the Horseshoe Falls. In a desperate attempt to save themselves, the men opened the bottom doors of the scow and flooded it. Fortunately, the scow became wedged against a rocky ledge, but due to the complicated nature of the rescue operation it was 19 hours later when the men finally were brought on shore.

gives some protection from the sun. And those who are afraid of heights should definitely stay on terra firma.

3850 Niagara River Pkwy., Niagara Falls, Ont. ℂ **877/642-7275.** www.niagaraparks.com/nfgg/aerocar.php. Admission C$11 (US$10) adults, C$6.50 (US$6.20) children 6–12, free for children 5 and under. Mon–Fri 9am–5pm; Sat–Sun 9am–6pm. Operation depends on wind and weather conditions. Last ticket sold 30 min. before closing.

White Water Walk ⚑ As you make your way down the boardwalk at the base of the Niagara Gorge (an elevator takes you down to the river level), you can hear the thunder of water all around you. Stand next to the Class V and VI Niagara River rapids, one of the world's wildest stretches of white water. The ever-changing display of waves, swell, foam, and spray is mesmerizing. Fidgety folks will do the walk amiably enough, but then ask what's next on the agenda. Others are drawn to the power of the water in motion and are quite content to stand and watch in fixed fascination, completely unaware of the passage of time.

Visit any time between April and November to see the rapids, but if you are in Niagara in the autumn, you absolutely must take this walk, as the wooden walkway is constructed under a canopy of deciduous trees. Warm autumn sunlight; orange, red, and gold leaves; the raging torrents of the rapids: it's a spectacular sight. And photographers take note—there are great nature shots here.

4330 Niagara Pkwy., Niagara Falls, Ont. ℂ **877/642-7275.** www.niagaraparks.com/nfgg/whitewater.php. Admission C$8.50 (US$8.10) adults, C$5 (US$4.75) children 6–12, free for children 5 and under. Apr–late Nov Mon–Fri 9am–5pm, Sat–Sun 9am–6pm. Last ticket sold 30 min. before closing.

ON THE AMERICAN SIDE
AMERICAN FALLS ⚑

The crest line of the American Falls, also sometimes referred to as the Rainbow Falls, is approximately 290m (950 ft.) wide; the depth of the water flowing over the crest line is only about half a meter (about 2 ft.). Just south of the main waterfall, there is a smaller waterfall, which is a mere 17m (56 ft.) wide at the crest line. This pretty waterfall resembles a bride's veil, hence the name Bridal Veil Falls, although it is also known as Luna Falls and Iris Falls. Bridal Veil Falls is separated from the American Falls by a thin strip of land called Luna Island. A massive amount of broken rock covers the base of the American and Bridal Veil Falls, contributing to their dramatic appearance. As the sun rises in the east, rainbows can often be seen as the light shines through the mist of the Falls. In order to feel the magnitude of the power of the churning water, you need to get up close and personal. Take the *Maid of the Mist* boat tour, which will take you past the American Falls and daringly close to the base of the Horseshoe Falls, walk along the pathway to the "Crow's Nest" at the base of the Observation Tower, or take the *Cave of the Winds* guided walking tour, which leads you along boardwalks down into the gorge—only 6m (20 ft.) away from the falling water at its closest point. Note, however, that the best views of the Falls are from the Canadian shore.

Cave of the Winds   This well-established attraction features a guided tour along wooden walkways at the base of the Bridal Veil Falls, and has recently been updated. Accessed from Goat Island, an elevator takes you 53m (175 ft.) down into the Niagara Gorge. Sporting a yellow recyclable waterproof poncho and Velcro-closure souvenir nonslip sandals, follow your tour guide along the boardwalks to the "Hurricane Deck," where you stand just 6m (20 ft.) from the thundering waters of Bridal Veil Falls. You are likely to get doused with a generous spray of water, so consider yourself warned. A second deck has been constructed 45m (150 ft.) away from the base of the Falls, designed especially for physically challenged visitors and adults carrying small children. For a really wild experience, descend after nightfall to see the illuminations surrounded by multicolored cascading torrents of water.

Goat Island, Niagara Falls State Park, Niagara Falls, NY. ✆ **716/278-1730**. www.niagarafallsstatepark.com. Admission C$9.50 (US$10) adults, C$7.35 (US$7) children 6–12 (must be at least 1.1m/42 in. tall), free for children 5 and under; those under 1.1m/42 in. tall must be accompanied by an adult and admission is restricted to certain areas of the walkway. Seasonal operation daily 9am–11pm.

Maid of the Mist ⚝   This is a must-do for visitors to the Falls—it might seem touristy, but it's well worth the trip. The *Maid of the Mist* operates on both sides of the Niagara Gorge, but each boat essentially provides the same experience, passing close to the base of the American Falls and into the horseshoe of the Canadian Falls. Boats on the American side dock at the base of the Observation Tower near Prospect Point in the Niagara Falls State Park. Recyclable blue rain ponchos are issued, which you can keep as a souvenir if you wish. Tickets include entry to the Observation Tower because access to the boat dock is via the tower elevators. Admission is included with the purchase of a *Passport to the Falls*. Tour lasts 30 minutes.

Inside Niagara Falls State Park, at the base of the Observation Tower, Niagara Falls, NY. ✆ **716/284-8897**. Admission C$14 (US$12.50) adults, C$8.60 (US$7.30) children 6–12, free for children 5 and under. Apr–Oct daily 10am–8pm (depending on weather conditions).

Observation Tower   Included with the Niagara Falls State Park Passport to the Falls, this 85m-high (280-ft.) tower has an outside observation deck that extends past the Niagara Gorge cliff face to allow visitors a bird's-eye view of the American Falls.

Fun Fact **The Original Cave of the Winds**

The original Cave of the Winds was a true cavern, located behind the Bridal Veil Falls. It measured approximately 40m (130 ft.) high, 30m (100 ft.) wide, and 9m (30 ft.) deep. Prior to the mid-1900s, tourists could enter the cave via a pathway. In 1954, a major rockfall occurred at Prospect Point, followed by several smaller rockfalls at Terrapin Point. Subsequently, an overhanging ledge of dolostone at the entrance to the cave was deemed to be in danger of collapse, and in 1955 the cave was demolished by a controlled dynamite blast.

Tips **Best Value Niagara Falls American Experience**

Take advantage of the special package put together by the Niagara Falls State Park to experience the top attractions and save a bundle at the same time. The **Niagara Falls State Park Passport to the Falls** grants you entry to the *Maid of the Mist*, **Observation Tower, Festival Theater, Aquarium of Niagara,** and the **Niagara Gorge Discovery Center.** Included with the pass is all-day transportation on the **Niagara Scenic Trolley,** which takes you on a 4.8km (3-mile) guided tour of Niagara Falls State Park, with frequent stops to allow visitors to hop on and off at the major attractions and scenic vistas throughout the park. The price of just C\$29 (US\$28) adults and C\$22 (US\$21) children 6 to 12 (free for kids 5 and under) is a fantastic bargain. The Passport to the Falls also includes discounted admission to Artpark, Old Fort Niagara, and the Historical Wax Museum. Discounts at snack centers and gift shops are also included. You can purchase the Passport at the Niagara Falls State Park Visitor Center, the Niagara Gorge Discovery Center, and at American Automobile Association (AAA) offices in Buffalo, Rochester, and Syracuse, New York.

Take the elevator to the top for the best views. The elevator also descends to the base of the gorge to provide tourists with access to the *Maid of the Mist* boat ride. At the base of the observation tower are a groomed pathway and stairs leading to the "Crow's Nest," an observation deck close to the huge boulders at the base of the American Falls—a unique perspective that is worth the journey.

Inside Niagara Falls State Park, just north of the American Falls. ℭ **716/278-1762.** Admission C\$1.20 (US\$1.15) adults and children 6 and over, free for children 5 and under. Late Mar–Dec daily 9am–8pm.

BEYOND THE FALLS

Aquarium of Niagara   Experience marine life up close at the Aquarium of Niagara, just a short walk over the bridge from the Niagara Gorge Discovery Centre, one of the stops on the Niagara Scenic Trolley route. Several times daily, you can watch the penguin feeding, sea lion shows, and harbor seal sessions. Tidal pool and shark feedings are available for observation on alternate days. Kids can buy a bucket of fish for C\$5(US\$4.75) and feed the seals. More than 40 exhibits contain a total of 1,500 aquatic animals from around the world. It's a great place to take the kids for a few hours. Not as extensive as Marineland, and there are no rides, but it's also less chaotic.

701 Whirlpool St., Niagara Falls, NY. ℭ **800/500-4609** or 716/285-3575. www.aquariumofniagara.org. Admission C\$9.45 (US\$9) adults, C\$7.35(US\$7) seniors, C\$6.30 (US\$6) children 4–12, free for children 3 and under. Late May–early Sept daily 9am–7pm; early Sept–late May daily 9am–5pm.

2 Museums & Historical Landmarks

From the War of 1812 to the American Revolution to the Underground Railroad for slaves, today's Niagara museums remain to tell the rich stories. The area boasts some of the best-reconstructed forts and historical sites in the country, as well as walking tours throughout the sites. **Chippawa Battlefield Park** marks the site of the bloodiest and longest battle during the War of 1812; visitors can walk a path reading storyboards placed around a memorial cairn. Walkers can access the trail to **Fort Mississauga,** a post-1812 defense site made from post-war rubble, on the corner of Simcoe and Front streets. Spanning from Niagara-on-the-Lake across to the Welland Canal, where thousands of ships come through every year, Niagara's museums present a broad range of artifacts and history that come to life with educational interpreters and costumed guides at some of the larger venues. Follow the descriptions below, as some sites are more worthy of your time than others.

NIAGARA FALLS, ONTARIO AND NEW YORK

Lundy's Lane Historical Museum   In this museum in a not-so-nice neighborhood, you'll find a collection of folklore and history pertaining to Niagara Falls. The limestone building dating back to 1874 includes everything from historical prints of the Falls to War of 1812 artifacts. Museum artifacts, such as the uniforms of soldiers and firefighters, are housed in glass cases, making for a lackluster presentation. A half-hour is enough to get a taste of this museum offering.

Outside the entrance, the Queen Victoria Memorial Fountain commemorates Victoria's reign of 64 years. Built in 1901 from 82 pieces of limestone, each stone represents a year of the queen's life.

5810 Ferry St., Niagara Falls, Ont. ✆ 905/358-5082. Fax 905/358-0920. www.lundyslanemuseum.com. Admission C$3 (US$2.85) adults, C$2.50 (US$2.40) students and seniors, C$2 (US$1.90) children 6–12, free for children under 6. Jan–May daily noon–4pm; May–Oct 31 daily 10am–5pm; Nov–Dec Tues–Sun noon–4pm.

Old Fort Niagara ✈ (Kids   Built as an outpost, it gradually became a fortress. Constructed in 1726 on the bluffs above Lake Ontario by the French, and strategically located at the mouth of the Niagara River, this fort held an important position that helped to shape Canada. The French maintained the first post here, but in 1759, during the French and Indian War, the British took over and retained control throughout the American Revolution. During the two world wars, Fort Niagara served as a barracks and training station. Restoration was completed in the mid-1930s.

Educational tours are available. Inside, costumed interpreters provide tours three to four times a day in the summer, which typically last an hour (tours are included in admission price). There are also fabulous fundraisers and events throughout the year; my favorite was the winter tour called Castle by Candlelight. It feels like you step back in time—bring your flashlight! Group tours are also available with advance notice only (between 1 and 2 hours). In the summer don't miss the musket firing demonstration. The gift shop is loaded with interesting historical literature.

Fort Niagara Historic Site, Youngstown, NY. ✆ 716/745-7611. www.oldfortniagara.org. Admission C$11 (US$10) adults, C$6.30 (US$6) children 6–12, free for children under 6. Daily 9am year-round; closing hours vary with seasons.

NIAGARA-ON-THE-LAKE AND QUEENSTON

For many history buffs, a collection of outdoor sites on well-groomed landscapes make for great picnic spots. Originally a group of 19 buildings acting as the British Indian Department site, **Butler's Barracks** was named after Colonel John Butler, the deputy superintendent. A handful of buildings are left—the Korean War building, the gun shed, and the officers' quarters, to name a few. Take a tour through the outside area, guided by interpretive plaques. This is worth a visit to get a history lesson. Another historical attraction with interpretive plaques is **Fort Mississauga.** Built to help defend the British against subsequent attacks from the Americans after the War of 1812, the fort is now home to the Niagara-on-the-Lake Golf Club. **Navy Hall** (26 Queen St., Niagara-on-the-Lake; ✆ **905/468-4257**) isn't open to the public but is of historical interest and is in a scenic spot. Originally a group of barracks buildings built in 1765, today only one building remains.

One building that is open to the public and is worth a quick visit is **Niagara Apothecary** (5 Queen St.; ℭ **905/468-3845**). It's one of the oldest continually operating pharmacies in Canada, having dispensed medicines from 1820 to 1964. Many of the original containers, prescription books, and account books have been recovered and are on display. Stop in for a peek while shopping on Queen Street.

Fort George ⭐ *Kids*　If you have time for only one fort on your trip, this is the one to see. As a headquarters for the British army during the War of 1812, this fort played a pivotal role in keeping the Niagara region in Canadian hands. Built between 1796 and 1799, this fort was constructed to complement the existing Navy Hall buildings in safeguarding the region. Commander-in-Chief Major-General Sir Isaac Brock was killed by a sniper when the Americans invaded Queenston in 1813 and destroyed the fort. The British reclaimed the fort and garrisoned the area. Reconstructed in the 1930s, the fort became a military base for the new Dominion of Canada Army until 1965.

Today, visitors can step back in time and relive the days of the War of 1812. Enter through the enormous main gates made of heavy timber secured with iron spikes. Tour through the elegant officers' quarters, offices, and the artificers, where war tools and artillery were made and repaired. Walk outside alongside the cannons facing the American Fort Niagara and get a sense of how intense the fighting must have been almost 200 years ago. During the main season, there are regular reenactments staged throughout the day, narrated by knowledgeable and highly entertaining costumed interpreters. See the "soldiers" prepare and fire the noon-hour cannon. Watch a musket drill or enjoy the military band. Children will enjoy being "enlisted:" wee soldiers receive a fake musket and a shilling for their duty.

26 Queen St., Niagara-on-the-Lake, Ont. ℭ **905/468-4257**. www.pc.gc.ca. Admission C$11 (US$10) adults, C$9.15 (US$8.70) seniors, C$5.45 (US$5.20) children 6–12, free for children 5 and under. May–end of Oct daily 10am–5pm; May and Nov weekends 10am–5pm.

Laura Secord Homestead　The former home of Laura Secord—a Canadian heroine of the War of 1812—is only a 10-minute drive along the Niagara Parkway from Niagara Falls. A visit to the homestead will give you a good sense of Secord's heroic journey and the local history of the era. The home includes examples of Upper Canadian furniture from the era (1803–35) along with remnants of dishes and other artifacts. Costumed staff add to the authenticity of the tours, which run every half-hour. Don't forget to stop by the small gift shop for refreshments and Canada's famous Laura Secord chocolates.

29 Queenston St., Queenston, Ont. ℭ **905/262-4851**. www.niagaraparks.com/heritage/laurasecord.php. Admission C$4.50 (US$4.30) adults, C$3.50 (US$3.30) children, free for children 5 and under. Mid-May to mid-Sept Wed–Sun 11am–4pm; Sept–May 9:30am–3:30pm.

McFarland House　Get a taste of living back—way back—in the 1800s in the old homestead of John McFarland. John and his sons constructed the house using bricks made in a kiln right on the property. The house later became a British military headquarters and then served as a makeshift hospital during the War of 1812 for both American and British soldiers. The home was badly damaged while McFarland was held prisoner during the war, and he was deeply saddened by its dilapidated state

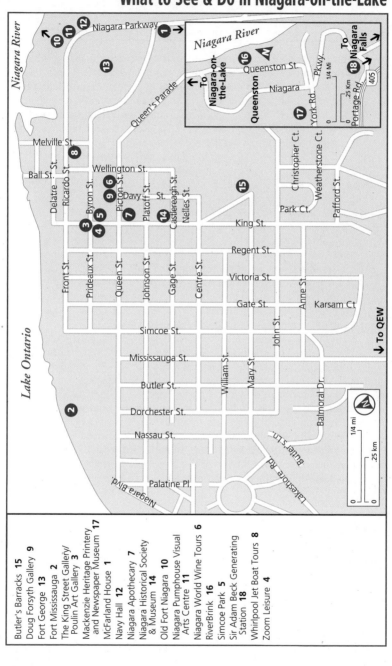

Butler's Barracks **15**
Doug Forsyth Gallery **9**
Fort George **13**
Fort Mississauga **2**
The King Street Gallery/
Poulin Art Gallery **3**
Mackenzie Heritage Printery
and Newspaper Museum **17**
McFarland House **1**
Navy Hall **12**
Niagara Apothecary **7**
Niagara Historical Society
& Museum **14**
Old Fort Niagara **10**
Niagara Pumphouse Visual
Arts Centre **11**
Niagara World Wine Tours **6**
RiverBrink **16**
Simcoe Park **5**
Sir Adam Beck Generating
Station **18**
Whirlpool Jet Boat Tours **8**
Zoom Leisure **4**

The Story of Laura Secord: It's Not Just about Chocolate

You may know the brand of chocolate, but its namesake is a lady with her own tale. Laura Ingersoll Secord, wife of British Loyalist James Secord, was born in Massachusetts but resided in Queenston, Upper Canada, during the War of 1812, as the Americans were fighting against the British (Canadians). In May 1813, three American soldiers invaded the Secord homestead in Queenston demanding lodging and food. As Secord tended to her husband, who suffered injuries from the Battle of Queenston Heights, she overheard the officers speaking: American Colonel Boerstler was planning a surprise attack on British Lt. Fitzgibbon at Beaverdams. The fate of the Canadian Niagara Peninsula was at stake. She told the soldiers she was going to visit her brother so as not to arouse suspicion, and in the morning began the 32km (20-mile) trek to warn the British of the invasion.

After walking through enemy lines and climbing the treacherous Niagara Escarpment, she finally met up with Natives allied with the British. The Natives took Secord directly to Fitzgibbon. Thanks to Laura Secord the American attack was thwarted, leaving the Niagara Peninsula in Canadian hands. There are many renditions of the story—some say Secord walked barefoot along the way; others reported that she brought a cow with her as an excuse to leave home. What is for certain is that Canada as we know it wouldn't be the same without her courageous feat.

Years later, at the age of 85, Secord finally received recognition: the Prince of Wales heard of her heroic act and gave her £100. In 1913, the centennial anniversary of Secord's journey, a small Toronto-based chocolatier named Frank P. O'Connor chose the name Laura Secord for his single Yonge Street location. O'Connor wanted his company to represent the same wholesomeness, purity, domesticity, and cleanliness that Laura Secord espoused. Today, her silhouette still appears as the company logo. Visitors to the Niagara region can visit the old Secord homestead, complete with costumed tour guides and a monument dedicated to Laura Secord, located in the Queenston Heights Park (14184 Niagara Pkwy.). And while Canadians may view this intrepid lady as a heroine, Americans may not hold the same view.

when he eventually returned from New York. Today the house, with re-created 19th-century herb garden, rooms, clothing displays, and teahouse, has been brought back to its glory days. Enjoy tea, home-baked goods, and light lunches while taking in the spectacle of flowers and greenery from the patio in the summer. Costumed interpreters educate visitors about the history of tea and the tumultuous history of the house and its era.

15927 Niagara Pkwy., Niagara-on-the-Lake, Ont. *C* 905/468-3322. Admission C$4.50 (US$4.30) adults, C$3.50 (US$3.30) children, free for children 5 and under. Mid-May to Labor Day 11am–5pm.

Mackenzie Heritage Printery and Newspaper Museum *★* *Kids*   See how far communication has come at Canada's largest working printing museum. Publisher William Lyon Mackenzie first printed *The Colonial Advocate* here in May 18, 1824.

Mackenzie championed land rights, fair court practices, and improved schools and roads from these very presses. See the Linotype in action as 5,000 moving parts work in conjunction to bring the news. Equally impressive is the 1760 "Louis Roy Press," known to be the oldest press in Canada and one of a very few wooden presses remaining in the world. The entire collection is composed of 10 operating presses ranging from the mid-1800s to the 1900s. Visitors can arrange their own type and print out pages using a hot metal typecaster.

1 Queenston St., Queenston, Ont. © 905/262-5676. www.mackenzieprintery.ca. Admission C$4.50 (US$4.30) adults, C$3.50 children (US$3.35), free for children 5 and under. Mid-May to mid-Sept Wed–Sun 11am–5pm.

Niagara Historical Society & Museum   This museum serves as a repository for artifacts and treasures from Niagara-on-the-Lake's history. The Niagara Historical Society, formed in the mid-1890s by a local retired schoolteacher, began collecting local artifacts and documents at a time when most museums were focused upon acquisition and display of foreign objects of interest. The museum is a rich source of local knowledge, offering guided tours of the town, lectures, and special exhibitions. If you're a history fan, this place will take a good hour or two to visit. Prearranged tours are available.

43 Castlereagh St., Niagara-on-the-Lake, Ont. © 905/468-3912. www.niagarahistorical.museum. Admission C$5 (US$4.75) adults, C$3 (US$2.85) seniors, C$2 (US$1.90) students, C$1 (US95¢) children 5–12, free for children 5 and under. May–Oct daily 10am–5:30pm; Nov–Apr daily 1–5pm.

Sir Adam Beck Generating Station   The Niagara River is one of the world's most important sources of hydroelectric power, generating clean, low-cost, renewable, and reliable electricity. Sir Adam Beck Generating Station No. 2, one of Ontario's largest hydroelectric facilities, is built into the side of the Niagara Gorge, 10km (6 miles) downstream from Niagara Falls near Queenston. Water from the Niagara River is delivered to the power plant through two 9km (5½-mile) tunnels built under the city of Niagara Falls. Take a comprehensive, fully guided public tour of the power station. Learn about the history of the station and how it was constructed and soak up plenty of statistics (the guides are engineers). The tour lasts approximately 40 minutes and includes a short film presentation. If you've never been to a generating station, this is a great overview of how one works. Note that all bags, including purses, must be secured in lockers during the tour. Good for all ages.

14000 Niagara Pkwy., Queenston, Ont. © 877/642-7275. www.opg.com. Admission C$8.50 (US$8.10) adults; C$5 (US$4.75) children 6–12, free for children 5 and under. Mid-Mar to early Dec daily 10am–4pm. June–Aug tours every 30 min., hourly remainder of the year.

ST. CATHARINES
Morningstar Mill   This site is a unique example of early Ontario milling heritage, and the mill and miller's house have been designated as buildings of historical and architectural interest and value under the Ontario Heritage Act. The Morningstar Mill Park, Interpretive Centre, and Museum are operated by volunteers. A number of buildings are on the site—the gristmill, a turbine shed, the miller's house, an icehouse, a barn, and a sawmill. The sawmill is a recently completed reconstruction, since the original building was abandoned during the 1930s and eventually completely dismantled. The volunteers who work to restore and maintain the site have been working on adding a blacksmith shop and carpentry shop. Bags of flour, bran, and cornmeal that have been ground on-site are on sale at the mill. Admission is free, although donations from visitors are always appreciated.

The Welland Canal Corridor

The 44km-long (27-mile) **Welland Canal** connects **Lake Ontario** with **Lake Erie** via a series of eight locks and roughly divides the Niagara region in half. The present canal, which is used primarily by bulk carriers transporting commodities such as grain and iron ore, was built in 1932. It is the fourth in a series of canals, the first of which was constructed in 1829.

At the head of the Canal sits the port city of **St. Catharines,** where you will find the **Welland Canals Centre** and **Lock 3 viewing platform** (see listing below). The **St. Catharines Museum** is also located at this site. Moving south along the Canal, **Thorold,** with its **Lock 7 viewing area,** offers another great observation spot as well as a tourist information center with lots of information on the Canal and the ships that sail up and down the waterway, a wooden outdoor deck for viewing, and a small snack bar (50 Chapel St. S.; ℭ **905/680-9477**). The world-famous Twinned Flight Locks are also located in Thorold, although there isn't a convenient place to stop and view them in operation. These locks raise and lower ships up and down the Niagara Escarpment (43m/140 ft.). This is the only place on the canal where there is two-way vessel traffic. Thorold also boasts an inn where you can stay and view the ships passing by your balcony. Farther south is the city of **Welland.** Finally, at the connection with Lake Erie lies the marine city of **Port Colborne.**

The Welland Canal is open between March and December. Call ahead for ship viewing times (ℭ **800/305-5134** or 905/984-8880).

2710 Decew Rd., St. Catharines, Ont. ℭ **905/688-6050.** www.morningstarmill.ca. Free admission. Mid-May to mid-Oct Tues and Thurs 9am–3pm, Sat–Sun noon–5pm; public holiday Mon noon–5pm. Since the Mill is run by volunteers, these hours are not guaranteed.

Welland Canals Centre at Lock 3   Here visitors can watch the ships pass by from a bird's-eye view atop a gigantic raised platform. Inside, watch the 15-minute film *Welland Canals Past and Present* to learn about the history of one of the tallest water staircases in the world—100m (328 ft.) high. This visit is worth at least a half-hour stop even if you're not a salty dog.

The **St. Catharines Museum,** housed in the same building, features an exhibit on the Underground Railroad as well as an impressive collection of maps, photographs, and more. Working models of the locks and bridges are on display. Don't leave without taking another half-hour to see this impressive museum.

1932 Welland Canals Pkwy., St. Catharines, Ont. ℭ **800/305-5134** or 905/984-8880. www.stcatharineslock3 museum.ca. Admission C$4.50 (US$4.30) adults, C$4 (US$3.80) seniors, C$3.25 (US$3.10) students (over 14), C$2.50 (US$2.40) children 6–13, free for children 5 and under, family discount 15%. Mon–Fri 9am–5pm; Sat–Sun 11am–4pm.

FORT ERIE AND PORT COLBORNE

Fort Erie Historical & Ridgeway Battlefield Site   In June 1866, Irish-American veterans of the U.S. Civil War fought Canadian forces in hopes of gaining Ireland's independence from England. Today there is a commemorative cairn built on

Highway 3, near Ridge Road, close to the old battlefield site; the site and cairn can be viewed at any time at the Ridgeway Battlefield Site. The Fort Erie Historical Museum tells a story dating back 10,000 years to the first aboriginal settlement—the outdated exhibits, viewed through glass cases, don't make it the most interesting visit but at least provide a thorough historical overview. The building, built in 1874, was once a jail turned town treasury, and still has the treasury vault. Ridgeway Battlefield Site is no longer a museum but instead an outside tour with interpretive plaques.

402 Ridge Rd., Ridgeway, Ont. (within town of Fort Erie). © 905/894-5322. www.museum.forterie.ca. Admission C$1.50 (US$1.40) adults, C50¢ (US48¢) children. Sept–May Sun–Fri 9am–5pm; June–Aug daily 9am–5pm. **Ridgeway Battlefield Site:** Hwy. #3 (Garrison Rd.), Ridgeway.

Fort Erie Railroad ✸   At one time, Fort Erie was the third-largest rail yard in Canada. The jet-black steam engine #6218 ran from its debut in 1948, into the early 1960s. Inside the museum, you'll find artifacts, such as tools and telegraphy equipment, and exhibits featuring photos and train-related paraphernalia. The original Grand Trunk Railway Station in Ridgeway and CN B-1 at one time monitored traffic movement over the International Railway Bridge. Today this relocated station, with wooden waiting chairs and stoves, re-creates the feel of a good old-fashioned train station from back when steam billowed from the engines. Worth a visit even if you don't have a train collection at home.

400 Central Ave., Fort Erie, Ont. © 905/871-1412. June–Aug 9am–5pm.

Mildred Mahoney Dolls House Gallery *(Kids)*   This historical home has more than 140 dollhouses from around the world—England, Europe, Japan, the U.S., and Canada. Peek at rare miniature houses dating back to 1780. Inside each house, you'll find antique miniature furniture and crocheted pieces—some even made by Mrs. Mahoney herself. Mrs. Mahoney kept all the dollhouses (37 years' worth) in her home until 1983, at which point they were moved to Bertie Hall—a historical landmark. The doll collection is a unique, charming, and homey tribute to a woman's childhood dream come true. Bertie Hall also served as a stopping point for black slaves seeking freedom in Canada during the time of the Underground Railroad. Little girls will adore this place.

657 Niagara Blvd., Fort Erie, Ont. © 905/871-5833. Admission C$6 (US$5.70) adults, C$5 (US$4.75) seniors, C$4 (US$3.80) students up to 16 years, free for children 5 and under. May–Dec daily 9:30am–3pm.

How Does a Lock Work?

In simple terms, here's how a ship "climbs" up the river. (Just reverse the steps for going down.)

- The boat approaches the bottom gates of the lock, which has a water level the same as the river on the downstream side.
- The lock gates swing open on the downstream side and the ship enters the lock.
- The lock gates are closed behind the boat.
- Valves on the upstream side of the lock are opened to let water into the lock until the water level in the lock is the same as the water on the upstream side.
- The gates on the upstream side of the lock are opened and the ship leaves the lock.

Old Fort Erie *Kids*   Built in 1764, this structure was the first British defense fort in the area. Only stone remnants of the original fort were used in the re-creation. The original building, built below the current structure, was a supply depot and port for ships along the Upper Great Lakes. Seeing battle during the American Revolution as a supply base for British troops, Loyalist Rangers, and Iroquois warriors, the tiny fort sustained much damage and another was built. During the War of 1812 the Americans occupied the fort, eventually destroying it when they vacated the premises. After the war, the fort continued to play an important role—most notably as a stop for American slaves seeking freedom in Canada during the mid-1800s. Today, visit impressively restored buildings such as the guardroom, soldiers' barracks, or the kitchen—where a fierce battle took place as the British tried to capture the fort from the Americans. The Curtain Wall that connected the two barracks together, with its 3m-thick (10-ft.) walls and wooden spikes, stands as an ominous reminder of a tumultuous era. Regular 1-hour tours are available with interpreters dressed in period costume; tours can be a tad dry because the young staff stick to the scripts and aren't always able to answer questions.

350 Lakeshore Rd., Fort Erie, Ont. ✆ **877/NIA-PARK** or 905/371-0254. Admission C$9 (US$8.55) adults, C$5 (US$4.75) children 6–12, free for children 5 and under. May–Sept daily 10am–5pm; July–early Oct daily 10am–4pm.

Port Colborne Historical and Marine Museum *Kids*   Inside the museum is a re-creation of the history of Port Colborne. The Heritage Village is complete with a network of paths and buildings, including the log schoolhouse, the Sherk-Troup log home, the FW Woods Marine Blacksmith shop, the Graf Loom, and the Carriage House gift shop. Artifacts inside the museum include photos, textiles, glassware, marine artifacts, housewares, and community archives related to Port Colborne and the Welland Canal. You'll also find Canada's Century Car, the Neff Steam Buggy. Made in 1901, this car is one of the oldest automobiles in Ontario and was built in Port Colborne. More exhibits within the museum cater to the sea buff—check out the Wheelhouse from the *Yvon Dupre Jr.* tug boat, the anchor from the *Raleigh,* and a real lifeboat from the SS *Hochelaga.* The museum also hosts many events: in the spring enjoy the Pie Social, the History Fair, and the Antique Road Show; in the summer, participate in Canal Days; in December savor the special Christmas pudding in Arabella's Tea Room—the original 1915 Edwardian-style homestead of Arabella Williams that serves steaming hot biscuits and homemade preserves. A great interactive village and educational museum to spend an hour or two with the kids. Tours are offered on request with knowledgeable locals.

The Museum, Heritage Village, and Gift Shop: 280 King St., Port Colborne, Ont. ✆ **905/834-7604.** Free admission. May–Dec daily noon–5pm, including holidays. **Arabella's Tea Room:** June–Sept daily 2–4pm, including holidays.

⌐ Fun Fact   The Hermit of Niagara

In 1829, a young man named Francis Abbott took up residence on Goat Island in an abandoned log cabin, despite not receiving permission to live there from the landowners. For the next 2 years he was the sole inhabitant of the island and often entertained tourists with his antics, such as balancing on the wooden pier leading to Terrapin Tower. He died by drowning in June 1831, while bathing in the Niagara River.

Niagara Freedom Trail (Underground Railroad)

The Niagara Freedom Trail is a tribute to the estimated 40,000 black American slaves who came to Canada seeking freedom in the 19th century when Canada passed the Slavery Abolition Act, making their way through Fort Erie and Niagara Falls and into St. Catharines. The Freedom Trail, as it stands today, isn't so much a trail as it is a series of markers, historical sites, and plaques. The trail is marked with a running-man symbol.

Fort Erie has a significant plaque—**The Crossing**—which marks the spot where many slaves crossed over into Canada from Buffalo. Also in Fort Erie is **Bertie Hall**—today the Mildred Mahoney Dolls House Gallery (p. 119). This home was a site for refugees seeking shelter and has a secret tunnel entrance that led from the house to the riverbank. Fort Erie is also home to "Little Africa." In the late 1700s the population grew from 80 to 200 black American slaves who made a living supplying lumber to the ferry and railway services. Here, Little Africa thrived—residents enjoyed working and farming walnut and hickory farms.

In Niagara Falls, the **Norval Johnson Heritage Library** houses more than 2,000 books by, about, and from black settlers on the subject of black heritage (5674 Peer St.; ☎ 905/358-9957). Next door is the **Nathaniel Dett Chapel,** built in 1836 and named after the church organist, a musician in his own right.

St. Catharines is home to the **Salem Chapel,** a British Methodist Episcopal church that served as a refuge safe haven (92 Geneva St.; ☎ 905/682-0993). Harriet Tubman, a former slave living in St. Catharines, helped an estimated 300 slaves to freedom and also attended the Salem Chapel. **The Anthony Burns Gravesite and Victorian Lawn Cemetery** honors Reverend Burns—the last man tried under the Fugitive Slave Act, which sent him back to slavery (Queenston St., west of Homer Bridge). He eventually moved to St. Catharines. The **Richard Pierpoint plaque** in Centennial Park commemorates an African-born slave who was brought to America and sold to a British officer. Pierpoint later joined the Colored Corps, an all-black military company, and was awarded land for his service.

If you can't tour the entire trail, the **St. Catharines Museum** at the Welland Canal Centre has a comprehensive gathering of facts and memorabilia, giving an impressive historical overview. The African Canadian Heritage Tour, the Central Ontario Network for Black History, and the Ontario Government have collaborated to produce a booklet outlining all 29 trail sites within the province.

3 Galleries

From landscape to contemporary, Niagara galleries host a small array of unique pieces. A few galleries also feature a creative mix of media and styles from artists in the region and across the country.

NIAGARA-ON-THE-LAKE

Doug Forsythe Gallery Doug Forsythe is an established Canadian artist. Many of his collections feature landscapes—a golden field or a vineyard–seascapes that include vivid blues and blacks, marine themes, and figure studies across Canada. He works in computer graphics, watercolor, oil, and acrylics, and is skilled in etching, engraving, dry point, collagraphs, woodcuts, serigraphs, and woodcarving. Local scenes include Niagara-on-the-Lake, Niagara Falls, and Niagara vineyards. Forsythe also creates intricate guitars and fine scale-model ships. His photo-realist paintings artfully capture nature.

92 Picton St., Niagara-on-the-Lake, Ont. *C* **905/468-3659.** www.dougforsythegallery.com. Admission is free. Apr–June 10am–5:30pm; July–Sept 10am–6pm; Oct 10am–5:30pm; Nov–Dec 10am–5pm; Jan–Mar Fri–Sun 10am–5pm, Mon–Thurs by chance or call.

The King Street Gallery/Poulin Art Gallery This gallery in a historical house in Niagara-on-the-Lake features works by Canadian artist Chantal Poulin. It's a small collection of about a dozen paintings and sculptures residing in a single room. Poulin's works range from portraits of children to landscapes of the Niagara vineyards, still life, and contemporary art. The gallery also displays other artists' work, including a number from Quebec.

153 King St., Niagara-on-the-Lake, Ont. *C* **905/468-8923.** Admission is free. Tues–Sun 10am–5pm.

Niagara Pumphouse Visual Arts Centre The work of local artists—a mix of traditional still life and floral paintings to bold abstract shapes on canvas using mixed media—is displayed in the salon. Exhibitions include raku ware and relief sculptures to etching, photography, and paintings. Lectures and programming for children and adults are offered throughout the year.

247 Ricardo St., Niagara-on-the-Lake, Ont. *C* **905/468-5455.** www.niagarapumphouse.ca. Admission is free. June–Aug daily 10am–4pm; Sept–May Sat–Sun 1–4pm.

RiverBrink *★* *Finds* Home of the Samuel E. Weir Collection (1898—1981), this gallery features a fascinating collection of over 1,000 pieces, consisting predominantly of Canadian works. Of particular interest are the works by Tom Thomson and the Group of Seven, who were the first artists to capture the power and spirit of Northern Canada. You'll also find many Quebec landscapes, Georgian portraiture, and War of 1812 pieces, plus a number of paintings of Niagara Falls, which give visitors a pristine view of the Falls and area before mass development. The collection also includes many antiques and an impressive 4,000-volume reference library. I recommend calling ahead to book a guided tour—you'll get great insight into Canadian history and the story behind the paintings. Exhibits change annually.

116 Queenston St., Niagara-on-the-Lake, Ont. *C* **905/262-4510.** www.riverbrink.org. Admission C$5 (US$4.75) adults, C$4 (US$3.80) seniors, free for children under 12 when accompanied by parent. Mid-May to mid-Oct 10am–5pm. After Oct by appointment only.

ST. CATHARINES

Rodman Hall Arts Centre The house and surrounding gardens are more interesting than the majority of the art inside. The Walker Botanical Garden includes plants from all around the world, such as blue atlas cedar from North Africa, cryptomeria and magnolia from Japan, and dawn redwood, dogwood, and blue fir from China. However, there are a few gems in the gallery's collection, including a whale-inspired piece by Newfoundland artist David Blackwood, and a landscape painting by B.C. artist Emily Carr. International paintings include a small piece by French artist Marc Chagall. The

> **_Fun Fact_ Hold the Foam**
> The brown foam you can see floating on the water below the Falls is not caused by pollution. It is simply a suspension of clay particles and decayed vegetative matter, originating mostly from the shallow eastern basin of Lake Erie. The foam is a natural consequence of the tons of water that plummet over the crest line of the Falls.

gallery features a permanent display of more than 850 works. Established in 1960, Rodman Hall recently became part of Brock University's School of Fine and Performing Arts.

109 St. Paul Crescent, St. Catharines, Ont. © **905/684-2925**. Admission is free. Sept–June Mon–Thurs noon–9pm; Fri–Sun noon–5pm.

JORDAN VILLAGE
Jordan Art Gallery 🛊   Quaint and local, this gallery is owned by a group of local artists who also staff the store, so there is always a knowledgeable and enthusiastic steward on hand to chat about the art on display. In addition to the showcased work of the gallery owners, other selected artists' works are exhibited. The styles and media of these artists are quite remarkable. This gallery should be marked as a must-see if you are in the Twenty Valley area.

3845 Main St., Jordan Village, Ont. © **905/562-6680**. Admission is free. Summer Mon–Sun 10am–6pm; winter Wed–Sun 10am–5pm.

GRIMSBY
Grimsby Public Art Gallery   This gallery features local work and promising young artists. Monthly exhibitions, tours, and programs are featured. Recent exhibitions include a tribute sculpture to Canadian ski legend Herman Smith-Johannsen and locally made folk-art boats.

18 Carnegie Lane, Grimsby, Ont. © **905/945-3246**. Admission is free. Mon and Fri 10am–5pm; Tues–Thurs 10am–8pm; Sat–Sun 1–5pm.

4 Niagara Falls for Thrill Seekers
AMUSEMENTS
CLIFTON HILL   Clifton Hill is a compact entertainment district wedged between Victoria Avenue at the top of the hill and Falls Avenue at the bottom. The lights, noise, and nonstop mayhem spill over its edges and seep along the side streets, but The Hill is without a doubt the center of the maelstrom. The contrast between the garish kitsch of the Clifton Hill district and the breathtaking natural beauty of the Falls could hardly be more extreme. The area is sensory overload both day and night. You'll either hate it or love it.

Just be sure to bring plenty of cash—admission prices for the novelty tourist attractions are steep. For example, **House of Frankenstein** (4967 Clifton Hill; © **905/357-9660**) charges C$10 (US$9.50) for adults and C$7 (US$6.65) for children, and **Ripley's Believe It or Not! Museum** (4960 Clifton Hill; © **905/356-2238**) will set you back C$15 (US$14) for adults and C$7 (US$6.65) for children. Often you'll find promotional brochures that contain discount coupons for some of the novelty attractions at hotels, some restaurants, and tourist information centers, so if you're planning to head to The Hill it's worth your while to hunt down one of these booklets before you step into the madness. If you plan to stay long enough to eat a meal or snack in the area, it also helps if you're a fast-food fanatic.

But beware: while some of the facades of these attractions may look enticing, new, and flashy, what's inside can be a huge disappointment. **The Louis Tussaud's Waxworks,** which feels like it hasn't changed inside since opening in 1949, does have well-constructed celebrity clones, if that's your style (5907 Victoria Ave.; ✆ **905/356-2238**). **Ripley's Believe It or Not,** despite its showcase of freaky events, people, and animals (a buffalo with eight legs), isn't worth the trip.

On a scare scale from least to most, the **Haunted House** and its fake ghoul sounds is the least scary but best suited for kids; the **House of Frankenstein** hires real actors to make sounds; and **Nightmares,** on Victoria Avenue, may give little ones actual nightmares—I don't suggest sending kids through.

The best of the rides includes the **Cosmic Coaster,** where you strap onto a moving floor and watch a futuristic roller coaster set to Grateful Dead–like music. For the really small ones, **Brick City,** made from over one-million Lego blocks, is fun (they even have the Falls made of Legos). For the older set, the view from the Niagara **Skywheel** is cool. The giant Ferris wheel (C$10/US$9.50) includes three turns, lasting 7 minutes, in an air-conditioned or heated gondola. Beware: On a sunny day, no amount of air-conditioning will keep this box cool.

THEME PARKS   Niagara Falls has many theme parks to keep the kids running around and the parents trying to catch up. The most popular is **Marineland,** where whales are the main attraction (7657 Portage Rd., Niagara Falls, Ont.; ✆ **905/356-9565;** www.marinelandcanada.com). Walkways allow visitors to view the marine mammals above and below water. Live performances featuring trained dolphins, walruses, and sea lions are scheduled several times daily. Fish, deer, black bears, and elk can also be seen. Marineland has an amusement park with a dozen or so rides, including roller coasters, a Ferris wheel, and a carousel. Day admission isn't cheap at C$39 (US$37) adults and C$32 (US$30) for children. A season's pass is available for an additional C$5 (US$4.75) when purchasing a regular-price day admission to the park. Younger kids can easily spend a full day here—but be sure to bring a lunch, as cafeteria prices are expensive and the food isn't especially healthy. However, older kids may find the rides tiresome, lacking the thrill factor in comparison to facilities that specialize in rides.

Martin's Fantasy Island (2400 Grand Island Blvd., Grand Island, NY; ✆ **716/773-7591;** www.martinsfantasyisland.com) is a seasonal amusement park with wet and dry rides, water slides, a wave pool, carnival-type rides, and live shows. Many of the attractions, such as Kiddie Land and a petting zoo, are geared toward the younger kids. The Silver Comet roller coaster is tame in comparison to other parks. One admission price covers all shows, rides, and attractions, including a petting zoo, canoes, and the water park. Parking is free.

Americana Conference Resort and Spa (8444 Lundy's Lane, Niagara Falls, Ont.; ✆ **800/263-3508;** www.americananiagara.com) is a 2325-sq.-m (25,000-sq.-ft.) indoor water park with beach-entry wave pool, tube slides, body slides, kiddy-pool interactive play structure, and whirlpools. There's an arcade and lounge area, but this facility isn't as large or fun as the outdoor counterparts. Young kids will appreciate half a day to get wet without insanely scary rides.

The Brave and the Foolhardy—Niagara's Daredevils

Barrel, tightrope, rubber tube, Jet Ski, kayak, or only the clothes on their backs—thrill seekers worldwide have used every conceivable contraption to go over, under, or through the Niagara Falls. Some made it—some didn't.

Captain Joel Robinson set out onboard the *Maid of the Mist II* to conquer the gorge rapids and whirlpool. During the ordeal, the smokestack snapped, but all crew and Robinson survived the journey in one piece. Their reward was a mere $500; Robinson retired soon after. **The Great Blondin,** aka Jean François Gravelot of France, balanced over the Falls on a precarious 335m-long (1,100-ft.) tightrope. On June 30, 1859, Blondin walked from Prospect Park in New York City to Oakes Garden in Niagara Falls. Subsequent walks included carrying his manager on his back and pushing a wheelbarrow across. On one occasion, Blondin cooked omelets on a small stove and lowered them on a cord to passengers on the *Maid of the Mist*. On her 63rd birthday on October 24, 1901, New York native **Annie Taylor** was the first human to go over the Falls in a barrel, without any prior experience. The widow emerged from the barrel saying: "No one ought ever to do that again."

But many more daredevil stunts followed, including those by **William "Red" Hill, Sr.,** who rode through the Great Gorge rapids and whirlpool in a steel barrel contraption. The 290-kilogram (640-lb.) red barrel had to be rescued from the whirlpool vortex. But ever determined, Red continued on to Queenston. Wishing to carry on his father's legacy, **William "Red" Hill, Jr.,** went over the Falls in a tower of inner tubes tied together precariously with fish net and canvas. "The Thing," as it was called, sank down into the bubbling water. Moments later, detached inner tubes surfaced—but no Red in sight. His body was recovered the next day.

In the "not intending to seek fame" category, on July 9, 1960, **Roger Woodward,** a 9-year-old American boy, was boating on the Niagara River with his sister and a family friend when the engine of their boat cut out and the force of the rapids propelled the boat toward the Falls. The 40-year-old family friend didn't make it, but Woodward, in what is dubbed "the miracle of the Falls," survived a trip over the Horseshoe Falls wearing only a life-jacket and bathing suit. His sister was rescued by horrified bystanders only seconds before she would have been swept over the brink.

Please note: It is illegal to perform any kind of stunt pertaining to the Niagara Falls under the regulations of the *Niagara Parks Act*. In addition to legal prosecution, individuals performing stunts can be fined up to $10,000.

Hours at the various parks vary, but all generally open late in the morning (11:30am) and close just before dark, while Marineland is open until 10pm.

THRILL RIDES

Niagara Helicopters Limited   What an exhilarating way to see the Falls on a clear day. A 9-minute ride covers 27km (17 miles): over the hydroelectric waterways system and Niagara Parks Botanical Gardens, along the Niagara River and Gorge to the American and Horseshoe falls, past Queen Victoria Park, and returning to base. Complimentary headsets with commentary are provided on the flight. Photographs taken as you enter the helicopter cost C$25 (US$24) and include pictures of the Falls from above.

3731 Victoria Ave., Niagara Falls, Ont. (℃) **800/281-8034** or 905/357-5672. www.niagarahelicopters.com. C$105 (US$100) adults (C$200/US$190 for 2), C$60 (US$57) children 2–12, free for children under 2. Family and group rates, call first. Daily flights 9am–sunset weather permitting.

Whirlpool Jet Boat Tours   This tour entails getting a little, or a lot, of splash from the Niagara River, depending on which boat you ride. You have a choice of two boats— a "Wet Jet" boat, which is open to the elements (you're going to get soaked), or a "Jet Dome" boat, which is enclosed. Life jackets, splash suits, and wet boots are provided, but a complete change of clothing is recommended for riders of the Wet Jet. The trip, about 1 hour on the water if you climb aboard at Niagara-on-the-Lake and about 45 minutes if you board at Lewiston, takes you upriver through the Niagara Gorge, the white water of Devil's Hole, and the famous Whirlpool. A photography team takes digital photos of the jet boat (offered on the Wet Jet and the Jet Dome) that are electronically transferred back to the dock for passengers to view upon their return, with an option to purchase. The Jet Dome has undergone a redesign to allow easier and safer boarding and seating on the boat. The original dome glass has been replaced in order to improve visibility for passengers. Book online for either experience, and you may get a discount of up to C$10 (US$9.50) per person. Jet Dome departs from Niagara Glen in June, July, and August and from Niagara-on-the-Lake in September.

61 Melville St., Niagara-on-the-Lake, Ont. (℃) **888/438-4444** or 905/468-4800. www.whirlpooljet.com. Access also available on the U.S. side (the dock is at the end of Center St. in Lewiston, New York). Admission C$56 (US$53) adults, C$47 (US$45) children (6–13 years and minimum height of 44 inches required for Wet Jet boat ride; children 4–13 years and minimum 40 inches tall for Jet Dome ride). Passengers under 16 years of age must be accompanied by a parent or guardian. Children under 6 are not permitted to ride on the Wet Jet boats and under 4 are not permitted on the Jet Dome boats. Reservations recommended.

5 Especially for Kids

Here's a lineup of the best things for kids to see and do in the Niagara region. It's a good mix of entertainment that will have kids either squealing with joy careening down a water slide or oohing and ahhing walking through a historical fort. There is a plethora of places to go with kids—it seems Niagara Falls was built with them in mind. But be wary of where you go—some are not worth a second glance. Here's our top picks that will make them want to return:

- *Maid of the Mist* (p. 106): You can't get much closer to the Falls than this. Kids will love the intense mist and thunderous sound of the Falls. They'll also appreciate the disposable poncho that matches the one you get.
- **Mackenzie Heritage Printery and Newspaper Museum** (p. 116): Kids can learn how to make a newspaper page the old-fashioned way. This museum is full of interactive and unique pieces that will have them busy for hours.
- **Marineland** (p. 124): Younger kids won't want to leave the rides and the magnificent animals here. It's one of the main draws for children in the area.
- **Fort George** (p. 114): Little soldiers will love the musket firing, cannons, and giant wooden wall fortifications, not to mention, they can enlist! Come on a July weekend, when kids can see reenactments of War of 1812 drills.

Niagara Region Attractions

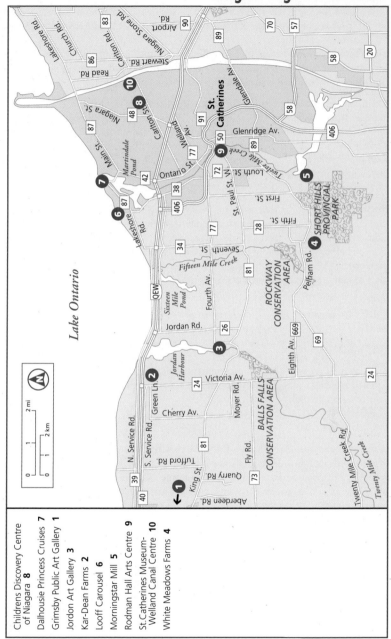

Childrens Discovery Centre
of Niagara **8**

Dalhousie Princess Cruises **7**

Grimsby Public Art Gallery **1**

Jordon Art Gallery **3**

Kar-Dean Farms **2**

Looff Carousel **6**

Morningstar Mill **5**

Rodman Hall Arts Centre **9**

St. Catherines Museum-
Welland Canal Centre **10**

White Meadows Farms **4**

- **Brick City** (p. 124): Famous structures such as the Statue of Liberty and the Greek Acropolis are made of over one-million pieces of Lego here. Kids can make their own creations.
- **White Meadows Farms** (p. 133): While in Rome, er, Canada, kids should experience the true Canadian experience of "sugaring off"—eating maple syrup poured on crisp white snow during February and March.

Children's Discovery Centre of Niagara   Open year-round, this is an entertaining educational experience for children of all ages and their families. The emphasis is on hands-on, interactive exhibits and galleries. A Wetland Park was installed in 2005. Key features include a dinosaur gallery, water conservation exhibit, recycling and environmental gallery, hydro gallery, and agricultural gallery.

360 Niagara St., St. Catharines, Ont. ⓒ **905/646-4365.** www.childrensdiscoverycentre.org. Admission C$6 (US$5.70), free for children under 2. Tues–Fri 10am–4pm; Sat 10am–5pm; closed Sun.

HorsePlay Niagara   Trail rides are available year-round. Take a 1- or 2-hour ride through the woods and past the ponds and abandoned quarries of adjacent Wainfleet Conservation Area. Themed activities include sunset rides and half-day adventures such as a cowboy cookout including wieners over an open fire. Children's play area includes a hay maze, playground, and petting zoo. Riders must be 6 years of age and up.

Hwy. 3, west of Port Colborne, Ont. ⓒ **800/871-1141** or 905/834-2380. www.horseplayniagara.com. One hour C$35 (US$33). Daily year-round 10am–5pm.

Looff Carousel   One of the largest and best-preserved examples of a Looff menagerie carousel, the carousel at Lakeside Park on Lake Ontario in Old Port Dalhousie is a fantastic sight. There are 69 carousel animals arranged in four rings. And the cost is only a nickel a ride! This beautifully preserved carousel celebrated its 100th birthday in 2005 and is one of only nine historic carousels in Canada. A recently constructed children's playground is situated between the carousel and the harbor walkway, in Lakeside Park.

Lakeside Park, accessed from Lakeport Rd., Old Port Dalhousie, St. Catharines. Admission C5¢ (US5¢). Mid-May to early Sept daily 10am–9pm.

Niagara Falls Aviary—Birds of the Lost Kingdom   This is a handy place to take the kids for some diversion, since it's within easy walking distance of the Falls as you travel upriver on River Road alongside the Niagara Gorge. Tropical plants, a waterfall, and moss-covered carvings combine to re-create a rainforest experience, complete with exotic species of birds from Australia, South America, and Africa.

Tips Keeping the Kids Entertained

When you're traveling with children, if you can put their needs first when planning your itinerary and include activities that all ages will enjoy then everyone will have a more pleasant vacation. Be sure to schedule plenty of time for relaxation (and naps, if your children are very young). The best advice you can follow is not to over-schedule. Don't expect your kids to act like adults—young children have short attention spans. When they start to wiggle and fidget, let them have a half-hour to blow off steam in a playground, sit with them on a park bench and lick ice-cream cones, or take them to a movie.

The Mystery of the Whirlpool—Solved!

The Whirlpool is a natural phenomenon in the Niagara River, occurring at the point where the river makes a sharp right-angled turn. The Whirlpool is a huge basin 518m (1,700 ft.) long by 365m (1,200 ft.) wide and 38m (125 ft.) deep at its deepest point.

When the Niagara River is at full flow, the water travels along the 1.6km (1-mile) stretch known as the Whirlpool Rapids, at speeds up to 9m per second (30 ft./sec.). The water enters the basin, and then travels counterclockwise around the pool and past the natural outlet.

As the water tries to cut across itself to reach the outlet, pressure builds up and forces the water under the incoming stream. This creates the whirlpool effect. The water then continues on its way to Lake Ontario.

More than 300 tropical birds are housed in the aviary—some free flying and some contained in observational exhibits. Newly added, the interactive Reptile Encounter allows kids to feel pythons, turtles, and more.

5651 River Rd., Niagara Falls, Ont. ☎ 888/994-0090 or 905/356-8888. www.niagarafallsaviary.com. Admission C$21 (US$19) adults, C$15 (US$14) seniors, C$10 (US$9.50) children 5–12, free for children under 5. July–Aug 9:30am–7pm; Sept–June 10am–5pm. Last admission is 1 hr. prior to closing.

Simcoe Park   This beautiful park has a gently rolling landscape, colorful flower beds, plenty of mature shade trees, and lush green lawns. There is a children's playground and a wading pool. Located in pretty Niagara-on-the-Lake.

Bordered by Picton St., King St., and Byron St. in Niagara-on-the-Lake.

Zooz   Kids love animals, and Zooz features more than 400 of them, both exotic and domestic, and all housed in natural habitats. Lots to keep young ones busy for hours on end—splash pad, Gator Express tram rides, catch-and-release fishing in a stocked pond, paddle boats, kite-flying, petting area, and children's play zone. Live interactive animal presentations and guided educational tours.

2821 Stevensville Rd., Stevensville, Ont. ☎ 866/367-9669 or 905/382-9669. www.zooz.ca. Admission C$18 (US$17) adults, C$16 (US$15) seniors, C$13 (US$12) children 4–12, children under 3 free. Seasonal operation: hours may change, so call ahead. Daily May 12–31 9am–5pm; June–Sept 3 9am–6pm; Sept 4–Oct 8 10am–4pm.

6 Parks & Gardens

NIAGARA PARKS COMMISSION

Despite the din of the Falls and the clamor of Clifton Hills, Niagara Falls offers a number of quiet oases. In the heart of Niagara Falls is the **Queen Victoria Park,** which features half a million daffodils in the spring. **Oakes Garden Theatre** marks the entrance to Queen Victoria Park, which extends south along the Niagara Parkway to the Horseshoe Falls. Many open-air concerts are held here throughout the summer season. **The Niagara Parks Greenhouse** (7145 Niagara Pkwy., Niagara Falls, Ontario; www.info niagara.com/attractions/green.html) is a 1025-sq.-m (11,000-sq.-ft.) greenhouse and surrounding gardens, located just a short distance south of the Horseshoe Falls on the Niagara Parkway. Themed horticulture events occur throughout the summer.

> **Tips Peek Inside the Clock**
>
> If you walk *behind* the Floral Clock (most people are much too occupied taking pictures of their family and friends standing in front of the clock to ever do this), you may be able to peek inside; the door is often open to allow visitors to see the drive mechanism of the clock. There is also a collection of photos of the clock in past years so you can compare the wildly different designs and colors as they change from year to year.

Those who like to dine al fresco have a number of spots to choose from. Originally formed by a glacier drift, today a labyrinth of trails and several bridges make **Dufferin Islands** a great place to picnic and explore for the day (7400 Portage Rd., Niagara Parks Commission, Niagara Falls, Ontario; © **877/642-7275**). These eight islands, connected by bridges, take about 15 minutes to walk, or less to bike; it's a quiet area of about 10km (6 miles) in total. **Kings Bridge Park** (7870 Niagara River Pkwy. © **877-NIA-PARK**), just south of the Falls near Chippawa, is another ideal picnic spot, with its picnic pavilion, picnic tables, washrooms, and playground and splash pad for children. On summer weekends and holidays, there is a parking fee of C$10 (US$9.50).

Perhaps the quietest retreat in the area is **Navy Island** (© **905/356-1338;** www.niagaraparks.com/nature/navyisland.php), which is accessible only via boat. Over 10,000 years ago, natives used the island for fishing and canoe building. Today you can find solace and wild raspberries, grapes, pawpaw, hickory, oak, and blue beech. Camping fees are C$8 (US$7.60) adult, C$4 (US$3.80) between 12 and 17 year-old, and free for children 12 and under.

One not-so-quiet stop that is visited by tour bus after tour bus is the **Floral Clock** (14004 Niagara River Pkwy., Niagara Falls, Ont.). The design is changed twice a year, with violas providing color in spring, followed in late May by a labor-intensive operation to install 16,000 carpet bedding plants to form the 12.2m-diameter (40-ft.) clock face. Spring is the best time to see the clock, with the intense smell of over 1,200 mature lilac trees representing 225 varieties.

Niagara Parks Botanical Gardens   This is one of the most endearing places to me in the Niagara region, particularly in the spring when the bulbs are in full bloom. The beds and borders have provided much inspiration over the years for my own gardening projects. The formal herb garden, planted in a symmetrical design, has benches tucked into niches in the clipped hedges that surround the display. On a warm summer's day, you can sit in contented solitude for a while, taking in the beauty of the plants or just dreaming about the future transformation of your own garden at home. There are numerous vegetable beds in an area adjacent to the herb garden and a rock garden. The plants in the perennial garden are handily labeled for reference, so bring a notebook and pen if you are a really keen green-thumber. The arboretum holds one of Canada's finest collections of ornamental trees and shrubs.

The Botanical Gardens were originally established in 1936 to provide a teaching facility for the School of Apprentice Gardeners. The site received its declaration as a Botanical Garden in 1990, as a result of the expansion of the variety and quality of the plant collections living in its extensive grounds. The Botanical Gardens continue to serve as a training ground for students of the School of Horticulture. The students gain practical experience through the maintenance and development of the gardens, although they also attend classroom lectures in horticultural theory.

The gardens are a short drive north of the Falls along the Niagara Parkway, about 9km (6 miles) north of the Horseshoe Falls. The site is serviced by the People Mover bus.

2565 Niagara Pkwy., Niagara Falls, Ont. © 877/NIA-PARK. www.niagaraparks.com/nature/botanical.php. Free admission. Daily dawn–dusk.

Queenston Heights Park   Only a few minutes' drive north of the Butterfly Conservatory and the Niagara Parks Botanical Gardens, this popular summertime destination is particularly good for families, history buffs, and those who enjoy hiking and cycling. Facilities at the park include two picnic pavilions, washrooms, and a band shell. During the summer a small snack bar is in operation. On hot summer days, let your kids wade in the shallow water of the splash pad or burn off their energy in the children's playground. There are plenty of mature shade trees and open grassy areas for ballgames and family fun. For those who like to hike and bike, you'll be pleased to learn that Queenston Heights Park is the southern terminus of the Bruce Trail, Canada's oldest and longest continuous footpath. The trail runs along the Niagara Escarpment, spanning a distance of 850km (528 miles); the northern terminus is at Tobermory in southwestern Ontario. See "Hiking & Biking," in the section titled "Outdoor Pursuits" later in this chapter for more details.

A walking tour of the Battleground of the Battle of Queenston Heights is clearly marked throughout the park, and takes about 45 minutes to 1 hour to complete, if you're walking at a leisurely pace. There are five plaques stationed along the way, which explain various stages of the battle and their consequences. See the section on tours later in this chapter for a more detailed description of the walking tour. **Queenston Heights Restaurant** provides an elegant setting with a spectacular view of the Niagara River, looking north toward Lake Ontario. The restaurant is perched on the edge of the Niagara Escarpment. For more detailed information on the restaurant, see the listing in chapter 6, "Where to Dine." To the right of the restaurant, you will find a monument dedicated to **Laura Ingersoll Secord,** who risked her life by taking a grueling 32km (19-mile) trek through trackless frontier forest to reach Lieutenant Fitzgibbon's headquarters and warn him of an impending attack on his forces by American soldiers.

Free parking is available on the left as you enter the park.

14184 Niagara Pkwy., Queenston, Ont. © 905/262-4274. Free admission to park.

Please Don't Feed the Geese

A breed of nonmigratory Canada Geese has made a comfortable year-round home throughout southern Ontario, thanks to the unwitting generosity of folks who feed them grain and bread. These geese have no natural predators, and their numbers are growing unchecked, causing city parks and walkways to be overrun with geese in some areas. Goose droppings, ripped-up sod, and damaged grass are just a few of the problems that have resulted. Park authorities are pleading with the public *not* to feed Canada Geese, in order to encourage them to fly south in the winter and keep the population in check.

NIAGARA FALLS, NEW YORK

The oldest state park in the United States, the **Niagara Falls State Park** (© 716/ 278-1796) is located on the eastern shore of Niagara River in downtown Niagara Falls, New York. It's a great spot to enjoy a snack or watch a short film on the history of the Falls (nominal admission fee charged to view the film). Attractions vary in their admission price; the best deal is to obtain a **Passport to the Falls** (see "Tips: Best Value Niagara Falls Experience" above). If you want to learn more about the natural and local history of Niagara Falls, and the Niagara gorge, the **Niagara Gorge Discovery Center** is located inside the Niagara Falls State Park. A multiscreen theater gives you a 180-degree perspective on how the Niagara Gorge was formed as the Niagara River eroded rock and soil over a time span of 12,000 years. The **Niagara Gorge Trailhead Building** is next to the **Discovery Center.** From this point, you can access hiking, walking, and cycling trails. Call © **716/278-1780** for more information. Also on the site is a 9m-high (30-ft.) outdoor climbing wall with three degrees of difficulty.

ST. CATHARINES

The city of **St. Catharines** has earned the title of Ontario's Garden City. More than 1,000 acres of gardens, parks, and trails are within the city limits, all open for the public to enjoy. One of St. Catharines' jewels is **Burgoyne Woods,** accessed from Edgedale Road, off Glendale Avenue. Families will find this park particularly appealing, as there are swimming and wading pools, a playground, and plenty of picnic areas and nature trails. Paved trails are wheelchair accessible. **Ontario Jaycee Gardens** is one of Niagara's prettiest garden displays and St. Catharines' largest single planting of annual and perennial flowering plants. The northern perimeter of the park overlooks Old Port Dalhousie, including Martindale Pond and the Royal Canadian Henley Rowing Course. The land was originally part of the third Welland Canal. The Gardens are located on Ontario Street, north of the QEW and south of Lakeport Road. On the edge of the downtown core, **Montebello Park** is designated under the Ontario Heritage Act. Noteworthy features in the park include a magnificent rose garden with more than 1,300 rose bushes, and a band shell and pavilion dating from 1888. Mature shade trees cast their majestic branches over walking paths, picnic tables, and a children's playground. The park is located at the corner of Lake Street and Ontario Street in downtown St. Catharines. Avid gardeners will enjoy the **Stokes Seeds Flower Trial Gardens,** one of the official sites of All-American Trial Gardens. July and August are the peak months for viewing the flowers, which are spread over several acres of farmland. It's located off Lakeshore Road, between Seventh and Fifth streets.

Kids A Playground for All

Along the Niagara Street frontage of Lester B. Pearson Park in St. Catharines, there is a special place. The Infinity Playplace, funded by the St. Catharines Kiwanis Club, is designed to offer play opportunities that can be enjoyed by all children, regardless of ability. A looped ramp system provides wheelchair access, visual orientation strips are placed at openings, and wide decks are featured. The entire surface is made of rubber to allow full accessibility.

Farm Living Is the Thing for Me

Experience the fruits of the earth up close—Niagara soil nurtures juicy fruit orchards, world-class vineyards, and expansive lush farms. As you drive around the Niagara region, stop by one of the many roadside stands for fresh produce, just hours from the vine or branch to the basket. Or spend a happy hour or two picking your own strawberries in June, sour cherries in mid-July, or pumpkins in October at farms such as **Kar-Dean Fruit Farms** (3320 First Ave., Vineland Station, Ont.; © **905/562-4394**), **Sommers' Family Farm** (290 Main St. W., Grimsby, Ont.; © **905/945-4448**), or **Mathias Farms** (1909 Effingham St., Fonthill, Ont.; © **905/892-6166**).

If you're interested in touring a working farm, try one of the many agri-tourism farms, such as **Puddicombe Estate Farms & Winery** (1468 Hwy. #8, Winona, Ont.; © **905/643-1015**; www.puddicombefarms.com). This 208-year-old family farm has lots to do. Learn about wine grapes on a wagon-ride tour, or taste estate wine while munching on some cheese and crackers on a wine tour on the farm, starting at C$10 (US$9.50). Pick your own in-season fruits or buy already-picked cherries, pears, or apples. Enjoy a hearty lunch at the bakery cafe and bring home some goodies from the general store.

For specialty food items visit the huge gourmet marketplace at **Kurtz Orchards,** located at 16006 Niagara Pkwy., Niagara-on-the-Lake, Ont. (© **905/468-2937**; www.kurtzorchards.com). In the marketplace, sample homemade mustards, specialty teas, maple syrup, Ontario honey, oils and vinegars, and chunky cookies. Watch how they're made at demonstrations, or try a work-shop—visit the website for event times. Tour the 100-acre farm on a tractor-pulled tram led by Mr. Kurtz himself, starting at C$20 (US$19), which includes a farm lunch.

White Meadows Farms (2519 Effingham St., Pelham, Ont.; © **905/682-0642**) is a maple syrup farm where visitors can get their fill of all things maple. They also grow grapes and raise dairy cows. White Meadows offers a year-round sweet shop, with maple sweets and syrup. Spring (Feb to mid-Apr) includes pancake weekends complete with preserves. When the sap starts to flow—February and March—join events revolving around "sugaring off," where visitors can make and taste fine Canadian maple syrup.

For something less sweet but also a good bet for the taste buds, visit the **Niagara Herb Farm** (1177 York Rd., Niagara-on-the-Lake, Ont.; © **905/262-5690**; www.niagaraherbfarm.com). Stroll through gardens with more than 350 varieties of culinary, medicinal, fragrant, and native herbs (book tours during summer months only). There is also a retail barn open March through December. Spend a summer Sunday afternoon at an herbal or craft workshop. Events include the Annual Open House, National Herb Week, and the Lavender Festival. Take home a satchel of lavender or jar of herbal jelly at the gift barn, open year-round.

7 Outdoor Pursuits

BIRDING

The **Niagara River Corridor** has been designated as a "Globally Significant Important Bird Area" by major conservation groups in Canada and the United States. The river is a significant winter feeding zone for migrating birds, since the swiftly moving water keeps the river free of ice at a time of year when many other waterways are frozen over. Gulls, in particular, use the Niagara River as a major stopping-off point on their migratory flights. Almost half of the world's 43 species of gull have been identified by birders along the Niagara River. Species that have been noted include Bonaparte's gull, Franklin's and Sabine's gull, and rarely seen species such as the California, Slaty-backed, and Ross's gulls. The best time of year to view gulls is from mid-November to mid-January.

The **Niagara Gorge** is a prime spot for birders, not only because small fish are abundant in the river, but also because large fish are sucked into the hydro turbines and chopped into pieces, which in turn attract gulls to the area. Overlooking the gorge at the site of the Sir Adam Beck power station, located on the Niagara Parkway north of the Butterfly Conservatory, many birds can be seen. The **Hydro Reservoir** is home to many gulls, ducks, geese, and herons. A footpath circles the reservoir and can be accessed from behind 2058 Stanley Ave. in north Niagara Falls, Ontario. Just upriver from the Horseshoe Falls on the Canadian side, opposite the Niagara Parks Greenhouse, a variety of birds may be seen, including purple sandpiper, harlequin duck, and red-necked and red phalarope. Other spots include the Niagara Glen Nature Reserve, the Niagara Parks Botanical Gardens, and the Whirlpool Rapids Overlook (by the Whirlpool Aero Car). **The Beamer Memorial Conservation Area** (mentioned below) is also a wonderful forest for exploring and watching wildlife—experience views of Forty-mile Creek Valley, Lake Ontario's shoreline, and the escarpment ridge.

BOATING

Opportunities for boating are plentiful in the Niagara Region, including the major waterways of **Lake Ontario, Lake Erie,** the **Niagara River,** and the **Welland Canal.** Numerous smaller waterways are suitable for canoes and kayaks. Docking and boat-launching facilities are of good quality and are situated along the Niagara River, Lake Ontario, and Lake Erie shores. For detailed information and contact addresses on all aspects of recreational boating in Niagara, obtain a copy of the annual *Ontario Marina Directory* by contacting the **Ontario Marine Operators Association** (**OMOA;** Village Square Mall, 2 Poyntz St., Ste. 49, Penetanguishene, Ont., L9M 1M2; © **888/547-6662;** omoa@omoa.com).

WELLAND CANAL   If you wish to navigate a leisure craft through the Welland Canal between Lake Erie and Lake Ontario, contact the St. Lawrence Seaway Management Corporation at © **905/641-1932** for information, regulations, and fees involved in traveling via the canal.

ST. CATHARINES   Canoeists, kayakers, and yachtsmen and -women are fond of the Lake Ontario shoreline and its connecting tributaries. Call © **800/305-5134** for more information, or visit **www.stcatharines.ca**. In 1999, St. Catharines was host to the World Rowing Championships and, since 1903, has been a major rowing attraction.

Cycling & Walking Tours

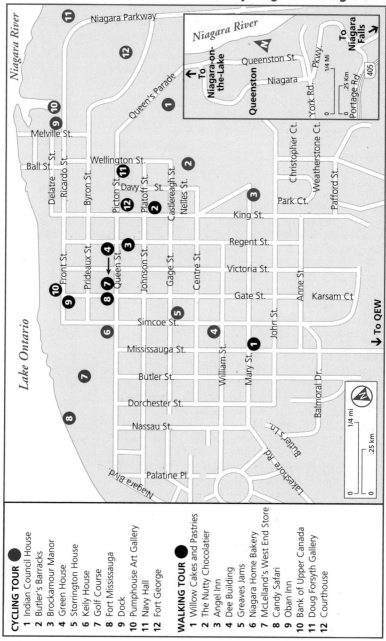

CYCLING TOUR
1 Indian Council House
2 Butler's Barracks
3 Brockamour Manor
4 Green House
5 Storrington House
6 Kelly House
7 Golf Course
8 Fort Mississauga
9 Dock
10 Pumphouse Art Gallery
11 Navy Hall
12 Fort George

WALKING TOUR
1 Willow Cakes and Pastries
2 The Nutty Chocolatier
3 Angel Inn
4 Dee Building
5 Greaves Jams
6 Niagara Home Bakery
7 McLelland's West End Store
8 Candy Safari
9 Oban Inn
10 Bank of Upper Canada
11 Doug Forsyth Gallery
12 Courthouse

PORT DALHOUSIE   You'll find **Martindale Pond** located between the Henley Bridge on the QEW and Port Dalhousie harbor. The **Henley Rowing Course** is home of the annual **Royal Canadian Henley Regatta** (www.henleyregatta.ca).

NIAGARA RIVER   If you are looking for a public marina on the river, the only one on the Canadian side is **Miller's Creek Marina** at 2400 Niagara Pkwy., Fort Erie, Ont. (✆ 905/871-4428), which allows Upper River access only. There are 135 seasonal docks, boat launch ramp, gas pump, showers, and washroom facilities.

PORT COLBORNE   Port Colborne is a popular center for sailing and power boat enthusiasts; the town hosts a number of sailing regattas and dockside events during the summer months. Port Colborne has three marinas, the largest of which is **Sugarloaf Harbour Marina,** featuring 350 seasonal berths, 150 guest docks, showers, washrooms, restaurant, four-lane boat launch ramp, and more (3 Marina Rd.; ✆ 905/835-6644).

CROSS-COUNTRY SKIING

The Niagara region has a multitude of trails, which can be accessed in the winter for cross-country skiing. The most easily accessible for visitors is the **Niagara River Recreational Trail,** which runs alongside the Niagara River Parkway between Fort Erie in the south and Niagara-on-the-Lake in the north. The trail is ungroomed, but it is popular with skiers and you are likely to find tracks to follow. Just park your vehicle in any designated parking area along the east side of the Niagara Parkway, step into your skis, and off you go. Many of the conservation areas are also open to skiers, including **Short Hills Provincial Park** in St. Catharines, **Balls Falls** in Vineland, and **Niagara State Park** on the U.S. side.

FISHING

Some of the best sport fishing in North America is found in Niagara, home to more freshwater species than anywhere on the continent. Game fish found in the waters of the Niagara region include coho salmon, rainbow trout, lake trout, walleye, yellow perch, smallmouth bass, northern pike, and muskellunge. Chinook salmon can be found in Lake Ontario between April and September; from September to November you can try your luck in the Niagara River. Some species have open and closed seasons; contact the Ontario Ministry of Natural Resources (see below) for more information. For information on dock fishing, boat launching, and annual fishing derbies, call the **Game & Fish Association** at ✆ 905/937-6335.

To fish in Ontario, those aged 18 and over must obtain a valid fishing permit, as stipulated by the Ministry of Natural Resources. Ontario residents, other Canadian residents, and nonresidents all need different licenses. More information is available by calling ✆ 800/387-7011, or visiting online at **www.mnr.gov.on.ca/MNR/fishing**. Fishing is permitted on the Welland River, along the Niagara River, and on Lake Ontario and Lake Erie. Note that there is a catch-and-release program in the Dufferin Islands, located just a short way upriver from the Falls on the Canadian side.

GOLF

The Niagara region is becoming a hot golf destination. Its varied topography and gentle climate are ideal attributes for hosting golf courses, and Niagara is teeming with them—more than 40 courses are contained within the Niagara Peninsula. The diverse landscape provides beginner and experienced golfers with a range of challenges on Niagara's well-designed and professionally maintained public and semiprivate golf courses.

The **golf season** in Niagara runs for 7 months, from April to October. Temperatures range from an average of 59°F (15°C) in April, to 82°F (28°C) in midsummer, and a comfortable 67°F (19°C) average monthly temperature in October. Greens fees vary widely, dependent upon the season, day of the week, time of day, whether it is an advance reservation or walk-in, and other factors. Expect to pay around C$100 (US$95) and up for a round, including a cart.

Thundering Waters Golf Club (6000 Marineland Pkwy., Niagara Falls, Ont.; *©* **905/357-6000** or 877/833-DALY; www.thunderingwaters.com), located just south of the Falls, is near Fallsview accommodations and the entertainment district in Niagara Falls, Ontario. Course designer John Daly attempted to hit a golf ball from Table Rock, next to the Horseshoe Falls in Canada, to Goat Island in the U.S., the island that lies between the Canadian and American falls. He failed, but the publicity was positive, and Daly proved to be a great ambassador for Niagara Falls and the new golf course. **Legends on the Niagara** (9561 Niagara Pkwy., Niagara Falls, Ont.; *©* **866/GOLF-NIA;** www.niagaraparksgolf.com/legends), another relatively new course, with 45 holes along the Niagara River, has earned a distinguished Platinum rating (based upon KPMG's scoring criteria). The course at **The Grand Niagara Resort** (8547 Grassy Brook Rd., Niagara Falls, Ont.; *©* **905/384-GOLF;** www.grandniagararesort.com) was designed by Rees Jones, one of the top golf course architects in the world. Currently there's an 18-hole course with a lounge and restaurant, and plans to expand into a hotel and more. **Royal Niagara Golf Club** (1 Niagara-on-the-Green Blvd., Niagara-on-the-Lake, Ont.; *©* **905/685-9501;** www.royalniagara.com) is situated alongside the Niagara Escarpment and is one of Niagara's most scenic courses. The **Whirlpool Public Golf Course** (3351 Niagara Pkwy., Box 150, Niagara Falls, Ont.; *©* **866/GOLF-NIA;** www.niagaragolftrail.com), on the Niagara Parkway, north of the Falls, is consistently ranked as one of the top public courses in Canada.

For more information on Niagara's golf courses, contact these online resources: the **Niagara Parks Commission** at **www.niagaraparks.com** and **www.niagaragolftrail. com**, the **Golf Association of Ontario** at **www.gao.ca**, or **Ontario's Online Golf Course Guide** at **www.ontgolf.ca**.

HIKING & BIKING

No matter what your speed—whether you like to take a leisurely bike ride stopping at every historical site, or if you love mud flying in your face while whipping down a "bum over the saddle" hill, Niagara's varied topography caters to all. If you're a hiker, spend a day in one of the more than 35 conservation areas, which vary from wetlands to waterfalls to lush forests full of rare and exotic wildlife. Most parks and conservation areas touch into the Niagara Escarpment and can make for challenging climbs—on bike or on foot. The Niagara Escarpment is a UNESCO World Heritage Site, hits heights up to 510m (1,675 ft.), and is home to more than 300 bird species, 53 mammals, 36 reptiles and amphibians, and 90 fish and flora, including 37 types of wild orchids. The sedimentary rock here formed more than 450 million years ago. What remains today is an outdoors enthusiast's playground. The escarpment rises near Rochester, New York, and runs west through the Niagara Peninsula, south of Lake Ontario and then to Hamilton, where it takes a turn north and heads straight up to the end of the Bruce Peninsula; see **www.escarpment.org**. Bring maps, water, and a friend, if venturing out.

The Niagara community has also made huge strides in organizing well-maintained, paved, multiuse paths that pass by various historical sites and waterways of the region.

And if you're so inclined, put a basket on the front of a rented bike, visit some wineries, and take home some goodies.

BIKE RENTALS

If you want to pick a path and go it alone, rent a bike from **Steve's Place Bicycle & Repair** (181 Niagara Blvd., Fort Erie, Ont.; © **888/649-BIKE**). Steve rents hybrid bikes (cross between a road and a mountain bike) for C$25 (US$24) a day or C$100 (US$95) for a full week. Rentals include a lock, but you must provide your own helmet. The store is just off the Niagara River Trail—great location. Another spot to pick up a bike is **Zoom Leisure** (2017 Niagara Stone Road [Hwy. 55], Niagara-on-the-Lake, Ont.; © **866/811-6993**). Choose from Trek hybrid bikes, tandems, kids', or mountain bikes for off-road riding. Every bike comes with map, helmet, and bike lock. Prices are around C$12 (US$11) per hour; C$20 (US$19) half-day up to 3 hours; or C$30 (US$29) for full day, until dark.

THE BRUCE TRAIL

The **Bruce Trail** is a meandering path that begins at Queenston Heights and ends almost 850km (528 miles) later in Tobermory, on the northern tip of the Bruce Peninsula. Hikers experience fantastic views overlooking waterfalls, opening up through lush fauna and flora and a kaleidoscope of colors (biking is not permitted on the trails). Opened in 1967, it is proudly the oldest and longest trail of its kind in Canada. For more information, including maps, visit the Bruce Trail Association website: **www. brucetrail.org**. Bring a map and follow the trail markings: single white blazes (15cm-by-5cm/6 in.-by-2 in. marking on tree, created by chipping off a piece of the bark) mean walk straight ahead, while a double blaze, with another slightly lower, indicates a turn ahead—look ahead for another single blaze to confirm the path's direction, or simply go in the direction of the upper blaze. Side trails are marked in blue.

The **Niagara Bruce Trail section** runs between **Beamsville** and **Queenston,** overlooks the Niagara River, and passes through countless orchards and wineries, yet feels secluded and wild. Within this area there are six recommended hiking routes. The first and most popular is the Brock's Monument to **Woodend Conservation Area.** An hour into the trek provides undulating terrain that requires proper hiking shoes. Stay on the single white–marked trail. The 18km (11-mile) hike, east to west, has parking on either side. You'll get a great workout here and perhaps a few blisters to boot! Starting at the east end of Queenston Heights Park from the cairn, you'll first come across the **Queenston Quarry** (Queenston Trails) 2km (1 mile) into the hike, which deviates onto its own set of trails that highlight more of the Niagara Escarpment. For mountain biking, the area's fat-tire mecca is **Short Hills Provincial Park** in Pelham— a multiuse trail system with more than 10km (6 miles) of single-track trails (call **Ontario Parks** at © **800/667-1940,** or **Short Hills Provincial Park** direct at © **905/774-6642** in summer or 905/827-6911 in winter). Visit **www.friendsof shorthillspark.ca** for a downloadable trail map. The expansive 735-hectare (1,820-acre) day-use park includes six trails and the Bruce Trail and has a distinctly different landscape from the rest of Niagara. Short Hills is a series of small but steep hills formed during the last ice age. The **Swayze Falls** (6.2km/3.9-mile) trail and **Black Walnut** (4.3km/2.7-mile) trail are open for mountain bikers, as well as hikers and horse riders—follow the yellow trail markers. The Black Walnut starts on a wide fire road with single-track trails that lead into the forest and loop back to the main fire road. With plenty of roots and steep climbs, these offshoots will please intermediate-level mountain bikers. Also note that the Scarlet Tanager, Hemlock Valley, Terrace Creek, and Paleozoic trails are for hikers only. The Terrace Creek is the best for hikers of intermediate ability (loads of hills). It takes about 2 hours to complete the trail and includes two waterfalls within the park. A great jumping-off point is the St. John's Education Centre.

A new mountain bike trail, maintained by local riders, is the **12-mile Creek** trail. It makes a 12-mile loop (obviously), which is about 20km of twisty single track. Starting at the foot of the Burgoyne Bridge, off Glendale Avenue in St. Catharines, the trail will provide hard-core riders a good fix. For a longer trail that follows the creek, park at Brock University, and start riding behind the school to access the 12-mile Creek trail.

In Lincoln County, just down the road from Rockway Glen, **Louth Conservation Area** has two magnificent waterfalls and a cornucopia of flowers. Intersecting with the Bruce Trail, there's also a 3km (2-mile) side trail with harder terrain. This place is quite secluded—don't be surprised if you don't see anyone. A far busier spot, and the touristiest, is **Ball's Falls Conservation Area,** which is just off the QEW. The trail is a flat, family-friendly jaunt that takes about 30 minutes to finish. The area is best known for its 19th-century hamlet—a barn, pavilion, church, and two waterfalls spread across 80 hectares (200 acres). The falls themselves are two-thirds the height of Niagara Falls, although the volume of water is considerably less.

OTHER TRAILS

GREATER NIAGARA CIRCLE ROUTE   Closer to civilization is the Greater Niagara Circle Route (© **905/680-9477;** campaignoffice@bellnet.ca), which is a 150km (90-mile), mostly paved path for cyclists, in-line skaters, and walkers—the 3m-wide (10-ft.) trail spans from Lake Erie to Lake Ontario. The trails are wheelchair accessible, save for a few railway crossings. The trail includes four sections:

- **The Friendship Trail,** part of the Trans-Canada Link Trail, extends from Port Colborne to Fort Erie along Lake Erie—about 14km (9 miles). The route can be accessed in Fort Erie near the Ridgeway Battlefield site (1km north on Ridge Rd.), and along Lake Erie on Windmill Point Road and Stone Mill Road. The trail follows the abandoned CN Rail line, passing through some quiet residential streets, and is great for a short ride or walking and jogging. Not the most picturesque ride.
- **The Niagara River Recreation Trail,** which spans all the way from Fort Erie to the tip of Niagara-on-the-Lake, is a great family ride, with plenty of grassy sections to stop and have a snack. Approximately 60km (35 miles), it is also part of the Trans-Canada Link Trail—access points include the north entrance from Fort George in Niagara-on-the-Lake. The trail is divided into four sections, each taking about an hour or two to complete on a bike: Niagara-on-the-Lake to Queenston is the busiest stretch and feels too congested on summer weekends; Queenston to the Whirlpool Aero Car; Chippawa to Black Creek; and Black Creek to Fort Erie (this is the least busy and frankly, just as scenic). While strolling or riding, take in the hundred or so historical plaques that tell of soldiers defending the frontier and of significant Upper Canadian historical sites such as Fort George, McFarland House, and early battle sites. Seasonal washrooms and free parking are available throughout.

- **The Waterfront Trail** picks up from the Recreation Trail going all the way to Brockville (outside of the Niagara Circle). But beware: During the majority of the Niagara-on-the-Lake section, there is neither waterfront nor a trail—riders are stuck on the side of the road and the lake is not even in view! Starting in St. Catharines, the trail signage to the gravel path is poor, but once you find your way, the trail finally follows the lake. The upside is that passing through more than 31 communities, including several farmlands and wineries, there's a chance to pick up wine and local fruit. In total, it spans 450km (280 miles). Access points include Lakeshore Road and another near Port Weller in Niagara-on-the-Lake, and Ansell Park in St. Catharines. For a detailed downloadable map, visit **www.waterfronttrail.org**.

- **The Welland Canal Recreation Trail** spans all the way from Lake Ontario to Lake Erie on a single paved path that hugs the canal waterway and passes through St. Catharines, Thorold, and Welland, finishing at Port Colborne. This is my favorite easy leisure ride. On hot days, a cool breeze comes off the water. Watching the ships in the canal is an added bonus. Access this section north of Lock 3 in St. Catharines or at the southern end of Seaway Park in Port Colborne. This trail is a bit busier, as it passes through towns and the sometimes-busy ports of the Welland Canal.

NIAGARA CONSERVATION AREAS ⚘ There are 36 separate conservation areas in the Niagara Region, operated by the **Niagara Peninsula Conservation Authority** (**© 905/788-3135;** www.conservation-niagara.on.ca). Visit the website for a complete list; and remember that these trails are open for hiking only! A good majority of the trails are for beginners and offer great scenery and wildlife viewing, but if you're a hiker, looking to cross streams and develop some well-earned blisters, I suggest the following.

The **Rockway Glen Conservation Area** is part of the Bruce Trail. The terrain features roller-coaster terrain crossing streams, rock faces, roots, and logs near a deep canyon; this is my idea of great hiking. Park your car at the Rockway Glen Community Centre (Pelham Rd., St. Catharines). Quite the opposite, in terms of terrain, but a spectacular place to view the escarpment, is **Beamer Memorial Conservation Area,** Ridge Road, Grimsby. The trail itself is a flat path that makes a loop and takes about 40 minutes to walk. There are also four lookout points—a great vantage point for bird-watching. Take the Lookout Trail to see the 23m (76-ft.) falls. Three wheelchair platforms lead to observation areas. About halfway through the loop, there's a side trail that jumps onto the Bruce Trail; the steep stairs going up the escarpment lead to a path that goes all the way into Grimsby. If you're looking for a harder climb, do the path to Grimsby and back to Beamer, which will take a couple of hours. Moving down the QEW to the east in Beamsville, there's another unique hike. Feeling more like Middle-earth (from *Lord of the Rings*) with trees strewn across the forest floor and giant ferns, I spent most of the time looking at the path to secure my steps on top of the mossy rocks at **Mountainview Conservation Area** (Mountainview Road, Beamsville). Occasionally there's a gap between the rocks leading to dark crevices—a Golem is rumored to live here. And still in the same area, **Louth Conservation area** (Staff Rd., Lincoln County) has undulating terrain, perhaps because a good chunk of it touches the escarpment; the trails also access the Bruce Trail. Louth is also blessed with two waterfalls.

Tips   **Scenic Drives along the Niagara Gorge and Niagara River**

On both sides of the border, you can take a leisurely drive alongside the Niagara River and Niagara Gorge. On the Canadian side (western shore), you can follow the Niagara Parkway all the way from Fort Erie at the southern end of the Niagara River to Niagara-on-the-Lake at the northern end, where it empties into Lake Ontario. On the U.S. side (eastern shore), start farther upriver, where the Robert Moses Parkway begins, first heading west at the junction with Interstate 90 and following it as it turns north with the natural bend in the river. You will pass through Niagara Falls State Park (or head through downtown Niagara Falls, although it is a less picturesque route), then through several other state parks, including Whirlpool, Earl W. Brydges Artpark, and Joseph Davis, ending at the northern end of the Niagara River in Fort Niagara State Park.

If you're in the Port Colborne area, I suggest the **Wainfleet Wetlands,** Quarry Road, Wainfleet. The area has informal trails, where hikers can see fossils—but please, don't take them home. **Wainfleet Bog,** Erie Peat Road, Wainfleet, near Port Colborne, has more than 800 hectares (2,000 acres) of land—be sure to bring a compass. Trails are short but the wetland scenery is worth the trek.

Niagara Glen Nature Reserve ★★   "The gorge" trail follows the river alongside rushing water. With side paths that take you onto flat rocks right at the water level, it's your best bet for an up-close view of the water at work—and it's free. It is located alongside the Niagara Gorge between the Whirlpool and the Niagara Parks Botanical Gardens, and you must descend the gorge to get to the trail, which is a steep, steep drop. There's a series of seven different pathways that link through this nature reserve ranging in length from .4km (a quarter-mile) to 3.3km (2 miles). Along the **Eddy Path** you will see the Wilson Terrace Passages, which are narrow passageways between huge boulders that toppled from Wintergreen Cliff many thousands of years ago. Along the **River Path,** you will see Devil's Hole, which is the narrowest point of the Niagara River. Rock beds cover a good portion of both paths so wear good shoes—I can't imagine running on these trails either. You'll know you have reached the end when you start to see painted blue symbols on trees. Then watch for a purple circle painted around the tree symbols. When you spot the one that says "Up," you'll start making your way up the side of the gorge to the top. Note that all of the paths, or the access to them, are steep in places (River Path is the flattest path, but you need to descend the cliff to reach it).

The Niagara Parks Commission produces an excellent small field guide (C$10/US$9.50) in a miniature hard-backed binder with a history and description of the Glen and listings of the trees, vines, flowers, insects, and birds to be found in this unique habitat, complete with beautiful color photos to aid identification of species as you explore the Glen. The reserve has a parking lot, gift shop, small cafe, and washrooms located at the side of the Niagara Parkway on a table of land known as Wintergreen Flats (1km/half-mile) north from Whirlpool Golf Course on Niagara Parkway, Niagara Falls, Ontario (*©* **877/NIA-PARK;** www.niagaraparks.com/nature/rectrail area.php).

8 Organized Tours

BY BUS

Grayline Niagara   I wouldn't necessarily stop at all the spots offered on these tours on my own, but I did appreciate the guide's commentary on the gorge, the Falls, and the history of the area. I recommend the Illumination Tour (6–10pm), which includes the Journey Behind the Falls, Skylon Tower, Sir Harry Oaks Gardens, and a view of the Whirlpool. But if you're used to doing your own research before you visit a place, I don't recommend this tour; besides the Journey Behind the Falls, the rest of the attractions are free. The oldest and largest of the bus tour companies, Grayline is accessible from selected hotel lobby desks or by prearranged pickup. Tours are also available through Expedia, Travelocity, and other Web search engines. A full-day tour, lasting 7 to 8 hours, includes similar sights and more, with dinner and boxed luncheon. Advance reservations or same-day reservations are accepted, and there are discounts for groups of 10 or more.

3466 Niagara Falls Blvd. N., Tonawanda, NY. ✆ 800/695-1603. www.grayline.com. Half-day from C$80 (US$76) adults, C$60 (US$57) children; full day C$230 (US$219) adults and children. Tours and times vary.

Niagara Airbus   This company offers bus tours to wineries, sightseeing tours, and packages that include lunch. The Niagara Falls tour, for example, includes lunch and a ride on the *Maid of the Mist* (or a journey behind the Falls in winter). See the Floral Clock, Botanical Gardens, Queenston Heights, and Spanish Aero Car Observation Area, then stop in Niagara-on-the-Lake for free time to stroll the pretty streets and do some shopping. Buses will pick up guests at any hotel or bed-and-breakfast in the region.

8626 Lundy's Lane, Niagara Falls, Ont. ✆ 905/374-8111. www.niagaraairbus.com. Tours start from C$60 (US$57). Book online and receive 10% discount.

BY BIKE

Niagara World Wine Tours   This is your best bet for leisure rides. The guide takes you through less-traveled (meaning away from the tourists) paths in the forest and behind the vineyards. The guide stops occasionally to impart some history and juicy gossip (about historical figures, of course). Tours are geared toward adults. Two bike tours are run a day; the one that leaves at 11:30am includes a lunch under a canopy in the woods and stops at four wineries (including two tours—a good mix of large and small wineries), while the later tour includes three wineries. For hard-core riders, there are longer tours offered in nearby Beamsville and Jordan.

92 Picton St., Niagara-on-the-Lake, Ont. ✆ 800/680-7006. www.niagaraworldwinetours.com. Tours C$65–C$120 (US$62–US$114).

Zoom Leisure   There's more *leisure* than zoom as you meander through the streets in between the vineyards on these tours—but that's just about the speed you need for tasting wines all afternoon. There are two tours a day and guides are matched to the personality of the riders; you can opt for a harder ride (i.e., more hills and faster terrain). Providing more than 100 bikes to choose from, Zoom Leisure provides child-friendly bike accessories such as trailers and child seats that mount on the bike. Other amenities include handlebar bags, bells, water-bottle cages, and kickstands. One tour leaves at 11am and includes a packed lunch—riders cycle for about an hour before having a big-spread picnic, and then it's on to three or four wineries for wine tastings, which may include a tour. The shorter ride, leaving at 1pm, includes three winery stops. Each bike has an optional basket in the front to bring home goodies from your voyage. Reserve tours in advance (48–72 hr. ahead for most).

2017 Niagara Stone Rd., Niagara-on-the-Lake, Ont. ✆ 866/811-6993 or 905/468-2366. www.zoomleisure.com. Tours start C$65–C$95 (US$62–US$90).

BY BOAT

Dalhousie Princess Cruises   Between May and September, enjoy historic Port Dalhousie harbor from a grand boat with an open deck. View the Welland Canal, wine country, and the southern shore of Lake Ontario. Have lunch or dinner or try a themed cruise, which may include Brit Night, fireworks dinner, or Hypnotist Dinner featuring Danny Zzzz (C$50/US$48). Book in advance—reservations for themed cruises must be booked a minimum of 48 hours prior to the cruise.

9 Lock St., St. Catharines, Ont. ✆ 905/937-BOAT. www.dalhousieprincess.com. C$45 (US$43) family pass, C$20 (US$19) adults, C$17 (US$16) seniors and students with ID, C$13 (US$12) children 6–12, free for children 5 and under.

9 City Strolls

Niagara-on-the-Lake is a picturesque town, so I've provided two tours, one for those equipped with a bike and the other for people wearing comfortable walking shoes, with plenty of chances to stop and shop. I also added a tour of St. Catharines, which is inland and has a different feel, for another tour of a historical area.

CYCLING TOUR	HISTORICAL NIAGARA-ON-THE-LAKE

Start:	Fort George parking lot, link onto Greater Niagara Circle.
Finish:	Fort George.
Time:	Plan to spend 1 to 2 hours, with time for stopping.
Best Time:	Take this tour in the morning as shops begin to open and the town is at its most peaceful.

This tour will take cyclists through some of the most historical areas of the town and Lake Ontario views.

① Cross Queen's Parade to the recreational pathway. This path is the Otter Trail. Near the small bridge stands the Indian Council House (ca. 1796), headquarters of the British Indian Department. During the War of 1812, British and Natives met here to discuss politics.

② The **Butler's Barracks** were constructed to replace Fort George after the War of 1812. It was here that soldiers trained to fight in the Boer War, World War I and World War II, and the Korean War. Turn right, crossing King Street, and continue on Mary Street.

③ At the corner of King Street and Mary Street stands **Brockamour Manor** (433 King St.). Here it is said that Sophia Shaw became engaged to General Sir Isaac Brock. Brock never returned home, coming to an untimely death at the Battle of Queenston Heights. The ghost of Sophia is said to walk the halls sobbing. Follow Mary Street to Simcoe Street and turn right.

④ First occupied as a private home, and then becoming a residential school, **Green House** (20 Simcoe St.) has been substantially altered and changed during its existence. Continue straight on Simcoe Street.

5 One of the first homes built after the War of 1812, **Storrington House** (289 Simcoe St.) was residence to Adam Lockhart, the secretary for the Niagara Harbour and Dock Company. Servants' quarters were built for the hired help.

6 Continue on Simcoe and cross Queen Street, passing by **Keily House** (ca. 1832). Built for lawyer Charles Richardson, this house is built on the soil of **Fort Mississauga.** The sweeping veranda around the house was built in the late 19th century. In the cellar there is a long vaulted chamber—a tunnel that connects to Fort Mississauga. The house is now operating as the Charles Inn.

7 Behind the Charles Inn is the **Niagara-on-the-Lake golf club,** the oldest golf course in Canada. Back in the day, golfers started here for 9 holes, and then moved on to Fort George to finish the game. Behind the Niagara-on-the-Lake golf course sits Fort Mississauga.

8 Built at the end of the War of 1812, **Fort Mississauga** was built to replace Fort George. A few parts of the tower were built from limestone from Ontario's first lighthouse, which was burned here by enemy forces in 1813.

9 Follow on to the end of Simcoe onto Front Street. Front Street is renamed Ricardo Street beyond King. To the left is the dock area used in the early 1780s. Many large steamboats were built in the yards of **Niagara Harbour and Dock Company.** Continue along until the end of the street.

10 At one time, the engine that pumped water into the town was housed at what is now the **Pumphouse Art Gallery.** Go straight along the Niagara Parkway.

11 Lieutenant-Governor John Graves Simcoe lived and worked for the Executive Council of Upper Canada on this site in 1792. American cannons destroyed the original buildings in 1813; they were rebuilt in 1815. To the right are ramparts of Fort George. At **Navy Hall,** Ricardo Street becomes the Niagara River Parkway, which leads all the way to Niagara Falls. Continue here to Queen's Parade, and cross the street to link up with John Street, where the path continues. Continue along the path, and then take a right to link up with the **Otter Trail** once again.

12 From 1796 until its capture by the American army in 1813, **Fort George** was the British military headquarters. Unfortunately, the Americans destroyed the original fort, and after the war it was completely abandoned by the British. In 1930, it was reconstructed. Stop by for a tour, complete with costumed guides and a history lesson or two.

WALKING TOUR 1	NIAGARA-ON-THE-LAKE SHOPPING DISTRICT

Start:	Willow Cakes and Pastries, corner of Mary and Mississauga streets.
Finish:	The Courthouse.
Time:	A slow 1-hour walk.
Best Time:	Midafternoon, when the lunch crowd has gone—stop for tea and browse the stores.

Niagara-on-the-Lake offers some one-of-a-kind stores filled with unique gifts and tasty delights. Stroll and enjoy.

1 Stop into **Willow Cakes and Pastries** (242 Mary St.) for coffee and a croissant. You can read the local paper and fuel up for your walk to come.

2 Just past Platoff Street, find **The Nutty Chocolatier** (233 King St.)—a great place to fill up on homemade fudge, truffles, and creamy Belgian chocolate. On Loonie Tuesday, stop in for a C$1 (US95¢) ice-cream cone.

❸ Proceed along Market Street and turn left onto to Regent Street. Pass by the **Angel Inn** (224 Regent St.; ca. 1825)—a fine place for a pint of ale or glass of Niagara wine. But beware—they say this house is haunted by a solider from the War of 1812. Turn left onto Queen Street.

❹ The **Dee Building** (54–58 Queen St.; ca. 1843), a two-story limestone building, has housed everything from a clothing store to grocers. Take note of the original shop front facing Regent Street.

❺ For a homemade souvenir, stop off at **Greaves Jams** (55 Queen St.; ca. 1845). Take note of the architectural features of this building—deep boxed cornices on the hip roof.

❻ And for something to put under the jam, pick up a bag of goodies from **Niagara Home Bakery** (66 Queen St.; ca. 1875). Enter the store through a double leafed door and enjoy the sunlight streaming in through the glassed transom over the doorway.

❼ Past Victoria Street is **McLelland's West End Store** (106 Queen St.; ca. 1835). To accommodate the boom in population during the 1830s, locals could pick up groceries and their fix of wines and spirits. The large T sign is a sign of a provisioner—the store that sold everything! The store expanded into 108 Queen St.

❽ The **Candy Safari** (135 Queen St.; ca. 1835) is a Gothic Revival house, originally built as a residence and shop for shoemaker and leatherworker John Burns. Today, it satisfies the sweet-tooth cravings of shoppers.

❾ Turn right onto Gate Street; on the corner of Front and Gate, take a peek at the **Oban Inn.** The original inn was built in 1822, and became a hotel in 1895. A fire destroyed the building in 1992. But, as with all good things, it came back and remains true to its original form.

❿ Turn right onto Front Street and walk toward 10 Front St.—the Bank of Upper Canada. With a stucco front and rough-cast side treatment, this old bank was rebuilt after the War of 1812. It still has the original steel vaults and is the location of a grand bed-and-breakfast now. Walk until Queen becomes Ricardo Street, then turn left onto Wellington Street and right onto Picton Street.

⓫ Stop in to browse the fascinating **Doug Forsyth Gallery** (92 Picton St.). Find unique etchings and paintings using fascinating print-making techniques.

⓬ Turn right on King Street, then right onto Queen Street to view the **Courthouse** (26 Queen St.; ca. 1847). This national historical site changed its function from a courthouse and jail cells to the town hall. The Shaw Festival was founded here and still performs in the Court House Theatre of the Shaw. From jail to theater—if only the walls could talk.

WALKING TOUR 2	HISTORIC DOWNTOWN ST. CATHARINES

Start:	Old Courthouse.
Finish:	Same location.
Time:	2 hours.
Best Time:	Take a midafternoon stroll through the area just after lunch.

Known as the garden city, St. Catharines' city streets are busting with color against the backdrop of well-maintained historical homes.

❶ Start at the **Old Courthouse,** constructed in 1849. Note the beautifully ornate stained glass transom and curving balustrades. On the St. James' side, notice the steer's head and wheat sheaf, recognizing the nearby market. The water fountain is a gift from Mayor Lucius Oille.

❷ Northeast on Church Street, you will find **St. Catherine of Alexandria Cathedral.** Built in 1845 for Irish Catholic immigrant workers—many working on the canal—the facade today is a wonderful example of English neo-Gothic.

❸ The lovely home at **134 Church St.** was a wedding gift from farmer Stephen Parnell to his daughter and son-in-law, local merchant James Wood, who would later become a prosperous merchant.

❹ Turn onto **King Street** and look for nos. **173–175.** This stream of row houses is typical of its era in 1860. Notice the red brick, popular frieze, and brackets at the roofline. Now, follow Academy Street east.

❺ Turn right onto St. Paul Street and note nos. **224–226.** This Italianate facade, with bulging exterior, reveals window shapes and large openings for windows, which were unique by 19th-century standards. It also resembles a palace on the Grand Canal in Venice, Italy.

❻ At **88 St. Paul St.,** built in 1869, marvel at the ornate decoration of the windows and the roofline with cast-iron markers on the facade.

❼ Turn onto **Ontario Street,** where nos. **37 and 39** are the former Masonic temple

buildings of 1873. Notice the cast-iron columns and window frames—a new material replacing brick and stone during its era.

❽ Returning back to St. Paul Street, overlooking Twelve-mile Creek to the south is the **statue of William Hamilton Merritt.** Merritt was a prominent businessman of the 19th century. He also conceived of a water channel from Lake Erie to Lake Ontario, which became the Welland Canal. Cross to Yates Street and enter into the **Yates Street heritage district.**

❾ **24 Yates St.** was the home of miller John Woodward. This home is representative of an elegant 19th-century style, in contrast to the Italian style mentioned above.

❿ Turn right onto Norris Place. A carriage maker built the home at **7 Norris Place;** its sidelights and transom above the doorway are typical of its day.

⓫ Turn left off Norris; on a diagonal you will see **105 Ontario St.,** where there's another example of row houses from 1860 built for Josiah Holmes and his partner W. W. Greenwood.

⓬ **83 Ontario St.** is the former home of J. F. Mittleberger, another prosperous businessman of his day. Take a look at the unique faces on the door.

⓭ Across the street is the **Welland Canal House Hotel,** built in the 1850s. Today it is a student residence. Walk 2 blocks farther to Queen Street and turn left.

⓮ The last house on the tour is **64 Queen St.,** former home of Chauncey Yale, an American manufacturer. Notice the familiar style of home and fence, which represents a traditional home (ca. 1851).

8

The Wine-Country Experience

Since its transformation over the past quarter of a century into a world-class wine-producing area, Niagara can step forward to stand proudly alongside venerable Old World and other New World wine regions. There are still improvements to be made and plans to execute, but the vision shared by the growers, producers, and merchants is strong and clear. Niagara's wine region is a rising star.

1 Introducing the Niagara Wine Region

HISTORY OF THE NIAGARA WINE REGION

Niagara's vibrant wine industry had humble beginnings, with the first European settlers making use of the native *Vitis labrusca* grapes, which were ideal for juice, preserves, and desserts but unfortunately did not produce the light, dry, sophisticated style of table wines that dominates the world's markets today. During the 1900s, Niagara vintners achieved modest success with Canadian hybrids.

During the 1960s and 1970s, a number of enterprising growers began planting *Vitis vinifera* vines, the so-called noble grape varietals that produce many of the world's finest wines, such as chardonnay, cabernet, gamay, and Riesling. Fertile, rich soils and a unique microclimate make Niagara a prime grape-growing region; and, contrary to the expectations of most, the vinifera vines thrived.

The biggest contributor to the transformation of Ontario's wine industry was the introduction of international trade agreements in 1988. The loss of tariff and retail price protection put the retail price of Ontario wines on a par with imports from the world's most respected and well-established wine regions. The industry had to reinvent itself as a worthy contender. Growers, wineries, and the provincial government decided to revitalize the wine industry, and together they rose to the challenge.

Between 1989 and 1991, growers removed almost half of Ontario's labrusca and hybrid vines and replaced them, over time, with traditional European varieties, as part of a government-initiated program to move toward increased production of higher-quality table wines. The focus was firmly and permanently shifted to *Vitis vinifera* production.

Today, Niagara has approximately 16,000 acres under vine, in an area stretching from Niagara-on-the-Lake in the east to Grimsby in the west. More than 70 wineries now make their home in Niagara, many with fine restaurants and boutiques on-site. A large number offer wine tasting and tours to the public. Niagara wines consistently bring home medals and awards from many of the world's most prestigious wine competitions.

Tips

When you purchase a Niagara wine in a restaurant, wine boutique, or retail store, check the label for the designation **VQA (Vintners Quality Alliance)**. Wine-producing regions around the world establish governing bodies to dictate the conditions under which that region's wine is produced. The VQA in Ontario requires that wines with this designation have been made exclusively with grapes grown in one of the four recognized Ontario viticultural areas—Niagara Peninsula, Lake Erie North Shore, Pelee Island, and Prince Edward County. In addition, the wine must be made entirely in Ontario from officially approved grape varieties. These specifications ensure the consumer will receive a quality product and serve to protect the wine industry's reputation.

World attention has turned to the Niagara wine industry, not least because of the superb quality of its icewine, a dessert wine produced from grapes that have been left on the vine after the fall harvest to freeze naturally. The frozen grapes are handpicked and immediately pressed to capture the thick, yellow-gold liquid, high in natural sugars and acidity.

THE HEART OF A WINE REGION'S SUCCESS—*TERROIR*

Winegrowing, or viticulture, is more or less restricted to two temperate bands around the world—where the summers are warm enough to consistently ripen the grapes and the winters are cold enough to allow the vines a period of dormancy.

Although the macroclimate of a district is the major factor determining whether grapes can be grown at all, it is the microclimate, soil, and topography, and the effects that each of these characteristics have on each other, that influence the type of wine that can be produced in a particular area. The French have coined a term for this combination of climate, soil, and topography as it relates to the world of winemaking: *terroir.*

The Niagara wine region is situated in one of the world's most northerly grape-growing regions. Despite Niagara's emergence onto the world wine stage over the last quarter-century, many people are still surprised to learn that the Niagara Peninsula is an ideal zone for the production of high-quality grapes. In fact, the growing season in Niagara enjoys a similar climate to that of Burgundy, France.

The area is designated a "cool climate viticulture region." However, although many vine growers in cool climates have to contend with summers that are not warm enough to fully ripen the grapes, the unique climate of the Niagara peninsula provides a more conducive environment. The moderating influence of Lake Ontario and Lake Erie protects the region from extreme temperature fluctuations. The presence of the escarpment further moderates the climate.

Finally, the soil in the Niagara Peninsula is composed of deposits of clay, loam, sand, and gravel, which vary by district. The soil is also rich in essential minerals and trace elements originating from the variety of bedrock present in the region, providing important nutrients to the vines and contributing to the complexity of the wines produced.

Niagara Region Wineries

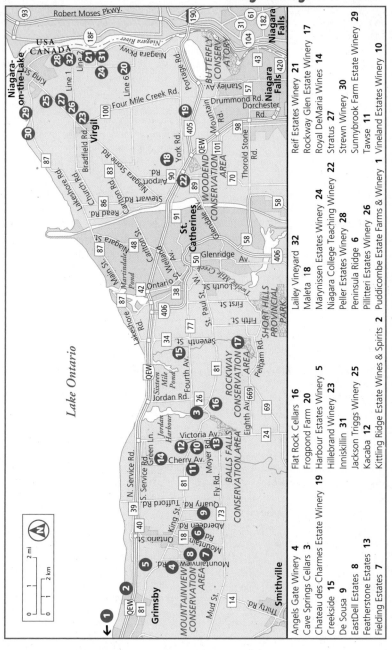

Angels Gate Winery **4**
Cave Springs Cellars **3**
Chateau des Charmes Estate Winery **19**
Creekside **15**
De Sousa **9**
EastDell Estates **8**
Featherstone Estates **13**
Fielding Estates **7**

Flat Rock Cellars **16**
Frogpond Farm **20**
Harbour Estates Winery **5**
Hillebrand Winery **23**
Inniskillin **31**
Jackson Triggs Winery **25**
Kacaba **12**
Kittling Ridge Estate Wines & Spirits **2**

Lailey Vineyard **32**
Maleta **18**
Marynissen Estates Winery **24**
Niagara College Teaching Winery **22**
Peller Estates Winery **28**
Peninsula Ridge **6**
Pillitteri Estates Winery **26**
Puddicombe Estate Farms & Winery **1**

Reif Estates Winery **21**
Rockway Glen Estate Winery **17**
Royal DeMaria Wines **14**
Stratus **27**
Strewn Winery **30**
Sunnybrook Farm Estate Winery **29**
Tawse **27**
Vineland Estates Winery **10**

2 Essentials

THE WINE REGION IN BRIEF

The Wine Council of Ontario has divided the Niagara Peninsula Wine Region into seven districts: Winona, Grimsby, Beamsville; Vineland, Jordan, St. Catharines, and Niagara-on-the-Lake. For ease of discussion, these districts have been used here, although the wine region extends seamlessly from Fifty Road in the west to the shores of the Niagara River in the east, bordered on the north by Lake Ontario and the south by the Niagara Escarpment. The entire area stretches about 55km (34 miles) from Fifty Road to the Niagara River, so if you were really keen to sample wines from right across the region it could be done in a day. However, it is much more relaxing to home in on a small section of the map and meander up and down the country roads at a leisurely pace.

GRIMSBY & BEAMSVILLE The highest point of this part of the Niagara Escarpment sits behind Grimsby. There are a few wineries in the extreme west of this area, but most are concentrated south of Beamsville, in an area bordered by Thirty Road on the west and Cherry Avenue on the east. The country roads winding up and down the escarpment are flanked by deciduous trees (not forgetting the vineyards!) and are particularly picturesque in the summer and fall.

JORDAN & VINELAND This winegrowing area extends roughly from Cherry Avenue in the west to the east side of the Welland Canal and the city of St. Catharines. The **Twenty Valley Creek** tumbles down the side of the escarpment, eventually flowing into Jordan Harbour and then Lake Ontario. With more than two dozen wineries, historical Jordan Village, and numerous sites of natural beauty, this area is a great place to be based for an overnight stay or weekend of wine-country pleasure.

NIAGARA-ON-THE-LAKE This wine area is bordered by the Welland Canal, Lake Ontario, the Niagara River, and the Niagara Escarpment. The wineries here are primarily in two clusters: one in the lee of the escarpment, the other in the northeast of the region, mostly on flat land surrounding Niagara-on-the-Lake. Many are located either right on the Niagara Parkway, along Niagara Stone Road (Hwy. 55), or on Lakeshore Road. The town of Niagara-on-the-Lake has a huge choice of accommodations; historical inns and heritage bed-and-breakfast properties are in abundance. Despite the large number of rooms in the town, it can be difficult, if not almost impossible, to secure a room at short notice, so book well ahead if you plan to stay there.

VISITOR INFORMATION

The **Wine Council of Ontario (WCO),** a nonprofit trade organization, produces an excellent map of Niagara's wine country with the official **Wine Route** clearly marked. As you drive along the highways and byways of the Niagara Peninsula, you will see these distinctive road signs, which feature the symbol of a bunch of white grapes against a deep blue background, often with names of vineyards, distances, and arrows added to aid your navigation. The map is available as a pocket fold-out and also appears as a pull-out centerfold in the annual **Official Guide to the Wineries of Ontario.** The guide and pocket map are widely available throughout the Niagara region—at tourism offices, wineries, and retail stores that carry wine. Visit their website at **http://winesofontario.org** for a wealth of information, including an events calendar, advice on matching wine and food, trip-planning advice, maps, a list of

Niagara Wineries in the U.S.

Nestled between the escarpment and Lake Ontario, in an area northeast of Niagara Falls, New York, lie a handful of wineries. A brochure entitled *Niagara Wine Trail USA,* with descriptions of the wineries and a map showing their locations, can be obtained from tourist information centers in Niagara Falls, New York, and at tourist information centers inside Niagara Falls State Park; or you can visit **www.niagarawinetrail.org**. Opening hours vary quite markedly among vineyards; some are limited to weekends in the colder months, so call ahead to avoid disappointment.

Eveningside Vineyards (4794 Lower Mountain Rd., Cambria, NY; ⓒ **716/867-2415;** www.eveningside.com) is a family-owned and -operated boutique winery. Production of their European-style wines is limited. **Niagara Landing Wine Cellars** (4434 Van Dusen Rd., Lockport, NY; ⓒ **716/433-8405;** www.niagaralanding.com) has vineyards dating back to the 1800s. They produce wine from native labrusca grapes and European viniferas. **Vizcarra Vineyards at Becker Farms** (3760 Quaker Rd., Gasport, NY; ⓒ **716/772-7815;** www.beckerfarms.com) is a family destination, with pick-your-own produce; a playground; and a store filled with pies, jams, and other treats in addition to their winery. **Warm Lake Estate Vineyard and Winery** (3868 Lower Mountain Rd., Lockport, NY; ⓒ **716/731-5900;** www.warmlakeestate.com) is located on the south shore of Lake Ontario. The winery offers a picnic area, winery tours and tasting, and numerous summer events.

winemaker members and their wineries, an explanation of the various grape varietals, and a history of Niagara's wine region—and much, much more.

Note: Not all wineries are members of the WCO. A number of establishments, either because they are smaller in size or brand-new, are not listed in the guide, although you will see signposts directing you to their properties as you tour around. Many of them produce award-winning wines and they all have their unique stories to tell. I urge you to venture into these wineries to enrich your experience of Niagara's wine country.

Each individual district of the wine region offers its own tourist resources. For year-round tourism information for the entire area, visit or call **Tourism Niagara at the Gateway Information Centre,** 424 South Service Rd. (exit 74 off the QEW), Grimsby, Ont. (ⓒ **800/263-2988** or 905/945-5444; www.tourismniagara.com). For Jordan & Vineland, Twenty Valley Tourism Association produces an excellent guidebook to the area called *Discover Twenty Valley,* which lists accommodations, dining, events, and more. Find out more at **www.20valley.ca**. The Welland Canals Centre at Lock 3 services the St. Catharines area (ⓒ **800/305 5134;** www.stcatharines.ca).

For information on wineries in Niagara-on-the-Lake (and loads of other tourist information on the immediate area), visit **Niagara-on-the-Lake Visitor & Convention Bureau,** 26 Queen St., Courthouse Building, Lower Level, Niagara-on-the-Lake, Ont. (ⓒ **905/468-1950;** www.niagaraonthelake.com).

This facility also operates an accommodations service, whereby you can give them your accommodations requirements and preferences and they will find a property for you (a small fee applies for this service).

Wine on the Radio

Check out **www.cheersniagara.com**, which is the online home of the syndicated "Cheers to Wine and Food" radio show, broadcast in the Niagara region on **91.7 Giant FM** at 7:25pm daily. Another great resource is wine expert Konrad Ejbich's 2-hour radio program, which is aired the last Friday of every month on **CBC** from noon to 2pm.

GETTING AROUND

Driving a car is probably the best way to see the wineries, as they are spread out over the entire Niagara region. Keep in mind that a tour of four to six wineries a day is more than enough. If you want to bike your way through your tour, choose a section and pick a couple of wineries. For example, the Greater Niagara Circle route (see chapter 7, "What to See & Do in the Niagara Region," for bike path info) hits many wineries en route. Another great option is to cycle the quiet country roads—they're wide open and there are not many road hazards. If you opt for the bus, note that public transit does not visit individual wineries. Instead, check out the bus tour options below that cater to the wine-hopping crowd.

WINE-TASTING TOURS

Crush on Niagara   Not just a regurgitated tour, your guide reveals unique facts and tidbits about the wineries and the town that you won't find in a brochure. And because the owner is a sommelier, this is the best bet for in-depth wine tours. For a unique experience, visitors get to taste wine straight from the barrel and then compare it with the same wine in a bottle. Tours depart in the morning or afternoon, last for 4 hours, and take you through the Niagara Escarpment or the wineries of Niagara-on-the-Lake. Choose from a three-winery tour with lunch, the Sip and Savour, from C$99 (US$94). Custom tours (with groups of six or more) are C$65 (US$62); the Sniff and Swirl tour includes four wineries for C$69 (US$66). An all-day tour (11am–4pm) is C$125 (US$119), with a three-course luncheon. Call ahead to reserve a ticket; Saturdays fill up fast. Crush will pick up guests at their hotel (within the wine region) or select a meeting place. Tours run twice daily, 7 days a week.

4101 King St., Beamsville, Ont. (administration office only) ✆ **866/408-WINE** or 905/562-3373. www.crushtours.com. Mon–Fri 9:30am–5pm; Sat 9:30am–2:30pm.

Niagara-on-the-Lake Trolley Wine Country Tours   Sit back and relax onboard a vintage trolley, while your tour guide narrates the way through Niagara's wineries. Tours are approximately 2½ to 3 hours long, inclusive of pickup and drop-off and wine tastings at the wineries.

48 John St., Niagara-on-the-Lake, Ont. ✆ **888/669-5566** or 905/468-2195. Tours C$55 (US$52). May–Oct daily. 2 tours each day.

Niagara World Wine Tours   These guys are the kings of tours, offering bicycle, van, or coach excursions through the Niagara wine region. Choose from winery tours, dinner and wine, or a gourmet wine and culinary tour, which is my favorite as it takes visitors through the rolling vineyards near the escarpment. The tour includes lunch at beautiful Peninsula Ridge and stops at some of the smaller wineries including Featherstone and Fielding. Areas covered include the Niagara Escarpment, the Niagara Peninsula, Jordan, and Beamsville. The cycling tour goes through Niagara-on-the-Lake, and be sure to ask about customized tours. If you prefer, tour the area in a luxury SUV, van, or minicoach, stopping at wineries, and then tasting fine cuisine at restaurants such as Terroir La Cachette. Packages are available.

92 Picton St., Niagara-on-the-Lake, Ont. ℂ **800/680-7006.** www.niagaraworldwinetours.com. Tours C$65–C$120 (US$62–US$114).

Zoom Leisure   With more than 100 bikes to choose from and a list of wine tours, this is a great place to start touring the region. Tour three wineries, sampling the wine as you go, or choose an extended package (with optional lunch), which includes four wineries. Each bike has an optional basket in the front to bring home goodies from your voyage. Group and custom tours, where you can choose different routes, and lunch and wineries are also available. Reserve tours in advance; call 48 to 72 hours ahead for most tours. If you want to purchase wine, the van will bring it back to the office for you.

2 Market St., Niagara-on-the-Lake, Ont. ℂ **866/811-6993** or 905/468-2366. www.zoomleisure.com. Tours start at C$60–C$115 (US$57–US$109).

STRATEGIES FOR TOURING NIAGARA'S WINE REGION

It would be impossible to visit Niagara's 70-plus wineries in one trip, unless you happen to have a couple of free weeks on hand and devote yourself to the task full-time. And touring the wine country is an activity that you must savor, not rush! My advice is to put together an itinerary before you arrive, but be flexible: be ready to pull into an enticing property that is not on your list, or to change your route to accommodate wineries with award-winning icewines, for instance, if that becomes your newfound passion during your visit.

Tour smarter, not harder are the words of advice to keep close to your heart as you leaf through this chapter in the process of planning your Niagara wine-country trip. First decide whether you would like to tour in your own vehicle, travel by bicycle, or join an organized tour. Bicycle rental companies are listed in chapter 7, "What to See & Do in the Niagara Region," and I look at a few tour options earlier in this chapter.

Begin with a guided tour of one of the larger wineries to get a good grounding in how wine is made. Next, I recommend taking part in a **tutored tasting.** Even if you are a seasoned wine aficionado, a refresher may well rekindle your passion for the noble grape. **Hillebrand Winery** (p. 163) offers several educational seminars daily. I highly recommend the **Art of Wine Making,** an hour of instruction that follows the grape from vineyard to bottle. It's a unique experience to learn about winegrowing, fermentation, and barrel aging.

As you draw up your shortlist of the wineries you will call upon, **aim for a balance** among the big guns and the mom-and-pop operations, the sophisticated estates and the modest weathered barn-board tasting rooms. And at least one meal in a **winery restaurant** is compulsory (in my opinion, at least).

Take it slowly—**aim to visit between three and six wineries** for a day's outing. You'll give yourself the opportunity to get to really know not only the wines but also the story behind each winery: its history, the types of wines it makes, where the grapes are grown, and the passionate people behind the scenes who make it all happen. Only by visiting the Niagara wine region will you gain a deep appreciation of the effort and experience that goes into every bottle produced. The winery staff are quite approachable and knowledgeable; it's not unusual to spend a half-hour chatting about the intricacies of a good bottle of Baco noir with a winemaker. You are likely to enjoy getting to know the winemakers just as much as the wines.

Tips **Never Drink & Drive**

There are lots of options to explore to ensure everyone gets to enjoy their visit to the wine country.

- Designate a driver. If you are staying more than a day, rotate the responsibility.
- Contact a tour company and allow them to transport you. You'll have the added bonus of a knowledgeable guide.
- If you are touring wineries in the Niagara-on-the-Lake region, there is a step-on/step-off bus service. Several wineries in the area provide shuttle buses, too.
- Become adept at tasting like a professional. Discipline yourself to expectorate the wine you taste and discard the remaining wine. There are vessels for just this purpose at every tasting bar.

And don't think you're okay as long as you're wobbling along on a bicycle—if you are under the influence of alcohol, you are a potential danger to yourself and other road or trail users.

If you are looking for the undivided attention of the tasting-room staff, **tour in the morning.** Most wineries open at 10am. Later in the day, when the winery parking lots are filling up with vehicles, you'll be enjoying an after-lunch espresso or *digestif* on the terrace of a winery restaurant nestled among the vines, or shaking the crumbs from your picnic blanket and contemplating an afternoon nap.

Beyond that, since the length of time you'll have to spend in the wine region and your level of wine knowledge are variables known only to you, it's impossible for me to provide you with a personalized touring strategy—you must devise your own itinerary that will best suit your intentions and wishes.

3 Niagara Region's Wineries

Many visitors may have heard of the larger, well-known wineries—those whose wines are offered globally. These big wineries, set on palatial venues, often have restaurants and offer a plethora of tours on how to pair wine and food. However, the Niagara region is peppered with smaller wineries whose vintages are equal to or surpass some of the larger ones. Yes, the big guys have some contenders, but I'm continually surprised by the quality of the wine produced at some of the smaller, more modest wineries. In smaller wineries, the wine makers often run the tours, which are casual and less scripted than those offered by the larger businesses. Having said that, the large wineries are a great starting point to learn. Make sure you visit a good mix of both to see the difference.

GRIMSBY & BEAMSVILLE

Angels Gate Winery   The name comes from the building's former life, as a convent. As you walk up to the winery door you pass by a tranquil garden. Wine production—from receiving to crushing and fermentation—is carried on underground, where temperatures are constant. A waterfall lends a peaceful element to the open-air garden room. Facing a fabulous view of Lake Ontario is a generous-sized terrace used for warm-weather dining until October. The Terrace lunch includes nibbles such as a tapas platter, cheese and artisan bread platter, and an herbed mushroom and goat cheese dip. On the wine side, Angels Gate is producing some fantastic full-bodied wines, including their flagship wine, Angels III, a merlot-dominant Bordeaux mix of two cabernets and estate-grown merlot. The 2006 Sussreserve Riesling garnered the Best White Wine award in the All Canadian Wine Championships. Tours, by appointment and costing C$5 (US$4.75), include a guided tour of the vineyards, cellar, and barrel rooms, followed by a tasting and cheese platter. Your fee is refunded if you purchase a bottle of wine. Sampling of four wines is free, and icewine samples are C$2 (US$1.90). Expect to pay between C$12 (US$11) and C$40 (US$38) for individual bottles of wine. Seminars are held on the hows and whys of decanting, how to build and stock a home wine cellar, and other wine-related topics.

4260 Mountainview Rd., Beamsville, Ont. ☎ 877/264-4283 or 905/563-3942. www.angelsgatewinery.com. June–Oct Mon–Sat 10am–5:30pm, Sun 11am–5:30pm; Nov–May Mon–Fri 11am–5pm, Sat 10am–5pm, Sun 11am–5pm.

De Sousa   This family-owned and -run winery is distinctly southern European in design, a feeling that is extended into the Old-World styling of the boutique and tasting room. The estate boasts a formal white villa with a red roof, manicured gardens with clipped shrubs, a terrace with a pond, and groves of trees surrounding the property. Traditional Portuguese wines and VQA wines are produced here. Mother De Sousa hosts wine tastings daily in the tasting room—ask for your tasting of red wine in the old-fashioned Portuguese clay cup. Once known for their jug-style bottle of Dos Amigos (a blend of Baco noir and Marechal Foch), the winery has replaced the jug with a 1.5-liter-bottle (about half a gallon), which you can only buy on-site. Other wines include the Cabernet Franc Reserve, which is also sold only at the winery. Samplings are free and available Saturday and Sunday only in the winter; tours, often by family members, are informal and inviting; the tours are offered from April to the end of October and are free. On weekends in July and August, partake of the vineyard barbecue fare. Wine prices range from C$9 (US$8.55) to C$50 (US$48).

3753 Quarry Rd., Beamsville, Ont. ☎ 905/563-7269. www.desousawines.com. May–Oct daily 10:30am–5:30pm; Nov–Apr Sat–Sun 10:30am–5pm. Daily tours May–Oct.

EastDell Estates   A very pretty country lane leads to EastDell Estates, a 34-hectare (85-acre) property with spectacular views over the countryside as it rolls down toward Lake Ontario—hence the restaurant's name, The View. The tasting room and restaurant are housed in a rustic building built entirely of wood and stone from the property. The C$5 (US$4.75) tour is one of my favorites in the region. Your guide will take you through the vineyards, to the Bruce Trail, and back. The informative talk covers

---

⌒ *Tips* Be Kind to your Palate

If you're planning on visiting several wineries in a day, and therefore potentially tasting one or two dozen wines (law dictates that each winery may serve up to four 1-ounce samples of wine), try narrowing your tasting choices in order to make the most of your olfactory and taste experience. The simplest plan is to stick to red or white. Beyond that, you could choose a vintage known to be a particularly good year locally, or a single varietal, or only light or full-bodied wines. Have fun with it—taste whites in the morning and reds in the afternoon, or stick to icewines and fruit wines. It's your choice!

the topography and geology of the region and how it contributes to the Bench's location as a prime grape-growing area. Tours are offered twice a day in the summer (usually around 2 and 4pm, but call ahead as schedules may change), and less often in the winter depending on the demand. You can educate your palate with one of several tasting seminars. Fees apply and schedules vary, so call ahead. Sampling is available free (icewine sampling is C$3/US$2.85), and wine prices vary between C$10 (US$9.50) and C$25 (US$24). You can rent a cute cottage year-round depending on weather conditions (big enough for only two) that perches right on the edge of a pond on the estate, surrounded by woodland and vineyards. There are more than 5km (3 miles) of hiking and cross-country ski trails accessible to visitors.

4041 Locust Lane, Beamsville, Ont. *C* **905/563-9463**. www.eastdell.com. Daily 11am–8pm; winter hours may vary.

Peninsula Ridge *★★*   An exquisitely restored and renovated Queen Anne–revival Victorian home at the end of the long, sweeping drive into the estate is the showpiece of this winery. The Restaurant at Peninsula Ridge is ensconced within the heritage building, and is highly recommended for lunch or dinner (see chapter 6, "Where to Dine," for listing information). The Winery Retail Shop is located in a meticulously restored 1885 post-and-beam barn. The atmosphere manages to be sophisticated and casual at the same time, making the space an inviting one in which to linger. Allow the staff to guide you through a tasting of VQA wines. Tastings are C$2 (US$1.90) for four samples, and C$2 (US$1.90) for one sample of icewine. No appointment for wine tours is necessary if you have fewer than 10 people in your party. Scripted tours of the winery production facilities are informative for beginners, but quite dull for anyone who knows a little about wine. The traditional underground cellar is available (C$5/US$4.75) at 11:30am and 3pm daily. Keep an eye out for their viognier—smooth, dry, and peachy. Icewine here is made with my number-one choice of grape for this delectable nectar—Cab Franc. The strawberry aroma and flavor is memorable. Wine prices vary between C$10 (US$9.50) and C$55 (US$52).

5600 King St., Beamsville, Ont. *C* **905/563-0900**. www.peninsularidge.com. May–Oct daily 10am–6pm; Nov–Apr Mon–Fri 11am–5:30pm, Sat–Sun 10am–5:30pm. Tours daily at 11:30am and 3pm.

Puddicombe Estate Farms & Winery *(Kids)*   This 120-hectre (300-acre) working farm was established more than 200 years ago by the Puddicombe family, who still own and operate the business today. Along with its family-based activities (including a petting zoo and agricultural train ride; see "What to See & Do in the Niagara Region," for more details), the Puddicombes offer a wine shop that's worth a visit. Prices range between C$9 (US$8.55) and C$28 (US$27). Award-winning wines are available to sample at the tasting bar at C$1 (US95¢) for four samples. Try the sauvignon blanc or raspberry fruit wine. Grapes grown in their vineyards include colombard, viognier, and muscats. Hikers take note—the farm property backs onto the Bruce Trail. Light fare is available in the licensed Harvest Café and Tea Room. Pick your own apples, cherries, and strawberries or choose a basket of prepicked fruit in season. Tours for 10 or more are available by appointment only and vary from regular winery tours; tastings are C$4 (US$3.80) per person and C$15 (US$14) will get you a wagon ride tour and more.

1468 Hwy. 48, Winona, Ont. *C* **905/643-1015** or 905/643-6882. www.puddicombefarms.com. Jan–Apr Mon–Fri 9am–5pm, Sat–Sun 10am–4pm; May–Dec daily 9am–5pm. Tours June–Oct daily 11am and 1pm; Nov–May by appointment.

JORDAN & VINELAND
Cave Spring Cellars *★*   Cave Spring Cellars' tasting room, wine shop, and cellars are located in a historical building (1871) on the main street in the village of Jordan,

Tips **Serve Your Wine at Its Ideal Temperature**

You may not be aware, but as you wander in and out of tasting rooms and winery bars, the wine you taste will (hopefully) have been carefully stored and served at the optimum temperature for its particular characteristics.

Pay heed to the following practical advice, if for no other reason than that the wines you taste while touring and then lug home by the caseload will simply not taste the same at home unless you serve them at their intended temperature:

- The cooler the wine, the less bouquet it will have, and conversely, the warmer the wine, the more bouquet will be detectable.
- Acidity and tannins are accentuated at lower temperatures and diminished at higher temperatures.

Here are some simple guidelines for serving temperatures. Light, sweet white wines and sparkling wine may be refrigerated for 4 or more hours. Most other white wines and light reds may be chilled for 1½ to 2 hours in the fridge. Full, dry white wines may be served slightly warmer—1 hour in the fridge will do. Medium and full, rich red wines should be served slightly below room temperature, and certainly no more than 18°C (64°F). If you do not have a temperature-controlled wine fridge (and not many of us do), then you will have to get creative as to how you cool your red wines for serving. In the Rhone Valley in France, for instance, you will see bottles of wine sitting outside the door of many a home in the early evening. This is not an offering to St. Vincent, the patron saint of French *vignerons,* but a practical method of coaxing the wine to the correct serving temperature in time for the evening meal, which is served much later in the evening in France than in North America.

And finally, don't mistreat the wine you have just purchased by letting it cook in your car on a hot summer's day. Bring a cooler and a few ice packs with you to protect your wine from deteriorating due to exposure to high temperatures.

which make it a great destination winery. Cave Spring Cellars has been producing wine from *Vitis vinifera* grapes for 20 years, on land first scouted by plane and chosen for its hillside location, heavy clay soils, and proximity to the moderating influences of Lake Ontario. Tutored tastings are held on weekends at 3pm Friday through Sunday in the winter, and noon and 3pm in the summer; expect a fun, lighthearted approach to wine. The Cabernet/Merlot (Beamsville Bench) 1998 is bottled heaven. Ripe berry and chocolate tastes are prominent. On the white side, the 2002 Chardonnay CSV has a strong nose of citrus. For tastings, expect to pay C75¢ (US70¢) per tasting and C$4 (US$3.80) for icewine. A late-harvest wine sample is C$2 (US$1.90). Tasting fees are waived if a bottle is purchased. Packages are available in partnership with the adjacent Inn on the Twenty (see chapter 5, "Where to Stay," for listing information) and its prestigious fine-dining restaurant, which include overnight accommodations, a winemaker's dinner, and a private tutored tasting. Bottles of wine cost C$13 (US$12) to C$30 (US$29) for table wines and up to C$60 (US$57) for icewines.

3638 Main St., Jordan, Ont. ℰ **905/562-3581**. www.cavespringcellars.com. June–Oct Mon–Thurs 10am–6pm, Fri–Sat 10am–7pm, Sun 11am–6pm; Nov–May Mon–Thurs 10am–5pm, Fri–Sat 10am–6pm, Sun 11am–5pm. Tours June–Sept daily noon and 3pm; Oct–May Fri–Sun 3pm.

Creekside   This place feels like a cottage in the woods, and its intimate setting is reason enough to visit. And if you like pinot noir, their Reserve Pinot Noirs—from 10- to 14-year-old vines—are some of the region's best, as are the shirazes, which are remarkably powerful. Inside there's an inviting tasting bar; outside, there's a covered deck for summertime dining and sipping. You are welcome to bring your own food, or enjoy the light fare on weekends from noon to 4pm. Menu items include suggestions for wine pairing. A variety of wines are produced here, using different production methods and grapes from their own on-site vineyards, vineyards along the St. David's Bench in Niagara-on-the-Lake, and several local growers. Their wines have a variety of price points, a mix of single varietals and blends, and are categorized into estate and reserve labels. Prices start at C$12 (US$11) for an Estate Wine Rose to C$35 (US$33) for a 2001 Grand Meritage Reserve Wine. Icewines top at C$40 (US$38) a bottle. Reserve wines are quite limited in quantity but worth investigating. If you're interested in acquiring wines for cellaring, ask the tasting-bar staff for recommendations. Samples are C50¢ (US45¢). Tours of the Estate are C$3 (US$2.85); C$5 (US$4.75) for reserve tours that include the barrel cellars and production facilities.

2170 Fourth Ave., Jordan Station, Ont. ℰ **877/262-9463** or 905/562-0035. www.creeksidewine.com. May–Oct daily 10am–6pm; Nov–Apr daily 11am–5pm.

Featherstone Estate Winery   The smallest full-time winery in Niagara, this laid-back family-run business is located in the owners' 1830s farmhouse. Featherstone is a small but earnest winery with high standards of land and crop management, resulting in wines of high quality, although limited quantity—3,500 cases (Jackson-Triggs produces 150,000!). The estate is a modest 9 hectares (23 acres), but its size makes it amenable to the personal care and attention lavished upon it. In their former life, the family owned a specialty-food store and they contend their wines are best served with food. Not coincidentally, the patio serves a fantastic selection of platters, including antipasto, cheese, and meat. Growing some of the oldest Riesling vines, the off-dry 2000 has a refreshing lemon-lime nose. Visitors looking for unique wines not available elsewhere would appreciate a visit here; this winery also subscribes to a natural philosophy: most recently a flock of New Zealand sheep have been enlisted to prune the lower vines—something unique to the region and fun to watch. The owners also provide tours, lasting about 40 minutes, for groups of eight or more people by appointment only. The C$5 (US$4.75) tour includes three samples. Three to four tasting samples, without the tour, are complimentary.

A surprisingly wide choice of wines is available, but some wines are limited in production to as few as 40 cases, so buy a case or two right there and then if there's a wine that really speaks to you. Individual bottles cost about C$12 (US$11) to C$30 (US$29). Food is served between 11am and 4pm Fridays to Mondays from late May to early September.

3678 Victoria Ave., Vineland, Ont. ℰ **905/562-1949**. www.featherstonewinery.ca. Apr–Dec Wed–Mon 10am–6pm; Jan–Mar by appointment or chance.

Fielding Estate Winery   Located on the Beamsville Bench near the Niagara escarpment on a secluded plot of land, a contemporary white cottage made of cedar, glass, and stone overlooks the vineyard and Lake Ontario in the background. "Better

Fun Fact Strange Sights and Sounds

As the grapes head toward their peak of ripeness in September and October, you will hear frequent bursts of a booming sound in the vineyards, the noise rolling and echoing as it spreads across the fields. No, the farmers aren't shooting the birds that flock to eat the ripening grapes—but you would be correct in thinking the noise is designed to scare the feathered creatures away. The boom is created by the firing of carbide guns, known as **"bird bangers."** You may also see **wind machines** in the vineyards. With the recent unusually harsh winters in the Niagara region, these are being installed in increasing numbers. When these machines are in operation, they help to break up layers of warmer and cooler air, moderating temperatures. Wind machines are quite effective at reducing winter damage to the vines.

a drop of the extraordinary than an ocean of the ordinary" is the philosophy of this winery, which produces a maximum of 10,000 cases a year. Because of this limited production, Fielding wines are available only through the on-site wine and gift shop, online, and through select LCBO vintage sections. The winery focuses on traditional wines of 15 varietals priced between C$13 (US$12) and C$36 (US$34) including merlot, Cabernet Franc, pinot noir, and syrah. The selection of white wines includes chardonnay, Riesling, pinot gris, and icewine. The C$5 (US$4.75) tour (10:30am and 1:30 and 3:30pm) is informative but not overburdened with information—you're invited to ask questions. Tours include three tastings—my favorite was an Alsatian-style 2006 Gewürztraminer Reserve, which was subtle yet fruity. Another favorite is the award-winning (including a Gold at the 2005 All Canadian Wine Championships) Cabernet Merlot Reserve. Named the Ontario legislature's official winery for 2007, this winery is producing some fine wines. Winter tours by appointment only.

4020 Locust Lane, Beamsville, Ont. (Ⓒ) **905/563-0668**. www.fieldingwines.com. May–Oct 10:30am–6pm; Nov–Apr 10:30am–5:30pm.

Flat Rock Cellars (✦) This young winery, opened to the public in spring 2005, has stunning architecture, surpassed only by the view from the generous floor-to-ceiling windows over the vineyards and across Lake Ontario. On a clear day you can see the CN Tower in Toronto. Perched up high, you get the feeling you're in a bird's nest. From the tasting bar, a short walk across a bridge takes you to the production facility. Tours are available for free and by appointment only and are highly recommended, since the production area is tour-friendly (a catwalk around the perimeter of the production area allows you to clearly see the various stages of production from an elevated position). The grapes, which have been deliberately restricted to simply Riesling, chardonnay, pinot noir, and vidal, are handpicked entirely from Flat Rock's own vineyards. The entire process from vine to bottle is handled as gently as possible—the juice for red wines is even hand-stirred while skins are in contact rather than using a mechanically operated stirring device. The 2003 Riesling "Nadja's Vineyard" (named after one of the proprietors) is a crisp, unique take on Reisling. A great take-home gift is a pinot noir gift set simply called The Clone Pack: four bottles in total, the first three are different clones of the pinot grape. The fourth bottle is a combination of the three clones. Tastings are C$3 (US$2.85) for four wine samples. To bring a bottle home, you'll pay between C$15 and C$30 (US$14–US$29) for table wine and up to C$40 (US$38) for icewine.

Tips   **The Ins and Outs of Shipping Wine Home**

Most of the wines you will encounter in the Niagara wine region are available only at the winery. A number of the larger producers do sell some of their series in Ontario retail stores across the province, and a few export selected wines to the United States. For the most part, however, the best way to get your case (or cases!) home is to arrange for the winery to handle shipment. Each winery has its own policy for delivery of wine—many deliver only in Ontario, some deliver across Canada and to selected U.S. states, still others are willing to send product overseas, while a few sell their wines only on the premises.

If you are a resident of Ontario, you can order Niagara VQA wines online from **www.winecountryathome.com**. Wine Country at Home was established in response to customer demand for wines that are not usually available for purchase at places other than the wineries themselves. It's also worth visiting the websites of individual wineries for information on ordering and shipping their wines.

2727 Seventh Ave., Jordan, Ont. © **905/562-8994**. www.flatrockcellars.com. May–Oct daily 10am–6pm; Nov–Apr Sat–Sun 10am–6pm or by appointment. Tours available upon request.

Harbour Estates Winery   These vineyards and winery are situated on land that was originally a fruit farm. The property was gradually converted to vines over a number of years. One of their most popular reds is a cabernet sauvignon/cabernet franc/merlot blend that is best described as "easy drinking." Their vineyards produce enough grapes to meet their annual target of 10,000 cases, but the owners and winemaker prefer to do some trading with other wineries in order to have access to a greater selection of grape varieties for the production of their wines.

The estate itself includes 549m (1800 ft.) of frontage onto Jordan Harbour with dinghy access, so that visitors are welcome to arrive by boat if they are out for a sail or cruise in the harbor or on the lake. There is even room for a helicopter landing. Visitors are also welcome to walk a self-guided tour route near the Carolinian forest on the property, along the Harbourside Trail and backwood paths. Guided walking tours of the estate are offered but must be booked in advance; cost is C$15 (US$14) per person. The retail shop and tasting bar have a down-to-earth country look; samples are free. Wines are modestly priced, with most bottles falling into the range of C$10 to C$15 (US$9.50–US$14). The owners eagerly share their knowledge of wines, vines, and the ins and outs of making an agricultural living on the Niagara Peninsula. A variety of events are held throughout the year, including concerts, art exhibits, and, yes, grape-stomping.

4362 Jordan Rd., Jordan Station, Ont. © **905/562-6279**. www.harbourestateswinery.com. June–Oct daily 10am–6pm; Nov–May daily noon–5pm. Tours available.

Kacaba Vineyards   Owner Mike Kacaba has Ukrainian heritage; a few years ago, then Ukrainian president Viktor Yushchenko paid a visit and was mighty impressed with the icewines. This boutique winery selects only 2 tons of the best syrah grapes for production, compared with the traditional 3 tons or more. Kacaba's syrahs are in a Northern Rhone style, creating a big, bold red. I suggest the 2002 with a hint of chocolate aftertaste. The reserve reds spend a year in new oak barrels, then several more months in used barrels. Grapes are thinned out regularly to ensure only the healthiest and robust survive. This is apparent in the sweet ripe Gamay Noir 2002 and the creamy Cabernet Franc Reserve of the same year. Wine prices range between C$10 and C$120 (US$9.50–US$114). Tours are informal and include a walk around the vineyard on a wide path. Tastings are free, except they charge C$8 (US$7.65) for reserve wines. The vineyard hooks up with the Bruce Trail and is close enough to cycle to other neighboring vineyards.

3550 King Street, Vineland, Ont., ✆ 905/562-5625. www.kacaba.com. May–Oct 10am–6pm; Nov–Apr 11am–5pm. Tours by appointment or chance.

Rockway Glen Estate Winery   This winery is somewhat unusual because it shares space with Rockway Glen Golf Course, an 18-hole championship course with full amenities, including a clubhouse restaurant (on the same premises as the tasting bar, wine boutique, and wine museum), driving range, and putting and chipping greens. The *musée du vin* is worth a visit, particularly if you opt for a guided rather than self-guided tour, since you will get a much more in-depth explanation of the artifacts on display and will have an opportunity to ask questions to further your knowledge of the history of the winemaking process. The museum's collection features a variety of antique implements and accoutrements from French vineyards, and depicts the journey of the noble grape from the vine to the bottle. The *musée du vin* is open 11am to 4pm daily. Guided tours must be prebooked. Admission fee is C$5 (US$4.75) per person, whether guided or self-guided. Three wine samples are complimentary.

Rockway Glen's Baco Noir (2005) is the best I've tasted and has the medals—such as the Silver at the 2007 Ontario Wine Awards and bronze at the All Canadian Wine Championships—to back it up. The Gewürztraminer 2006 is also a fine wine with a tropical fruit taste and a refreshing grapefruit finish. Wine prices range between C$10 and C$30 (US$9.50–US$29) for a special reserve merlot and C$40 (US$38) for icewines.

3290 Ninth St., St. Catharines, Ont. ✆ 877/762-5929 or 905/641-1030. www.rockwayglen.com. Mon–Sat 11am–7pm, Sun 11am–5pm.

Tawse Winery ⍟   The modern architecture of the Tawse winery building features clean, simple lines, making its presence in the landscape unobtrusive. A large pond is situated in front of the winery, providing the building with geothermal energy for heating and cooling. Due to its position on the bench, the winery is able to use the hillside terrain to its advantage, and uses a six-level gravity-feed system for its winemaking process. The winery plans to focus on traditional Burgundy-style wines, and its chardonnays are certainly stirring the hearts of local wine critics. Small amounts of cabernet franc, pinot noir, and Riesling wines are also produced here. Many of the grapes used for Tawse wines are from old-growth, low-yield vines, which have a tendency to yield greater depth of character when vinified. The 2004 Robyn's Block Estate Chardonnay is buttery and smooth. Tours of the innovative production facilities, which include sampling in the winery store and in the barrel cellar, cost C$20 (US$19) per person and must be booked in advance. In the tasting room, you can get two 2-ounce samples for C$5 (US$4.75). Wines hover around the C$30 to C$40 (US$29–US$38) mark.

3955 Cherry Ave., Vineland, Ont. ✆ 905/562-9500. www.tawsewinery.ca. May–Oct 10am–6pm; Nov–Apr 10am–5pm. Call ahead to confirm opening hours.

⌒ *Fun Fact* **Tasting a Flight**

A *flight* is an array of wines, with each showing different characteristics ranging from the origin of the grapes used and production methods to the year the wine was produced and the producer her or himself. Tasting a flight allows you to get a sense of how influences such as age, production, origins, year of harvest, and winemaker styles can affect the bouquet and flavor. It's a great way to become more familiar with a particular **varietal**. You can also experience a **vertical tasting,** which includes several vintages of the same wine, or a **horizontal tasting,** which includes several producers' products from the same vintage.

Vineland Estates Winery ★★★ Set on a reconstructed Mennonite village, Vineland Estate's stone-clad coach house and adjacent buildings create an ambience of romance and sophistication. Vineland Estates is one of the largest wineries in Niagara, and is an excellent ambassador of the region. You will find Vineland wines in the U.S., U.K., Japan, and many other countries around the world. In their stylish wine boutique, there are many wine accompaniments such as salsas and oils, as well as stemware and Polish glass. Try several vintages—the large tasting bar has a good selection of wines and the staff are eager to share their knowledge and personal points of view on the various wines available for tasting. Summer lunch on the shaded terrace of the restaurant, which serves among the very best of Niagara cuisine, will give visitors a taste of the tranquil and intimate atmosphere that is Vineland's specialty. (See chapter 6 for more information about the winery's restaurant.) The 2006 Gamay Noir has tones of sweet cherry and blueberry, and the semidry Riesling is a fine drink.

Organized tours and tastings are available, ranging from a basic tour of the vineyards, production area, and cellars to tour and tasting combinations that include wine and cheese, or specialized icewine tours and tastings. Tours, which cost C$6 (US$5.70), run twice daily between May and October, at 11am and 3pm; weekends only at 3pm in the fall and spring. Tours are available between January and March by appointment only. Lower-priced wines can be sampled free of charge; a nominal fee applies for premium wines. Bottles range from C$10 to around C$250 (US$9.50–US$238).

3620 Moyer Rd., Vineland, Ont. ⌒ **888/846-3526** or 905/562-7088. www.vineland.com. May–Dec daily 10am–6pm; Jan–Apr daily 10am–5pm. Tours late May–Oct daily 11am and 3pm; Nov to mid-May Sat–Sun 3pm.

NIAGARA-ON-THE-LAKE

Chateau des Charmes The Bosc family's French roots permeate one of Niagara's original wineries. Paul Bosc, Sr., helped transform the Niagara wine landscape, planting the largest single vinifera in Ontario in 1978. Gone were the days of Baby Duck (an embarrassing but popular Canadian sparkling wine from days gone by), thanks in part to the vision of Paul, Sr. Today, the 113 hectares (279 acres) of vineyard, located on four different properties, emphasize single vineyard bottles. The vineyard continues to break new ground, offering wines unique to the area, including the only vinifera clone in Canada, called the Gamay Noir Droit; the deviant gamay vine ripens later than gamay and is higher in sugar. Their pinot noir, chardonnay, gamay, and aligote are notable. For a tasting treat, try the Equuleus, a bold blend of cabernet sauvignon, cab franc, and merlot. Unlike at the other large wineries in the region, the Bosc family are often on the premises—sometimes Paul, Sr., rides his horses alongside the vineyard; the family has tried to preserve an old-world feel about the château—it feels very

European and homey at the same time. Tours start with a hearty welcome from staff at the door and include a traditional tour of the winery and production facilities as well as a peek at the vines and a bit of history of the grapes. Daily tours start at 11am and 3pm; tours in French available at noon. Reservations are not required.

1025 York Rd., St. David's, Niagara-on-the–Lake, Ont. © **800/263-2541** or 905/262-4219. www.chateaudescharmes. com. Daily 10am–6pm.

Frogpond Farm ✯   This small country winery produces the only certified organic wine in Ontario. The proprietors are on hand to enthusiastically discuss their organic farming methods and offer free tastings of their organic Riesling and cabernet merlot. The country screen door slams behind as you enter the small room with a thick wooden table set up for tastings. Try the oak-aged Riesling, which has been aged in huge 2,500-liter (660 gal.) oak casks, an unusual treatment for a Riesling (it is much more common to find oak-aged chardonnay). The barrels are old, so they allow air to reach the wine but do not impart the typical vanilla, toast, or caramel notes you would find from a young oak barrel. Rather, the flavor is richer and more complex than an unoaked Riesling. Prices are reasonable, ranging from C$12 to C$16 (US$11–US$15).

If you are in a position to transport them home, when you drop in ask if there are any eggs for sale that day. You will even see the chickens they came from, running around the farmyard. And when the peaches and cherries are ripe, they're free for the picking. The self-guided tour takes you around the property, past the frog pond (yes, there are frogs in the pond!) and vines. There are a few benches where you can sit and relax.

1385 Larkin Rd., Niagara-on-the-Lake, Ont. © **905/468-1079**. www.frogpondfarm.ca. Tues–Sat 1–5pm. Free guided tours on Sat afternoons or by appointment.

Hillebrand Estates Winery ✯✯   This winery is a great starting point for a tour of the wine country because of its extensive facilities, which just underwent a $3-million renovation. With the addition of more outdoor tasting areas, including the Winemaker's Lookout—a two-story stone structure that overlooks the vineyard—the cobblestone village feels like it's growing. Established in 1979, Hillebrand is one of the original wineries in the area, and as such, has mastered the art of tours.

If you want to unveil the mysteries of how a wine interacts with your senses of sight, smell, and taste, then I recommend the Winery Experience Seminars (C$10/US$9.50 per person). The "Art of Winemaking" seminar is suitable for wine novices, but experienced oenophiles may find this to be a welcome refresher course. Led by Hillebrand's knowledgeable and charismatic resident wine consultants, the seminar is a lesson on the inner workings of winemaking. Other seminars include specialized sparkling wine and icewine sessions and an explanation of cellaring, with tips for identifying wines that will benefit from aging. My favorite seminar is "*Trius*—The Art of Red"—visitors can create their own red wine blend: working in a team, you choose how much cabernet or merlot you want in your bottle as the winemaker takes you through the steps of creating a blended red wine. At the end, you can then create your own label, name it, and take it home.

The tasting bar offers a flight of three preselected wines for C$5 to C$10 (US$4.75–US$9.50), or you can select your own wine to sample. Table wine prices run from C$10 to C$80 (US$9.50–US$76). Hillebrand Estates Winery Restaurant is one of the top Niagara wine-country dining destinations, open for lunch and dinner. See the listing in chapter 6, "Where to Dine."

1249 Niagara Stone Rd., Niagara-on-the-Lake, Ont. © **800/582-8412** or 905/468-7123. www.hillebrand.com. Daily 10am–6pm; varies slightly by season.

Niagara's Jewel—Icewine

Icewine is a truly sensational experience for the palate. Its key characteristic is a perfect balance of sweetness and refreshing acidity. Icewine delivers delicious aromas, ranging from lychee, apricot, pear, and vanilla in a vidal icewine to strawberries and raspberries in a cabernet franc. Complex fruit flavors explode in the mouth with each and every sip. Officially classed as a dessert wine, icewine also may be served as an aperitif with pâté or foie gras or on its own.

The grapes used to produce icewine are left untouched on the vines and covered with a layer of protective netting once the fruit has reached full ripeness in October. Close attention is paid to the falling temperatures as winter envelops wine country. When the temperature drops below 17°F (−8°C; although most vintners prefer to operate at temperatures a few degrees colder) and the grapes are frozen solid, there is a sudden flurry of activity in the vineyards. Dozens of volunteers arrive, usually at midnight or later, when there is the least danger of the temperature rising.

The grapes are handpicked and quickly transported to the winery to be de-stemmed and crushed, then immediately pressed while still frozen. The water in the grape juice remains frozen, and a relatively minute amount of sweet juice is extracted, so concentrated that its consistency is like honey.

After the sediment has been cleared, the juice undergoes a slow fermentation process, which takes several months, and is then aged. Both fermentation and aging take place in stainless-steel containers at cool temperatures in order to maximize fruit concentration.

Icewine was first discovered in Germany in the late 1700s by farmers trying to rescue their semifrozen grape crop after a sudden cold snap. However, German winters are not consistently cold enough to freeze the grapes—it happens only once or twice every 10 years or so. Moving forward to Niagara in the mid-1980s, insightful and enterprising winemakers realized that Ontario's cold winters would provide just the right conditions for producing an annual icewine vintage.

Hillebrand Estates was the pioneer of icewine production in Niagara, beginning in 1983. A year later, Inniskillin made its first vintage of icewine. By the early 1990s, Niagara's icewine entered the world stage when it began attracting favorable attention at international wine competitions, including the prestigious Vinexpo in Bordeaux, France.

Niagara icewine is always produced as a varietal, with the majority being made from vidal and Riesling. Other varieties include Gewürztraminer, cabernet franc, merlot, pinot gris, chardonnay, muscat ottonel, and gamay. Winemakers vary slightly in their recommendations for serving. Chill the bottle for 1½ to 3 hours in the fridge, which will bring the serving temperature down to between 5°C and 10°C (41°F–50°F). Serve 1 to 2 ounces per person in a small tulip-shaped glass, which will encourage the wine to flow over the tip of the tongue (where most of the sweetness-detecting taste buds are concentrated) as you taste. A small white wineglass is an acceptable alternative.

Inniskillin 🦆   Inniskillin is one of the largest Niagara wineries, producing about 150,000 cases a year, and with that size, it's a venue that has something to offer a variety of tastes, from wine and food to architecture. The winery added a new tasting area in 2007; the Founders' Hall includes a new demonstration kitchen where you can learn about wine and food pairings firsthand. The interior is rustic but sleek, with a glass facade, high beams, and a large open space with various tasting stations. Architecture buffs may appreciate the influences of Frank Lloyd Wright and J. D. Larkin in the winery's buildings. For tastings, samples are offered at C$1 (US95¢) for table wines—more for icewines. Bottles range from C$12 to C$30 (US$11–US$29). Guests are able to sample and go or linger and sit down for a formal flight tasting.

Guided tours are offered for C$5 (US$4.75) daily between May and October until 4:30pm and until 2:30pm in the winter and include two tasting samples of table wines. If available, try their Pinot Noir Founders' Reserve for a truly classical taste of earthy plums and cedar. The winery has a well-stocked wine boutique housed in the barn, with gifts and accessories. Visit during the harvest (Sept–Oct) and you will be rewarded with the heady, blissful aroma of fresh juice as the grapes are gathered and processed right alongside the main visitor entrance.

S.R. 66, R.R. 1 Niagara Pkwy., Niagara-on-the-Lake, Ont. ✆ **888/466-4754** or 905/468-2187. www.inniskillin.com. May–Oct daily 10am–6pm; Nov–Apr daily 10am–5pm.

Jackson-Triggs Niagara Estate Winery   If you have a keen interest in technology, you will be intrigued by the tour at Jackson-Triggs. Their state-of-the-art, gravity-flow-assisted production is one of the most technologically advanced in Canada. Hour-long tours are available for C$5 (US$4.75; refunded with purchase of wine) and include three tastings. Individual bottles of Jackson-Triggs wine range between C$9 and C$30 (US$9.50–US$29) for table wine and between C$45 and C$75 (US$43–US$71) for icewine. Although there isn't a restaurant on-site, the winery holds special food and wine events throughout the year—including their popular "Savour the Sights," a unique dining experience with several courses, each served at different locations within the winery. Tucked away beyond the rear of the winery lies an open-air amphitheater, which resembles an inverted potato chip with rows of curved stone seating built into the grassy hillside. Seasonal entertainment is on offer between July and September—call ahead for details of who is performing and when. There are two tasting rooms—it's C$1 (US95¢) per sample at the tasting bar within the boutique, and at the premium tasting room with an outdoor terrace, each sample has a price tag of C$3 to C$4 (US$2.85–US$3.80). Cheese platters can be purchased to accompany wines by the glass. Keep your eyes open for the half-dozen or so sample rows of different grape varietals growing in front of the winery. It's a great opportunity to see the vines and their fruit at close quarters.

2145 Niagara Stone Rd., Niagara-on-the-Lake, Ont. ✆ **905/468-4637**, ext. 3, concierge desk. www.jacksontriggs winery.com. Summer daily 10:30am–6:30pm; winter daily 10:30am–5:30pm.

Lailey Vineyard   A simple wood building with a glass facade marks this unpretentious and unique spot. Stand at the spotlessly clean counter, learn a little about the wines on offer from the approachable, knowledgeable staff, and enjoy an interesting variety of wines. Samples may include an unoaked chardonnay (with an extremely pleasant green apple note), dry Riesling, cabernet/merlot blend, or their icewine. Lailey Vineyard and its winemaker Derek Barnett were the first commercial vintners to release wines fermented in Canadian oak barrels—their 2001 chardonnay. Four additional varietals have now been added to the Canadian oak method. The family has

Tips Affordable Icewine?

There's no denying the fact that icewine is expensive. In 2007, Royal DeMaria Wines sold a 2000 chardonnay for $30,000, making it the worlds' most expensive icewine. But producers say the cost is justified by several hard facts. The grapes are at the mercy of nature in every vintage, and vintners cannot predict or control how much fruit will be left on the vines when the time for harvest eventually arrives, or what condition the grapes will be in. The process is labor-intensive, since the grapes are handpicked within a brief timeframe. Labor costs are high, since trained workers (depending on the winery) must be enticed to go into the vineyards at short notice, in the middle of the night in extreme cold, to pick the frozen grapes. Yields are small—it takes 3 to 3.5kg (6.6–7.7 lb.) of grapes to make one 375mL (12.7-oz.) bottle of icewine. The same amount of grapes would make three 750mL (25.4-oz.) bottles of table wine.

Having said all of that, if your wallet will not stretch to icewine's price tag, seek out one of the new, smaller 200mL (6.7-oz.) bottles. Watch out for sales of older vintage icewines in the winery boutiques.

For exceptional value, try a select late-harvest dessert wine. This is made from the second pressing of the grapes, after they have thawed for several hours. The resulting wine retains much of icewine's delectable aromas, but approximately one-third of the sugar content—and one-third of the price.

---

been making their exclusively estate-grown *Vitis vinifera* wines for more than 35 years, but the tasting room is a relatively recent venture where most samples are free. Wines start at C$12 (US$11) and reach $45 (US$43). Because the winery is small, tours are available by prior appointment only. You're in for a treat if the winemaker or one of the owners conducts the tours (call ahead to ensure they conduct the tour)—they speak with passion, which is something that is missing from the tours at the larger wineries. Basic tours cost C$5 (US$4.75), which includes four samples; tours including a cheese platter, four samples, and two icewines cost C$15 (US$14).

15940 Niagara Pkwy., Niagara-on-the-Lake, Ont. ✆ **905/468-0503**. www.laileyvineyard.com. May–Oct daily 10am–6pm; Nov–Apr daily 10am–5pm.

Maleta Vineyards & Estate Winery   Don't let the garish pink house (Quonset hut) prevent you from trying out this winery. Daniel Pambianchi, technical editor of *Wine Maker Magazine* and author of *Techniques in Home Winemaking* (Véhicule Press, 2002), purchased the family winery in 2004 and has since revamped the selection of wine to include a larger breadth, which really sets it apart from other small wineries. But he doesn't want to get too big for his britches: production—from picking the grapes to turning the bottles—is still done by hand. The only speedy mechanization is the labeling machine. Some of the best wines are derived from the 1.5 hectares (4.5-acres) of Riesling grapes, planted in 1969. I recommend a bottle of the 2004 Grape Brain Cabernet Merlot; it's light on the tannins and has nice body. With wine glass in hand, Daniel or other well-informed staff takes visitors on tours through the vineyard; tours include an informal wine and cheese pairing tutelage and a walk through the vineyard, for $5 (US4.75)—it's one of the more interesting tours in the area. Wines range between C$16 and C$34 (US$15–US$32).

450 Queenston Rd., R.R. #4, Niagara-on-the-Lake, Ont. ✆ **905/685-8486**. www.maletawinery.com. May–Oct 31 Thurs–Mon 10:30am–5:30pm; Nov–Apr 30 Sat–Sun 11am–5pm or by appointment.

Marynissen Estates Winery   Trundle along the pretty Concession 1 side road and pull into the cozy, welcoming, weathered wood–clad tasting room and wine store. This small estate vineyard is family-owned and -run—you are likely to meet family members across the tasting-bar counter. Some of the oldest vines in Canada thrive in the vineyards here. Winemaker John Marynissen was the first grower to successfully cultivate cabernet sauvignon grapes in Canada, at a time when the belief was firm that the Ontario climate was too harsh to support vinifera grapes. John's daughter Sandra is now the head winemaker and makes Sandra's Summer Blend, a nice light summer white wine made from chardonnay, sauvignon blanc, and vidal. Because the winery is small, there are no formal tours available. From 10am to 5pm daily, come in for a taste for C50¢ (US45¢)—no charge with purchase of wine. Varietals include sauvignon blanc, gamay, merlot, and their prestigious cabernet sauvignon, ranging from C$9 to C$24 (US$8.55–US$23). The Rolling Stones ordered several cases of Marynissen's wines when they were performing in Toronto.

R.R. 6, 1208 Concession 1, Niagara-on-the-Lake, Ont. ✆ **905/468-7270**. www.marynissen.com. May–Oct daily 10am–6pm; Nov–Apr daily 10am–5pm.

Niagara College Teaching (NCT) Winery   Members of the public are welcome to visit the Glendale Campus of Niagara College and see the students in action at the Niagara College Teaching Winery. There is a vineyard and winery on the campus, where students practice what they learn in the classroom. Their award-winning VQA wines are available for purchase at the wine boutique located near the entrance to Niagara College's Culinary Institute Dining Room (see chapter 6, "Where to Dine," for more information on the restaurant). Expect to spend between C$12 and C$50 (US$11–US$48) for a bottle and between C$1 and C$3 (US$.95–US$2.85)for samples. With Terence van Rooyen on board as the new winemaker (from Stonechurch Winery), the college is expecting exciting new wines. My choice would be the 2005 Meritage, which won Silver at the 2007 Finger Lakes International Wine Competition. While at the college, enjoy the beautiful multilevel display gardens designed to mimic the Niagara Escarpment, which forms a backdrop to the college. The Bruce Trail can be accessed nearby, and there are walking and biking trails on campus. The campus greenhouse is open to the public as well. Locals flock here to buy a wide variety of plants for home and garden, particularly in the spring bedding-plant season and in the weeks leading up to Christmas, when the greenhouse is filled with brightly colored poinsettias. For groups of eight or more, book a tour—choose from a half-hour guided walk with three samples for C$4 (US$3.80) or an hour-long educational tour for C$16 (US$15; minimum 15 people).

Niagara College, Glendale Campus, 135 Taylor Rd., Niagara-on-the-Lake, Ont. ✆ **905/641-2252**. www.nctwinery.ca. Winery and retail store Mon–Sat 10am–5pm; Sun 11am–5pm.

Peller Estates Winery ⚝⚝⚝   One of Canada's largest producers of wine, Peller Estates is a grand property that echoes the distinguished chateau estates of the Old World. The interior of the main entrance immediately evokes a feeling of stepping into a splendid hotel lobby. Sweeping staircases, comfortable upholstered seating, a giant fireplace, wood paneling, warm caramel walls, and spacious public spaces all contribute to the luxurious setting. Excellent seminars are on offer, and they are carefully coordinated with nearby Hillebrand seminars so that they complement each other rather than repeat content between the two wineries. "The Art of Wine & Food" is an hour-long seminar that pairs three canapés with three wines. In a formal boardroom, visitors are lead through a tasting and encouraged to give their opinions and to ask questions. Winery tours are offered year-round for C$5 (US$4.75) and include two VQA tastings. Tours start at 10:30am in the summer, running on the half-hour every hour, typically until 7:30pm. In the winter, tours start at 11:30am and run until 5:30pm. Individual samples range from C$1 to C$5 (US95¢–US$4.75)for icewine selections. The reserve wines are reliably first-rate. If you are a sauvignon blanc devotee, make sure you taste one or more here. Wine prices start at C$10 (US$9.50) and top at C$40 (US$38) for table wine selections. Icewines can hit C$95 (US$90). Peller Estates Winery Restaurant, led by Chef Jason Parsons, is quite simply one of the best in Niagara's wine country. See chapter 6, "Where to Dine," for more detailed information. A shuttle service is available between Niagara-on-the-Lake's old town district and the winery—call the winery for details. Packages that include lunch or dinner at the winery restaurant, tickets for the Shaw Festival, and overnight accommodations are available.

290 John St. E., Niagara-on-the-Lake, Ont. (C) **905/468-4578** (winery) or 888/673-5537 for information on events in and around the vineyard. www.peller.com. Daily 10am–6pm; extended hours in summer.

Reif Estates Winery   With a new retail space, Reif finally has a venue befitting its wine. Enter the European country cottage through oversized oak doors, which lead to a large cherrywood tasting bar. Outside, not far from the water fountain, a wine sensory garden was created with help from local horticulture students: four sections of flora and plants are meant to mimic the aromas and styles of each wine. A light-bodied white such as Riesling has pear smells, and a bold red has the smell of bell peppers. This attention to horticulture is natural to Reif Estates; their wines are produced using only grapes from their own vineyards. The first tasting sample is free, and it's C$1 (US95¢) for subsequent tastings. Icewine is C$4 (US$3.80) per sample. Reif is well known for its Late Harvest Vidal, and its Riesling, vidal, and cabernet franc icewines (high-end varieties cost C$55/US$52 per bottle). Wine prices vary between C$9 and C$50 (US$8.55–US$48; for premium first-growth reds).

The wine boutique has gifts as well as locally made jams, jellies, and fudge. There is a limited selection of Canadian cheese and crackers available for takeout if you decide on an impromptu picnic. Facing the car park are sample rows of the types of grapes grown at Reif, so you can get a close-up view of the vines and fruit. Winter tours are not available, but in summer two daily tours are on offer for C$5 (US$4.75): 11:30am and 1:30pm. The price includes three tastings, one of which is an icewine. No appointment is required. Tours are generic but the new venue is worth visiting.

(Tips **Dining Out Wisely**

Dining at a winery restaurant can be quite a hedonistic experience, not least due to the many courses you will undoubtedly be tempted to order and the variety of wines available to sample. It's best to plan to have one extended, leisurely meal (lunch and dinner both have their unique charms), and picnic or snack the rest of the day. A few delectable cheeses served with fresh bread make a perfect light meal or snack to have on hand while touring the wine country.

Dine Among the Vines

A number of wineries have restaurants or cafes on their premises. As you would expect in a wine region, the cuisine is exceptional. Opening days and times vary considerably depending on the property and the season, so call ahead. Reservations are recommended, although not required. For reviews and full descriptions of the following dining destinations, see chapter 6, "Where to Dine."

The region's longest established estate winery restaurant is **Inn on the Twenty Restaurant and Wine Bar,** located in the center of pretty Jordan Village, across the street from Cave Spring Cellars (3836 Main St., Jordan Village, Ont.; ✆ **905/562-7313**). **The Restaurant at Peninsula Ridge** can be found in a historical Queen Anne–revival Victorian house on the grounds of Peninsula Ridge Estates Winery (5600 King St. W., Beamsville, Ont.; ✆ **905/ 563-0900**). There are picnic and patio facilities at **Henry of Pelham Family Estate Winery** (1469 Pelham Rd., St. Catharines, Ont.; ✆ **877/735-4267** or 905/684-8423); their **Coach House Café** offers casual light fare, cheese platters, and picnic baskets. **Hillebrand Winery Restaurant** is open for lunch and dinner (1249 Niagara Stone Rd., Niagara-on-the-Lake, Ont.; ✆ **800/582-8412** or 905/468-7123). For great value, sample the fare and service of the students of Niagara College at the **Niagara Culinary Institute Dining Room** (135 Taylor Rd., Niagara-on-the-Lake, Ont.; ✆ **905/641-2252,** ext. 4619). Enjoy the creations of Marc Picone and his culinary team in a picturesque setting at **Vineland Estate Winery Restaurant** (3620 Moyer Rd., Vineland, Ont.; ✆ **888/846-3526,** ext. 33 or 905/562-7088, ext. 33). At the western end of Niagara's wine region, along the Beamsville Bench on the Niagara Escarpment, lies EastDell Estates's **The View Restaurant,** named for its panoramic view of the surrounding vineyards and Lake Ontario (4041 Locust Lane, Beamsville, Ont.; ✆ **905/563-9463**). Wine-country cuisine awaits at **Peller Estates Winery Restaurant** (290 John St. E., Niagara-on-the-Lake, Ont.; ✆ **888/673-5537** or 905/468-4678). **Terroir La Cachette Restaurant & Wine Bar** features Provençal-style cuisine and is located within Strewn Winery (1339 Lakeshore Rd., Niagara-on-the-Lake, Ont.; ✆ **905/468-1222**). Angels Gate Winery (4260 Mountainview Rd., Beamsville, Ont.; ✆ **877/264-4283**) as well as Featherstone Estate Winery (which has a beautiful wraparound patio) has seasonal lunches that include cheese platters to have with your wine (3678 Victoria Ave., Vineland, Ont.; ✆ **905/562-1949**).

15608 Niagara Pkwy., Niagara-on-the-Lake, Ont. ✆ **905/468-7738.** www.reifwinery.com. Apr–Oct daily 10am–6pm; Nov–Mar daily 10am–5pm. Tours May–Oct daily 11:30am and 1:30pm; Oct–Apr by appointment only.

Stratus ✿✿   Stratus is urban, high-end, and sleek. It's well worth the experience; just be sure to wear black. With a futuristic steel facade, the winery became the first Leadership in Energy and Environmental design (LEED) building in Canada, and the first LEED-certified winery in the world. In addition to such features as geothermal heating and cooling technology and a system for composting organic waste, the winery is four

Microbreweries

If you'd rather gulp a frosty brew, don't weep in your empty pint glass. Here are three microbreweries amongst the grapes.

Visitors to Niagara-on-the-Lake can have a tasting and production tour of the production facilities at **TAPS** (10 Walker Rd., Virgil, Ont.; ✆ **905/468-TAPS;** www.tapsbeer.ca). Choose from Red Cream Ale, a premium lager, or, for the true aficionado, a vanilla wheat beer offered seasonally. If you're around during September's Grape and Wine Festival, try TAPS's wine barrel lager, which is aged in stainless steel, then in red wine barrels. Tastings and tours are free. Call ahead to make sure they're not busy (summer Wed–Sat 11am–6pm, Sun 11am–5pm; winter Wed–Sat 11am–6pm).

St. Catharines is home to two microbreweries. **Niagara's Best** has become popular for their West-Coast inspired Blonde Premium Ale. Tasting rather hoppy with a full body, this beer is a favorite with the beer connoisseur. Their lager, which caters to the everyday beer drinker, is a light refreshing drink. Tours of the production facility and samplings are free. (75 St. Paul St., St. Catharines, Ont.; ✆ **905/684-5998;** www.niagarasbestbeer.com). **The Merchant Ale House** is a pub that has hopped (forgive me) into the micro-brewing business in the past few years. Sadly, their beer is only sold on the premises (98 St. Paul St., St. Catharines, Ont.; ✆ **905/984-1060;** www.merchantalehouse.ca). Featuring between five and seven beers at any time, one staple is strawberry blonde fruit ale that tastes just like it sounds. The Drunken Monkey, which has prompted locals to bring in a slough of stuffed monkeys that sit above the bar, is a chewy tasting dark oatmeal stout. The Old Time Hockey ale is an easy-drinking ale brewed with lager malts and English hops (chocolate was used to enhance its flavor). The Extra Special Bitter is dubbed the "King of English ales," and the Blonde Bombshell is a lager/malt that is combined with ale. The Merchant Ale House also offers seasonal beers such as their Halloween favorite, pumpkin beer.

stories high to allow a gravity-feed production system to function, a necessity on the relatively flat landscape of the Niagara-on-the-Lake region. Premium prices have been set for the narrow range of wines on offer. The French-born winemaker has chosen to create two signature blends, Stratus White and Stratus Red, with a small number of single varietals including chardonnay and merlot. Wine critic Konrad Ejbich has only one complaint of Stratus's Riesling icewine. Garnering a 99 out of 100, its only imperfection was bottle size: it wasn't large enough. Table wines typically run between C$30 and C$40 (US$29–US$38), and C$55 (US$52) for the highest. Tastings are offered from Wednesday to Sunday and no reservation is needed. Sample three wines for C$10 (US$9.50). Tours are by appointment only and cost C$15 (US$14) per person.

2059 Niagara Stone Rd., Niagara-on-the-Lake, Ont. ✆ **905/468-1806.** www.stratuswines.com. Daily 11am–5pm. Seminars held weekly; call for times and to reserve a space.

Strewn Winery ✿   Your first impression as you pull into the parking lot at Strewn may leave you feeling a little puzzled; the industrial nature of the site is in stark contrast to many of the wineries in the district. You'd be right in thinking industrial, since the concrete-block winery buildings, in fact, are located in what was once an abandoned cannery. Step inside, however, and you will find a wood-clad wine boutique on your left, a state-of-the-art cooking school on your right, and to the rear of the building, a tasting bar and restaurant, serving Provençal-inspired cuisine and backing onto the picturesque woodland bordering Four-mile Creek. Public tours of the vineyard, barrel cellar, and production facilities are daily at 1pm for groups of 10 or more—call to make an appointment first. Tours are an informal walk through the property. No scripted lines here. Ask for owner Joe Will if he's around—he's a hoot.

Special events are held throughout the year; check the website for up-to-date information. Past events have included invitations to take part in pruning the vines in early spring, a fall participation event that includes grape picking, assisting with the grape crushing and a sample of grape juice to take home, and an interactive seminar on identification of the characteristics of wines made from different grape varieties. *Terroir la Cachette* is Strewn's winery restaurant, featuring the French-Provençal cooking expertise of Chef Alain Levesque, with an emphasis on local ingredients. The Wine Country Cooking School offers a variety of classes that feature food and wine. One-day classes, 2-day culinary weekends, and 5-day culinary vacations are available. (See chapter 6, "Where to Dine," for more detailed information on the restaurant and the cooking school.) To walk in and sample a wine, tastings range between C50¢ to C$2 (US45¢–US$1.90) for icewine varieties. To take a wine home, expect to pay between C$11 and C$34 (US$10–US$32) per bottle.

1339 Lakeshore Rd., Niagara-on-the-Lake, Ont. © 905/468-1229 (winery), 905/468-1222 (restaurant), or 905/468-8304 (cooking school). www.strewnwinery.com or www.winecountrycookingschool.com. Daily 10am–6pm. Free tour daily 1pm.

Sunnybrook Farm Estate Winery   Sunnybrook Farm, a short drive west of Niagara-on-the-Lake along the southern shore of Lake Ontario, is unique among the Niagara wineries because it exclusively produces fruit wines, many of which are made with fruit from their own orchards. This small family-owned and -operated fruit winery is proud of the many awards its wines have accumulated over the years. When you visit the cozy tasting room, you will see the bottles displayed on the shelves with their medals hanging around their necks. No formal tours are available, but staff are ready to pour samples 7 days a week—it's C$2 (US$1.90) for four tastings. Notable wines include blackcurrant, spiced apple, and black raspberry. Peach, pear, and other fruit wines, many of them dry or off-dry, are a nice refreshing alternative to—or change from—grape wines. Their Ironwood Hard Cider has received critical praise. All of Sunnybrook's wines are Quality Certified (QC), which is the fruit wine equivalent of VQA for Ontario grape wines. Prices to pick up a bottle range from C$15 to C$30 (US$14–US$29).

1425 Lakeshore Rd., Niagara-on-the-Lake, Ont. © 905/468-1122. www.sunnybrookfarmwinery.com. May–Oct daily 10am–6pm; Nov–Dec daily 10am–5pm; Jan–Feb Thurs–Mon 10am–5pm; Mar–Apr daily 10am–5pm.

OTHER WINERIES

A few other notable wineries scattered along the Wine Route include **Kittling Ridge Estate Wines & Spirits,** 297 South Service Rd., Grimsby, Ont. (© 905/ 945-9225); **Pillitteri Estates Winery,** 1686 Niagara Stone Rd., Niagara-on-the-Lake, Ont. (© 905/ 468-3147); and **Royal DeMaria Wines,** 4551 Cherry Ave., Beamsville, Ont. (© 888/ 562-6775 or 905/562-6767), whose entire operation is devoted to icewine.

9

Shopping

You can find pockets of great shopping in the Niagara Region, without having to resort to a commemorative Niagara Falls snow globe or pack of playing cards. My favorite places require a little driving, but once there you'll find lots to bring home. I've provided some suggestions in the "Shopping A to Z" section below, where the better retailers have been ferreted out and listed for your shopping pleasure.

1 The Shopping Scene

From a shopping standpoint, the Niagara region serves both the huge influx of tourists and its diverse regional population base. As a result, there tend to be extremes in the shopping landscape. The area immediately surrounding Niagara Falls on the Canadian side of the border is awash in souvenir shops, with a cluster of upscale stores attached to the recently opened Fallsview Casino. The economically depressed Niagara Falls, New York, has little to offer in the way of shopping, with the exception of The Outlets at Niagara Falls USA, a mall that features Manhattan-style shopping destinations with everyday discounts of up to 60%. Niagara Falls, Ontario, also has an outlet complex, on Lundy's Lane.

Heading to the more sophisticated tourism areas, you will find boutique-style shopping with unique products. Niagara-on-the-Lake's style of clothing and gifts are a tad conventional: you're buying quality, certainly, but it comes with a hefty price tag. Jordan Village, although much smaller in scale, also offers an upscale shopping experience. Old Port Dalhousie on the Lake Ontario shoreline is one of my favorite towns for unique finds. Antiques lovers will find irresistible hunting in the Twenty Valley district and in the vicinity of the town of Virgil, just south of Niagara-on-the-Lake.

The malls and shopping centers in the Niagara region tend toward the practical and predictable—you won't find anything you can't find at home, but these stores have true factory outlet prices.

2 Great Shopping Areas

JORDAN VILLAGE

Jordan Village is compact enough to explore on foot. Two large, century-old warehouses have been converted into an eclectic assortment of retailers, punctuated by a luxurious inn, an award-winning fine-dining restaurant, and a well-established Niagara winery. In addition, there are numerous retailers scattered along Main Street and Nineteenth Street, bounded on the south by Highway 81 (King St.) and on the north by Wismer Street. Shopping is higher-end in focus, with a mix of art galleries, designer fashions, giftware, antiques, home and garden accessories—and even a shop catering to dogs.

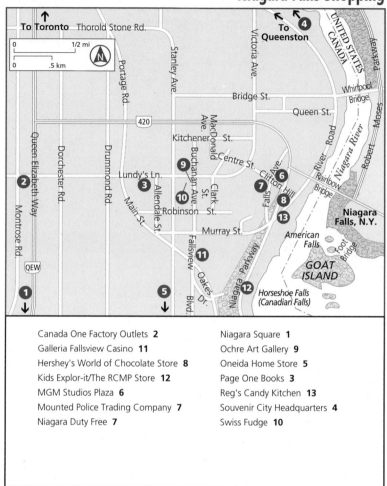

Niagara Falls Shopping

Canada One Factory Outlets **2**
Galleria Fallsview Casino **11**
Hershey's World of Chocolate Store **8**
Kids Explor-it/The RCMP Store **12**
MGM Studios Plaza **6**
Mounted Police Trading Company **7**
Niagara Duty Free **7**

Niagara Square **1**
Ochre Art Gallery **9**
Oneida Home Store **5**
Page One Books **3**
Reg's Candy Kitchen **13**
Souvenir City Headquarters **4**
Swiss Fudge **10**

NIAGARA FALLS

If you are a souvenir hound, you don't need a guidebook to give you suggestions for where to buy souvenirs. You will see trinkets at every turn as you stroll around the tourist areas by the Falls. If you want upscale shops, visit the Galleria inside the Niagara Fallsview Casino Resort. For duty-free shopping, see section 3 below.

NIAGARA-ON-THE-LAKE

Niagara-on-the-Lake, dubbed "Canada's prettiest town," boasts great shopping along a stretch of road through the middle of town, spilling over onto a few of the cross streets. This area will appeal to an older, affluent, shopper. Clothes are top quality but they wouldn't necessarily make it down a runway any time soon. You'll find indulgences such as homemade fudge, Brit imports, kitchen gadgets, wine, fine dog

Niagara-on-the-Lake Shopping

Angie Strauss Gallery **7**
The Bark and Fitz **2**
Beau Chapeau Hat Shop **8**
Dansk **5**
Doug Forsythe Gallery **17**
Irish Design **4**
Just Christmas **10**
Moggridge Studio **1**
Newark Shoes **6**

Old Niagara Bookshop **15**
The Copper Leaf **13**
The King Street Gallery/Poulin Art Gallery **11**
The Nutty Chocolatier **16**
The Romance Collection Gallery **12**
The Viking Shop **9**
Tickle Your Fancy **3**
Valle Verde **14**

apparel, and bathing products so good you'll want to eat them. There are benches thoughtfully placed at regular intervals along the flower-bedecked sidewalks, and some shady spots for hot summer days. Refreshments are easy to come by, whether your idea of a pick-me-up is a cup of tea, a mug of joe, or a double-scoop ice-cream cone. The town sparkles in the winter and is a bit less frantic than the summer crowd.

PORT DALHOUSIE

This waterfront village, nestled on the south shore of Lake Ontario, has attracted some interesting boutiques and specialty stores. Its market is a hodge-podge of stores and features a memorable bakery. Port Dalhousie is small enough that you can park the car in one spot and walk around the village center. There are restaurants and bars in addition to gift stores, women's fashions, and a candy emporium.

3 Malls & Shopping Centers

NIAGARA FALLS, ONTARIO AND NEW YORK

Canada One Factory Outlets   True factory outlet deals can be found here; items are up to 75% off regular retail prices. Stores include Roots, The Body Shop Depot, Club Monaco Outlet Store, Samsonite Company Stores, Tootsies Factory Shoe Market, Esprit, and Mexx. The number of retailers here is only a fraction of those at the huge outlet mall in Niagara Falls, New York, but if you're looking for Canadian or European-based stores (for example Roots, The Body Shop, Rocky Mountain Chocolate Factory, or Mexx), then Canada One will serve you better. Call ahead or visit the website before your trip for an up-to-date listing of retailers. The outlet is open Monday to Saturday from 10am to 9pm (from Jan to Apr the outlet closes at 6pm on Sat). On Sundays and holidays, the hours are 10am to 6pm. 7500 Lundy's Lane (at QEW), Niagara Falls, Ont. ✆ 905/356-8989. www.canadaoneoutlets.com.

Galleria Fallsview Casino   The architecture, decor, and construction materials are all luxurious, in keeping with the upscale money, money, money atmosphere of the casino—although some of the styles can be a bit garish. Whether you're a shopper or not, it's worth a wander around the Galleria. Stroll up past the shooting fountains and waterfalls with their ever-changing multicolored lights and enter by the main doors. You'll come face to face with Hydro-Teslatron, a monstrosity of a "living" sculpture. At regular intervals, H-T comes alive with a sound and light show, leaving some bystanders bemused, although many seem to be fascinated by this imaginative structure. At the rear of the Galleria is a huge rotunda under a magnificent multistory glass-domed ceiling. Retailers lean toward the high end, including Swarovski Austrian crystal, Linda Lundström designer women's fashions, and Philippe Artois imported Italian menswear. For souvenirs, check out Canada's Finest, the official supplier of souvenir RCMP clothing and accessories, or First Hand Canadian Craft & Design, which stocks arts and crafts by Canadian artists. From Sunday to Thursday, the stores are open from 10am to 11pm; on Fridays and Saturdays, they close at 12am. 6380 Fallsview Blvd., Niagara Falls, Ont. ✆ 905/371-3268. www.fallsviewcasinoresort.com.

Niagara Square   This regional shopping center is anchored by The Bay and Sport Chek. A separate Cineplex Odeon movie theater complex is on-site. A small food court serves shoppers. Several mall stalwarts cover the women's fashion scene, including Cotton Ginny, Suzy Shier, Tabi, La Senza, and Tan Jay, but men's and youth fashions are not as well represented. Bargain stores include Payless ShoeSource and Dollarama. The mall is open Monday to Friday from 10am to 9pm, Saturdays from 9:30am to 5:30pm, and Sundays from 12pm to 5pm. 7555 Montrose Rd. (corner of McLeod Rd. and the QEW), Niagara Falls, Ont. ✆ 905/357-1110. www.niagarasquare.com.

The Outlets at Niagara Falls USA   This huge outlet mall is crazily busy, and you may find yourself cruising the parking lot for a while, especially on a weekend, to find a parking space. It's worth it, though. Many Canadians make the trek across the border to this clean and well-designed mall. The closest border crossing is the Rainbow Bridge, but you can zip up Highway I-90 from Fort Erie or down from the Lewiston–Queenston Bridge. Around 150 brand-name stores offer everyday discounts on their stock, up to as high as 60% off the regular retail prices. If it's famous, it's here. Polo Ralph Lauren, Guess, Gap, Calvin Klein, Burberry, Liz Claiborne, Rockport, and Jones New York are just a handful of the women's fashion retailers. Housewares include Mikasa, Pfalztgraff, and Corningware Corelle Revere. Kid's clothing can be found at OshKosh B'Gosh, The Children's Place, Nautica, and more. Luggage, accessories, shoes, and menswear are well represented throughout. Specialty stores include a Fragrance Outlet, KB Toy Outlet, and OFF 5TH Saks Fifth Avenue Outlet. You can browse the shops from 10am to 9pm Monday to Saturday, and 11am to 6pm on Sundays. 1900 Military Rd., Niagara Falls, NY (take Hwy. I-90 to exit 22 to Factory Outlet Blvd.). ✆ 800/414-0475 or 716/297-2022. www.fashionoutletsniagara.com.

Duty-Free Shopping

Check for the current duty-free allowances before making your purchases. Canadian residents, please note: if you are traveling to the U.S., you may purchase goods you wish to bring back to Canada at duty-free stores before leaving Canada. If you will be out of Canada for 48 hours or more, you may also purchase duty-free alcohol and tobacco. U.S. residents may purchase up to $200 of duty-free goods (excluding alcohol and tobacco) for trips across the border that are less than 48 hours. U.S. residents who stay in Canada for 48 hours or longer can bring back up to $800 worth of duty-free goods, which can include one liter of liquor and one carton of cigarettes. Please note that customs rules and regulations are subject to change, and visitors to both sides of the border should check current rules and regulations before making out-of-country purchases they intend to bring home with them, whether those goods were purchased duty-free or not.

Niagara Duty Free An array of duty-free goods are available, including perfume, cosmetics, jewelry, Swiss watches, china, crystal, chocolate, wine (including Niagara wines and icewines), and liquor. There is a currency-exchange service. Save up to 50% on regular retail prices. Located beside the Rainbow Bridge on the Canadian shore—the closest duty-free store to the Falls. The Rainbow Bridge is the shortest route to Interstate 90 from Niagara Falls, Ontario, and is a truck-free route. 5726 Falls Ave. (beside the Rainbow Bridge), Niagara Falls, Ont. ℂ **905/374-3700.** www.niagaradutyfree.com.

Peace Bridge Duty Free Billed as North America's largest duty-free shopping complex, the Peace Bridge Duty Free has a wide variety of items and is open 24 hours. In addition, there is a handy Travel Services Center, which offers currency exchange, customized maps, tourist information, and business services. Other amenities include a food court with branded fast-food outlets, bathrooms, an ATM, and phones. Duty-free goods include Canadian souvenirs, leather goods, imported chocolate and gourmet foods, perfumes, china and crystal, wine, icewine, beer, liquor, and tobacco. 1 Peace Bridge Plaza (beside the Peace Bridge), Fort Erie, Ont. ℂ **800/361-1302.** www.dutyfree.ca.

Peninsula Duty Free This duty-free shop is next to the Queenston–Lewiston Bridge, the most northerly of the three public border crossings in the Niagara region (the Whirlpool Bridge is reserved for frequent travelers). Beside the Queenston–Lewiston Bridge, Queenston, Ont. ℂ **905/262-5363.**

ST. CATHARINES

Fairview Mall   This mall serves local residents and features around 60 stores and services. Anchors are Zellers, Chapters, Mark's Work Wearhouse, Future Shop, and Zehrs. Winners clothing store and HomeSense home furnishings are new additions. Mall hours are Monday to Friday, 10am to 9pm, Saturday, 9:30am to 5:30pm, and Sunday, 12pm to 5pm. 285 Geneva St. (near the QEW—take the Lake St. exit), St. Catharines, Ont. ℂ **905/646-3165.**

The Pen Centre   This large indoor mall has approximately 180 stores and is the largest mall in the Niagara region. Anchor stores include The Bay, Gap, Pier 1, Sears, Zehrs, Zellers, HomeSense, Sport Chek, Winners, Old Navy, and my favorite spot for trendy and cheap clothes: H&M. There are a half-dozen full-service restaurants, a food court, and numerous snack retailers. If you want a break from shopping, there is a Famous Players Silver City on-site with eight movie theaters. There are dozens of women's and unisex fashion stores; less in the way of children's and men's fashions. More than 93,000 sq. m. (1-million sq. ft.) of shopping. The mall is open Monday to Fridays from 10am to 9pm, Saturdays from 9am to 6pm, and Sunday From 11am to 6pm. Hwy. 406 and Glendale Ave., St. Catharines, Ont. ✆ **800/582-8202** or 905/687-6622. www.thepen centre.com.

WELLAND

Seaway Mall   Serving Welland and district, Seaway Mall has a cinema complex and is anchored by Sears, Winners, and Zellers. A good selection of mall chain sportswear, shoes, unisex fashions, and women's fashion retailers can be found here. There are also banks, a post office, and a food court. Shopping hours are 10am to 9pm, Monday to Friday, Saturdays, 9:30am to 5:30pm, and Sundays from 12pm to 5pm. 800 Niagara St., Welland, Ont. ✆ **905/735-0697**. www.seawaymall.com.

4 Shopping A to Z

ANTIQUES & COLLECTIBLES

Bartlett House of Antiques   This antiques store specializes in historical military paraphernalia, china, jewelry, and fine furniture. 1490 Niagara Stone Rd., Niagara-on-the-Lake, Ont. ✆ **905/468-1880**.

Blue Barn Antiques & Collectibles   Located in an old barn in the Twenty Valley antiques district, this store offers two floors of antiques and collectible treasures. 4107 Cherry Ave., Vineland, Ont. ✆ **905/562-4606**.

Forum Galleries Antiques & Collectibles   A variety of dealers showcase their wares at this large 745-sq.-m (8,000-sq.-ft.) antiques market. Furniture from Canada and Europe is available, with many different eras represented—from Victorian and country to Art Nouveau, Art Deco, '50s and '60s, and much more. You name it, they've probably got it—jewelry, glass, books, lamps, art, silver, china, toys, fine antiques, Canadiana . . . lose yourself for an hour or so as you wander the aisles. 2017 Niagara Stone Rd. (Hwy. 55), Niagara-on-the-Lake, Ont. ✆ **905/468-2777**. www.forumgalleries.com.

Granny's Boot Antiques and Country Pine   Hand-crafted country pine pieces are a specialty at Granny's Boot. You'll also find a great selection of folk art, unique antiques, rustic furniture, and primitives. 3389 King St., Vineland, Ont. ✆ **877/211-0735** or 905/562-7055. www.grannysbootantiques.com.

Harp & Swan Gallery   Located "on the bend" of Main Street inside the Jordan Village Guest Manor, this location specializes in Group of Seven reprints, quilts, antique European furniture, and reproductions. Collectibles are also featured. Hours vary, so call ahead. 3864 Main St., Jordan Village, Ont. ✆ **905/562-8269**. www.bbstay.biz.

Jordan Antiques Centre   This village marketplace carries inventory from 25 antiques dealers and features a permanent show year-round. Specialized items include antique toys, Christmas decorations, jewelry, and silver. The Centre has a sound local reputation as a gift resource and showcase for large pieces of antique furniture. 3836 Main St., Jordan Village, Ont. ℭ **905/562-7723**. www.jordanantiques.com.

Nothing New Antiques   This is the place for Canadiana, country furniture, and accessories. 1823 Niagara Stone Rd., Niagara-on-the-Lake, Ont. ℭ **905/468-7016**.

Prudhomme's Antique Market   On the shores of Lake Ontario stands a restored turn-of-the-20th-century farmhouse that is home to a wide selection of antiques and collectibles, representing multiple vendors. 3319 North Service Rd., Vineland, Ont. ℭ **905/562-5187**.

S&B Antique Gallery   This store specializes in fine furniture, decorative arts, and collectibles. On display you will find dining-room suites, bedroom suites, occasional furniture, china and glass, estate jewelry, prints, paintings, and lighting. 3845 Main St., Jordan Village, Ont. ℭ **877/337-4577** or 905/562-5415.

Vineland Antiques   Housed in the original general store in the village of Vineland, this antiques market is a multidealer enterprise. 4227 Victoria Ave., Vineland, Ont. ℭ **905/562-9145**.

MORE ANTIQUES STORES   There are more antiques and collectibles destinations to check out, including **Europa Antiques,** The Old Red Brick Church, 1523 Niagara Stone Rd., Niagara-on-the-Lake (ℭ **905/468-3130**). **Lakeshore Antiques & Treasures,** 855 Lakeshore Rd., Niagara-on-the-Lake (ℭ **905/646-1965**), or **Antiques of Niagara-on-the-Lake,** 1561 Niagara Stone Rd., Niagara-on-the-Lake (ℭ **905/468-8527**) offer multiple dealers in a marketplace setting.

ART GALLERIES

Angie Strauss Gallery   Local artist Angie Strauss creates oil and watercolor paintings and has a line of women's fashions (see below). In the recently expanded gallery, one of the largest private galleries in the Niagara region, you will find limited editions, prints, and originals. Strauss paints popular local scenes and landmarks, florals, landscapes, and country collages. 129 Queen St., Niagara-on-the-Lake, Ont. ℭ **888/510-0939** or 905/468-2255. www.angiestrauss.com.

Doug Forsythe Gallery   Doug Forsythe is an established Canadian artist. Many of his collections feature landscapes, seascapes, marine themes, and figure studies. He works in computer graphics, watercolor, oil, and acrylics, and is skilled in etching, engraving, dry point, collagraphs, woodcuts, serigraphs, and woodcarving. Local scenes include Niagara-on-the-Lake, Niagara Falls, and Niagara vineyards. Forsythe also creates intricate guitars and fine scale-model ships. 92 Picton St., Niagara-on-the-Lake, Ont. ℭ **905/468-3659**. www.dougforsythegallery.com.

First-Hand Canadian Crafts   This store features Canadian-designed and handcrafted arts. Categories include Inuit sculpture, art glass, ceramics, jewelry, and folk art. Galleria, Niagara Fallsview Casino & Resort, Niagara Falls, Ont. ℭ **905/354-2006**.

Jordan Art Gallery ⊀   This gallery is owned by a group of local contemporary artists who also staff the store, so there is always a knowledgeable and enthusiastic steward on hand to chat about the art on display. In addition to showcasing the work of the gallery owners, other selected artists' works are exhibited. Joyce Honsberger creates large whimsical fiber and metal sculptures, while Mori MacCrae's paintings are playful takes on portraits—think funky Mona Lisa. There's jewelry, wearable art, paintings, dishes, sculptures, and more—what a place! 3845 Main St., Jordan Village, Ont. ℭ **905/562-6680**.

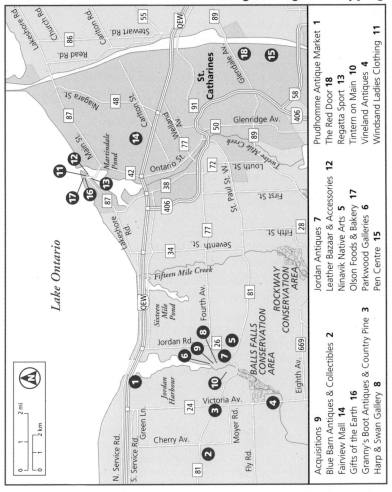

Prudhomme Antique Market **1**
The Red Door **18**
Regatta Sport **13**
Tintern on Main **10**
Vineland Antiques **4**
Windsand Ladies Clothing **11**

Jordan Antiques **7**
Leather Bazaar & Accessories **12**
Ninavik Native Arts **5**
Olson Foods & Bakery **17**
Parkwood Galleries **6**
Pen Centre **15**

Acquisitions **9**
Blue Barn Antiques & Collectibles **2**
Fairview Mall **14**
Gifts of the Earth **16**
Granny's Boot Antiques & Country Pine **3**
Harp & Swan Gallery **8**

The King Street Gallery/Poulin Art Gallery   This gallery in a historic home in Niagara-on-the-Lake features works by Canadian artist Chantal Poulin. Poulin's works range from portraits of children to landscapes, still life, and contemporary art. A number of vineyard landscapes are available. The gallery also displays other artists' work, including sculptures from Quebecois collaborative artists Yann Normand and Nancy Ferland, and Olivier Henley. 153 King St., Niagara-on-the-Lake, Ont. ℭ **905/468-8923.**

Moggridge Studio   In a quiet residential area with a view of Lake Ontario, this gallery and framing studio handles a huge variety of categories. In addition, the work of Canadian wildlife artist Robert Bateman is available here. Other Canadian artists whose work you'll find here include Bev Doolittle and Trisha Romance. 285 Niagara Blvd., Niagara-on-the-Lake, Ont. ℭ **800/265-4889** or 905/468-2009. www.artlineetc.com.

Antiquing in the Niagara Region

There are many fine antiques dealers in the Niagara region—although many have retired in the last few years—but if you want to hit a few places in a single neighborhood, then head for Virgil, a village just a few kilometers south of Niagara-on-the-Lake on Niagara Stone Road. Another good hunting ground is the Twenty Valley—its antique retailers are located mainly around Jordan and Vineland. If you're a country-drive kind of person who likes to pull over now and then when an antiques market catches your eye, cruise along Victoria Avenue between the QEW and Fly Road (if you turn onto the North Service Rd. first, you can catch Prudhomme's 25-vendor market before heading south on Victoria toward Vineland), or Niagara Stone Road (Hwy. 55) between the QEW and Niagara-on-the-Lake.

Take note that opening hours for antiques retailers differ from typical shopping hours. Many are closed on Mondays (except holiday Mon) and some also close Tuesday and Wednesday, although most are open 7 days a week in July and August. As always, if there is a particular vendor you wish to visit, call ahead to avoid disappointment.

Ninavik Native Arts ☆   This beautiful store features an impressive collection of Native art and sculpture. Initially the focus was purely on Inuit works, but the owners have expanded their product line to include Iroquois artists. Stunning pieces by established Native sculptors run as high as five figures. Works from younger, up-and-coming indigenous artists are also featured. Soapstone, ivory, bone, and antler are used to create the works of art. Fabrics, prints, pottery, paintings, and masks are also on display. Pieces may be purchased in person or online. 3845 Main St., Jordan, Ont. ℭ 800/646-2848 or 905/562-8888. www.ninavik.com.

Ochre Art Gallery   Original paintings by Canadian artists are available for sale in this gallery within the Doubletree Resort in Niagara Falls. Paintings have been selected to reflect the beauty of nature and the great Canadian outdoors. 6039 Fallsview Blvd. (inside the Doubletree Resort Spa Fallsview), Niagara Falls, Ont. ℭ 800/730-8609 or 905/354-4132.

Wyland Galleries   Canadian marine life artist Wyland creates bronze sculptures and paintings in a variety of media. Wyland's own work is featured along with other internationally recognized artists. Wyland Galleries is part of a large chain, most of whose stores are in the U.S. Galleria, Niagara Fallsview Casino Resort, 6380 Fallsview Blvd., Niagara Falls, Ont. ℭ 905/354-7474.

BOOKS

Chapters   Chapters has become a familiar name and favored destination for Canadian book lovers. They offer an extensive selection of books and magazines; larger stores carry CDs and a growing selection of giftware. Fairview Mall, 285 Geneva St., St. Catharines, Ont. ℭ 905/934-3494.

Coles   Under the umbrella of Chapters Indigo, Coles is a mainstream general bookseller that favors mall locations. A wide selection of new and established titles and authors, book-related accessories, and gifts. Niagara Square Shopping Centre: 7555 Montrose

Rd., Niagara Falls, Ont. ℭ **905/357-1422.** The Pen Centre: Hwy. 406 and Glendale Ave., St. Catharines, Ont. ℭ **905/685/4961.** Seaway Mall: 800 Niagara St. N., Welland, Ont. ℭ **905/735-6146.**

Old Niagara Bookshop   This independent bookstore carries literary works, specializing in Canadiana and children's books. Most titles are new. They carry some out-of-print and collectors' items, but not secondhand books. 233 King St., Niagara-on-the-Lake, Ont. ℭ **905/468-2602.**

Page One Books   Most of the books in stock here are used rather than new. Since they serve a relatively small community, the subject areas are wide-ranging—they try to carry a little bit of everything. Fun for a browse. 5984 Main St., Niagara Falls, Ont. ℭ **905/354-9761.**

CDS, MOVIES & MUSIC

Larger shopping malls have at least one store specializing in CDs and DVDs, although they tend to limit their selection to mainstream bestsellers and charge full price. Three of the most popular chain stores in the Niagara region are **HMV Canada, Music World,** and **Sunrise Records.**

MGM Studios Plaza   If you're a film buff, you will enjoy the MGM store. Besides a wide selection of DVDs and CDs, there is a range of interesting movie memorabilia and licensed movie-themed gifts and clothing. Great collection of James Bond, Pink Panther, and Rocky stuff. 4915 Clifton Hill Niagara Falls, Ont. ℭ **905/374-2663.**

CHOCOLATES & SWEETS

Hershey's World of Chocolate Store *Kids*   As you stroll along Falls Avenue at the foot of Clifton Hill, keep your eyes open for the gigantic silver-colored Hershey's Kiss that marks the location of this sweet treat emporium. If you have a sweet tooth, you'll be delighted with the free samples of Hershey products—milkshakes, fudge, truffles, Kisses, and more. The 650-sq.-m (7,000-sq.-ft.) store's shelves are loaded with calories. Fudge-making demonstrations happen on-site. Parking is available in a garage immediately adjacent to the store. 5701 Falls Ave., Niagara Falls, Ont. ℭ **905/374-4444.**

Laura Secord   Named after a local heroine of the War of 1812, Laura Secord is Canada's largest and best-known chocolatier. If you are looking for chocolate-themed gifts, Laura Secord is a winner. Every major holiday in the calendar has a theme at Laura Secord. They stock gift-wrapped boxes of chocolates, and their gift baskets are second to none. Niagara Square: 7555 Montrose Rd. (corner of McLeod Rd. and the QEW) in Niagara Falls, Ont. ℭ **905/357-1110;** www.niagarasquare.com. The Pen Centre: Hwy. 406 and Glendale Ave., St. Catharines, Ont. ℭ **800/582-8202** or 905/684-1227; www.thepencentre.com.

The Nutty Chocolatier   Fashioned after a Victorian candy store, this shop has antique candy bins and mahogany cases. Imported chocolate, candies, and fudge. 233 King St., Niagara-on-the-Lake, Ont. ℭ **905/468-0788.**

Olson Foods + Bakery *✶*   Your nose immediately follows the trail of chocolate, pastry, and warm bread into Olson's bakery. Author and host of the Food Network's *Sugar,* Anna Olson can be found on a busy Saturday behind the kitchen counter rolling pastry and talking to visitors. Yummy chocolate raspberry pâté, caramel chocolate tart, chocolate strawberry cake, white chocolate blueberry parfait, and fresh cream cannoli cakes. If you're still hungry, there's a sandwich counter serving hot pressed *panini* and salad. For the discerning foodies, there are condiments galore. 17 Lock St., Port Dalhousie, Ont. ℭ **905/938-8490.**

Reg's Candy Kitchen   Reg Wall has been making fudge at this location for more than 36 years. You can watch him at work in his candy kitchen. Delicious flavors include chocolate mint, butterscotch, maple walnut, and vanilla. The shop is just one block from the *Maid of the Mist,* along River Road, right under the Rainbow Bridge. Rainbow Bridge Plaza, Niagara Falls, Ont. ℭ **905/356-4229.**

Swiss Fudge   High-quality chocolate and candy from around the world is featured in this scrumptious shop in the Galleria shopping complex inside Niagara Fallsview Casino Resort. Swiss Fudge has been making fudge in Niagara Falls since 1966. Whether your sweet tooth craves English, American, Italian, Canadian, or French candies, it will be satisfied here. Plenty of prettily packaged sweet gifts on display. 6380 Fallsview Blvd., Niagara Falls, Ont. ℭ **905/356-5691.**

Toute Sweet Ice Cream & Chocolate   I always say you can never have too much ice cream, and if you are touring around the Twenty Valley, this cute little ice-cream parlor (with a natty outdoor patio for summer pleasure) in Jordan Village is just what you need. You can customize your ice cream by choosing fresh fruit, brownies, cookies, chocolate, or nuts, and they will blend it with their premium ice cream on a frozen granite stone while you wait. Chocoholics should stop by, too, for hand-molded Belgian chocolates. Icewine truffles on the premises. Yum. 3771 Nineteenth St., Jordan, Ont. ℭ **905/562-9666.**

CHRISTMAS STORES
Just Christmas ✦   You might think a store that sells only Christmas decorations wouldn't do much trade outside of the Christmas season, but you'd be wrong. People don't just browse out of season here, they buy. And the store is like Doctor Who's Tardis (deceptively small outside, very large inside). Every Christmas decorating theme you could imagine is here for you to discover as you make your way from room to room, following the crowds of shoppers. 34 Queen St., Niagara-on-the-Lake, Ont. ℭ **905/468-4500.**

DEPARTMENT STORES
The Bay   Established in the Canadian North more than 300 years ago as a fur-trading post known as The Hudson's Bay Company, The Bay carries standard department-store collections of fashions and housewares. Sales and promotions are frequent, and merchandise is good quality. The Bay occupies an anchor spot at two Niagara-region malls—the Pen Centre in St. Catharines, and Niagara Square in Niagara Falls, Ontario. The Pen Centre: 221 Glendale Ave., St. Catharines, Ont. ℭ **905/688-4441.** Niagara Square Mall: 7555 Montrose Rd., Niagara Falls, Ont. ℭ **905/668-4441.**

Sears   Offering a comprehensive range of consumer goods, Sears anchors the Pen Centre in St. Catharines and Seaway Mall in Welland. Like The Bay, sales and promotions are offered on an ongoing basis. The Pen Centre: 221 Glendale Ave., St. Catharines, Ont. ℭ **905/682-6481.** Seaway Mall: 800 Niagara St., Welland, Ont. ℭ **905/732-6100.**

FASHION, MEN'S
Phillip Artois   Exclusively Italian-made, high-end menswear, Phillip Artois specializes in smart casual clothing, including shirts, slacks, sportswear, and sweaters. Leather shoes, accessories, better suits, dress shirts, and sports jackets round out the selection. Galleria, Niagara Fallsview Casino Resort, 6380 Fallsview Blvd., Niagara Falls, Ont. ℭ **905/356-7400.**

FASHION, MEN'S & WOMEN'S

Irish Design   Find Irish books and music, Shetland wool sweaters, and Celtic jewelry at this shop. Irish descendants will appreciate exports such as Taytobrand chips, Inis Energy of the Sea lotions and perfumes, and Claddagh heart rings. The Irish tearoom in the back has Irish favorites such as Barry's imported teas, homemade scones, salmon dill fish cakes, and Bushmill's Irish coffee with a cinnamon shamrock served in your foam. 75 Queen St., Niagara on the Lake, Ont. ✆ **905/468-7233.**

Roots   Although Roots has been a well-known Canadian label for many years, their sponsorship of the Nagano Winter Olympic games several years ago catapulted their coats, sweaters, and caps into the world spotlight. Demand has grown for their clothing line since that time, particularly in the United States. This casual clothing, in infant to adult sizes, washes and wears well. Only selected stores carry kids' merchandise. Roots has expanded their product line to include fragrances, jewelry, leather goods, and shoes. Table Rock Complex: Queen Victoria Park, Niagara Falls, Ont. ✆ **877/642-7275.** Canada One Outlet Mall: 7500 Lundy's Lane, Niagara Falls, Ont. ✆ **905/371-2322.**

FASHION, WOMEN'S

Angie Strauss Fashions   Featuring the creations of fashion designer and local artist Angie Strauss, this boutique stocks clothing, hats, jewelry, and accessories. Styles are aimed at more mature women; plus-sizes are available. Mix and match separates. Some items feature Strauss's watercolor paintings. Accessories and gifts include gift cards, desk clocks, tote bags, silk scarves, aprons, and paper tole kits. 129 Queen St., Niagara-on-the-Lake, Ont. ✆ **888/510-0939** or 905/468-2255. www.angiestrauss.com.

Nantucket   Casual and high-fashion clothing and home and garden accessories. Fashion advisor Jennifer Thrasher fills the store with imports from Europe and handcrafted items from the south to create an eclectic assortment of merchandise. 3836 Main St., Jordan, Ont. ✆ **905/562-9281.**

The Red Door   This tiny white and red painted store features a mix of funky, yet conventional women's clothes—women in their 30s or 50s can shop here for clothes, but there's also costume jewelry, frames, dishes, cute and brightly colored bath mats, and a wall of bath soaps and Fruit Frappe lotions. On the trendier side, the purses are fun and well priced. 45 Front St., S., Thorold, Ont. ✆ **905/680-2045.**

Tintern on Main   Designer and boutique owner Jacqueline Del Col, under the label of Tintern Road, is a gracious host. Del Col's work utilizes higher-end fabrics and fine detailing, yet strives to combine style with practicality. A number of other fine designer labels, selected by Del Col, are also available and include Franco Mirabelli, Michael Kors, and Virani. Find some funky dresses and classy business-casual wear that is a trendier option than the majority of the stores in the area. 3836 Main St., Jordan Village, Ont. ✆ **905/562-5547.** www.tinternonmain.ca.

Valleverde   Nothing form fitting here; instead it's flowing, airy dresses and other women's clothing. Fine linens and flax organic materials make some naturally beautiful pieces of clothing. 55 Queen St., Niagara on the Lake, Ont. ✆ **905/468-3698.**

Windsand Ladies Clothing   Ladies' wear for casual living, with an emphasis on quality, comfort, and function. A boutique with clothing from small to extra-large. 26 Lakeport Rd., Port Dalhousie, St. Catharines, Ont. ✆ **905/646-3322.**

GARDENING

The Copper Leaf   Gardeners will happily browse here for ages, wandering among the statuary, garden tools, furniture, garden decor items, and a small selection of live plants. 3845 Main St., Jordan, Ont. ℂ **905/562-0244**; 10 Queen St., Niagara-on-the-Lake, Ont. ℂ **905/468-5323**. www.thecopperleaf.com.

GIFT & SOUVENIR SHOPS

The Canada Store   One of Jordan's most recent Main Street retailers, The Canada Store has plenty of souvenirs and Canadian-made crafts. 3636 Main St., Jordan, Ont. ℂ **905/562-9714**.

Gifts of the Earth   Just around the corner from the sweet-smelling Olson Foods housed in the Lock & Main Market, Gifts of the Earth has lots of treats of the non-edible variety: amber, amethyst, and garnet stone (to name a few) earrings, rings, and necklaces; incense from exotic countries; chimes; and crystals. Also includes books and candles in a myriad of smells and sizes. Lock & Main Market, 17 Lock Street, Port Dalhousie, Ont. ℂ **905/937-7171**.

Heritage Gift Shop   Proceeds from sales at this shop support the Jordan Historical Museum of the Twenty, which is just 2 minutes down the road on the valley side of Main Street. The museum has several old restored buildings and artifacts, a cemetery where a number of pioneers are buried, and access to the Twenty Valley hiking trails. In the shop, which is fully staffed by volunteers, you will find an assortment of gift items and pieces for the home, many of them with a Victorian flavor. Choose from china, pottery, glassware, candles, linens, and decorative seasonal florals. At the back of the store there is a fudge counter with slices of freshly made sweet, creamy fudge. 3836 Main St., Jordan, Ont. ℂ **905/562-4849**.

Mounted Police Trading Post   Royal Canadian Mounted Police collectibles and souvenirs abound in this small shop along with bears, figurines, hats, shirts, and a plethora of tacky souvenirs. 5685 Falls Ave., Niagara Falls, Ont. ℂ **800/372-0472**. www.mounted policetradepost.com.

The RCMP Store   This is one of four specialty boutiques within the Table Rock Complex located on the Niagara Parkway, near the lip of the Horseshoe Falls. Merchandise is themed around the Royal Canadian Mounted Police. Shops of Table Rock, Queen Victoria Park, Niagara Falls, Ont. ℂ **877/642-7275**.

Souvenir City Headquarters   This is a high-volume tourist souvenir stop packed to the rafters with trinkets such as tacky mass-produced beads and totem poles, valor eagle paintings, and personalized Niagara Falls coffee mugs. Groups and buses travel here in droves. The Chocolate Factory serves up fast food. The chocolate fudge is actually worth buying, and some of the maple syrup products (cookies) are also quite good. 4199 River Rd., Niagara Falls, Ont. ℂ **905/357-1133**.

Swarovski   This store's world-famous fine Austrian lead crystal figurines can be dust collectors, but the crystal jewelry is quite fashionable, modern, and stylish. The prices, for the quality of necklaces and earrings, are also quite reasonable. Galleria, Niagara Fallsview Casino Resort, Niagara Falls, Ont. ℂ **905/354-0118**. www.swarovski.com.

Tickle Your Fancy   For Canadian-made sweets, gifts, cards, jewelry, and original art, head for this store. Their specialties include gourmet chocolate, fudge, and maple-flavored indulgences. 106 Queen St., Niagara-on-the-Lake, Ont. ℂ **905/468-9939**.

The Viking Shop   If you're an avid collector of ornaments, head here. The Viking Shop carries Hümmel, Royal Doulton, Precious Moments, Lilliput Lane, Peter Rabbit, Willow Tree Angels, Wedgwood, Waterford Crystal, Boyd's Bear, Cherished Teddies—the list goes on. Garden deck chimes and knickknacks abound. 42 Queen St., Niagara-on-the-Lake, Ont. © **905/468-2264.**

HATS

BeauChapeau Hat Shop ☞   They declare that there is no such thing as a bad hair day, just a good hat day. There are literally thousands of hats in the store. Say fedora, homburg, bowler, or safari, they're all here. And that sexy number Harrison Ford sports in those Indiana Jones movies—yep, officially licensed Indiana Jones wool felt and genuine fur hats are available. Women's hats range from inexpensive knitted beanies to handmade cloches, with berets, upturns, buckets, and wide brims filling out the selection. 126 Queen St., Niagara-on-the-Lake, Ont. © **905/468-8011.** www.beauchapeau.com.

HOME DECOR

Acquisitions   For those who love to decorate their homes, room by room, with dedication to detail, look no further than Acquisitions, a retail store that also offers a professional interior design service. Fabrics, wall-coverings, decorative accents, custom furnishings, lighting, mirrors, and artwork can all be found here. 3836 Main St., Jordan, Ont. © **905/562-1220.**

L'Esprit Provence/Tableclothsetc.com   This store originally exclusively sold products imported from the South of France. They recently relaunched the business as Tableclothsetc.com to focus on tablecloths, napkins, and coordinating products for dressing the dining table. The product line has been expanded to include products from Italy, Spain, and South Africa. Fabric by the yard is available for most of the patterns they carry. They will send fabric swatches by post, and they do custom orders if required. If you can't get to Europe, stop in here. Besides a wide range of tablecloths, placemats, runners, and so on, they carry lamps, wireware, bathing products (including the marvelous Marseille soaps), books and magazines, music, and kitchen knives. 106C Queen St., Niagara-on-the-Lake, Ont. © **905/468-1817.** www.tableclothsetc.com.

Santa Fe Lifestyle[em]Home decor items and furniture abound here, but you will also find casual clothing, hand-blown glass, and jewelry. The theme is American Southwest, and there is a mix of authentic and reproduction pieces. K. John Mason, a third-generation blacksmith and sculptor (whose ironworks studio is close by and may be toured by prior appointment) exhibits his work here. Custom ironwork is available, as is pottery from parts of the Southwestern states. 3836 Main St., Jordan, Ont. © **905/562-3078.**

KITCHENWARE

Dansk   The distinctive bright colors and simple lines of Dansk tableware and linens are displayed with flair in this lovely shop. Drinkware, cookware, gifts, home accessories, dinnerware—it's all here for the cook and those who love to entertain at home. 91 Queen St., Niagara-on-the-Lake, Ont. © **905/468-2614.**

Oneida Home Store   This outlet store features Oneida-brand hollowware, stainless-steel flatware, and silver-plate flatware. Savings can be substantial, but some merchandise is imperfect and some patterns are ones that have been discontinued. 8699 Stanley Ave. S., Niagara Falls, Ont. © **905/356-9691.** www.oneida.com.

LEATHER

The Leather Bazaar & Accessories   Leather goods of all kinds, from belts, pouches, and gloves to handbags, shoes, and clothing are on offer. 50 Lakeport Rd., Port Dalhousie, St. Catharines, Ont. ℂ **905/938-5016.**

PERFUME

The Perfume Factory   If you plan to cross the border as part of your trip, you can purchase perfume products at duty-free shops. Or you can head to the Perfume Factory on York Road near the Niagara-on-the-Lake exit of the QEW. Brand-name fragrances (more than 1,000 to choose from) are offered at discounted prices; the store claims most prices are lower than duty-free. Tax rebate forms are available at the store for nonresidents. Sterling silver jewelry and men's and women's watches are also available. 393 York Rd., Niagara-on-the-Lake, Ont. (close to the Niagara-on-the-Lake exit from the QEW, not in the town). ℂ **800/463-0012** or 905/685-6666. www.perfumefactory.ca.

PETS

The Bark and Fitz   Doggie treats for the upscale dog: a bakery (behind a sneeze guard) includes doggie biscotti, cannoli, and holiday Easter and Christmas goodies. Find brand-name dog accessories, such as Fou Fou Dog and Planet Dog, and removable charm collars for the discerning pooch, as well as chocolate- and peanut butter–scented chew bones and bribery bits dog treats. The franchise carries only all-natural products. The scented poop bags are a little over the top—but some owners might appreciate the citrus smell while scooping! 106 Queen St., Niagara-on-the-Lake. ℂ **905/468-0305.**

SHOES

Arezzo Shoes   Boutique styles in footwear, plus accessories and lingerie. Exclusively for women, this is a "girls'-day-out" kind of shop, where you can ooh and ahh together to your heart's delight. 3836 Main St., Jordan, Ont. ℂ **905/682-9419.**

Newark Shoes   This upscale casual shoe store features shoes by Clarks, Birkenstock, Josef Seibel, and more. Leather handbags, gloves, wallets, and other accessories are also available. 122 Queen St., Niagara-on-the-Lake, Ont. ℂ **905/468-7637.**

SPORTS EQUIPMENT & CLOTHING

Regatta Sport   Whether you're a recreational athlete or national champion, you will find this specialist clothing and equipment store quite fascinating. Training and racing gear for rowers, dragon-boaters, cyclists, runners, and other types of athletes. 50 Lakeport Rd., Port Dalhousie, St. Catharines, Ont. ℂ **905/937-7858.** www.regattasport.com.

TOYS

Kids Explor-it *Kids*   Inside the Table Rock Complex located on the Niagara Parkway, near the lip of the Horseshoe Falls, is this shop just for children, designed to be an interactive store and play center. Shops at Table Rock, Queen Victoria Park, Niagara Falls, Ont. ℂ **877/642-7275.**

Turtle Pond Toys *Kids*   Play areas are set up around the store to encourage kids to try out the merchandise. Higher-quality toys, games, and puzzles for children of all ages. Galleria at Niagara Fallsview Casino Resort, 6380 Fallsview Blvd., Niagara Falls, Ont. ℂ **905/357-7710.**

WINE & SPIRITS

Most of Ontario's wine, some beer, and all spirits are purchased through the provincial government-owned **Liquor Control Board of Ontario (LCBO)** retail stores. There are locations throughout the Niagara region. Look for the vintages section for the best selection of wines from around the world. Individual winery boutiques are also licensed to sell wine, but you can't buy alcoholic beverages in a grocery or convenience store in Ontario. Beer is also available at The Beer Store, a provincially owned and operated business with plenty of locations in the region.

10

Niagara Region After Dark

When night falls in Niagara Falls, by far the best entertainment is the spectacular view of the illuminated cascading waters of the American and Horseshoe falls. The light show happens nightly all year. Beginning at dusk and ending at midnight, an ever-changing rainbow of color floods the Falls. During the main tourist season, the lights are accompanied by a fireworks display on Friday and Saturday evenings.

The nightlife has picked up in Niagara Falls—younger visitors can dance to Brazilian bands in the summer heat or vogue to electric vibes at some new venues. Other than the theater, Niagara-on-the-Lake shuts down after 6pm. The Shaw Festival, with its productions of plays by George Bernard Shaw and his contemporaries—from Oscar Wilde and

Noel Coward to Chekhov, Ibsen, and Brecht—is a cerebral treat. You'll find stylish places in Niagara-on-the-Lake's compact town center, where you can relax with a glass of wine or a cocktail before or after the show.

If you're looking for live music or somewhere to dance the night away, St. Catharines has some unique places for the 30-something crowd, while Niagara Falls offers youths and older places to dance and sip pricey drinks. This chapter will give a sampling to suit every party mood, whether you want to relax and listen to music or get sweaty in a crammed dance club.

Tip: Keep an eye out for ***Niagara Hot Spots,*** the free entertainment guide to what's happening around Niagara, or visit **www.niagaranights.com**.

1 The Performing Arts

Since the lion's share of visitors to Niagara Falls come in the warmer months, the region has a thriving summer theater presence. The biggest draw for theatergoers is the fabulous **Shaw Festival.** Throughout the year, concerts, plays, and dance recitals are held in the **Centre for the Arts** at Brock University (500 Glenridge Ave., St. Catharines, Ont.; ✆ **905/688-5550**). Other events in the performing arts arena take place as part of various festivals held in Niagara's many towns and villages (see "Calendar of Events," chapter 2).

THEATER

Shaw Festival ✫✫✫ The Shaw Festival is unique, exclusively producing plays by George Bernard Shaw and his contemporaries, and plays about the period of Shaw's lifetime (1856–1950). Shaw's long life provides the festival with a nearly bottomless source of material to present each year, and their eclectic offerings range from intimate dramas to rollicking musicals.

The Festival, whose season runs from April to November, has three venues in Niagara-on-the-Lake. The largest is the flagship **Festival Theatre,** which features a cafe and shop. The **Court House Theatre,** where the Festival began in 1962, is located on the site of Upper Canada's first Parliament. The **Royal George Theatre,** at 85 Queen St., was originally built as a vaudeville house in 1915, for the purpose of entertaining troops stationed on the Commons in the town during World War I.

To enrich your Shaw experience, plan to attend one of the many theatrical events that take place throughout the season. **Backstage tours** are held Saturday mornings from June to October. Between May and August, informal **preshow chats** give an introduction to the evening's play prior to most performances. On most Tuesday evenings, post-performance, the audience is invited to remain in the theater for an **informal Q&A session.** The public can **engage in discussions with members of the theater company** on selected Saturdays during July and August prior to the matinee performance. **Free concerts** are held on selected Sundays throughout the season in the lobby of the Festival Theatre at 11am. The festival also offers staged readings and workshops throughout the season; check their website for more information.

The Shaw announces its festival program in September. Tickets are difficult to obtain on short notice, so book in advance. Contact the box office at the Festival Theatre for tickets for all three venues. 10 Queen's Parade, P.O. Box 774, Niagara-on-the-Lake, Ont., L0S 1J0. ℂ **800/511-SHAW (511-7429)** or 905/468-2172. www.shawfest.com.

REPERTORY & DINNER THEATER

Firehall Theatre   The Niagara Falls Music Theatre Society is a community theater group, performing a selection of musicals, drama, and comedies. They stage a three-play season through the fall and winter months. 4990 Walnut St., Niagara Falls, Ont. ℂ **905/356-4953.**

Greg Frewin Theatre   This 700-seat dinner theater presents a Las Vegas–style magic show, complete with large cats, showgirls, and astounding illusions by Greg Frewin, the award-winning International Grand Champion of Magic. Matinees start at 1:30pm (preshow lunch at 12) and the evening show starts at 8pm all year; optional preshow dinner is served at 6:30pm. Suitable for the entire family. 5781 Ellen Ave., Niagara Falls, Ont. ℂ **866/779-8778** or 905/356-0777. www.gregfrewintheatre.com.

Gypsy Theatre, Fort Erie   Primarily a summer theater company, the Gypsy Theatre has a permanent professional acting company that performs an eclectic range of shows. Past performances include vivacious *Freedy Vette and the Flames,* a musical featuring an eight-piece band; *The Wizard of Oz,* with a cast of 50; and *Educating Rita.* 465 Central Ave., Fort Erie. ℂ **877/990-7529** or 905/871-4407. www.gypsytheatre.com.

Niagara Falls Grand Dinner Theatre   The Niagara Grand offers lunch and dinner shows. Plays are selected for their suitability for all ages; recent shows included the comedy "Greetings," by Tom Dudzick, and "Drinking Alone," by Norm Foster. The season runs from March to December. Queenston Heights Restaurant, Queenston Heights Park, 14184 Niagara Pkwy., Niagara Falls, Ont. ℂ **866/845-7469** or 905/357-7818. www.niagarafallsgrand dinnertheatre.com. Queen Victoria Place, 6345 Niagara Pkwy.

Oh Canada Eh! Dinner Show   An evening of Canadian comfort food and squeaky-clean musical entertainment awaits. During the main tourist season, the "Oh Canada Eh!" show plays daily. Starting at 6:30pm (ending at 9pm), guests pass around four courses (just like home) during the performance, while actors double up as servers to clear the table. Matinees are scheduled on some days beginning at 3pm. You'll hear Newfie jokes and a host of Canadian songs made popular by such artists as Shania Twain and Anne Murray. Canadian audiences might appreciate—or cringe—from the Mounties, hockey players, lumberjacks, and even *Anne of Green*

Moments   The Falls by Night

The spectacle of the **Falls illuminations** must not be missed. Imagine gigantic northern lights rippling color back and forth. It's best viewed from above; so take a trip up the **Konica Minolta Tower** or **Skylon Tower.** If you're lucky enough to have a **falls-view hotel room,** crack open a bottle of bubbly and watch the ever-changing pattern of rainbow colors from the comfort of your home away from home.

Twenty-one xenon lights illuminate the Falls, each with a 76-cm (30-in.) diameter. Eighteen lights are located at the Illumination Tower beside Queen Victoria Place, and three are located below street level in the Niagara Gorge, opposite the American Falls.

The show starts between 5 and 6:30pm in winter, between 7 and 8:30pm in spring and fall, and at 9pm in summer, and runs until at least 10pm from January through April and until midnight the rest of the year. All times are approximate and subject to change according to light conditions; feel free to call ahead or visit **www.niagaraparks.com** if you're on a tight schedule but don't want to miss the show—and you *don't* want to miss it, believe me (© **800/563-2557** or 905/356-6061).

The Falls were first illuminated in 1860 in celebration of a visit by the Prince of Wales, using calcium, volcanic, and torpedo lights and an assortment of fireworks. Electric-powered lights were first used in 1879, and the lights have operated almost continuously since 1925—when the Niagara Falls Illumination Board, a joint venture between Canada and the U.S., was established to finance and operate the light show.

In addition, enjoy a **free fireworks display** over the Falls every Friday and Sunday evening at 10pm from late May to early September (weather permitting). During the major Canadian and U.S. holiday weekends, they kick it up a notch.

Gables references, but American visitors can appreciate a bit of border humor, too. For the most part, the jokes are quite corny and the constant clapping and screaming out "EH!" may not be for everyone. 8585 Lundy's Lane, Niagara Falls, Ont. © **800/467-2071** or 905/ 374-1995.

Port Mansion Dinner Theatre ✯   I belly-laughed and was on the verge of tears watching the shows here—the theater is engaging and heartfelt. You can watch the play with a glass of wine at your table in the balcony-style seating—very cozy. The dinner beforehand is standard fare (steak, pasta, salmon) and might be worth skipping. The adjacent 88-seat cabaret-style Theatre in Port provides an intimate theater experience all year, performing musicals, comedies, and dramas. Lively nightlife hops nonstop at the PM nightclub. In the summer, PM stages theme nights, including Friday Miami Nights and Band Night Thursdays; and DJs from local radio stations spin tunes on Wednesdays and Saturdays. 12 Lakeport Rd., Port Dalhousie, Ont. © **866/452-7678** or 905/934-0575; www.portmansion.com.

Showboat Festival Theatre   A variety of comedy, drama, mystery, and musical performances are produced during the spring and summer season by the Showboat Festival Theatre. Professional shows include *BOARDWALK! A Doo-Wop Musical* and *The Flying Bandit*. The intimate 220-seat theater-in-the-round is located in the historical setting of the Roselawn Centre for the Living Arts, a facility that incorporates Roselawn, a stone-and-brick 1860 Victorian building. 296 Fielden Ave., Port Colborne, Ont. ℭ **888/870-8181** or 905/834-0833

MUSIC

Although the Niagara region offers great live theater, its options for a night of music are a little more limited. **Pop performers** with a decidedly retro bent often perform for baby boomers at the Avalon Ballroom in the **Niagara Fallsview Casino Resort** (6380 Fallsview Blvd., Niagara Falls, Ont.; ℭ **888/836-8118**). More diverse fare, from folk to rock to classical, can be found during July and August at the 500-seat open-air amphitheater at Jackson-Triggs Winery (2145 Niagara Stone Rd., Niagara-on-the-Lake, Ont.; ℭ **866/589-4637**).

Even the spoiled urban aficionado of symphonic and choral music will appreciate the professional offerings of **Chorus Niagara** and the **Niagara Symphony,** both of which perform at the **Centre for the Arts,** Brock University (500 Glenridge Ave., St. Catharines, Ont.; ℭ **905/688-5550**). Chorus Niagara's repertoire includes a diverse range of choral programs, from full orchestra accompaniment to a cappella, and from ancient music to premiere performances. The Niagara Symphony Orchestra plays both classical and pop concerts.

2 The Club, Live Music & Bar Scene

Downtown Niagara Falls, Ontario, pulses with noise and crowds, particularly along Falls Avenue and Clifton Hill. Niagara-on-the-Lake is much quieter, offering cozy and elegant hotel bars and a pub or two. St. Catharines caters to the student crowd. Outside of these places, the region is rather sedate.

Dance clubs, bars, and live entertainment venues, by nature, are constantly evolving, as they try to keep up with or keep ahead of their patrons' latest passions in terms of music and drinks. By the time you visit some of the venues listed here, they may have changed the type of music they offer, the decor, the beer, or even their name. Amble on out for the evening and take a gamble—you never know what you might stumble upon.

COMEDY CLUBS

House of Comedy   Stand-up comedians entertain in the House of Comedy's new venue, which is a larger and brighter space than the previous basement location. Those with tender ears should be warned that comedians can be quite raw in their subject matter—cursing is rampant. Entertainers from both sides of the border make appearances. Shows are Friday and Saturday nights while the bar is open, during select evenings. 4189 Stanley Ave., Niagara Falls, Ont. ℭ **905/357-SHOW.** www.thehouseofcomedy.com.

DANCE CLUBS & LOUNGES

Club Rialto   One of the few places catering to the over-30 crowd, with music that's a little less hip-hop and a little more Billy Joel. DJs and karaoke rule. You'll find it tucked away at the back of the Casa d'Oro Restaurant. 5875 Victoria Ave., in Casa d'Oro Restaurant, Niagara Falls, Ont. ℭ **905/356-5646.**

Shooting the Falls

If you're a film buff, check out *Niagara* (1953) and *Superman II* (1980). *Niagara*, starring Marilyn Monroe, is a movie in the "film noir" genre, advertised in its day with the slogan *"Niagara and Marilyn Monroe: The two most electrifying sights in the world!"* The film reveals the Falls in its mid–20th-century glory, before much of the commercial building got underway. *Superman II,* starring Christopher Reeve and Margot Kidder, gives moviegoers a peek into hokey honeymoon heaven, complete with a heart-shaped bathtub and vibrating bed. And, naturally, it also features a couple of dramatic Superman rescue scenes—first, a young boy who falls into the water, closely followed by a foolhardy Lois Lane who flings herself into the rapids in what turns out to be an unsuccessful attempt to prove that Clark Kent is Superman.

CopaCabana's Brazilian Steak House   Imagine sipping a minty mojito on a hot summer night to a live Brazilian band and the Rio Samba Divas dancing. Every weekend there's live Brazilian music with tasty—but expensive—Caribbean drinks. For eats, there's a Brazilian favorite: a "full rodizo"; waiters come around with giant skewers of meat (12 kinds of Angus-grade beef) and drop it on your plate. A glass facade opens up to a large patio and outdoor grill in the summer. 6671 Fallsview Blvd., Niagara Falls, Ont. © 905/354-8775. www.copacabana.ca.

Dragonfly   Long red velvet curtains and exceedingly tall dark metal doors give this Asian-inspired nightclub an ominous and sensual feel. Over 930 sq. m (100,000 sq. ft.), this is Niagara's place to be for young sophisticates (20s and up). Open only on weekends; Orchid Fridays ($10 cover) is ladies' night, featuring a DJ spinning R&B, house, party mix, and rock; Saturdays ($15 cover) offer rock, club anthems, and R&B. Doors open at 10pm; call ahead to reserve a spot to avoid the notorious line. The place gets hopping around 11pm. 6380 Fallsview Blvd., Concourse Level, Unit 109. © 905/356-4691. www.dragonflynightclub.com.

Hard Rock Club   Can't decide what you want to do tonight? The Hard Rock Club has a dance floor with doors that open to the street, so you can see the Falls while you boogie. Not in the mood for dancing? Relax in the retro lounge, accented with red plush velvet, or check out the martini bar. The outdoor patio is popular in the summer. Local trendy 20- and 30-somethings like to hang here. 5701 Falls Ave., Niagara Falls, Ont. © 905/356-7625.

Rumours Night Club   If you've got the energy to dance, dance, dance, then head to Rumours, smack in the middle of the carnival atmosphere of the "Street of Fun" at the top of Clifton Hill. This perennially popular club regularly sees lines out the door. Huge video screens, blasting sound, and a laser show on are tap here. Music ranges from retro '80s and '90s to top-40 tunes, with an all-request mix on Sunday nights. Dress to impress. 4960 Clifton Hill, Niagara Falls, Ont. © 905/358-6152. Cover $5 (Canadian and U.S. currency).

ECLECTIC
After Hours   This restaurant and lounge is frequented by an easygoing 30-plus crowd, dropping in for appetizers, dinner, or Niagara wines and willing to take in

whatever music is on offer. Entertainers include vocalists, quartets, and bands, singing and playing everything from Celtic tunes, acoustic guitar, and rock to jazz and blues. 5470 Victoria Ave., Niagara Falls, Ont. ℭ **905/357-2503.**

The Moose & Goose   This student hangout has hosted some great live rock bands, including Billy Talent, Finger 11, Kim Mitchell, The Tea Party, and The Trews. 54 Front St., Thorold, Ont. ℭ **905/227-6969.**

365 Club   Located just steps away from the action on the vast gaming floor of the Niagara Fallsview Casino Resort, this intimate lounge and bar has no cover charge. The 365 Breeze martini is a great fruity cocktail to sip (amongst other cocktails) while being entertained by a variety of cabarets, lounge singers, and other live stage acts. From Thursday to Sunday, a local band plays '60s and '70s tunes for an older crowd, from 8:30 until 10:30pm. Another band plays top-10 radio picks until 2am. Inside the Niagara Fallsview Casino Resort, 6380 Fallsview Blvd., Niagara Falls, Ont. ℭ **888/FALLS-VU (325-5788).**

JAZZ & BLUES

St. Catharine's is emerging as a great nightspot in the Niagara area. There are two great places to hang out late into the evening.

Café Etc.   This cafe-cum-jazz-bar swings with live music on Friday and Saturday nights. 462 Third St., Niagara Falls, NY. ℭ **716/285-0801.**

Stella's   Imagine an industrial open-spaced apartment: brick walls, exposed wooden ceilings, and an expansive hardwood floor for dancing to DJ-spun top-40 tunes on the weekend. There's a VIP area in the back and high-backed booths on either side for the 25-plus crowd to take a break. Nightly specials include half-priced drinks from 11am till 8pm on Friday, and half-priced martinis on Thursdays. An extensive menu includes fantastic Italian fare. 45 James St., St. Catharines, Ont. ℭ **905/685-3000.** www.stellasdowntown.ca.

3 Film

IMAX

IMAX Theatre   IMAX technology is a Canadian invention. The screen is more than six stories high, which is almost overwhelming in terms of visual stimulation. Add 12,000 watts of digital surround sound, and you've got the whole picture. The film *Niagara: Miracles, Myths, and Magic* has been the star of the theater for many, many years and has become a little dated, but it nevertheless gives tourists who are unfamiliar with the Falls and all its history a broad appreciation of the seventh forgotten wonder of the natural world. The re-creation of such spectacles as the Great Blondin's tightrope antics over the gorge, Annie Taylor's foolhardy yet brave plunge over the Falls in a barrel, and the daring folks who have shot the rapids makes for interesting viewing.

Tips   **Save on IMAX Tickets**

Discounts on IMAX tickets are plentiful—if you know where to look. Most hotels offer discounted tickets—just ask at the reception desk. You can also purchase tickets online at a lower price than the box office. Another way to save (if you are planning a trip up the nearby Skylon Tower) is to buy a Sky-Max combo ticket.

There is an impressive collection of original daredevil barrels and other historical artifacts in the **Niagara Falls Daredevil Gallery,** which is free whether you have movie tickets or not. The containers are open for viewing and visitors are invited to touch, unlike most museums. Also on-site is a **National Geographic** gift shop. 6170 Fallsview Blvd., Niagara Falls, Ont. ✆ 905/374-IMAX (374-4629).

REPERTORY CINEMA

If you're a fan of independent, foreign, and second-run films, check out events at **Brock University,** 500 Glenridge Ave., St. Catharines, Ont. (✆ **905/688-5550**). Brock University Film Society screens films on Sunday evenings in the David S. Howes Theatre on campus. Visit **www.brocku.ca/cpcf/bufs/BUFSmain.html** for schedules, pricing, and parking details.

The **Niagara Indie Filmfest** is held annually in June at various downtown St. Catharines locations. The festival showcases Canadian short film and video works. For more details, visit **www.niagaraindiefilmfest.org**, or call the **Festival Hotline** (✆ **905/ 685-8336**).

4 Gaming

Casino Niagara   Niagara's original casino, this casino features more than 2,400 slot and video poker machines on two gaming levels. With its fake palm trees, joker face masks, and less contemporary carpets, this garish setting is reminiscent of old-style Las Vegas. The dress here is quite casual—jeans and sneakers. And even though the casino went nonsmoking, the smell still lingers in the carpets. Table games include blackjack, roulette, craps, Sic-Bo, Pai-Gow, baccarat, mini-baccarat, three-card poker, and Let it Ride. Lower-limit tables and an exclusive high-limit gaming area are offered on-site. Beginners can play the slots with ease; there are plenty of machines to go around, even on a busy night. You have a choice of valet parking or Park'n'Ride shuttle service from a nearby parking lot. Dining choices include Perks Café, the Market Buffet, and the Quench Bar. Lucky's Steakhouse offers a dark and romantic hideaway for some quiet time. The casino is open 24 hours a day, every day of the year. 5705 Falls Ave., Niagara Falls, Ont. ✆ 888/WIN-FALL (946-3255).

Fort Erie Racetrack & Slots   The Fort Erie Racetrack, more than 100 years old, features live thoroughbred racing in a season that stretches from late April to early November; the outdoor track runs around a beautiful garden and pond. The racetrack hosts one of the Canadian horse-racing season's most prestigious events, the Prince of Wales Crown, which is the second leg of Canada's Triple Crown. Simulcast racing is also available. Inside, the venue isn't as pretty, to say the least, but it is popular with an older crowd. Those who like to gamble on the slots will find 1,200 slot machines to keep them occupied. Dining ranges from all-you-can-eat buffets to roadhouse-style menus. Bertie St., Fort Erie, Ont. ✆ 800/295-3770. www.forterieracing.com.

Niagara Fallsview Casino Resort   Romanesque in style—gold trim on the ceilings and crown molding, grand light fixtures and marble floors—this upscale casino is full of people who dress up and want to be seen. It features a 18,580-sq.-m (200,000-sq.-ft.) casino that operates 24 hours a day, every day of the year. There are 150 gaming tables and more than 3,000 slot machines in the vast gaming area; high rollers can enter the private salon (most tables start at $100) with a members lounge. If you want to take a break from the gambling, catch icons such as Diana Ross and

> ### *Tips* Gambling Should Be Fun, Not Obsessive
>
> Many people enjoy playing games of chance for entertainment. But for a minority of people, gambling becomes a real problem, and they find themselves unable to control the amount of money they spend. Information on dealing with a gambling problem can be obtained by calling the **Ontario Problem Gambling Helpline** at © **888/230-3505.**

Wayne Newton at the Avalon Ballroom or watch some live local entertainment while having a drink at the 365 Club. There is a 368-room hotel, a full-service hotel spa, and a luxury shopping galleria. A unique hydroelectric water sculpture dominates the main entrance to the resort. In front of the complex, a series of waterfalls provides an ever-changing display, complete with colored lighting after dark. Ten dining options—including some of the area's best sushi and Italian—ensure every pocketbook and palate is represented. 6380 Fallsview Blvd., Niagara Falls, Ont. © **888/FALLS-VU.** www. fallsviewcasinoresort.com.

Seneca Niagara Casino & Hotel   This American casino feels a bit raw: waitresses, dressed in short hockey jerseys, serve free alcohol amidst thick cigarette smoke. There are 3,200 reel-spinning and video slot machines and almost 100 gaming tables on the large floor that once was a convention center, including blackjack, craps, roulette, and more. A separate poker room is available for play. Above the bar, in the center of the room, a band plays most nights; the music is geared toward an older crowd. Parking is free, as are all beverages. Patrons must be 21 years of age or over and must have photo ID available. Hungry gamblers can choose steak, buffet, or sports pub–style food. 310 Fourth St., Niagara Falls, NY © **877/873-6322** or 716/299-1100. www.senecaniagaracasino.com.

Appendix A: The Niagara Region in Depth

The Niagara region's rich history spans an extensive period of several thousand years, although its modern-day existence as one of the world's best-known tourist destinations began less than 2 centuries ago. The fascinating story of this landscape of remarkable beauty, encompassing Niagara Falls, the Niagara River and Gorge, the environmentally significant Niagara Escarpment, and the burgeoning wine country, has been condensed in the next few pages.

1 History 101

FROM HUNTING GROUND TO BATTLEFIELD

The history of the Niagara Region stretches back 10,000 years, to the time when the glaciers of the last ice age retreated north. Vast herds of game roamed the boreal forests surrounding Lake Ontario and its environs, bringing tribes of hunters to the area. For several millennia, the first peoples of Niagara survived as hunters, fishers, gatherers, and eventually agriculturalists.

The first Europeans arrived in the mid-1600s, driven by the desire to expand the fur trade and led by French explorers and missionaries. Although several white men visited the Falls prior to Father Louis Hennepin, he was the first to record a description of the mighty wonder of nature following his visit in 1678. His account of the Falls was a dramatic exaggeration, leading to the production of a hand-tinted engraving that depicted the Falls much higher and narrower than in reality, with mountains rising in the distance. This misrepresentation became the standard pictorial representation for many decades to follow.

For the next hundred years or so, the Niagara area remained populated by various Native groups, although their numbers were increasingly depleted by European-borne diseases and clashes with warring tribes.

Dateline

- **1678** Father Louis Hennepin is the first person to record a description of the Falls.
- **1721** A trading post is established by the French at Lewiston to protect the fur trade.
- **1726** The French build a sturdy stone fort on the east bank of the Niagara River at the point where it flows into Lake Ontario, called Fort Niagara.
- **1759** Fort Niagara is attacked by the British. Nineteen days later, the French surrender and withdraw from the Niagara Peninsula.
- **1764** Fort Erie is constructed by the British.
- **1792** John Graves Simcoe is appointed Governor of Upper Canada and the town of Newark (now known as Niagara-on-the-Lake) is established as the capital.
- **1793** The first Parliament of Upper Canada passes a bill that prevents further slavery in Upper Canada.
- **1812** The War of 1812 commences when the fledgling country America declares war on Britain, sending U.S. forces north into Canada. Because of its proximity to the border, Niagara becomes the focus of a major offensive.
- **1813** The first wave of freedom-seeking black slaves

French and British troops fought for control of the continent during the first half of the 18th century. During this period, Fort Niagara was built by the French on the east bank of the Niagara River, at the point where it flows into Lake Ontario. At the end of the Seven Years War in 1763, all of New France was ceded to Great Britain, and the British established control of the Niagara River. Fort Erie was built in 1764 on the west side of the mouth of the Niagara River and Lake Erie.

The next wave of newcomers to the district were the United Empire Loyalists, who fled to Upper Canada seeking sanctuary from the fierce fighting of the American Revolution of 1775 to 1783. When the war ended, remaining Loyalists were expelled from American territory and many of them settled along the western shore of the Niagara River.

At the end of the American Revolution, Fort Niagara, on the eastern side of the Niagara River, was in the hands of the United States. To protect their interests in Upper Canada, the British constructed a fort on the opposite side of the river. In 1802, Fort George was completed and became the headquarters for the British army, local militia, and the Indian Department.

The War of 1812 was the last military confrontation between Canada and the U.S. Eager to expand the nation, the United States declared war on Britain in June 1812. By attacking on four fronts, one of which was Niagara, the Americans hoped to achieve a swift victory. Several bloody battles ensued over the next 2 years, but the eventual outcome was a stalemate. The Treaty of Ghent, signed on Christmas Eve 1814, brought the hostilities to a close and the Niagara River was reestablished as the border between Upper Canada and the U.S. Throughout the region, historic forts, monuments, and memorials stand as reminders of the war.

Upper Canada became the first place in the British Empire to abolish slavery, when Governor General John Graves Simcoe introduced legislation in 1793. In the years that followed, the country became a haven for black men and women escaping from slavery in the American South. To enable the freedom seekers to reach safety, supporters of the abolition of slavery throughout America and Canada provided secret "safe houses," where escaping slaves were given food, shelter, and directions north. The routes that passed by the safe houses became known as the Underground Railroad. Niagara was one of the main termini for the freedom seekers. Fugitive men, women, and children were transported

arrives in the region via the Underground Railroad.

- **1814** The War of 1812 comes to an end upon the signing of the Treaty of Ghent. The Niagara River is reestablished as the border between Upper Canada and the United States.
- **1820** The Falls become a sightseeing attraction for the burgeoning tourist class.
- **1827** The establishment of a strip of hotels between Robinson Street and Table

Rock marks the beginning of uncontrolled commercial development.

- **1829** The first Welland Canal is completed, opening a shipping lane between Lake Ontario and Lake Erie.
- **1845** The second Welland Canal opens, with 27 locks of cut stone replacing the 40 original wooden locks.
- **1846** The first *Maid of the Mist*, a steamboat carrying passengers daringly close to

the American and Horseshoe Falls, is launched.

- **1848** The Niagara River ceases its flow and the Falls stop for 30 long, silent hours when millions of tons of ice at the source of the river block the channel. The ice dam is eventually released by the forces of nature and a solid wall of water crashes over the brink of the falls.

across the Niagara River at Fort Erie. Niagara Falls, Niagara-on-the-Lake, and St. Catharines became important settlement areas for refugee slaves. From the early to the mid-1800s, thousands of fugitive slaves made their way into Canada through Fort Erie.

THE BIRTH OF TOURISM AT THE FALLS

Tourists first began to visit the Falls in the 1820s. Official guides were available to take sightseers on a tour of the major points of interest in the area. By the time the first *Maid of the Mist* steamboat was launched on the American side of the Falls in 1846, with its accompanying water-powered Inclined Railway to take passengers down the face of the gorge to the boat dock, the Falls were welcoming 50,000 summer visitors a year. A mere decade later, following the completion of the world's first railway suspension bridge, which included a plank roadway for foot passengers and horse-drawn carriages on its underside, Niagara Falls became the best-known tourist destination in North America.

One of the main attractions in those early days of tourism was Table Rock, a large platform of dolostone at the edge of the Horseshoe Falls. Although the overhang dramatically collapsed in 1850, the landmass remains the most beloved

vantage point on the Canadian side. Just over a century later, most of Prospect Point, the prime location to view the Falls on the American side, collapsed and 185,000 tons of rock crashed into the gorge below.

As the crowds grew, a rowdy strip of concession stands, hotels, and carnival booths sprung up, all eager to grab a piece of the tourist dollar. Despite the popularity of these attractions, many members of the public were concerned at the desecration of such a wonder of nature. Accordingly, in 1878, Lord Dufferin, then Governor General of Canada, proposed that a strategy be developed to preserve the natural beauty of Niagara Falls. Seven years later, the Niagara Parks Commission was founded. Its mandate was to preserve and enhance the natural beauty of the Falls and the Niagara River corridor. On the U.S. side of the border, the New York State Reservation at Niagara Falls was established in the same year. But the kitsch could not be suppressed, and to this day, Niagara audaciously exhibits both extremes of the tourist experience—the majesty and grandeur of the Falls, surrounded by beautifully groomed parks and pristine gardens, and the noise and clutter of the Clifton Hill district and Lundy's Lane, with its neon lights, fast food, carnival atmosphere, and motel strip.

- **1850** The Falls entertain 60,000 visitors a year.
- **1855** With the completion of the first railway suspension bridge across the gorge, and arrival of the steam train in the town of Clifton, Niagara Falls becomes the best-known tourist destination in North America.
- **1859** Frenchman Jean Francois Gravelet, known as "The Great Blondin," is the first

tightrope walker to cross the gorge of the Niagara River.
- **1860** Funambulist Bill Hunt, from Port Hope, Ontario, billed as "Signor Farini," challenges Blondin's position as the champion of Niagara.
- **1881** The third Welland Canal is constructed. Part of the route is altered, and contrary to the previous two canals, the banks are kept free of mills by government policy.

- **1885** The Niagara Parks Commission is founded. Its mandate is to preserve and enhance the natural beauty of the Falls and the Niagara River corridor.
- **1888** The Niagara Parks Commission opens Queen Victoria Park, a 62-hectare (154-acre) park adjacent to the Horseshoe Falls.
- **1895** The first large-scale hydroelectric station in the world begins operation in the

NIAGARA'S OTHER INDUSTRIES: SHIPPING AND AGRICULTURE

The commercial growth at the Falls was not restricted to the tourist industry. Engineers and scientists of the 19th century eagerly contemplated the potential of the powerful rapids and waterfalls. Since the 1700s, mills had made use of the water to drive their machinery, but the full potential of Niagara to produce hydroelectric power could not be realized until the invention of the alternating current system, the basis of the long-distance transmission of electricity. In 1891, Nikola Tesla, who had invented alternating current dynamos, transformers, and motors, sold his patents to George Westinghouse. Together, they designed generators for the first large-scale hydroelectric plant in the world, the Adams Station. Since then, a number of power stations have been constructed in Canada and the U.S., and in total, the Niagara River now generates approximately 4,400 megawatts of electricity. In order to protect the thunder of the Falls as a major tourist attraction, only half of the river's flow is available for power, mostly at night. But only the most perceptive of tourists can distinguish the difference in flow.

The other major endeavor that boosted the area's economy was the construction of a shipping canal between Lake Erie and Lake Ontario. The St. Lawrence River and the Great Lakes form the largest inland waterway in the world, extending 3,700km (2,300 miles) from the Atlantic Ocean to the heart of North America, and a canal was needed to bypass the Niagara River corridor and establish a mighty commercial shipping route.

The first canal was completed in 1829. Consisting of 40 wooden locks, the canal served its purpose for only a few years before deterioration of the wood and the increasing size of ships required a second canal to be built. The Second Welland Canal had 27 cut stone locks and went into operation in 1845. In 1881, a third canal was built, following the same route as previous canals in the southern part of the region, but taking a new line in the north. The banks of the Third Welland Canal were kept free of industry by government decree. The fourth canal, known as the Welland Ship Canal, was completed in 1932. The number of locks was drastically reduced to eight and the canal adopted a direct north-south route over the escarpment.

Agricultural development of the region was aggressively pursued due to the unique combination of climate, physical geography, soil, and location. More than 50% of the Niagara land base is farmed,

Niagara Gorge, using alternating-current generators.

- **1900** Irish-American Fenian sympathizers target Lock 24 of the Welland Canal in an unsuccessful bombing attack.
- **1901** Schoolteacher Annie Taylor is the first person to conquer the Falls, when she plunges over the Horseshoe Falls in a barrel. She survives, gaining fame but not the fortune she had eagerly sought.
- **1912** Three tourists lose their lives on the "ice bridge" when it suddenly breaks up, and from this point people are prohibited from crossing the frozen Niagara River during the winter.
- **1914** More than one million tourists a year visit the Falls.
- **1922** The Clock Tower, now a well-known landmark on Queen Street in Niagara-on-the-Lake, is erected as a memorial to the Niagara men who died in World War I.
- **1925** The Falls are illuminated for the first time, setting off a nightly event that has continued uninterrupted since that time, much to the delight of millions of visitors.
- **1930s** The government takes on a series of projects to boost tourism to Niagara, including the construction of the roadway now known as

although increasing pressure for urban expansion and urban-type land use is a threat. Fruit trees dominate the agricultural landscape, although greenhouses and agri–food processing industries (including wineries) generate the most revenue in the agricultural sector of Niagara's economy.

The thriving Niagara wine industry had humble beginnings, with the first European settlers making use of the native labrusca grapes, which unfortunately did not produce palatable table wines. Modest success was achieved with Canadian hybrids, and the grape industry became established in Niagara during the early 1900s. By midcentury, six million vines were growing in the province, with the bulk of them in Niagara. French hybrids were becoming more popular, as consumer taste shifted toward dryer, lower-alcohol table wines and away from sweeter table and dessert wines.

By the 1970s, several enterprising growers had already begun planting *vitis vinifera* vines, the so-called noble grape varietals that produce many of the world's finest wines, such as chardonnay, cabernet, gamay, and Riesling. Fertile, rich soils and a unique microclimate make Niagara a prime grape-growing region, and contrary to popular public opinion of the proposed outcome, the *vinifera* vines thrived.

The biggest contributor to the transformation of Ontario's wine industry was the introduction of international trade agreements in 1988. The loss of tariff and retail price protection put Ontario wines on par with imports from the world's most respected and well-established wine regions, and the industry was faced with surrendering its market share or reinventing itself as a worthy contender. Growers, wineries, and the provincial government decided to revitalize the wine industry, and together they rose to the challenge.

Today, Niagara has approximately 6,500 hectares (16,000 acres) under vine, in an area stretching from Niagara-on-the-Lake in the east to Grimsby in the west. More than 70 wineries now make their home in Niagara, many with fine restaurants and boutiques on-site. A large number offer wine-tasting and tours to the public. Niagara wines consistently bring home medals and awards from many of the world's most prestigious wine competitions. World attention has turned to the Niagara wine industry, not least because of the superb quality of its icewine, a dessert wine produced from grapes that have been left on the vine after the fall harvest to freeze naturally. The frozen grapes are handpicked and immediately pressed to capture the thick, yellow-gold liquid, high in natural sugars and acidity.

Queen Elizabeth Way and the reconstruction of Fort George, which had been destroyed in the War of 1812.

■ **1932** The fourth Welland Canal, consisting of eight concrete locks in a direct north-south route over the Niagara Escarpment, opens.

■ **1940s** Hybrid grape varieties are introduced to Ontario and a fledgling wine industry is born.

■ **1950** The Floral Clock, consisting of 15,000 plants, is constructed along the Niagara Parkway north of the Botanical Gardens.

■ **1953** Niagara Falls becomes the backdrop for the Marilyn Monroe film *Niagara*.

■ **1954** Prospect Point, the most famous viewing point for the Falls on the American side, collapses into the gorge below.

■ **1960** A 7-year-old boy is swept over the Horseshoe Falls

following a boating accident in the upper Niagara River, wearing only a lifejacket. He survives and is rescued by the *Maid of the Mist* tourist boat.

■ **1962** The Shaw Festival stages its first two productions in the old courthouse in Niagara-on-the-Lake.

■ **1969** The flow over the American Falls is stopped completely for several months while the feasibility of removing much of the

NIAGARA TODAY

The Niagara Region today has a population of more than 400,000, living in 12 municipalities, ranging from large urban, industrial, and service centers to rural locations. The area is very well placed for accessibility to major markets in North America and around the world. Niagara is within a 1-day drive of approximately half of the population of Canada and the United States. Its major industrial sectors include tourism, manufacturing, telecommunications, agriculture and greenhouse production, and service industries. Locals and visitors alike enjoy a wealth of golf courses, wineries, parks, and marinas under a sun that shines more than 2,000 hours annually.

Niagara as a region has great potential for prosperity. The word "Niagara" has global brand recognition, and its diverse economic base ensures a degree of stability. Recent investments have been huge, from the multitude of new wineries and hotels to the $1-billion Niagara Fallsview Casino Resort. Niagara's outstanding natural beauty, crowned by the Falls and its proximity to the border, are exceptional attributes.

Despite Niagara's strengths, the region on both sides of the border tends to perform below its economic potential. A 5-year economic growth strategy, projected to the year 2010, has been crafted by business, government, and community stakeholders and is already underway, helping to steer the region toward a more prosperous future.

loose rock from the base of the waterfall is investigated. It is decided that the expense would be prohibitive.

- **1970s** Local grape growers begin planting *viniferas,* the so-called noble grape varietals that produce many of the world's finest wines—cabernet, chardonnay, gamay, and Riesling.
- **1973** The purpose-built Shaw Festival Theatre opens in Niagara-on-the-Lake.

- **1975** Niagara-based Inniskillin Wines is granted the first new winery license in Ontario since 1929.
- **1979** Niagara Falls finds Hollywood fame once again when scenes from *Superman II* are filmed there.
- **1988** The introduction of international trade agreements induces the Niagara wine region to reinvent itself as a worthy world competitor in order to survive.

- **1989** The Vintners' Quality Alliance appellation system is introduced to ensure standards of excellence in Ontario winemaking.
- **1996** The 150th anniversary of the launch of the first *Maid of the Mist* is celebrated.
- **2004** The $1-billion Niagara Fallsview Casino Resort opens.
- **2007** An astounding 10 million visitors a year pour into the Niagara region.

Appendix B:
Wine 101

By John Thoreen and Louise Dearden

For those who wish to enrich their experience of Niagara's wine country, here is a taste of everything you wanted to know about wine but were afraid to ask. As you venture into Niagara's wineries, though, don't be shy. Niagara's winemakers are enthusiastic and genuinely hospitable folk, eager to lend a helping hand as you discover the world of wine.

1 Introduction to Winemaking

Transforming grapes into a rudimentary wine is a relatively simple process. Ripe grapes contain sugar, which, in the presence of certain yeast organisms, is converted into alcohol and carbon dioxide. For thousands of years, this process was carried out in a fairly crude manner, with early vintners making passable—but certainly not great—wines.

The science called *oenology*, which revolutionized winemaking, was developed after Louis Pasteur's work with fermentation and bacteriology around 150 years ago. Only in the past few generations have winemakers acquired intensive technical training and earned PhDs in viticulture (the science of grape growing) in a concentrated effort to deepen their understanding of wine and winemaking. In Niagara, Brock University in St. Catharines and Niagara College Teaching Winery at the Glendale Campus of Niagara College in Niagara-on-the-Lake offer a variety of programs related to the grape-growing and wine industry.

GROWING GRAPES

The rebirth of Niagara's wine industry occurred a quarter of a century ago; the majority of the vineyards are fewer than 15 years old. Many of the vines are planted in a north-south orientation in order to take full advantage of the sun and reap the maximum benefits of the moderating air currents that flow from above Lake Ontario toward the Niagara Escarpment. The fertility of the grape variety and soil type determines how the growers train the vine canopy, in a perpetual search for the perfect balance between quality and volume of yield. Growers also employ canopy management techniques to control and prevent mildew, mold, and insect damage. The immense efforts that take place in the vineyard are directed to producing the best possible grape for the *terroir* and specific weather and other environmental conditions, since the quality of the grape can be improved only while it is actively growing on the vine.

Grapes can be incredibly fussy, and growers face a perpetual struggle against the vagaries of weather and pests. Organic grape farmers, while striving to minimize environmental impact and reduce the amount of pesticides that wine drinkers imbibe, face even greater challenges, although the results are rewarding both for the conscience and the palate.

The majority of the vineyards in Niagara are independently owned by growers, with about 6,500 hectares (16,000 acres) under vine, a number that is increasing yearly. Most growers live on their property, farm the land themselves, and sell their grapes to nearby wineries under contract.

THE WINEMAKING PROCESS

Production facilities in the Niagara region rank among the world's best in terms of technology and allow the area to compete with other cool-climate wine regions around the globe. Increasingly, the area is attracting knowledgeable and respected international winemakers, who work alongside the region's established vintners to bring innovation and experience to Niagara's wine industry.

During the winemaking process, many decisions must be made by the winemakers in order to craft wines that are unique to their winery. When to pick the grapes; whether to pick by hand or machine; whether to sort, de-stem, and crush the grapes; the duration of skin contact; which method to use to press the grapes or pulp; which type of yeast to implement; which sort of container to use for fermentation and whether to use a warm or cool fermentation process; how much exposure to air should be allowed; and which methods of stabilization and filtration to use are all critical decisions that contribute to the personality of the wine. There are many more variables to consider during the winemaking process, many of them specific to certain styles and types of wine. It's no wonder that today's winemakers attend educational programs in oenology and viticulture in addition to hands-on acquisition of knowledge in the wineries themselves. Modern wines truly are a blend of art and science.

WHITE WINES   For white wines, the winemaker wants only the juice from the grapes. (For red wines, both the juice and skins of the grapes are essential—see below.) Grapes are picked either by hand or machine and brought to the winery as quickly as possible. Just as the cut surface

of an apple turns brown when left open to the air, grapes oxidize—and can even start fermenting—if they are not processed quickly. At some wineries, the clusters go through a "de-stemmer–crusher," which pops the berries off their stems and breaks them open (not really crushing them). The resulting mixture of juices, pulp, and seeds—called *must*—is pumped into a press (a widely used technique called, logically, *whole-cluster pressing*).

Most presses these days use an inflatable membrane, like a balloon, and gently use air pressure to separate the skins from the juice, which is then pumped into fermenting vessels. In the recent past, most white wines were fermented in stainless-steel tanks fitted with cooling jackets. Cool, even cold, fermentations preserve the natural fruitiness of white grapes. Wooden barrels are sometimes used for fermentation of white wines, especially chardonnay. This practice reverts to old-style French winemaking techniques and is believed to capture fragrances, flavors, and textures not possible in stainless steel. However, barrel fermentation is labor-intensive and the barrels themselves are expensive.

After white wines are fermented, they are clarified, aged (if appropriate), and bottled, usually before the next harvest. Simpler white wines—Riesling and sauvignon blanc, for example, are bottled first. A small number of white wines, usually chardonnays, undergo 15 to 18 months of barrel aging, producing richly flavored, complex, and expensive wines.

RED WINES   The chief difference between white wines and red wines lies simply in the red pigment that's lodged in the skins of the wine grapes. So, while for white wines the juice is quickly pressed away from the skins, for rosés and reds the pressing happens after the right amount of "skin contact." That can be anywhere from 6 hours—yielding a rosé or very light red—to 6 weeks, producing

Grape Varietals in Niagara's Wine Country

Because growers in the Niagara wine region do not have the luxury of generations of experience to draw upon when deciding which grape varieties are best suited for its *terroir,* they experiment, with more than four dozen varieties planted throughout the region. Below is a list of the most prevalent grape varietals found in Niagara's wine country.

RED GRAPE VARIETIES

BACO NOIR & MARECHAL FOCH   These French hybrids were developed in the early 1900s to suit the climate of northeastern North America. Strawberry can be detected in these wines, which are often made from older vines and aged in oak barrels.

CABERNET FRANC   This is the most widely planted red vinifera grape variety in Niagara. Cab franc is often overshadowed by the better-known cabernet sauvignon, but this French black grape is well suited to Niagara's *terroir,* being winter-tolerant and high-yielding. In hot growing years, excellent medium- to full-bodied wines are produced. Cabernet franc tends to be lighter in color and tannins than cabernet sauvignon and matures earlier in the bottle. These wines have a deep purple color with an herbaceous aroma.

CABERNET SAUVIGNON   This well-known transplant from Bordeaux has small, deep-colored, thick-skinned berries and is harvested in late October to early November in Niagara. The grape produces complex, medium- to full-bodied red wines that are highly tannic when young and usually require a long aging period to achieve their greatest potential. "Cab," as it is often affectionately called, is frequently blended with other related red varietals such as merlot and cabernet franc to produce classic full-flavored Bordeaux-style wines. Cabernet is a good match with red-meat dishes and is delightful with a well-constructed cheese board.

MERLOT   This varietal is traditionally used as a blending wine to smooth the rough edges of other grapes, due to its soft and fruity nature and lower tannin levels. The merlot grape is a relative of cabernet sauvignon, but it tends to be less complex, with a black cherry bouquet. Merlots are drinkable at an earlier age than cabernet sauvignons, though they will still gain complexity with age. Merlot may be paired with any dish that a "cab" would complement.

PINOT NOIR   Made famous by the film *Sideways,* pinot noir is a difficult grape to grow. Even in their native Burgundy, the wines are excellent only a few years out of every decade, and they are a challenge for winemakers to master. During good years, pinot noir produces light- to medium-bodied red wines with low tannins and silky textures, making some of Niagara's most elegant and expensive table wines. Pinots are fuller and softer than cabernets and can be drinkable at 2 to 5 years of age, though the best improve with additional aging. Pinot noir is versatile at the dinner table, but it goes best with lamb, duck, turkey, game birds, semisoft cheeses, and even fish.

WHITE GRAPE VARIETIES

CHARDONNAY   Chardonnay is the most widely planted white vinifera grape variety in Niagara (and, interestingly, also in California). The grape is relatively winter-hardy and one of the earliest-ripening Niagara varieties, typically harvested toward the end of September. It produces exceptional medium- to full-bodied dry white wines. Chardonnays range from delicate, crisp wines that are clear and light in color to fruity, buttery, oaky wines that tend to have deeper golden hues as they increase in richness. No other wine benefits more from the oak-barrel aging process than chardonnay. This highly complex and aromatic grape is one of the few grapes in the world that doesn't require blending—it is also the principal grape in sparkling wine. Chardonnay goes well with a variety of dishes, from seafood to poultry to pork, veal, or pasta with cream- or butter-based sauces.

GEWÜRTZTRAMINER   This grape produces white wines with a distinctive, powerful floral aroma, often described as rosewater. Slightly sweet yet spicy, its flavor is reminiscent of lychee nuts. The varietal is particularly appreciated for its ability to complement Asian foods; its sweet character stands up to flavors that would diminish a drier wine's flavors and make it seem tarter. The vine is somewhat labor-intensive to grow in Niagara since it produces abundant foliage that must be controlled in order to prevent mildew problems.

RIESLING   The grape from which most of Germany's great wines are made, Riesling is a consistent performer and was one of the first commercially planted vinifera grapes in Niagara. This versatile grape produces some outstanding sparkling, dry, off-dry, semisweet, and icewine styles. Well-made Riesling wines have a vivid fruitiness and lively balancing acidity, leaving the palate refreshed, even when made into late-harvest dessert wine. Suggested food pairings include crab, pork, sweet-and-sour dishes, and anything with a pronounced citrus flavor. Asian-influenced cuisine also pairs well with Riesling.

SAUVIGNON BLANC   This varietal produces crisp, dry whites and has become increasing popular in the region. Its predominant notes are grassy, fruity, and herbaceous when grown in a cool climate. The plant is a vigorous grower and is typically harvested during mid- to late October. Because of its acidity, sauvignon blanc pairs well with shellfish, seafood, and salads.

VIDAL   This varietal is the most favored for the creation of Niagara's famous icewine and late-harvest wines, since it produces large bunches of thick-skinned grapes and maintains its acidity throughout the winter months.

a red that has extracted all the pigment from the skins and additionally refined the tannin that naturally occurs in grape skins and seeds.

Almost all red wines are aged in barrels or casks for at least several months, occasionally for as long as 3 years. Most wooden containers—collectively called *cooperage*—are barrels now made of North American or French oak and recently from Canadian oak.

The aging of red wines plays an important role in their eventual style because several aspects of the wine change while in wood. First, the wine picks up oak fragrances and flavors. Second, the wine, which leaves the fermenter in a somewhat murky condition, complete with suspended yeast cells and bits of skin, clarifies as the particulate matter settles to the bottom of the barrel. Third, the texture of the wine changes as the tannins interact and begin to make the wine suppler. Deciding just when each wine in the cellar is ready to bottle challenges the winemaker every year. And, to make the entire process even more challenging, every year is different.

Unlike white wines, which are usually ready to drink shortly after bottling, many of the best red wines improve with aging in the bottle. Red wines generally have a "plateau" of several years when they are at their best condition for consumption, rather than a peak. There are no rigid rules surrounding when it's time to pop the cork. Only by consistently practicing the art of tasting will you find your own sense of when a wine is ready to drink by your standards.

2 The Art of Wine Tasting

At its simplest, all you need to become a wine taster is a glass and the willingness to focus your attention fully on the wine with your senses of **sight, smell,** and **taste.** To an expert, such details as the time of day and amount of humidity in the room can affect how a wine is perceived, but for the vast majority of wine drinkers, such subtleties are irrelevant.

PREPARING FOR TASTING

What is important is to have a **clean palate** before you begin. During your wine tour, **don't chew gum** or suck on minty sweets as they will interfere with the taste of the wine. Water is always available in a jug on tasting room counters; it is a good idea to **take a sip or two of water** before beginning your tasting session, but not necessary in between samples. Some people like to chew a **small piece of bread** or a few plain, unsalted **nuts** (walnuts are favored) prior to tasting to **neutralize the palate.**

To **clear the olfactory area** at the top of your nose before or between tastings, wine experts often favor a sniff of coffee beans—don't ask me how or why it works, but apparently it does the job. The untrained nose in particular can suffer from sensory overload if too many wines are nosed in too short a time, so take it easy in order to gain full enjoyment of the experience.

You are now ready to approach the glass. About **an ounce of wine** is sufficient for a tasting, although a more generous serving is perfectly acceptable. **Pick up the glass by the stem** (or the base if that feels more comfortable for you) but never cradle the bowl of the glass in your hand, as it will change the temperature of the wine.

SIGHT

Your first assessment is **visual.** Although this is the least important (and less enjoyable than smelling and tasting), it nonetheless can give you significant clues about the characteristics of a wine. Tilt the glass away from you and hold it against a neutral background—white if possible.

Check its **clarity.** For the most part, wines ought to be clear, even brilliant, although a few unfiltered wines bear a slight haze. Filtration for clarification is, however, standard practice. Next, observe the **shades of color,** especially at the rim where the age of a wine tends to show itself. The browner a wine is, whether red or white, usually the older it is. Red wines range from purple (often a sign of young wine) through to ruby, garnet, and tawny. The depth of color of red wines lightens as they age, but in order to assess that accurately you would need to know what to expect of that particular wine at a younger age, since lighter shades are also specific to certain grape varieties. White wines vary in hue from pale greenish yellow to straw to deep gold. Better-quality wines seem to show a luster, or sheen, while those at the opposite end of the scale may appear dull and monochromatic.

SMELL

Smelling the wine is the next step, and is vital to enjoyment of a glass of wine. Indeed, to take full pleasure of a wine that speaks to you, we encourage you to "swirl and sniff" before every sip. That may feel pretentious at first, but it makes perfect sense. The olfactory bulb at the top of the nose can detect several thousand scents, but the tongue can discern only four tastes: sweet, sour, bitter, and salty.

The reason that many wine drinkers who do not take the time to smell their wine still reckon they get quite a lot of satisfaction from their wine is twofold. First, wine naturally vaporizes quite easily, so molecules drift up your nose as you drink from a glass whether you encourage them or not. Second, aromas reach the olfactory area via the *retro-nasal passage* at the back of the mouth as you swallow.

A decently shaped wineglass with a bowl that slopes toward the rim will help to direct the heady aromas to your nose (not to mention helping the wine to stay in the glass as you swirl it). Inhale the aroma, and then pause for a moment. Take a second sniff, and this time try to identify distinctive scents. Don't worry if you have difficulty trying to describe what your nose smells. The best you can do is find descriptive words that remind you of the smell, although often they are woefully inadequate and sometimes are downright amusing. The **aroma wheel,** a groundbreaking graphic developed by Professor Ann. C. Noble and colleagues at the University of California, contains a battery of terms commonly used to describe a wine's aroma, bouquet, and flavor and can nudge you toward a wider vocabulary when propping up a tasting bar.

The basic aromas include floral, spicy, fruity, caramel, woody, earthy, mineral, and vegetal, among others. These descriptions can be further subdivided, which often then begins to identify particular grape varieties. For example, chocolate and Shiraz, raspberry and young pinot noir, and green apple and chardonnay.

One final point on smell—the words *aroma* and *bouquet* possess widely recognized, distinct meanings when used to describe wine, although they are commonly used almost interchangeably in normal conversation. **Aroma** refers to the characteristic simple, often fruity smell or flavor of a young wine, often a single varietal, for example the distinctive "gooseberry and cat's pee" of sauvignon blanc. **Bouquet** is used to describe the complex, multilayered smells or flavors that develop with aging and therefore from sources other than the grapes, such as the characteristic vanilla fragrance of French oak barrels.

TASTE

Now, it's finally time to **taste.** Take a mouthful of wine and try to cover your entire palate. If you are able to **draw a little air into your mouth** while it's full of wine, without dribbling or otherwise making a spectacle of yourself (some people pick this technique up fairly quickly;

for others it's a bit messy), then you will intensify the flavor and encourage the vapor to rise up the retro-nasal passage at the back of your mouth. This is particularly useful if you are going to spit out the wine rather than swallow it.

While the wine is in your mouth, notice its qualities of **sweetness, acidity, and alcohol** and whether any bitterness, tannin, or gassiness is present. Do you find the balance of these elements pleasing? **If you are swallowing, note the "finish."** How long did the impact of the wine last after you swallowed it? Did you notice further scents and flavors during or after swallowing?

It's up to you how seriously you want to take the practice of wine tasting. There are no right or wrong feelings toward a particular bottle of wine. No one other than you can ever understand exactly how a wine will excite your senses. What you *will* find after conducting several wine tastings is that you quickly acquire a sense of the types of wine that appeal to your palate. So let that be your goal and your guide as you travel the quiet country roads of Niagara's wine country.

Index

See also Accommodations and Restaurant indexes, below.